EASTERN COYOTE

The Story of Its Success

Gerry Parker

D1453973

NIMBUS PUBLISHING

Nimbus Publishing Limited
P.O. Box 9301, Station A
Halifax, N.S. B3K 5N5
(902)455-4286

Designed by Arthur B. Carter, Halifax
Cover photo: Dale Wilson Photography, Eastern Passage
Printed and bound in Canada

Canadian Cataloguing in Publication Data
Parker, G. R.
Eastern coyotes
ISBN 1-55109-111-9
1. Coyotes. I. Title.
QL737.C22P37 1995   599.74'442   C95-950055-3

CONTENTS

To the memory of David Cartwright.

FOREWORD

During the mid to late 1800s, most of the land in eastern North America was cleared for agriculture, destroying both habitat and populations of large prey that provided food for wolves. The loss of eastern populations of bison, woodland caribou, and elk, coupled with great reduction in distributions and populations of moose and white-tailed deer, left wolves with little to eat except domestic stock. By 1900, widespread persecution of the few remaining wolves led to the extinction of the species in the east, except for portions of Quebec, Ontario, and Labrador.

Meanwhile, coyote populations were expanding in both range and numbers in the northcentral states and prairie provinces of Canada. Coyotes were able to flourish because of the significant decline in wolf populations and because of their ability to thrive on the small prey, fruit, and agricultural crops associated with the clearing and tilling of land.

Shortly after the turn of the century, a resurgence in productive, young forests associated with widespread abandonment of farms created more prime coyote habitat teeming with small rodents, snowshoe hares, and fruit. Burgeoning populations of coyotes in the northcentral states allowed the species to thrust eastward into southern Ontario, Quebec, New York, and northern New England during the early 1900s, where they could take advantage of an unfilled niche that was relatively free from com-petition. Populations of coyotes grew slowly and inconspicuously in these areas into the 1930s and 1940s.

Fueled by the forces of exponential growth, populations expanded rapidly during the 1950s through the 1970s. As populations began to approach saturation in Que-bec, New York, and northern New England, a second wave of expansion moved into New Brunswick and Nova Scotia, and even to large offshore islands such as Mount Desert Island in Maine, and the provinces of Prince Edward Island and Newfound-land in Canada(during the1980s). Populations in the northeast also turned south into the states of Connecticut, Rhode Island, New Jersey, Pennsylvania, and Mary-land. In the mid-Atlantic states, the population expanding from the north merged with a second wave of expansion from the southwest. This southern colonization involved populations from Texas, Louisiana, and Arkansas that moved east of the Mississippi to colonize Florida, Alabama, Georgia, and the Carolinas during the 1960s through the 1980s.

By 1990, the coyote had become established in all of the eastern states and Cana-dian provinces and had pushed the limit of its eastern range onto many large offshore islands. The wide range of habitats colonized in the east provide new opportunities to observe the coyote's ability to adapt its life history characteristics and behaviours to local environments.

Despite its presence in the west for thousands of years, only recently have we begun to understand the coyote's biology and ecological relationships there. In 1951, S. Young and H. Jackson published the first scientific book that attempted to describe the characteristics, behaviour, and life history of the species. This book greatly increased awareness about the coyote but was largely restricted to anecdotal observations and "coyote lore" because of the premature nature of scientific research on the species. M. Bekoff edited a contributed volume on the coyote in 1976 that represented the first compilation of available information from scientific research. Chapters in that book were devoted to the limited information that was available then for the expanding populations of coyotes in southeastern and northeastern United States. Since 1976, much outstanding research has been conducted throughout North America on various aspects of coyote biology. Although defined patterns are emerging that describe the behavioural and ecological responses of coyotes under different ecological conditions, most of this information resides in technical reports and scientific journals that may not be readily available to many wildlife managers, sportsmen and casual naturalists.

Coyotes in the east are often described as being unique within the species' historic range. This has generated great interest and controversy among scientists, wildlife managers, sportsmen, outdoor enthusiasts, and the press. Although everyone seems to have an opinion about the coyote, myth and hearsay have often substituted for informed knowledge. I have conducted more than two hundred public presentations or media interviews about eastern coyotes and have been astounded by the regularity with which several common questions and issues emerge from the audience. The most common inquiries are summarized as follows:

-Why are eastern coyotes larger than their western counterparts?

-Are eastern coyotes unique to their species, and if so, do they represent a coyote-wolf or coyote-dog hybrid?

-Do coyotes in the east fill the vacated niche of the wolf, and if so, does the behaviour of eastern coyotes more closely resemble wolf behaviour than coyote behaviour?

-What is the relationship of coyotes to their principal prey, and specifically, how do coyotes influence white-tailed deer populations?

-Do eastern coyotes form packs?

-What is the relationship of newly established coyotes to other native predators such as bobcats and red foxes?

-How will coyotes affect farming and livestock management in eastern North America?

-What are the options for management and control of coyotes?

These outwardly simple, but ultimately complex questions are addressed in *Eastern Coyote: The Story of Its Success*. Thus, this book should satisfy various informational needs about the species within the broad divisions of general knowledge, academic interest, and applied management.

Although a few popularized books on the eastern coyote have previously been published, content has generally relied little on scientific inquiry and has relied heavily on personal perceptions. An exception was a volume edited by A. Boer in 1992 that presented invited papers from a scientific conference on the eastern coyote. Those proceedings are an outstanding reference. However, several chapters feature results that are specific to a particular topic of research, and thus, may be of greatest interest to the trained scientist. Drawing upon multiple disciplines and a wide range of information sources, *Eastern Coyote: The Story of Its Success* brings together available scientific information on the classification, life history, interspecific relationships, and management issues associated with this unique animal in new environments. The approach is emperical and unbiased, leaving the reader with the necessary information on which to base informed conclusions. The author should be commended for a comprehensive presentation and synthesis that should make this book a valuable reference for scientists, biologists, sportsmen, and casual naturalists.

Daniel J. Harrison
Associate Professor of Wildlife Ecology
University of Maine, Orono, Maine.

PREFACE

"...there is no American predator that approaches the coyote in its ability to veer at times from the expected, and do just the opposite. This versatility is many of the answers to the animal's ability to persist, exist, depredate, and increase in the face of what seems like unsurmountable odds and obstacles to its existence and extension of its range, where it may be either an asset or a very detrimental creature."

The great American naturalist Stanley P. Young penned this early tribute to the western coyote over 50 years ago, and the coyote's adaptability remains the basis of the controversy and debate which has followed this fascinating wild dog throughout its remarkable journey. This historic journey has seen the coyote extend its range outward from the western prairies to occupy most of the continental United States and southern Canada. Even more remarkable has been the occupation within the past several decades of that vast expanse of eastern land beyond the Mississippi River in the south and throughout New England and Atlantic Canada in the north. It has been a story of unparalleled range expansion made even more incredible by the immense and costly programs of control and eradication which have followed the coyote step for step.

My interest in the eastern coyote began in 1982 when studying wildlife populations in the spruce-fir forests of northern New Brunswick. On forested-wilderness lands managed for timber, coyotes were common. They had only recently become the focus of controversy, and here, among the thick spruce and pine plantations, their favourite food, the snowshoe hare, was abundant. White-tailed deer were also common, wintering among the mixed woods and pockets of eastern white cedar along the slopes of the Salmon River. Here was an opportunity to study the interactions of coyotes and their two major prey. My colleagues and I followed the activities of coyotes through the seasons. We camped there in the winter and followed coyote trails with snowmobile and snowshoe, reading the stories of life and death imprinted in the snow, a recorded moment in time, until a new storm wiped the record clean.

Like many others, I have watched the story of the coyote unfold. This predator, seemingly unlike any other, inspires strong emotional debate. Most people agree that coyotes can and do kill white-tailed deer and snowshoe hare, and, when conditions permit, sheep and other domestic animals. What is less certain is the specific impact on prey by coyotes in given regions under given conditions.

I have talked about the eastern coyote with outdoor groups throughout the Maritimes, and I am always impressed by the interest generated by those discussions. With that interest, however, is a general lack of understanding of the eastern coyote and the role that this predator has assumed in the natural ecosystems of the northeast.

Although the news media have given the coyote considerable attention, most of their information is general in nature with minimal research documentation. As a scientist with access to most information on wildlife in the region, I could find only two published accounts of the eastern coyote, both with limited distribution to the general public.

The first was a book entitled *America's New "Wolf,"* written by Gene Letourneau and published in 1984 (Gannett Books, 390 Congress Street, Portland, Maine). The second was the proceedings of a workshop on the eastern coyote held in Fredericton, New Brunswick, November 7-9, 1991. Those proceedings (*Ecology and Management of the Eastern Coyote*) were published by the Wildlife Research Unit of the University of New Brunswick in Fredericton. Neither publication was widely distributed or readily accessible to the general public. These books represented opposing philosophies toward the eastern coyote and its management.

Gene Letourneau has been an outdoor columnist in Maine for over 40 years and, in his words, has been on a "20-year campaign" to control coyote numbers and increase deer populations. He sees little need for more research by government biologists and considers the use of radio telemetry to study movements and habits of coyotes a poor use of the taxpayer's dollar. He advocates giving deer all the protection available, including "... predator control that is sound, definite, organized and supervised."

In contrast to the emotionally charged book by Letourneau, the proceedings of the symposium held in Fredericton represent the results of many years of scientific research on eastern and western coyotes by scientists from across North America. I strongly recommend it for readers who would like more detail on coyote research and management and the applicability of that knowledge to coyotes in the northeast. I referred to these proceedings often while doing research for this book. However, although many aspects of coyote biology and management were addressed at that symposium, it does represent 12 individual papers, some quite technical, and many aspects of coyote biology and natural history of interest to the public were not addressed. The need remains for a source of information on the taxonomy, colonization, natural history, and management of the eastern coyote. I hope this book fills that need.

Although I studied coyotes for several years I do not consider myself an authority on the animal. This book represents the results of research on eastern and western coyotes by a great many scientists across North America. Results and conclusions are often presented in their own words. This not only allows the reader to appreciate the passions and emotions of each author but also serves to avoid real or imagined misinterpretation. Guy Connolly, a scientist who has studied coyotes and coyote predation at the Denver Wildlife Research Center, warned that a sufficiently selective review of the literature can reinforce any desired view on the subject of predation. I began this review with no particular cause for or against the coyote, or predators and predation in general. I have, at one time or another, been both trapper and hunter, although not particularly proficient at either. I also respect those whose opinions on the role of predators may differ from my own. Throughout this study I have tried to remain unbiased to allow readers to interpret information for themselves. I have, however, taken a degree of literary licence and have myself interpreted some information in a manner which I feel is both rational and objective. Others might disagree.

This book is meant to serve as a reference on the eastern coyote for both the scientist and the general public. A generous amount of documentation is necessary in a book of this nature and, for those who would have preferred an easier read, I extend my regrets. Usually I provide the reader with an option to pursue a specific point, fact, or issue further by giving references to the relevant studies.

Although I have tried to avoid any extreme points of view, parts of this book will have their critics. On the controversial question of coyote predation on white-tailed deer, I have presented the information that I found. I have also made some personal interpretations and comments relative to the situation in Atlantic Canada; here I made every effort to identify such comments as mine alone. Most of the book, however, should not be controversial. It is intended to serve as an information source on this new and interesting predator of eastern North America.

There have been few studies of the eastern coyote in Atlantic Canada. Most information comes from populations established to the south and west, which may not always apply. The application of results from studies of coyotes in Pennsylvania, for instance, to coyotes on Prince Edward Island is risky, but until regional information becomes available, we must go with the best we have. If nothing else, this exercise may serve to isolate and identify areas where new information is required for management of the resource.

The differences between regional populations most important to management may well be behavioural, and this field of study has been largely ignored. I frequently examine an issue (e.g., food habits) in a geographical context, and use the term northeast in reference to the northeastern portion of its range, which includes Atlantic Canada. I also refer to the northeastern states, which, of course, refers only to that portion of the United States.

So let us begin to explore what is known about this native wild dog of North America that we call the eastern coyote. We will review its ancestry and early historical development, the whens and whys for its colonization of most of North America during the past century, and take a glimpse at the undeclared war on the prairie coyote which provides an explicit, although not commendable example of the futility of most wildlife control and bounty systems. We will review what is known of the impact of the eastern coyote on native wildlife species and populations and explore the real, perceived and potential interaction between coyotes and white-tailed deer. We will examine coyote predation on domestic animals from other regions and the implications for the northeast. We will review means for reducing coyote predation on domestic stock, especially sheep, and potential dangers this new predator poses to humans. Lastly, we will summarize our deliberations and look ahead to the future and how the changing values being placed on all forms of wildlife may affect not only coyote populations but the integrity of the ecological systems in general.

This is a book that I have thoroughly enjoyed preparing. I feel that it addresses an information gap and that in itself makes the exercise personally rewarding. I hope that the reader develops an appreciation of the eastern coyote, truly one of the most remarkable members of our wildlife fauna, and one deserving of greater understanding.

INTRODUCTION

The successful colonization by the coyote of most of North America south of the closed boreal forest over the past 100 years is unparalleled by any other species of terrestrial mammal in recent history. The process of colonization by this medium-sized predator has been remarkable for its swiftness and the near total occupation of all available agricultural and forested habitats, an accomplishment which assumes greater significance when we consider the massive and extensive efforts of control and eradication that have haunted the coyote throughout its history of range expansion. Extensive landscape change and urban sprawl, which have led to population declines and loss of habitat for so many wildlife species, appear to have presented little challenge to the coyote. In fact the coyote has expanded its range into some of the most radically changed landscapes and heavily populated industralized centres of northeastern North America.

So how impressive has this phenomenon of coyote range expansion been? In the mid-1800s (about 150 years ago) the coyote was limited to the open grasslands and prairies of western United States and southwestern Canada. Since then this amazing wild dog has moved north into Alaska, crossed the Rocky Mountains to the Pacific Ocean, travelled south into central Mexico, and swept east across the Mississippi River to the Atlantic coast to occupy most lands from the swamps of Florida to the spruce barrens of Newfoundland. How this remarkable accomplishment has been achieved is the major topic of this book. It is a success story, one of ecological and behavioural flexibility, which has seen the coyote capitalize on the smallest of opportunities to successfully multiply and move on to occupy new territories.

But first let us look at what is known of the origins of this jackal-sized predator that we call the coyote. What do the archaelogical records show, and how can they enlighten us on the reasons why this predator in particular has proven so successful in spite of man's obsessive efforts of control and eradication?

Although fossil records shed important and interesting information on the early development of plant and animal species, most of the information provides us with only a brief glimpse into the biological richness and diversity of the animals and plants which flourished during the evolutionary process. Species evolved, colonized, and then disappeared only to be replaced by more adaptable, or perhaps more specialized, forms of life. Dinosaurs lorded over the land and sea for more than 100 million years, only to suddenly, in geological terms, literally vanish from the face of the earth. Whether this decline in abundance was cataclysmic (eg., a dramatic weather change from a celestial collision) or more gradual (eg., a longer-term global climatic change) is uncertain. What is known is that a small and inconspicuous form of "mammal-like reptile" began to colonize the vacant niches left by the declining numbers of larger and dominant reptiles.

At the close of the Mesozoic era, some 70 million years ago, these mammal-like reptiles began to increase in abundance and variety and their mammalian descendents developed into the dominant creatures on earth. A divergent evolutionary path from early reptilian stock saw the development of birds and their occupancy and dominance of the skies above the earth. The true separation point between birds and mammals and their reptilian ancestors was the development of the unique process for maintaining body temperature. The development of birds and mammals into "warm blooded" creatures removed a significant and formidable barrier in the evolutionary process and provided enormous opportunities for specific development and subsequent occupancy and colonization of most of the earth's habitats.

The taxonomists, whose charge it is to develop a scheme of classification within which all living creatures can be conveniently placed, often based on unique skeletal or physical characteristics, have placed all mammals in the Class *Mammalia*. In Class *Mammalia*, the Order *Carnivora* contains the flesh-eating beasts of prey, mammals characterized by their dentition of comparatively small incisors, large canines, and often a modified and enlarged cheek tooth in the upper and lower jaws giving a scissor or shearing action. Carnivores are a numerous and ancient order that existed in the

Millions of years ago, early ancestors of the coyote fought the sabre-toothed tiger for spoils of the kill (Young and Goldman, 1964).

early Palaeocene, and were probably derived from a late Cretaceous insectivore (feeding largely on insects).

The wild dogs (canids) belong to the taxonomic Family Canidae and first appeared in the Eocene era some 60 million years ago. Today there are 15 genera in the Family Canidae containing 35 natural species.[1] Fossil records suggest that the open plains of North America were the main centre for the evolution and dispersal of the canids. The North American coyote, *Canis latrans*,

> *"was present during the Pleistocene as a species distinct from* Canis lupus, *the wolf. Evidence of distribution and numbers of Pleistocene coyotes is so fragmentary as to be of little interpretative value except to limit the species to North America."*[2]

The present-day coyote resembles the early ancestral and less specialized forms of *Canis* more closely than does the wolf. This may explain the capacity of the coyote to adapt and proliferate under a wide variety of habitats and environmental stresses. Specialized species tend to be more vulnerable to environmental change.

> *"The coyote (*Canis latrans*) is strictly an American mammal, and in fact might well be termed strictly North American since so far as is known it occurs nowhere south of Costa Rica. It has close relatives in the Eastern Hemisphere, particularly in the jackals which it resembles somewhat in structure and habits. In fact, on account of this close resemblance the coyote has frequently been referred to as the American jackal by the early explorers and naturalists. Less wary than its big brother the timber wolf and always more abundant in most of its range, it*

The Asiatic jackal is a close relative of the North American coyote (M. Bekoff, 1975).

became more familiar to the early settlers of the Plains than the true wolf. Where both species occurred in the eastern part of the coyote's range as, for example, in the upper Mississippi Valley, the coyote was generally known as the brush or prairie wolf, in contrast to the name timber wolf for the true wolf. Coyote was a Spanish name for the animal that was later applied by explorers and naturalists after they came in contact with the southwestern Spanish settlements."[3]

Coyote is a modification of the Aztec word "coyotl."[4] The name *Canis latrans* ("barking dog") was first given to the prairie coyote by Thomas Say in 1823 after examining specimens collected in Nebraska.[5]

"Both the coyote and jackals are relatively small animals averaging closer in size to the foxes than to the gray wolf. The skull of the coyote, like that of the foxes, is comparatively narrow; the jaws have not spread to develop the great grasping power needed by a predator to attack an animal larger than itself. The sagittal crest is usually low or even flattened, indicating that the muscles controlling the jaws are relatively, if not absolutely, weak. The molar teeth of the coyote are deeply sculptured, retaining the primitive cusps and cones, and having large chewing surfaces. Such features suggest that the species still depends to some extent on vegetation for food, and has not become so specialized for flesh eating as the wolves. These various characteristics should not be considered handicaps, in the evolutionary sense. Its smaller size, and capability to utilize small prey and vegetation more efficiently, may help the coyote survive periods of adverse conditions under which the wolf would perish. Indeed, this process may be occurring today as the wolf progressively declines through competition with man, while the coyote continues to thrive and even expand its range.... The coyote might be considered part of the same central stock of unspecialized canids that has formed the basis of the evolution of the family [Canidae] ... These small animals seem to have maintained themselves with relatively little change, while the canids that became large, and specialized in habits, have disappeared. The [prehistoric] bear-dogs ... , the hyena-dogs ... , and the great dire wolf ... , have all fallen by the wayside. Now even the gray and red wolves may be moving in this same direction, but the coyote shows no sign of becoming a has-been."[6]

"The coyote...was well-represented in Aztec art and folklore ... indicating an understanding of its biology but attaching many mystical properties to it. Indians of the Great Plains had "dogs" that served as beasts of burden or as food for special feasts when Spaniards visited the area in the 17th century. Some 'Indian dogs' appeared to be only partially domesticated coyotes, somewhat modified by selection. Whether or not Indians moved or bartered their coyote-type 'dogs' beyond the ranges of coyotes is not known.... By 1850, the range of the 'prairie wolf' was quite clearly established as extending from the Mississippi River, west into the Sierra Nevada Mountains, north into Alberta, and south to southern Mexico."[7]

I recently coauthored a paper on colonization of the coyote in eastern North

America,[8] in preparation for which I reviewed many articles on the coyote, both scientific and popular, which addressed the expansion of coyote range east. I have drawn extensively from that paper in the preparation of the chapter on colonization for this book. The sequence of colonization is based on the "best available" sources of information. Although some people believe that coyotes were introduced into the northeast, that does not appear to be the case. A popular and widely circulated rumour says that coyotes were brought into the east by various interests to decrease the numbers of snowshoe hares. This, according to popular belief, might limit the damage by snowshoe hares to young seedlings in spruce and fir plantations. Although there were releases of coyotes in scattered locations in the eastern United States (for reasons other than the above), they seem to have found their way into most regions of the northeast on their own.

I wrote the respective wildlife agencies of most states east of the Mississippi River, and all provinces and territories in Canada, for information on the historic and current status of coyotes in each jurisdiction. To those many wildlife researchers and managers who responded so generously, I am very appreciative. I am also indebted to Jean Sealy, Librarian at Canadian Wildlife Service, Sackville, New Brunswick, for her patience and perseverance in helping to track down many of the elusive references. My special thanks to colleagues Randy Dibblee, Barry Sabean, and Rod Cumberland, respective furbearer biologists for the provinces of Prince Edward Island, Nova Scotia, and New Brunswick, and to Brent Patterson of Acadia University for reviewing the manuscript and making many helpful comments and suggestions. However, although acknowledging the considerable contributions made by many individuals it is the author alone who assumes full responsibility for the final product.

1 TAXONOMY

Most people want to know what kind of wild canid the eastern coyote represents and how it got here. It is difficult to separate the two questions because the eastern coyote is a result of genetic and environmental influences experienced during the period of eastern dispersal and colonization. For that reason it was difficult to choose which subject to deal with first. It is also for that reason that the reader should consider both subjects as one issue. The taxonomy, or genetic classification, of the eastern coyote can be considered the "product" which has resulted from the "process" of colonization. In that respect perhaps it can be said that I have placed the cart (product) before the horse (process). However, I encourage the reader to bear with me until you read the chapter on colonization, after which you should have a greater appreciation and understanding of this "chicken or egg" dilemma.

I also treat the process of eastern expansion of coyote range as two geographically separable events: the *northern* front of colonization and the *southern* front. I arbitrarily recognize the Ohio River valley as a convenient (although not absolute) line of demarcation between these two fronts. And I take the liberty of using that convenient dividing line when dealing with taxonomy, not only for the obvious reason of continuity, but also because of very real differences in genetic lineage. The question of genetic origin of the eastern coyote has received considerable attention from the scientific community, and those are the studies with which we will deal here. To set the table, so to speak, I will begin with a caution to those expecting a clearly defined genetic path and absolute taxonomic label for the eastern coyote.

> *"Natural hybridization [interbreeding] between sympatric [occupying the same area] mammalian species is relatively rare. The family Canidae appears to be an exception. Within the past 70 years in several parts of North America, wolves both Canis lupus [northern gray wolf] and Canis rufus [southern red wolf], have been largely replaced by canids that appear to be predominantly coyotes, but with admixtures of wolf and/or dog ... Apparently, as widespread habitat changes were brought about by man and as the wolf populations were decimated by hunting and trapping, reproductive barriers between coyotes and wolves and/or dogs broke down and widespread hybridization occurred."* [1]

NORTHERN FRONT

There is some speculation that the coyotelike predators now established throughout the northeast originated from wild canids which survived human settlement, landscape change, and persecution in small relic populations in remote regions of New York, Pennsylvania, and Maine. However, it is more likely that they are the product of eastern dispersal and colonization which began with the coyote *Canis latrans thamnos* and originated from northern Minnesota and Manitoba sometime near the turn of the century.

Fifty years ago Hartley Jackson referred to *C. l. thamnos* as the northeastern coyote, or brush wolf.[2] This distinguished it from the timber wolf, the natural wild canid of the northern forests. The distribution of the northeastern coyote was given at that time as eastcentral Saskatchewan, Manitoba, extreme eastern North Dakota, Minnesota, Iowa, northern Missouri, and easterly through western Ontario, Michigan, Wisconsin, northern and central Illinois, northern Indiana, southern and eastern Ontario, to extreme southern Quebec. That distribution, especially throughout much of the Great Lakes region, was after 50 years of eastern expansion, mainly from Minnesota and Manitoba.

The somewhat smaller plains coyote, *C. l. latrans*, occupied the open prairie to the west. The type specimen of the northeastern coyote was collected from Wisconsin in 1919[3] and was, therefore, most likely a product of earlier interbreeding between the small plains coyote and gray wolves.

Jackson gave us the following description of early specimens of northeastern coyotes collected from Ontario, Manitoba, Quebec and the Great Lakes States:

> *The coyote was known to the early settlers of this [Great Lakes] region sometimes as the "prairie wolf," but more often as the "brush wolf," hence the scientific name* thamnos, *I have given to it, meaning brush or scrub. It is a large dark coyote but is quite in contrast with the huge timber wolf of the Great Lakes country, though many of the adult individuals weigh more than 30 pounds each."*[4]

The North American coyote is a medium-sized predator whose small size, large ears, and pointed muzzle give it a more doglike appearance than the larger and fuller-bodied wolf (G. Parker).

7

Somewhere the coyote which dispersed from the open grasslands of southern Minnesota in the late 19th century bred with gray wolves in the forested wilderness regions of northern Minnesota and western Ontario. Exactly when is uncertain, and the process was most likely not a one-time affair, so to speak, with interbreeding occurring as the eastern coyote "forerunners" dispersed ahead of the main front of colonization through northern Minnesota and across western and southern Ontario. Historical records suggest that coyotes were common across the southern and south-western prairies of Minnesota in the late 1800s but rare throughout the northern forests. Occupancy of the northern two-thirds of that state by coyotes has been associated with changing landscapes caused by logging, fire and land clearing around the turn of the century.[5] At that time wolves occupied the forests of northern Minnesota. It may have been here, then, that early breeding between the plains coyote and timber wolves occurred, and the process of eastern dispersal and colonization by the northeastern coyote, or brush wolf, began.

The gray wolf, a close relative of the coyote, was the dominant large canid predator of the closed forests of northern United States and Canada (G. Parker).

Henry Hilton of the Maine Department of Inland Fisheries and Wildlife summarized our knowledge of the development and ecology of the eastern coyote and showed that:

> "1) the coyote as a species has or is occupying most of the former wolf range in the east; 2) traditional wild Canis isolating mechanisms are apparently being broken down; 3) the eastern coyote has a unique taxonomic position among the Canis species; 4) growth and behavior of the eastern form are different than that of previously classified [coyotes]; and 5) the feeding strategy of the coyote may be expanding from the traditional role as an opportunistic scavenger and predator of small mammals to more frequently include larger prey where it is available."[6]

These considerations are critical in our assessment of the eastern coyote and in understanding how the apparent breakdown in reproductive isolating mechanisms within the genus *Canis* has contributed to the biological and ecological uniqueness of this new wild canid in the northeast. Hilton summarized his research of coyote expansion into the northeast by stating,

> "In short, dispersal of coyotes into the East was, and to some degree still is, obscure."[7]

I will now "walk you through" the sequence of studies which have addressed the issue of taxonomy of wild canids in the northeast. Early attempts to name-tag wild canids created considerable confusion and misinformation. In the 1940s a ratio was developed from skull measurements to separate dogs and coyotes in the western United States.[8] However, when applied to early wild canids in the northeast, subsequent ratios suggested significant influence from domestic dogs. It was later realized that many of these early "coydogs" had probably been misidentified by inappropriate application of skull measurement ratios.[9]

Hilton expands on this early period (1940-1950) in the northeast, when wild canids were becoming more frequent and attempts at identification, although sincere, were often based less on science and more on popular belief and hearsay.

> "Almost from the beginning of the expansion eastward, the concept of coyote-dog hybridization was promulgated both popularly and scientifically. For example, coyote-dog crosses were reported as early as 1885.... The implications of such crosses occurring in the Northeast often were exaggerated, and in some cases erroneously derived."[10]

The first successful mating of a captive female coyote and a domestic male dog was reported from Michigan in 1937. The length of that pregnancy was between 58 and 62 days although the 3 hybrid pups died in the first year of life.[11] Many years later the husband and wife team of Walter and Helenette Silver studied the growth and behaviour of a litter of 5 wild canids found in New Hampshire in 1960, and kept in captivity through 1966.[12] The subsequent 2 generations of offspring from the original wild canid pups were also studied, as well as a litter of western coyotes from Colorado, and several litters of wild canid and domestic dog hybrids. These behavioural observations suggested that the wild canids from New Hampshire most closely resembled coyotes although males and females averaged twice the weights of captive western coyotes from Colorado.

Behaviourly the eastern wild canids were less aggressive towards their mates, had greater tolerance of litter mates, and were generally more social than the western coyotes. The breeding pattern was typical of wolves and coyotes; i.e., the female came into heat once a year and the male was capable of breeding from January to March (approximately). This differs from the breeding cycle in domestic dogs, where males can breed year-round and females normally come into heat twice a year. The New Hampshire study found no evidence for breeding between wild canids and domestic dogs in the wild. Crossing captive wild canids with domestic dogs advanced the breeding season; the resulting nonsynchrony of breeding cycles provides further evidence for the unlikelihood of successful mating between wild canids and domestic dogs in the wild. The authors concluded their study with the following summary.

1) The New Hampshire wild canids resembled large coyotes. In appearance, wild canid and domestic dog hybrids could not be distinguished from domestic dogs.

2) New Hampshire wild canids and coyotes (captive western) had a single annual breeding season in February. Hybrids (wild canid and domestic dog) also had a single season, but bred 3-4 months earlier. Litters from hybrids breeding in the wild would therefore be born in January or February with little likelihood for survival.

3) The unidentified wild canids were more nearly like coyotes but possessed some wolflike and/or doglike characteristics. They believed that these animals evolved from coyotes with the introduction of some dog and/or wolf genes sufficiently long ago for the population to have become stabilized.

4) The New England canids should be considered a form of coyote. The authors suggested that they be designated *Canis latrans* var., and be called eastern coyotes.

About this time (mid-1960s) a technique for identifying wolf, coyote and domestic dog skulls was developed by reducing 15 measurements to a single value.[13] This method was later applied to the wild canids raised in the New Hampshire study as well as additional wild canids collected from the northeast[14]. That study concluded that the wild canids sampled were predominantly coyote with some probable dog/wolf ancestry. The wild canids differed significantly from known dog-coyote hybrids, which were intermediate between the two parent stocks. The New England wild canids were closely related to coyotes from Minnesota. Results from the body measurements of wild canids from the northeast were in agreement with the behavioural studies in New Hampshire, and the authors agreed that this new wild canid should be called *Canis latrans* var. and be referred to as the eastern coyote.

These early studies of northeastern wild canids implied a degree of genetic pooling among coyotes, wolves, and possibly domestic dogs sometime during the process of colonization east from Minnesota and Manitoba. However, the suspected lack of reproductive synchrony between coyotes and domestic dogs, as well as between coyotes and first generation coyote and domestic dog hybrids suggested that successful breeding between the two species of *Canis* in the wild, especially in the northeast, was unlikely. Although there was a degree of similarity between northeastern wild canids and wolves, and although the species had similar breeding cycles, they also displayed little tolerance for each other, especially wolves towards coyotes. New studies were needed to confirm or refute the possibility for coyote and dog and coyote and wolf interbreeding in the wild. Two timely studies addressed that very issue.

A study in Kansas during the late 1960s compared observations and measurements of first and second generation coyote and domestic dog captive hybrids.[15] Results of that study suggested that small second generation litters might indicate reduced productivity in these hybrids. Both sexes of hybrids entered breeding condition in December, suggesting that the young of animals presumably less fit than coyotes would be born in midwinter. Another study of coyote and dog hybrids in Colorado during the mid-1960s also found hybrid females entering breeding condition in December.[16] In contrast to coyotes, but similar to domestic dogs, adult male hybrids do not help the female raise the young which further reduces the chances for survival of young born in winter.

During a series of controlled breeding experiments in Ontario during the mid-1960s a female wolf mated with a male coyote and twice successfully gave birth to hybrid litters.[17] In size and general appearance the hybrids resembled coyotes more closely than they did wolves, and most displayed the characteristic grizzled colour pattern characteristic of most eastern coyotes and southern timber wolves.

Results of these studies during the 1960s were interpreted by Henry Hilton of Maine to suggest *against* a coyote and domestic dog hybridization and *for* a coyote and wolf hybridization as the most plausible genetic lineage for the eastern coyote.[18] Hilton expands on this argument with 3 factors which would most likely prevent establishment of successfully reproducing coydog populations in the northeast: 1) the phase shift in breeding period would cause young to be born in the middle of winter; 2) unlike wild *Canis* the male parent does not usually assist in the care of the young; and 3) successive generations would continually lose the adaptive characteristics of wild *Canis*, particularly coyotes, and would not be so competitive in the wild.

In the mid-1970s Helen McGinnis, a graduate student at Pennsylvania State University, conducted an extensive study of specimen material from recently established populations of wild canids in that state.[19] Skull and tooth characters were compared visually and by statistical analyses. She found 9 of 76 skulls of Pennsylvania canids were probable coyote and dog hybrids, the rest were coyotes. Pennsylvania coyotes were smaller than wolves but larger than western coyotes. They were also larger and more doglike and/or wolflike than specimens examined from Upper Michigan and northern Wisconsin, Illinois, and Lower Michigan, Indiana, and Ohio. Coyotes from Pennsylvania were comparable in size to coyotes from New York, New England, and southern Ontario, but the trend towards dog and wolf was less pronounced. The most likely origin for wild canids in Pennsylvania was south from New York during the 1940s and 1950s. This origin would provide genetic ties with early colonizers from southern Ontario, and greater similarities with wild canids in New England than with coyotes to the west in Indiana, Illinois, and Ohio.

In the early 1980s researchers in Ontario studied physical measurements of wolves and coyotes collected in that province from 1959 to 1969.[20] Measurements of wolves and coyotes were also collected from Minnesota with the objective of identifying physically distinct groups of canids in Ontario and establishing their origin. They found 3 distinct groups of coyotes present in Ontario. The southeastern and Algonquin type coyotes appeared to have originated from coyote and wolf hybrids and resembled the large eastern coyote, as described by earlier studies in New England,[21] rather than coyotes found in Minnesota. Morphological features of dogs were not common in Ontario coyotes, suggesting that any dog characteristics common to coyotes in northeastern United States and Atlantic Canada were probably picked up through coyote and dog hybridization after wild canids crossed over from Ontario and Quebec.

A more recent study in Ontario examined the original coyote and wolf measurements from 1959 to 1969 and compared them to later measurements collected in 1983-84.[22] The results are quite interesting. In the brief interval between collections (approximately 15 years), coyotes had become larger and wolves had become smaller, at least in southeastern Ontario where the 1983-1984 collection was from. The earlier study had also shown that coyotes from central Ontario were smaller than coyotes from southeastern Ontario. The authors attempted to sort out this rather confusing situation with several possible explanations. Following European settlement and subsequent landscape change, the caribou and moose (large ungulates, i.e., hoofed grazing mammals) were replaced by white-tailed deer (small ungulates) as prey in southeastern Ontario. This decrease in size of available prey might explain the observed decrease in size of wolves, and increase in size of coyotes (from small game to deer). The two large predators converged on a single prey base. Wolves in central Ontario, still having access to moose and caribou, maintained their larger body size. This does not completely answer the question of why coyotes in central Ontario, which appear to be the product of coyote and wolf hybridization, have not increased in size at least proportionate to the size increase of southeastern coyotes. The authors suggested that this apparent discrepancy might be a consequence of higher environmental productivity (i.e., richer soils, warmer climate, greater abundance and variety of food) in southeastern Ontario.

One recent study compared weights of coyotes from Alaska with published weights of coyotes from various geographic areas.[23] That study concluded that the larger body size of eastern coyotes was best explained by enhanced food supply, that the fields and forests of the northeast supported a greater variety and abundance of food than the western prairies. This theory was later questioned and reasons given why greater body size was most likely a response by coyotes in the northeast to increased reliance on larger prey.

> "... we believe that the larger size of eastern coyotes constitutes an evolutionary adaptation to a larger prey, namely, the white-tailed deer, and that the increased size reflects a genotypic response. The larger size of coyotes results from either hybridization with gray or red wolves ... or from natural selection."[24]

One final study will conclude our review on the taxonomy of the eastern coyote in the northern front of colonization. This recent study relies on advances in biochemistry and may represent the final word on the clouded ancestry and taxonomy of the wild canid now firmly established throughout the northeast. Mitochondrial DNA (mtDNA) analysis (genetic fingerprinting) was applied to samples of organs and/or blood from 350 gray wolves and 327 coyotes from the northern United States and Canada and 87 canids from the southcentral United States.[25] Results of those sophisticated analyses can be summarized as follows.

1) Hybridization between gray wolves and coyotes occurs in the wild in eastern North America.

2) There may have been 2 distinct hybridization episodes, one between Minnesota and southwestern Ontario wolves and coyotes and a later event between more eastern populations of the 2 species (as postulated by earlier studies). Coyotes in southeastern Ontario, Quebec, and New England and Atlantic Canada may be part of the later hybridization episode.

3) More than half the gray wolves in Minnesota and southwestern Ontario and all

12

wolves sampled to the east of these localities have mtDNA genotypes that are likely derived from hybridization with coyotes.

4) Hybridization may be the primary cause of morphological variability among gray wolves in eastern North America.

5) The mtDNA genotype frequency data suggest that coyotes which immigrated into eastern Canada and New England had a similar origin.

6) The only genetic trace of the first migration remains in extant gray wolves with coywolf genotypes from Minnesota and southwestern Ontario.

7) Coyotes of the second wave likely have genetic contributions from eastern gray wolves.

8) Because the mitochondrial genome is maternally inherited, the absence of gray wolf genotypes in coyotes suggests that hybridization is asymmetric such that successful hybridization occurs only between male wolves and female coyotes. (Note: This is interesting given the successful breeding of a female wolf and male coyote in Ontario).[26]

9) Hybridization between coyotes and wolves was widespread and likely common in eastern North American populations. The genetic composition of the eastern coyote is not clear because of the maternal mode of mitochondrial DNA inheritance and an apparent interspecific mating asymmetry.

This completes our search for the ancestral roots of the coyote in the northeast. Let us now turn south and briefly review studies of the taxonomy and origin of coyotes which swept across the Mississippi River and became established throughout the southeastern United States over the past 30 years.

SOUTHERN FRONT

Although the origin and identification of coyotes which composed the initial eastward advance out of Texas, Arkansas, and Louisiana, differed from those of coyotes which moved east through the Great Lakes region and into the northeast, the process and subsequent product are remarkably similar. The original subspecies of coyote which occupied the southeastern portion of open prairie land was recognized as *Canis latrans frustror* and called the southeastern coyote.[27] Its range lay south of that occupied by *C. l. thamnos* (the northeastern coyote), the subspecies which moved east from Minnesota and represented the original coyote stock of the present wild canid in the northeast. The southeastern subspecies was the largest of the races of coyote, and was probably the result of genetic flow from adjacent populations of gray and red wolves.

The history of the genus *Canis* in the southeast is generally recognized as complex, with coyotes, dogs, and at least 3 species of wolves having occupied the region, at times simultaneously, over the past 10,000 years.[28] However, we will begin our short review near the turn of the last century, at which time the gray wolf had been eliminated from most of the eastern United States, the southern red wolf was virtually extinct, and wild canids (the southeastern coyote with red wolf genetics from early interbreeding in eastern Texas and parts of Arkansas) had not yet crossed the Mississippi River. Thus, in the early 20th century, the vast area east of the Mississippi River and south of the Ohio River valley was virtually empty of large wild canids (with the exception of feral domestic dogs), very similar to most regions of the northeast. In retrospect, and aware of the dynamics and interactions of wild canids in the southeast over the past 10,000 years, the question should not have been why but rather when wild canids of some ancestry would reoccupy these vacant lands. The wolf, a specialized predator not tolerant of environmental change and human disturbance, had not been able to adapt and cope. It was therefore left to the opportunistic and adaptable coyote to seize the opportunity and successfully colonize those eastern lands of plenty.

By 1950 the large southeastern coyote showed indications that hybridization with the dwindling numbers of red wolves was well under way in such states as Arkansas and Missouri.[29] By the early 1960s there was concern that the red wolf had already been replaced by the coyote west of the Mississippi River,[30] and the red wolf was subsequently placed on the list of rare and endangered species by the United States Fish and Wildlife Service in 1965.

A number of studies in the 1960s and 1970s attempted to clarify the taxonomy of Canis west of the Mississippi, and the interrelationships and hybridization among populations of coyotes, red wolves, and domestic dogs.[31] Suffice to say that the issue remained unresolved, and as in the northeast, the process of hybridization between coyotes, wolves and domestic dogs caused great variation in body size and colour of canids west of the Mississippi River through the first half of this century. The sequence of coyote occupation of the vast and diversified landscape east of the Mississippi is described under "Colonization" and I will not repeat it here. Once coyotes crossed the Mississippi River in the early 1960s, however, occupation of most of the southeast was rapid.

An examination of specimens collected in Alabama from 1917 through 1978 agreed with an earlier study which suggested that the population of wild canids in Alabama in the late 1970s, other than feral dogs, was predominantly coyotelike but suggested a slight shift in characters towards the red wolf.[32] The origin of the red wolf and whether it now represents a true species of wolf (Canis rufus), a subspecies of the gray wolf (Canis lupus) or a hybrid resulting from interbreedings of gray wolves and coyotes remains a contentious issue. Genetic integrity of a species is important when debating the merits of reintroducing captive-born stock back into formerly occupied ranges. Phillips and Henry summarized their recent discussion on red wolf taxonomy with the following:

> "In terms of behavior, ecology, and morphology red wolves have never exhibited the variability one would expect if the species originated from interbreedings of gray wolves and coyotes.... Data concerning red wolf form and function support that contention that red wolves possess wolf-derived nuclear DNA that produces a wolf-like rather than a hybrid-like organism. Thus, it seems that Canis rufus is a valid taxon or, at the very least, a subspecies of Canis lupus."[33]

Several hundred specimens of wild canids from Tennessee were examined in the 1980s to establish their identity and origin.[34] This study attempted to determine whether the newly founded population of coyotes in Tennessee most closely resembled C.l.frustror to the west or C.l.thamnos to the north. Using statistical procedures,

5 pelage and 20 skull measurements were compared. Not surprisingly, given the complicated ancestry already documented for eastern colonizing populations of wild canids, both subspecies of coyotes were identified. A multiple origin for coyotes in Tennessee was suggested, but one having a greater affinity with *C.l.frustror* than with *C.l.thamnos*. This agrees with my interpretation of the process of colonization on northern (*C.l.thamnos* origin) and southern (*C.l.frustror* origin) fronts.

In summary, most scientific evidence points to a mixed ancestry for the wild canids now occupying eastern North America. In the northeast, taxonomists have chosen to label the wild canid as the eastern coyote and identified it as *Canis latrans* var. In the southeast, although the genetic origin and evolvement of wild canids is very similar, taxonomists have remained content to refer to it as a regional variation of the original southeastern coyote and labelled it *C.l.frustror*. Given the documented process of hybridization and colonization of wild canids throughout most of eastern North America over the past 100 years, and given the remarkable similarity in the process of hybridization between coyotes, wolves, and possibly domestic dogs from Ontario to Mississippi, it is surprising that some taxonomic identification of this new wild canid has not been proposed. The genetic input from red wolves in the south has probably long been diluted and southeastern populations of wild canids are now breeding true similar to wild canids in the northeast. The need for a wider geographic sampling of wild canids, especially from north to south, is apparant, and a biochemical mitochondrian DNA analysis needs to be applied.

The red wolf, formerly distributed throughout much of the southern United States, had become virtually extinct by 1960 and was placed on the list of rare and endangered species in 1965 (H. J. Stains, 1975).

2 COLONIZATION

We begin the story of our "littlest hobo" before the turn of the century, when "wild canid" in the northeast meant timber wolves, and lonely coyotes sang to the prairie heavens as they entertained the cowboys round their evening campfire. More recently Wiley Coyote has found new ways to make us laugh at his ineptness at catching the roadrunner in television cartoons. Much has changed in the past few decades. Through all this time, however, certain people observed, studied, and documented the event as coyotes entered, occupied and moved on through a particular county, state, province or region. The arrival of the coyote generated much speculation, rumour, and general misinformation, and this new predator became the object of special attention by sportsmen, biologists, outdoor writers, and the general public. New records for coyotes in each state were reported by local newspapers. Editorials and letters-to-the-editor would pronounce, and often denounce, its impact on everything from deer to human safety, and the public would demand that "something be done" about this unwanted intruder. It raided chicken houses in Mississippi, destroyed watermelons in Alabama, ate stray housecats in New Hampshire, and, of course, preyed on deer in the northeast. It's arrival in Atlantic Canada was heralded with equal publicity, controversy, and concern. Who would have thought a few short years ago that coyotes would soon roam the highlands of Cape Breton Island and the spruce barrens of Newfoundland? But they are there today, and most likely will be there tomorrow, and it is in our best interest that we learn as much about our new guest as we possibly can.

PRE-SETTLEMENT DISTRIBUTION

The early distribution of coyotes in North America, prior to the arrival of Europeans and subsequent landscape change and alteration, was mainly restricted to the prairies and grasslands of the mid-western portion of the continent (*Figure 1*), although precise boundaries remain uncertain.[1]

As was pointed out earlier, the coyote is one of the few animals that has been able to extend its range within historic times, and this in spite of tremendous efforts of control and eradication. Stanley Young, in the classic book *The Clever Coyote*, was convinced that the coyote was originally an animal of the open plains, which, with the arrival of settlement, followed livestock and game into the forested areas of the mountains. The pre-European southern range limit was probably central Mexico. In the 16th century, with the introduction of livestock by the Spaniards, coyotes travelled south through Mexico and into the Central American Republics.[2]

The closed forests west of the Mississippi River represented the eastern pre-European boundary. Small fingers and pockets of coyote occupation probably extended farther east, especially in those states adjacent to the Mississippi River and south of the Great Lakes. This development probably also applies to the western and northern limits of coyote range. We must remember, as mentioned elsewhere, that coyotes and wolves do not make good bedfellows, and wolves frequently kill coyotes which happen to intrude into their territory.

Thus, prior to European occupation and the decline and subsequent elimination of wolves (a result of human persecution and displacement), coyotes did not wander far from the open prairie. This soon changed, and the interspecific barrier that discouraged coyotes from expanding their range was removed. It is interesting to note, especially for those who may feel that the coyote is a recent intruder into the east, that fossils resembling coyotes have been found in Pleistocene deposits in Maryland[3] and from a 1969 dig at Passamaquoddy Bay, New Brunswick.[4] In that era, climates, landscapes, and native plants and animals were probably quite different from those of today. Perhaps, then, we should consider the arrival of the coyote as a "reoccupation" of former range and see ourselves, in that respect, as the intruders!

EARLY EXPANSION (1800-1900)

This was an era of slow coyote range expansion, especially to the north and south (*Figure 2*). It was a period in American history often referred to as "when the west was won," a time of rapid land settlement and landscape change. The limited available records do not suggest a substantial shift in coyote range to the east, but, during the years 1860-1885, an extensive program of coyote control was in effect from central Saskatchewan and Manitoba south through Montana and the Dakotas and deep into the state of Texas.[5] What effect the removal of hundreds of thousands of coyotes had on their abundance, distribution, and range expansion is uncertain.

Coyotes did expand their range to the northwest, where they followed the trail of clearings, waste, and garbage left by the gold rushes north into the Yukon Territory and the state of Alaska during the late 1800s. By 1850 the range of the coyote extended from the Mississippi River west into the Sierra Nevada Mountains, north into Alberta, and south to southern Mexico.[6] Coyotes were numerous at that time, and according to some reports, several hundred might be seen during one day's travel. By 1900, however, coyote populations were substantially reduced by programs of control and the general reduction of large mammals on the prairies.

"About 1850, coyotes extended their range into Illinois and Michigan, Yucatan, northern California and the Pacific Northwest. The 1880s saw the great northern expansion during the Alaskan gold rush as the coyotes followed the trail of dead horses headed for the Yukon."[7]

Brian Slough, Furbearer Biologist for the Yukon Territory places the date when coyotes arrived there at around 1910, somewhat after the gold rush years.[8] This is

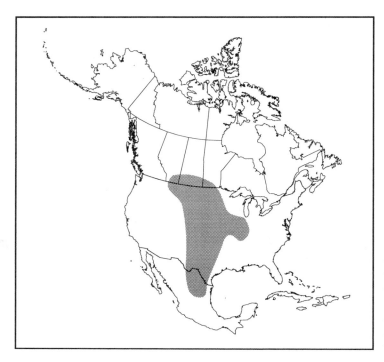

Figure 1: Prior to European settlement the coyote was restricted to the prairies of northcentral Mexico, the central United States, and southwestern Canada.

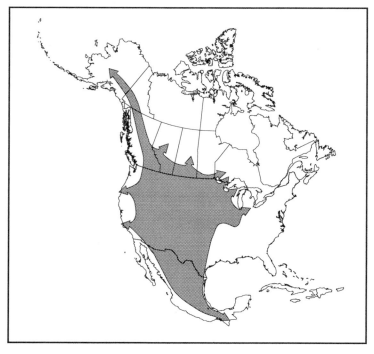

Figure 2: By 1900 coyotes had pushed south through Mexico into Central America, west into the Rocky Mountains, and northwest into Alaska following the trail of garbage and dead horses left by the gold rush of the late 1800s. Colonization of the eastern half of the continent did not begin until the early part of this century.

confirmed by A.L. Rand in his 1949 book *Mammals of Yukon, Canada*.

> *"Most people in Yukon say the coyote is a recent addition to the fauna, appearing in Pelly Valley about 1912."*[9]

Phil Koehl, Alaska Department of Fish and Game, writes:

> *"Coyotes were first noted in the state shortly after the turn of the 20th century. Populations were reported on the mainland of southeastern Alaska, then slowly expanded northward into the upper Tanana Valley from which they radiated in all directions. A population peak occurred around 1940, but since that time numbers have declined in many areas. There are few records of the coyote north of the Yukon River, although they probably wander into that area occasionally. Portions of the state with the highest densities of coyotes are the Kenai Peninsula, Matanuska-Susitna Valley, and the Copper River Valley. The coyote is scarce or absent from offshore islands of southeast Alaska, the arctic slope, and west of a line extending from Kotzebue Sound to Cook Inlet."*[10]

Winthrop Staples, a graduate student studying lynx at the Kenai National Wildlife Refuge (KNWR), Alaska, told me that coyotes there are closely tied to human development, and often rely on small game, road kills and garbage.[11] In more remote areas, wolves are common, and radio-marked coyotes in the KNWR have experienced up to 25% mortality from predation by wolves. Examination of coyote scats (fecal droppings) show a high reliance on moose, all of which would be from scavenging, much of it on moose killed by wolves. Predation by wolves on coyotes often occurs when coyotes attempt to scavenge moose carcasses. Another source of food is salmon, and coyotes in Alaska have been seen eating salmon and digging for old carcasses in the ice and snow along riverbanks throughout the winter. Staples speculates that because of the coyote's high dependence on moose killed by wolves, it might have difficulty surviving in Alaska without the benefits (food and protection) afforded by human activity.

The situation in Alaska is relevant to the habits and survival of coyotes which have recently become established on the island of Newfoundland. It has been suggested that in the extreme northeastern portions of its range many coyotes depend upon the availability of white-tailed deer to survive through the winter when environmental stress is most severe. Winters in Newfoundland can be severe but there are no white-tailed deer. Moose and caribou are common but, in contrast to Alaska, there are no wolves to act as primary predators and provide carcasses on which coyotes can scavenge, particularly in winter. Neither, of course, are there any wolves to prey on coyotes.

A high harvest of moose from hunting in Newfoundland ensures some carrion for coyotes, but how much of that remains available in late winter is uncertain. Direct predation by coyotes on moose in winter is unlikely. Direct predation on adult caribou is also unlikely, although limited predation on juveniles and crippled and diseased adults is possible. Caribou are often gregarious and nomadic, making that source of food unreliable to adult coyotes, which often remain within fixed territories. Predation by coyotes on young caribou and newborn moose in spring is certainly possible, but hardly dependable, and is only available for a short time of the year. (See

"Coyotes and White-Tailed Deer - Predator removal studies" for information on coyotes and caribou in Quebec.) Snowshoe hares are found throughout the forests of Newfoundland, and the availability of that food source will likely control coyote numbers there. However, given the coyote's history of adapting to new environments and new sources of food, its colonization of Newfoundland, and possible subsequent changes in social behaviour, feeding habits, and perhaps even morphology (larger body size for larger prey) will be interesting to follow.

Prior to 1900 the distribution of the coyote east of its presettlement "prairie range" was minimal. The major advance east through the Lake States and western and southern Ontario did not gain momentum until the early 1900s.

EASTERN COLONIZATION

I have tried to simplify the process of colonization of eastern North America by the coyote with a fairly basic "no frills" illustration based upon my interpretation of the literature and personal contacts (*Figure 3*). Arrows serve only to illustrate the approximate origin and direction of immigration while the dates show when colonizing coyotes first began to appear in areas where populations subsequently increased. The arrival and increase of coyotes in various states and provinces is dealt with in greater detail in the text. As in the previous section on taxonomy, I have chosen to describe the colonization of eastern North America by the coyote as two distinct, but in many respects related, geographical events: 1) the northern front of eastern expansion and 2) the southern front.

The northern front began at the turn of the century, and by the 1950s, the "wild canid" referred to as the eastern coyote had reached New England and had veered south into Pennsylvania and New Jersey. The southern front began later. To the west of the Mississippi River coyotes moved east out of Texas and Oklahoma and into Arkansas and Louisiana through the 1940s and 1950s. These canids were most likely coyote and red wolf hybrids and, as they progressed east, absorbed isolated pockets of red wolves, and any small centres of coyotes that may have developed from earlier liberations. This southern front of coyote and red wolf hybrids (similar to the coyote and gray wolf hybrids of the northern front) crossed the Mississippi River in the early 1960s and rapidly occupied the states of Mississippi and Alabama. Colonization continues into the 1990s, and the front has now reached all states south of the Ohio River valley, although populations are low and dispersed in such states as Virginia, North Carolina, and Florida.

Figure 3 also shows possible expansion of coyotes east and southeast from Ohio, Indiana, and Illinois. There may have been pockets of coyotes in those states since presettlement; at any rate, numbers there have increased substantially over the past 20 years. The extent of emigration out of those states and into western Pennsylvania, Kentucky, and western Tennessee is uncertain, but, especially in Tennessee, the direction of advance was from west to east. With the highway deaths of two coyotes in Delaware in 1993,[12] the species now appears established in all states east of the Mississippi River.

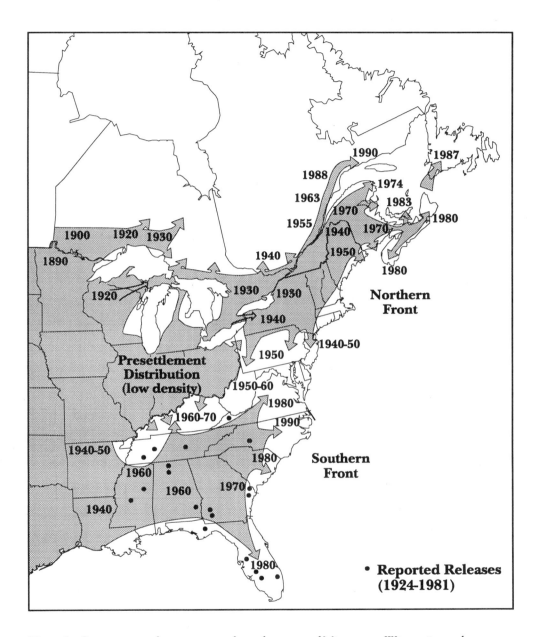

Figure 3: Coyotes moved east on a northern front out of Minnesota, Wisconsin, and Manitoba into Ontario in the early 1900s, but the southern front out of Louisiania and Arkansas did not sweep across the Mississippi River and flood the southeastern states until the 1960s. Colonization of the southeast may have been supplemented by releases of captive western coyotes.

The reader should understand that even though the gray wolf was absent from most of the eastern United States and Atlantic Canada in 1900, this vast tract of forested wilderness and agricultural landscape was not completely empty of wild canids prior to the arrival of coyotes a half century later. The red wolf, formerly distributed throughout much of southern United States, was still found in the Ozark Mountain region of Missouri, Arkansas and southeastern Oklahoma and in outlying sections in Louisiana and Texas by the early 1940s.[13] Although this southern wild canid was recognized as a separate species of wolf in early taxonomical studies, more recent collections of specimens suggest that it is probably a race of the gray wolf.[14] Three subspecies of the red wolf are recognized, but the similarity in size and skeletal measurements between red wolves and coyotes in Texas in the 1960s led to the conclusion that, at least in that state, the red wolf and coyote were the same species.[15] With the recent colonization of coyotes throughout the southern United States in the past 30 years, it is most likely that the red wolf has been absorbed into this new "wild canid" through hybridization, and that the wild canids south of the Ohio River valley represent a coyote and red wolf hybrid with possible western coyote influence from introductions and releases. There have also been a number of releases or escapes of coyotes brought in from western states for various purposes. (See *Figure 3*.) Add to this the possibility of interbreeding between red wolves, coyotes, and domestic dogs, including scattered feral domestic dogs, and the complexity of wild canid identification in the southern United States becomes further confounded.

For our purposes here, the reader need only have an appreciation of the complexities when attempting to trace the origin and taxonomy of wild canids in the southern United States. Suffice to say that the subject remains confusing, but as with the colonization of southern Ontario, New England, and Atlantic Canada, there is convincing evidence for a mixed origin. Through the process of range expansion to the east, what began as a race of western coyote has developed into an eastern coyote with a blend of coyote, wolf, and perhaps domestic dog. This applies equally to the northern and southern populations of eastern coyote. I addressed this issue more thoroughly under "Taxonomy." We will now review the process of recent colonization in more detail.

NORTHERN FRONT

The presettlement eastern limit of coyotes north of the Ohio River valley appears to have been the prairies of Iowa and southern Minnesota, with small pockets further east as far as the Lower Peninsula of Michigan[16] and Illinois.[17] It is possible that coyotes existed as far east as Indiana prior to European settlement[18] although, with both gray and red wolves present, they were probably never very plentiful. Coyotes began to extend their range east around the turn of the century. Although prior to this time coyotes most likely occupied pockets of favourable habitat in Wisconsin, Michigan, Illinois, Indiana, and Ohio, their numbers and range limits remained relatively stable.[19] The most likely explanation for the colonization by the coyote eastward through the forests and fields of southeastern Canada and the northeastern United States was the development of favourable habitat (and food supplies) and the extirpation of the wolf from much of its former range.

ONTARIO / LAKE STATES

We begin this important era in the early development of the eastern coyote around 1900 far from the Atlantic coast and deep into the northern forests of Minnesota and western Ontario. For reasons not fully understood, an early and quite rapid expansion of coyote range began out of northern Minnesota and southeastern Manitoba.

"There appear to have been two main routes of invasion into Ontario. One, which originated in Manitoba and extreme western Ontario and northeastern Minnesota, extended eastward along trans-continental railway lines and roads in the late 1920s and early 1930s. This invasion is evident from the great increase in the numbers of pelts of "prairie wolves" which were traded at Hudson Bay Company stores throughout northern and central Ontario during this period. Few, if any, had been trapped in these areas prior to this time. The peak in this eastward expansion probably occurred in 1928, and it appears that this movement, although relatively short-lived, was rapid and extensive and was responsible for the establishment of coyote populations in the farming areas of the Clay Belt and their occurrence locally in northern Ontario as far north as James Bay and other parts of the Hudson Bay Lowlands. Undoubtedly, this eastern movement also contributed to coyotes now established west of Lake Superior and along the north shore of Lake Huron and Georgian Bay.... A more extensive and longer-lived eastward expansion of range followed the southern shores of the Great Lakes. It also originated in the prairies and had been steadily progressing eastward across the "Lake States" prior to the northern invasion of the 1920s. The first evidence of this movement into Ontario were the coyotes, mentioned earlier, which probably crossed Lake Huron or Lake St. Clair. Branches from this eastward movement may have extended north at the western end of Lake Superior, entered Ontario from populations now established along the north shore of Lake Huron and on Manitoulin Island. The main extension of range eastward throughout southern Ontario has tended to follow the shores of the Great Lakes and most of the cleared areas of southern Ontario now have well-established coyote populations." [20]

A 1929 booklet on the mammals of Ontario commented that,

"The brush wolf [i.e., coyote] ranges over the greater part of the province, from the Manitoba boundary as far east as Ottawa, south as far as the Kawartha lakes and north as far as the main line of the Canadian National Railway... The brush wolf is smaller than the timber wolf and usually has finer fur of a more reddish hue." [21]

A review of the physical similarities and possible origins of wolves and coyotes in Ontario concluded that "Evidently, there is considerable confusion about the identity and origin of various canids in southern Ontario as well as the origin of wolves in northern Ontario."[22]

By 1975 the following types of wolves were recognized in Ontario: the northern

Hudson Bay wolf of the Hudson and James Bay coastal areas, the Boreal type found in the northern and central forests, the Algonquin type of the southern deciduous-coniferous forest, and the small Southern Tweed wolf with some coyotelike characteristics. The precise origin of the smaller Tweed type wolf remains in question, although they closely resemble large coyotes.[23]

A 1985 study of body and skull measurements of all these forms of wild canids in Ontario concluded that coyotes in southern and southeastern Ontario descended from coyotes that hybridized with wolves, most likely the smaller Algonquin type. The small Tweed wolf may also be the consequence of early hybridization between resident wolves and coyotes moving east from Minnesota and Manitoba in the early 1900s.

> *"Hybridization between coyotes and wolves may result when there is a breakdown in reproductive barriers such as interspecific agonistic behaviour and differing habitat preferences which normally maintain these species in reproductive isolation."*[24]

It was in southern Ontario, then, sometime early in this century, that coyotes of the western race *C. l. thamnos,* during early colonization eastward, most likely interbred with the smaller Algonquin race of gray wolf. Consequent breeding of hybrids back with wolves may have produced the present day small Tweed race of wolf. Similarly, breeding by hybrids back with colonizing coyotes, most likely produced what we now refer to as the eastern coyote, *Canis latrans* var.

QUEBEC

Coyotes were first reported from the Ottawa River area of the province of Quebec in 1944, when a specimen was captured near Luskville, in the southwestern part of the province.[25] Subsequent captures in the counties of Huntington (1952, 1954, and 1957), Argenteuil (1955), Beauce and Frontenac (1957), and Brome (1958) confirmed the coyote's progressive colonization of that province.[26] By 1963, the coyote could be found as far east as L'Islet on the south shore of the St. Lawrence River and as far as La Malbaie on the north shore. In 1971 this new predator was reported at Rivière-du-Loup, and in 1973 a wild canid captured near Ste-Anne-des-Monts, in the Gaspé region, was positively identified as an adult male coyote.[27] In October 1974 two other coyotes were captured near St.-Ulric, southwest of Matane.[28] Today the coyote occupies most regions of Quebec south of the 50th degree of latitude, from remote areas such as Abitibi-Temiscaming to the north shore of the St. Lawrence across from the island of Anticosti.[29]

NORTHEASTERN UNITED STATES

The exact sequence of colonization, hybridization, backcrossing and continued colonization remains unclear, but we do know that early specimens of wild canids began to appear in New York by the 1920s[30] and in Maine by the 1930s.[31] Some of these early records may well have been coyote and dog hybrids (coydogs) that did not represent true specimens of colonizing eastern coyotes. It is this early thrust of coyotes through southern Ontario, the likely interbreeding with wolves and subsequent appearance of wild canids in the northeastern states that makes this early period in the history of colonization most important. Coyotes moved across the St. Lawrence River and into New York perhaps as early as the 1920s, into Maine by the 1930s, and into New Brunswick by the late 1950s.

This sounds fairly straightforward, but the precise sequence and mechanics of colonization by the eastern coyote was probably anything but. Early accounts of wild canids in the northeast suggest that many may have been crosses between coyotes and domestic dogs (coydogs).[32] As we reviewed earlier, coydogs seldom breed successfully in the wild, and most appear at the forefront of early coyote colonization when densities are low and mate selection difficult.

Besides the penetration of coyotes into New York from Ontario, coyotes from small pockets of occupation in Illinois, Indiana, and Ohio may have also moved east into Pennsylvania and north into New York. The importance of coyotes from those states to the process of colonization in the northeast is uncertain, but it was probably not significant. Coyotes from those sources would have soon met, and interbred with, coyotes moving south through New York and thus have been integrated into the eastern coyote race.

In the late 1970s skulls from coyotelike wild canids from Pennsylvania were compared with samples of western coyotes, domestic dogs, gray wolves from the Great Lakes region and southeastern Canada, coyote and dog hybrids, coyote and wolf hybrids, and other coyotelike canids from other parts of the Great Lakes region and the northeastern United States.

> "Nine of 76 skulls of Pennsylvania canids were identified as probable ... coyote x dog hybrids, the rest as coyotes.... The typical Pennsylvania coyote is larger and more dog- and/or wolflike than those in samples from Upper Michigan and northern Wisconsin, Illinois and Lower Michigan, Indiana, and Ohio. They are comparable in average size to coyotes in New York, New England, and southern Ontario.... Pennsylvania coyotes are similar to New England coyotes....Coyotes which occasionally appeared in Pennsylvania at the turn of the century probably ... had been imported from the west and later escaped or were released from captivity.... By the late 1930s wild coyotes were scattered across the northern half of the state. Some may have originated in southern Ontario, crossing the Niagara River and southwestern New York. Others may have come from Ohio."[33]

The rather circuitous development suggested for eastern coyotes which colonized Pennsylvania is probably not unusual, and a "composite" ancestry for coyote populations in many other regions of North America is probably responsible for so much confusion in attempts to sort out the "family tree." Bill Severinghaus, longtime deer biologist for the state of New York, provides us with these early observations on the presence of wild canids in that state during the 1930s and 1940s.

> "During the years from 1937 to 1940, the author [Bill Severinghaus] travelled extensively during the winter through and in the vicinity of deer wintering areas in the central Adirondacks [of New York]. Although [I] saw an occasional bobcat track and an abundance of porcupine tracks, [I] could find no fisher or signs of

coyotes.... [I]t is evident that coyotes were present along the northern side of the St. Lawrence River in Ontario after about 1935 and in Quebec by 1944. Thus it is possible for coyotes to reach New York by crossing the St. Lawrence River."[34]

Coyotes may have occurred in Vermont and New Hampshire in the 1930s and in Maine about 1936.[35] The earliest verified specimen from New Jersey was in 1948, although that 36-pound male was thought to have escaped or been released from captivity. The first "wild-type" canid was not confirmed in New Jersey until 1958[36] and it has been suggested that New Jersey coyotes entered the state from New York; they may also have crossed the Delaware River from Pennsylvania.

The period from 1940 through the mid-1950s was one of slow population growth and expansion of coyotes north of the Ohio River valley. Colonization in the extreme north appears to have moved up the St. Lawrence River valley through southern Quebec. Following the first record of a coyote in Quebec in 1944,[37] colonization along both sides of the St. Lawrence River was quite rapid. Early pioneering coyotes had already moved into New York, Vermont, Maine, and New Jersey and their numbers slowly expanded during this era. It was also during this period that colonizing populations of eastern coyotes began breeding true and the incidences of coydogs became less frequent.

"By 1942 and 1943 ... wild hybrid canids were being shot and trapped [in the Adirondacks].... The author saw more than 10 of these. They were big animals weighing 35 to 50 pounds.... By 1950, the gray wild canids were present in most localities of the central Adirondacks and were being seen more frequently in the peripheral sections. The population was definitely expanding its range.... During the late 1940s and 1950s, hundreds of coydogs were seen at deer checking stations in the Adirondacks.... During the 1950s, animals essentially coyotelike in appearance became predominant in the wild canid population in the Adirondacks.... In recent years, hybrids have become more and more infrequent."[38]

Coyotelike animals were reported from Maine during the 1930s, some being identified as coyotes, some as dogs, and others as hybrid offspring (coydogs) of dogs and coyotes.[39] From 1936 to 1944 the Maine Cooperative Wildlife Research Unit received the carcasses of 35 wild canids; all but 2 were identified as dogs. Sixteen more canids were killed and sent to the Coop Unit for identification between 1944 and 1953; 15 of these were dogs but one was identified as a dog-coyote cross. There are few records of wild canids in Maine from 1953 to 1962, suggesting a time of population stability from the 1930s (when they first appeared in Maine) to when they began to rapidly increase in the early 1960s. This 30-year period of only scattered reports is difficult to explain, especially when considering the speed of colonization in other states and provinces during the 30-year period from 1960 to 1990 (e.g. Mississippi, Pennsylvania, Nova Scotia).

It would appear, then, that the vanguard of eastern coyote colonization did not reach the northeast much before the 1950s. Prior to that most of the wild canids recorded were probably feral domestic dogs and coyote-dog hybrids. Juvenile coyotes can disperse hundreds of kilometres, and it is quite probable that a trickle of dispersers reached the northeast from southern Ontario long before the main population front arrived. Many early dispersers may have bred with domestic dogs, but the coydog offspring, although being seen and trapped occasionally, could not successfully breed and establish viable populations. Once coyote numbers reached densities that allowed successful pairings among coyotes, and breeding territories became established, populations would rapidly increase, and this appears to have happened in the 1960s and 1970s throughout much of the northeast.

It is quite probable that, more by accident than design, occasional coyotes were "liberated" into the northeast from western sources. There is evidence to suggest a release of several western coyote mascots by troops from Oklahoma and Texas stationed in New York in 1941.[40] Such occasional releases would not have significantly contributed to growth in coyote populations because of the rarity of potential mates in the region at that time, and the consequent production of coydogs if reproduction occurred at all.

> "...Reports suggest that throughout the East it was not uncommon for captive western coyotes to escape or be released. These animals may have been the progenitors of small localized populations of alien coyotes which then died out, were killed, or were genetically assimilated into existing populations. This would account for the seemingly spontaneous occurrence of local "pockets" of coyotes in Maine ... New York ... and Pennsylvania.... Such groups of animals, for the most part, cannot be considered part of the principal coyote dispersal into the East."[41]

The spread of coyotes in Vermont (first specimen in 1942) and New Hampshire (first specimen in 1944) closely paralleled that described for New York and Maine, although somewhat later.[42] Coyotes were not identified in Massachusetts until 1957-1958.[43] About the same time (late 1950s) coyotes first appeared in Connecticut.[44] Although a coyote was shot in Maryland as early as 1921, it was 40 years (1961) before a second specimen was identified.[45] The first coyote was shot in New Jersey in 1939 and the second, which was believed to have been released or escaped from captivity, in 1948.[46] In 1958 the first eastern coyote was shot by a deer hunter in northwestern Passaic County, New Jersey; today coyotes are distributed throughout the state.[47] Coyotes were found across the northern half of Pennsylvania by the late 1930s, and by the 1950s eastern type coyotes began to spread into southern sections of that state. The origin of these coyotes is believed to have been southern Ontario via the Niagara River and New York, though some may have crossed over from Ohio.[48]

The history of colonization of the eastern coyote into West Virginia is not well documented and numbers have remained low.[49] However it is probable that coyotes dispersed into West Virginia from Ohio and Pennsylvania in the 1950s or 1960s. Coyotes may have been in Ohio during presettlement; if so, numbers were low. The earliest reported occurrence of coyotes in Ohio was in 1919.[50] Occasional reports continued from 1934 to 1961, although none were reported for the period 1961 through 1971, perhaps because to see them was no longer a novelty.

ATLANTIC CANADA

In his 1968 book *The Mammals of New Brunswick*, W. Austin Squires comments on early reports of coyotes in that province.

> "For nearly fifty years there have been reports of the occasional wild dog or wolf being seen in New Brunswick forests and several of these have been trapped or shot. Few of these have been examined by experts qualified to identify them.... However, one killed near Sussex in 1958 has been identified definitely as a coyote, and another taken in Kent County appears to be a coyote but is not supported by a skull."[51]

The first confirmed coyote in Atlantic Canada referred to by Squires was shot at Sussex on Boxing Day of 1958. The following account of that incident appeared in the January 1, 1959 issue of *The Kings County Record*.

NO MORE MARAUDING OR HOWLING BY THIS ANIMAL—BUT WHAT IS IT ?

> It could be a timber wolf, a coyote, a wild dog or a number of other animals of that general description, and until its head and skin are received and studied by wild life authorities at Fredericton there will be that intriguing doubt.

> 'Twas the Night After Christmas', instead of the classical 'Before,' when the marauder which had been bothering Albert Freeze and his family and neighbours, on Maple Avenue extension, finally met its doom. He fell to a blast from a shotgun in the hands of Bob McFarlane, of Penobsquis, who was visiting Mr. Freeze. The latter was so cold, after long standing in the outdoors to get a bead

Albert Freeze holds the first confirmed coyote in New Brunswick, which was shot at Sussex by Bob McFarlane in 1958 (A. Freeze).

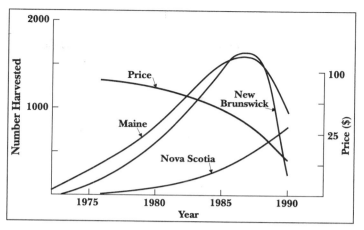

Figure 4: The harvests of coyotes in Maine, New Brunswick, and Nova Scotia reflect the trend in population expansion east. Declines in the harvest of coyotes in the late 1980s were most likely caused by a decline in the value of fur and reduced trapping effort.

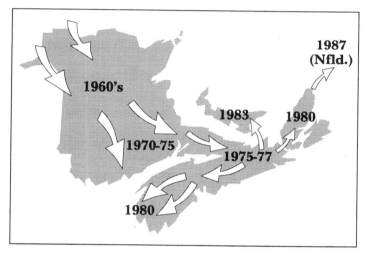

Figure 5: Viable breeding populations of eastern coyotes probably entered northwestern New Brunswick from Maine and Quebec in the 1960s and reached southwestern Nova Scotia by 1980. Coyotes were first reported on Prince Edward Island in 1983, and had reached Newfoundland, probably on winter ice, by 1987.

on the visitor, that he could not hold a rifle steady. A third member of the posse was Roy Carhart, a neighbour of Mr. Freeze.

The animal, viewed by hundreds of people since it was caught, weighed between 30 and 35 pounds, was black and greyish brown in color, had a large 'heavy' head and a bushy tail, much like a fox appendage. He was of the general size of a smaller breed of police dog and was in excellent condition. Mr. Freeze explained that it probably had found food in material discarded from the slaughter house he operates, and it had been known to steal the family's chickens from time to time, and rabbits which the children were raising.

Practically every one of the hundreds of people who visited the Freeze home to view the animal had his, or her, own opinion of its 'identity.' One Sussex couple, who had resided in the West for some years and were familiar with coyotes, were quite certain it was not an animal of this type; another resident felt it

29

looked very much like a timber wolf. Others were of the opinion it had quite a bit of police dog ancestry. Mr. Freeze had the animal skinned on Tuesday and was preparing to send it to Bruce Wright, noted authority, at Fredericton. Mr. Wright's conclusions will be eagerly awaited.

Mr. Freeze, while pleased that the animal was finally caught, was sorry that, because he was 'chilled to the bone' he could not fire the telling round himself." [52]

Bruce Wright confirmed that the Sussex animal was indeed a coyote, and the pelt is now in possession of the Biology Department at the University of New Brunswick.

Although there were several subsequent reports of "coyotelike" wild canids being seen in the province, it was not until 1966 that the next specimen was killed by a car near Woodstock, not far from the Maine border. The earliest reports and specimens in New Brunswick suggest an initial movement into the province from Maine, probably beginning in the 1950s. However, these early dispersers did not successfully establish breeding populations in the province, for only 2 more were killed between 1966 and 1972. (One was shot near Moncton in 1970 and the other was trapped near Edmundston in 1972.) Thus in the first 14 years (1958-1972) of confirmed coyote presence in New Brunswick only 4 were known to have been killed. This extended period of low coyote numbers in New Brunswick was similar to the situation in New York during the 1930s and 1940s. As mentioned earlier, dispersers from established populations, usually juveniles, may enter and occupy new territory long before the vanguard of the true breeding population arrives. The low densities of dispersers makes mate selection difficult, and often impossible, thus preventing successful colonization.

Five wild canids trapped in scattered locations throughout New Brunswick in 1973-74 were identified as 2 coydogs, 2 coyotes and 1 suspected coyote-wolf cross. Weights for those 5 canids varied from 26 - 48 pounds (12 to 22 kg). David Cartwright, furbearer biologist for the province at that time, reported that sightings of coyotelike canids in 1974 were restricted to those counties bordering the state of Maine. [53] Four more coyotes were killed in Carleton County (next to Maine) in 1975. A successful breeding population was probably established in New Brunswick by the early 1970s.

Trapping records show that the New Brunswick population grew rapidly during the 10 years from 1976, when 30 were killed, to 1987, when 1,633 were killed (*Figure 4*). Harvests have subsequently declined. Most of that decline probably reflects a drop in fur prices and decreased trapping effort. However it may also indicate a stable or declining coyote population. The provincial deer herd, which peaked around 1985 (based upon hunter harvest), began to decline in the late 1980s, a decline which has continued into the 1990s. If many coyotes in the northeast depend upon white-tailed deer for survival in late winter, as the literature suggests, then a decline in deer would affect coyote productivity, survival and numbers. Disease, especially mange, may also have contributed to a decline of coyotes in New Brunswick by the early 1990s. The "increase in coyotes - decrease in deer" scenario in New Brunswick during the 1980s was not new, and the response it generated from the public, particularly deer hunters, was typical of public response during times of coyote expansion in Maine, New York, and other regions of the northeast.

The first confirmed coyote in Nova Scotia was trapped in the winter of 1976-77 by Howard Porter (right) of Country Harbour Mines, Guysborough County (*The Chronicle-Herald*, Halifax).

Johnny MacCormack holds the first confirmed coyote on Prince Edward Island, which he trapped near Souris (*Canadian Press*).

The first confirmed coyote in Nova Scotia was trapped by Howard Porter in Country Harbour Mines, Guysborough County, during the winter of 1976-77.[54] Harry Mowatt, a provincial ranger at the time, shot the second coyote in Pictou County in July 1977. That coyote had been killing sheep in the area for over a year (as many as 70 sheep kills were credited to that particular coyote) and Harry had tried various means for its capture. He finally shot it at night with a rifle fitted with a night scope. Coyotes probably entered the province from New Brunswick by the early 1970s and early records were restricted to the northern counties of Guysborough, Pictou, and Antigonish. Total occupation of Nova Scotia was rapid, and within 4 years of the first record coyotes were distributed from Yarmouth County in the extreme southwest to Cape Breton Island in the northeast (*Figure 5*). The rate of increase in coyote harvest was similar to that in New Brunswick 5-10 years earlier.

The first confirmed coyote on Prince Edward Island was trapped by Johnny MacCormack in 1983.[55] That coyote, a male, was trapped north of Souris Township in Kings County, probably having crossed Northumberland Strait from Nova Scotia on the ice in winter. Confirmed deaths of coyotes on Prince Edward Island from 1987-88 through 1993-94 were 1, 2, 5, 17, 26, 95 and 131,[56] indicating a rapidly expanding population in that province. There are reports of coyotes reaching Newfoundland by 1985 although the first specimen was not confirmed until 1987. Bill Power commented on the arrival of coyotes in that province in his "Outdoors" column of the St. John's *Evening Telegram* (May 23, 1992).

> *"As to how they arrived, officials are about 99.9 per cent sure coyotes established here by crossing on sea ice in the Cabot Strait from Nova Scotia. It's believed they were attracted by the smell of seal carcasses left on the ice by Magdalen Islanders or Newfoundland landsmen. A small pack of three to five animals was reported coming ashore in the Port au Port area in 1985 and the next year three animals were seen less than a mile offshore by a Stephenville harbor master. The first coyote specimen taken in Newfoundland was a juvenile struck by a vehicle and killed in the Hughes Brook area near Deer Lake in 1987."*

The reports of 30 others killed in that province up to 1994[57] suggest that the eastern coyote has now established a breeding population throughout most of Newfoundland.

SOUTHERN FRONT

The Ohio River valley is not a significant barrier to dispersing coyotes, but it does serve as the approximate boundary between the northern and southern fronts of eastern coyote colonization. Although the red wolf was eliminated from most of its former range in the southern United States by the turn of the century, there may have been limited crossbreeding between red wolves and the first colonizing or introduced coyotes.[58] Skulls examined from wild canids in Arkansas illustrated the confusion in present-day taxonomy of wild canids in many of the southern states because of the interbreeding among coyotes, dogs and red wolves.[59]

> *"In the last 50 years the coyote has become the predominant wild canid in Arkansas, although the red wolf and dog characteristics are obvious in the present canid population.... By the early 1920s coyotes had extended their range into northwestern Arkansas.... As coyotes advanced eastward across the state the red wolf population declined and became confined to inaccessible mountains and swamp bottomland forests. In the late forties only scattered family groups of red wolves remained.... The present wild canid population appears to approximate a panmictic unit with coyotes, dogs, possible red wolves and intermediates of these forms at times mating with each other and producing offspring.... We feel that the advancing coyote population in Arkansas may have absorbed both red wolves and dogs....*

> *"It seems that the red wolf is extinct in Arkansas and its genes have been incorporated into the gene pool of the predominant coyote population."[60]*

In 1939 few coyotes were to be found in that vast expanse of the continent south of the Ohio River valley and east of the Mississippi River. There had been introductions of western coyotes and isolated pockets of wild canids, some of which probably represented coyote and dog hybrids, but eastern colonization had not yet crossed the Mississippi River. Between 1925 and 1987 there were at least 20 cases of early liberations of western coyotes into southeastern United States (see *Figure 3*).[61]

The main thrust of dispersal on the southern front moved across the Mississippi River in the early 1960s, swept through Alabama and north into Tennessee by 1970, through Georgia during the 1970s and into Florida by the 1980s. Dispersal continued northeast into South Carolina by 1980 and into North Carolina and Virginia during the 1980s. A more gradual trickle of dispersers entered Kentucky from expanding populations in Ohio, Illinois, Indiana, and Missouri during the 1960s and 1970s, perhaps bolstered by dispersers from West Virginia and north from Tennessee. All of this was probably supplemented by canids of various ancestry radiating out from local areas of release or escape.

We will now look more closely at the occupation by coyotes of most of the southeastern United States during the 30-year period from 1960 through 1990. The reader should be aware that the colonization of the southeastern United States by wild canids was independent (at least in origin) from colonization of the northeast that occurred predominantly during the 30-year period from 1950 to 1980.

Coyotes first entered Louisiana in the late 1940s and quickly became established throughout the state. It is probable that coyotes interbred with remnant populations of red wolves in Texas prior to their arrival in Louisiana.

> *"Most authorities agree that due to the near extirpation of the red wolf from 1920 to 1940 through extensive loss of forest habitat, the bounty system, government control operations, and intensive hunting, the niche or space for another large predator became available. This was quickly filled by the coyote....* [H]*ybridization between coyotes from Texas and surviving red wolves has produced the coyotelike canid present in Louisiana today."*[62]

This all sounds very familiar. Although the northern front of dispersing coyotes which passed through the Great Lake States and southern Ontario in the 1920s and 1930s was quite separate from the front which moved into Louisiana from Texas in the 1940s, the contributing factors were similar. The interbreeding between early colonizing coyotes and rapidly declining red wolves in the south was remarkably similar to the interbreeding between coyotes and gray wolves in southern Ontario.

Coyotes may have moved into northwestern Arkansas in the 1920s, somewhat earlier than their arrival in Louisiana, had spread beyond the central part of the state by the 1950s and had reached the most southeastern county by 1964.[63]

> *"...The advancing coyote population in Arkansas may have absorbed both red wolves and dogs."*[64]

By 1964 coyotes had reached the Mississippi River and had crossed over into the state of Mississippi by 1966.[65] The increase of coyotes in Mississippi was remarkable. The number harvested increased from 177 in 1977 to 29,742 by 1984, at which time the state coyote population was estimated at 200,000. By 1988 the harvest had reached 40,000 and the population was estimated at 400,000.[66]

Coyotes appeared in Alabama as early as 1924 but, as in other southern states, most early records are attributed to releases.[67] The first documented release in that state, however, was not until the late 1950s.[68] The "front" of colonization out of Mississippi reached Alabama in the 1960s. Only 8 coyotes or coyote hybrids were known from Alabama prior to 1970.[69] Annual harvests increased from 300 in 1977 to 600 in 1979 and to 10,000 by 1983. These new wild canids commonly exceeded 31 pounds (14 kg), supporting the theory of interbreeding with the larger red wolf.[70]

In Georgia the first coyotes were seen as early as 1929,[71] but like other early observations of wild canids in the southeast, these were probably releases of western coyotes. By the mid-1980s coyotes had moved into that state from the west and colonized at least 3/4 of the counties. Western coyotes were brought to Florida as pets in the 1920s, but by 1980 only 26 wild coyotes had been recorded in that state although eventual total occupation was predicted.[72] A resurvey in 1988 determined that

> "Coyotes now occur throughout most of Florida and appear to be well established across the panhandle and into north-central Florida. Although there are scattered reports of coyotes throughout the central peninsula...it does not appear that coyotes are firmly established in the central and southern portions of the state. It is expected that coyotes will continue to expand their distribution in Florida. Although there are rumors that coyotes continue to be illegally imported and released, we suspect that further range expansion will result primarily through the dispersal of coyotes born within the state."[73]

Coyotes were first sighted in South Carolina in 1979.[74] The annual harvest of coyotes expanded from 0 in 1985 to 16 in 1990, at which time the state population was expanding rapidly. Perry Sumner, Furbearer Project Leader for the North Carolina Wildlife Resources Commission, believed that in 1991 coyotes were just becoming established in that state.

> "Coyotes in the western counties appear to result from range expansion while the coyotes occurring in the eastern two-thirds of the state probably have come from illegal releases."

The first coyotes were reported in western Tennessee in the early 1960s, and they moved easterly through that state during the following two decades. By 1989 coyotes were well established in western Tennessee and some central parts, and they were expected to increase in the eastern regions of that state.[75]

The earliest written account of a coyote in Kentucky appeared in 1949. The next report was not until 1965, but by 1987 coyotes were widely distributed throughout the state. It seems the appearance of coyotes in western Kentucky was shortly preceded by their presence in southeastern Missouri and Illinois. Just shortly after the mid-1960s the coyote began showing up along the southeast border of Indiana. By the mid-1970s there were reports of coyotes in nearly every county in the western one-third of Kentucky. In general terms, coyote population levels have been greatest in western Kentucky and lowest in the east. Monthly roadkill totals for the state increased from 11 in 1981 to 91 by 1986 and 166 in 1988.[76]

Specimens of wild canids shot in Kentucky as early as 1948-49 probably originated from coyotes of Texas stock which escaped from a farm. Thus it appears that the vanguard of coyote colonization in Kentucky moved from west to east and probably originated in Missouri, Illinois, and Indiana.

By now you should have some appreciation of the complexities, and remaining mysteries, which surround the genetic origins of the eastern coyote, and of the magnitude of its development throughout the past century. The arrival of the coyote in the northeast, particularly in Atlantic Canada, has been the final act in a drama of continental proportions. Coyotes now lick at the bones of moose from the arctic slopes of Alaska to the black spruce bogs of Newfoundland and feed on white-tailed deer from the closed spruce-fir forests of the highlands of Cape Breton Island to the open scrublands of southern Texas. No other large carnivore can boast such a record. So let us now look at this animal which has presented itself to us, for better or for worse, depending upon your point of view. How has this particular animal been so successful at a time when others are losing their battle for survival?

3 PHYSICAL CHARACTERISTICS

"Whether one accepts literally the explanation of Creation in Genesis, or inclines toward acceptance of modern biological theories which spring largely from the concepts of Darwin, there can be no disputing the reality that animals are superbly adapted to the special lives they lead." [1]

Contrary to popular belief, the coyote of Atlantic Canada is not the monster of the northern woods. Although larger than its western cousin, it is only slightly heavier than coyotes in Kansas and Minnesota and no larger than coyotes in New England. In fact, coyotes in the southeastern states are as large, if not larger than coyotes in the northeast. This is not to suggest that northeastern coyotes are small, for a 35-40 pound (16-18 kg) wild predator is large anywhere, but weights from samples of coyotes east of the prairies show remarkable consistency.

The original northeastern coyote, which moved out of northern Minnesota some 100 years ago, was nearly as large as coyotes now distributed throughout the northeast. Although interbreeding with the red wolf in the southern states and with the gray wolf to the north has no doubt contributed to the development of larger body size, most coyotes in forested habitat are, as a rule, larger and darker than prairie coyotes. Some large specimens may reach 50 or 60 pounds (23-27 kg), but this is unusual, and 30- or 40- pound (14-18 kg) coyotes seem to be the average. Coydogs, or coyote-domestic dog hybrids, are most common during early coyote colonization, and records suggest that some of these early specimens reached 60 or 70 pounds (27-32 kg). The occasional old male eastern coyote might reach those weights as well, but this would be uncommon. The following accounts serve to give the reader an appreciation of the size and coloration of North American coyotes in general, and the eastern coyote in particular.

Dr. C. Hart Merriam, an ambitious turn-of-the-century American taxonomist, left us the following meticulous description of the western coyote.

> *"... Muzzle dull and rather pale fulvous, finely sprinkled with gray hairs (chiefly above) and with black hairs (chiefly on the cheeks); top of head from front of eyes to ears grizzled gray, the pale rufous zone of underfur showing through,*

The eastern coyote is believed to have interbred with wolves, but these 2-year-old coyotes at Shubenacadie Wildlife Park—captured as pups in northern Nova Scotia—have typical coyote features. They display here a sociality that is characteristic of eastern coyotes (G. Parker).

but the gray predominating; ears deep rich fulvous, sparingly sprinkled with black hairs; upper parts from ears to tail coarsely mixed buffy gray and black; under parts and upper lip whitish; long hairs of throat sparingly tipped with blackish, giving the broad collar a grizzled appearance; fore-legs and feet dirty whitish; becoming dull clay color on outer side of leg; hind legs and feet dull fulvous on outer sides, white on inner side and on dorsal surface of feet, the change from fulvous to white rather abrupt; tail narrowly tipped with black, its under side whitish basally, becoming pale fulvous on distal half and tipped and edged with black." [2]

Stanley Young provides an early account of coyotes found on the western prairies of the United States in the early 1900s.

"The coyote, which sometimes is commonly called brush wolf, and also the American jackal, because of its close resemblance to that South European and African mammal, and such other names as prairie wolf, heul wolf, and steppen wolf, is a small wolf weighing usually between 13 to 30 pounds, or about a third as much as the average sized gray wolf. Many coyotes resemble the modern collie dog in appearance, or the so-called 'toy-sheperd.' However, it has slenderer proportions, including a long, narrow, pointed nose; small rounded nose pads; large pointed ears; slender legs; small feet; and a bushy tail, which gives it somewhat the appearance of an animal midway between a fox and a wolf. With its fox-like contours goes an acute fox-like mentality that serves it well in its struggle for existence." [3]

Even in those early years Young acknowledged the frequent misjudgements by the public when estimating sizes and weights of prairie coyotes.

"Often one may be easily misled about the weight of coyotes. A matured adult of either sex taken when the fur is prime appears, when first looked upon, to be comparable in weight of the gray wolf forms.... Generally speaking, the coyote weighs somewhere between 18 and 30 pounds. Exceptionally heavy individuals occur.... A male coyote taken near Jackson, Michigan, weighed 53 ½ pounds. The heaviest coyote among the records obtained by the Fish and Wildlife Service is that of male weighing 74 ¾ pounds killed near Afton, Wyoming.... Other weights are: 446 male coyotes from New Mexico averaged 24.4 pounds; 383 female coyotes from the same state averaged 22.2 pounds." [4]

Sexual dimorphism (differences between sexes) is the rule among canids, and the coyote is no exception. Male coyotes are larger and heavier than female coyotes throughout its range.

"The predominant hair color is a light gray and red fulvous interspersed over parts of the body with black and white which holds generally for the species, with certain modification in some of the races. Altitude of habitat is a factor in coyote coloration, those found at the higher elevations tend toward gray and black, while those on desert areas are more fulvous, or often a whitish gray, a color that is generally protective from its blending with so much of the desert growth.... It is interesting to note that of a total of 750,000 coyotes killed by

Federal and cooperative hunters between March 22, 1938, and June 30, 1945, only two albinos [white] were captured in the main United States range of the animal... Among 1,672,604 coyotes taken by hunters of the Fish and Wildlife Service for the period July 1, 1915, to June 30, 1945, only 6 were albinos. ... This record is one per 278,767 coyotes captured."[5]

Iowa coyotes have been described as rather shaggy and doglike in appearance with erect pointed ears and a bushy, bottle-shaped, drooping tail, not unlike coyotes described for other western states. The Iowa coyote has the characteristic gray color with yellowish tint and scattered black patches throughout the pelage.[6]

Male and female coyotes in Iowa average 29 and 25 pounds (13 and 11 kg), respectively, comparable to 30 and 24 pounds (14 and 11 kg) for male and female coyotes in Minnesota and 31 and 26 pounds (14 and 12 kg) for coyotes in Kansas.[7] These midwestern weights are heavier than male and female weights of 24 and 21 pounds (11 and 10 kg) for coyotes in California but lighter than the 35 and 30 pounds (16 and 14 kg) for males and females from Maine, supporting the generally accepted theory that coyotes are larger and heavier in the eastern and northeastern sectors of the continent.[8] This regional trend in weight and size is similar to a regional trend in densities (described elsewhere), and probably home range sizes. Some people have suggested that coyotes in the northeast have assumed the appearance and behaviour of timber wolves, (greater dependence on ungulates; prolonged family units (packs) through the winter) although that suggestion is not shared by all.

The colour of coyotes in Ontario ranges from creamy to dark rufous, but the tawny-gray agouti pattern is the most common.[9] Throat and belly areas are light gray or white while a shoulder saddle or mane of black-tipped hairs is typical as are black-tipped hairs on the dorsal surface of the proximal third of the tail. This is the typical colour pattern of coyotes in the northeast. However, there may be considerable variation in colour even within litters, with extremes ranging from black to blond. Henry Hilton classified 54 coyotes collected in Maine during the mid-1970s into 4 colour types. The proportions of that sample in each colour type were: dark brown=15%; brown=41%; gray=33%; blond=11%. As in other regions of its range, the coyotes molted once a year, beginning in late spring.[10]

The wild canids that colonized the southeastern states over the past 30 years are quite large in build, and, as suggested elsewhere, probably resulted from hybridization among ingressing coyotes, domestic and feral dogs and red wolves. Southeastern male coyotes weigh about 30 pounds (14 kg) while females are slightly smaller. The average weight of 113 adult male coyotes collected in Arkansas from 1968 through 1972 was 34 pounds (15 kg), and 28 pounds (13 kg) for 62 adult females.[11] Total body lengths ranged from 42-54 inches (107-137 cm) for males and from 40-49 inches (102-124 cm) for females. Tail lengths ranged from 12-15 inches (30-38 cm) for males and 11-13 inches (28-33 cm) for females. Coats of that sample of wild canids from Arkansas were typical salt-and-pepper gray.

Black canids (melanism) are occasionally reported throughout the southeast. The frequency of melanistic coyotes in the southeast is probably a function of interbreeding between coyotes and red wolves. Melanism has been considered a diagnostic feature of red wolves, useful for distinguishing red wolves from coyotes. Approximately 25% of the red wolves taken in the western Ozark Mountains of Arkansas during the 1930s were melanistic.[12]

There are two possible sources of melanism in coyotes and coyotelike canids in the southeast.

> "Genes for melanism may have been present in eastern coyote populations in Texas, Oklahoma, and Missouri before coyotes from these areas extended their range eastward. Environmental factors in the Southeast could have provided some selective advantage for melanism permitting an increase in black pelage among coyotes. This hypothesis is supported by the fact that 12 of the 24 black coyotes from Arkansas could not be differentiated from coyotes. The second possibility is that melanism was derived from red wolves and/or dogs through hybridization which occurred as coyotes extended their range across the western edge of the Southeast. Genes for melanism were probably passed to some hybrid offspring which, in turn, became a part of the gene pool of the present interbreeding canid population."[13]

Adult male coyotes in Minnesota normally weigh 28-30 pounds (13-14 kg); adult females 26-27 pounds (12 kg).[14] Coyotes in Illinois have been described as being "exceedingly large, with weights to 40 pounds and reports of weights up to 50 pounds. This large size has caused many who know the small coyote in the West to call this animal in Illinois a wolf."[15] Five hundred and ninety-six coyotes were collected from trappers in Kansas during the winters of 1974-76.[16] The heaviest animal was a 45-pound (20-kg) male, while average weights for males and females were 29 pounds (13 kg) and 24 pounds (11 kg).

In the northeast, the average weights for adult male and female coyotes collected from Massachusetts and Vermont during the mid-1970s were 37 pounds (17 kg) and 32 pounds (15 kg) respectively. Body lengths (including tail) varied from 44 to 54 inches (112 to 137 cm) for males and 43 to 59 inches (110 to 151 cm) for females.[17] Henry Hilton, a biologist with the Maine Department of Inland Fisheries and Wildlife, has studied coyotes extensively in that state and provides the following detailed description of coyotes found in the northeastern United States.

> "The most distinctive physical characteristic of the eastern coyote is its large size which is, nonetheless, often overestimated in the field. Erroneous reports of 60-80 pound (27-36 kg) coyotes are not uncommon. On several occasions I have weighed animals reputed to exceed 70 pounds (31 kg), and found them to weigh only 35-40 pounds (15-18 kg). The average weight of coyotes throughout the East is less than 40 pounds, and authenticated reports of coyotes exceeding 48 pounds are uncommon.... The external appearance of eastern coyotes, basically, is not unlike that of western coyotes and wolves, while external characteristics of domestic dogs (e.g., curled tail, irregular markings, tipped-over ears) are absent. The ears are erect, the tail is full and straight, the black tail-gland spot is conspicuous, and the chest is narrow. In addition, a broad (8-10 cm), black tail tip, and a prominant V-shaped shoulder harness are

characteristic.... Four color phases can be distinguished ... which range from dark brown to blond or reddish blond, but the most common (typical) is an overall gray-brown, with tan legs, rufous flanks, rich rufous ears, and grizzled gray frontals. A light eye ring was particularly evident on several blond-coloured (cream) specimens."[18]

Weights and measurements of coyotes from Atlantic Canada are similar to those from other regions of the northeast. One of the earliest collections was 73 coyotes from New Brunswick during the winters of 1979-1981, made by Gary Moore, then a graduate student at the University of Western Ontario. The mean weight for adult males (adjusted whole weights from skinned carcasses; skinned carcasses may weigh 15% less than whole weights) was 36 pounds (16 kg) and for adult females 33 pounds (15 kg).[19]

We also have weights and measurements of early colonizing coyotes from Nova Scotia. The mean skinned weights of males and females collected between 1977 and 1981 were 37 pounds (17 kg) and 24 pounds (11 kg), respectively. The mean skinned weights of males and females collected in 1981-82 were 27 pounds (12 kg) and 23 pounds (10 kg). Both samples combined adults and juveniles. The lengths (tip of nose to base of tailbone) of males and females in the 1981-82 sample were 35 inches (89 cm) and 34 inches (87 cm), respectively.[20] Weights of coyotes submitted for bounty in 1985-86 and collected by the Nova Scotia Wildlife Branch (males = 29 pounds; females = 24 pounds) were similar to the weights (unskinned) from New Brunswick and the 1981-82 collection from Nova Scotia.[21]

A useful collection of whole (unskinned) weights of coyotes trapped in Kings County, Nova Scotia from 1989-90 through 1992-93 (4 years) was kindly made available to me by Lloyd Duncanson, retired Curator of Mammals at the Nova Scotia Museum. (*Table 1*).

Table 1: Whole weights (pounds) of coyotes collected in Nova Scotia by Lloyd Duncanson, 1989-90 through 1992-93.

Year	Number	Males	Females
1989-90	14	41.4	33.3
1990-91	14	34.1	31.6
1991-92	36	36.5	30.1
1992-93	25	33.9	28.5
Totals	89	36.3	30.2

Two female coyotes trapped by Duncanson in Nova Scotia were black (melanistic). The heaviest coyote was a 47-pound (21-kg) male. [Note: In early December, 1993, Lloyd Duncanson caught and weighed a 51¼ pound female coyote. The swollen condition of the uterus revealed that the female was into or entering breeding condition. The early date of breeding suggests that this animal may have been a coyote and domestic dog hybrid (coydog), although the pelt was typical coyote].

Three hundred and fourteen coyote carcasses were collected from trappers by the Nova Scotia Wildlife Branch during the winter of 1992-93.[22] Mature (1.5 years +) males and females averaged 34 and 28 pounds (15 and 13 kg), respectively. Immature (0.5 years) males and females averaged 26 and 23 pounds (12 and 11 kg), respectively. The heaviest coyote was a 48-pound (22-kg) adult male and the lightest was a 10-pound (4.5-kg) juvenile female. Adjusted whole weights of 90 skinned coyotes (all ages) killed on Prince Edward Island from 1991 through 1993 were 35 pounds (16 kg) for males and 32 pounds (15 kg) for females. A large male shot in Prince Edward Island on May 30, 1994, weighed 55 pounds (25 kg).[23] Two adult males trapped on the island of Newfoundland each weighed 30 pounds (13.7 kg).[24]

In summary, although coyotes in the northeast are large, they are comparable in size and weight to coyotes throughout the eastern United States. For example, a col-

lection of male coyotes from Arkansas averaged only several pounds lighter than male coyotes from Nova Scotia, and there are occasional reports of 60- to 70-pound (27-32 kg) coyotes from Minnesota to Alabama. Although large male eastern coyotes may reach 50 pounds (23 kg), the average adult male weighs 35 to 40 pounds (16 to 18 kg), while 50- to 60- pound (23-27 kg) coyotes are rare. Adult females usually weigh 5-10 pounds (2-5 kg) less than males.

Alfred MacDonell with a large 57-pound coyote that he trapped near Elmsdale, Nova Scotia (H. Mowatt).

4 Food Habits

"The coyote's favorite food is anything he can chew."[1]

One reason for the rapid colonization by the coyote of most of eastern North America is its ability to adapt its feeding habits to the available food supply. Few will argue that the coyote is an extremely efficient and opportunistic predator. It is a generalist, a fact which has allowed it to adapt to changing environmental conditions and stresses and to be flexible rather than rigid in its living requirements. The coyote is not alone in its ability to exploit habitats altered by humans; included in this group are common species such as robins, starlings, house sparrows, various species of gulls, raccoons, and a host of others. These species have managed to increase in numbers and expand their ranges while less adaptable species struggle within a changing world. Much of that change is from intervention and habitat alteration by humans. The coyote, however, appears equally successful whether in the mountains, plains, deserts or forests. To provide an exhaustive review of the feeding habits of the coyote across its range is beyond the scope of this book. Given the wide diversity in diet, both seasonally and geographically, the reader could soon become swamped and utterly confused. However, there are seasonal and geographical trends in coyote diets, and these patterns might be more useful in understanding its feeding ecology, on a continental scale, than to confuse the issue with questionable detail.

This chapter reviews studies on the diet of coyotes from food items in samples of stomachs and scats and summarizes those data regionally to show trends interpreted by discussion on food availability, season and climate. It presents summaries of dietary studies in the United States from the west, midwest, southcentral, Great Lakes and northeast, and in Canada from New Brunswick and Nova Scotia. It also shows the regional trends for 5 major food classes: 1) hares and rabbits; 2) deer (and antelope); 3) rodents; 4) fruits, berries, and vegetation; and 5) domestic animals (*Figure 6*). Although there are exceptions to these trends, the following serves as a summary and general account. Readers wishing greater detail should refer to the sources provided.

There are errors with food studies based on occurrence of food items in samples of coyote stomachs and scats. The relative amounts (weights, volumes) of food items are more meaningful, but due to the problems of quantification, most studies have limited their results and discussion to percentage occurrence values. Thus, although most contents of a stomach sample might be of deer, and only a single toenail present from

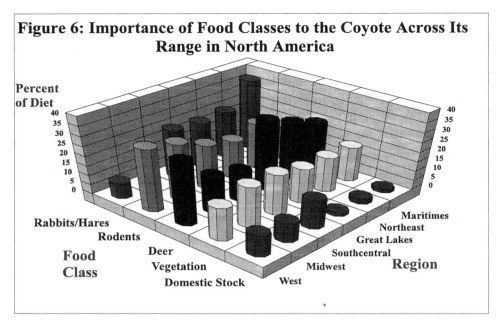

Figure 6: Importance of Food Classes to the Coyote Across Its Range in North America

Figure 6: In the northeast, coyotes rely on snowshoe hares year-round and on rodents, fruits and berries in summer and fall; in forested wilderness regions they may rely on white-tailed deer in late winter.

a meadow vole, both food items would receive equal value. Also, stomach samples are often from trapped coyotes, in which food items may represent bait, or from dispersers, whose diet would most likely be of smaller mammals or other items readily available (e.g., carrion, garbage). Given these inadequacies, however, the method has remained popular due to the ease of collecting and processing samples. The value of the exercise is enhanced when large data sets are compared for spatial and seasonal trends, as I have done here. I will give a general review of studies by region, and, where appropriate, discuss how they may have been influenced by environmental conditions and food availability.

UNITED STATES

WEST

In most western states there is an abundance and variety of prey for a medium-sized predator such as the coyote. One early study of coyote scats in California listed 14 species of rodents, 13 types of birds, 3 reptiles, and 3 invertebrates, along with assorted berries, vegetables, egg fragments, pika, jack rabbit, cottontail rabbit, mule deer, domestic sheep, badger, and domestic cat—all in all, a very well balanced diet![2] Rodents were also important to coyotes in Washington where 80% of rodents eaten were ground squirrels.[3] Deer were also well represented, with fawns and yearlings being most vulnerable to predation, although mortality on deer was considered to be compensatory. (Deer killed by coyotes would probably have died from other causes.) Climatic stress on coyotes is minimal and their prey base is abundant and diversified. Hares and rabbits are not as important to the coyote here as they are in most other regions, probably due to the abundance of rodents. Predation on domestic stock, especially sheep, can be significant.

MIDWEST

Here on the prairies the coyote has a broad food base of small to medium-sized prey, especially cotton rats, pocket gophers, ground squirrels, jack rabbits, cottontail rabbits, mice, and voles.[4] Winters can be stressful and predation on ungulates can be significant, especially young pronghorn antelope in spring and summer. Deer eaten in winter is mostly from carrion, although some predation may occur. Predation on domestic stock, especially cattle, sheep, and chickens, can be significant locally. Berries and fruits are commonly eaten in late summer and fall.

SOUTHCENTRAL

When coyotes expanded into the southcentral United States, they entered the land of plenty, and soon proved to have a significant impact on many domestic animals and crops. They have been especially troublesome in some areas by feeding on poultry (much believed to be carrion), newborn calves on open range, and free-ranging pigs, sheep and goats,[5] while damage to watermelons can be significant seasonally. The main wild prey are cottontail rabbits and rodents, especially mice, voles, woodchucks, cotton rats, and squirrels. Predation on deer is usually restricted to fawns in spring and early summer (with a consequent decline in consumption of rabbits and rodents) although the coyote's impact upon deer is not considered significant. Persimmons, blackberries, wild grapes, huckleberries, and wild plums are important in late summer and autumn, and climatic stress is minimal to absent.

GREAT LAKES

Coyotes began to penetrate the forests of Michigan and Wisconsin near the turn of the century. It was here that the coyote adopted lifestyle changes to ensure survival and allow continued colonization into the northeastern United States and southern Canada, and it was also here that studies first began to detect significant dependency by coyotes on white-tailed deer, especially in winter.[6] As early as 1956 white-tailed deer were found to be the coyote's primary winter food in northern Michigan, although most deer were thought to be carrion.[7] Biologists related increased consumption of deer by coyotes to increased vulnerability of deer during long periods of deep snow and low availability of browse to them. When snowfall was light, and deer were in good physical condition, predation was considered minimal, and healthy deer were thought to be quite capable of escaping from coyotes. Most predation was considered compensatory, and coyotes selected the smallest and weakest animals.

A high consumption of deer by coyotes in winter was confirmed by further studies in Wisconsin, although here too biologists also concluded that "most deer appearing in coyotes' winter and spring diet are carrion."[8] Coyote scats in the spring, however, contained substantial amounts of fawn hair, similar to other studies in more western and southern states. Lagomorphs, represented in this region by the snowshoe hare, are important to coyotes throughout the year but, with few exceptions (mainly autumn samples) its importance is less than white-tailed deer. Although the abundance and variety of rodents available to coyotes is less than in western and southern states, rodents are fed upon regularly and are important to the overall diet. A 3-year all-season collection of coyote scats from Wisconsin showed rodents only slightly less important than deer and hare. Rodents were less important in winter to coyotes in both Wisconsin and Michigan probably because of low availability due to deep snow cover.[9]

Rodents, fruits and vegetables were most important to coyotes in summer and fall. Important rodents included the meadow vole, white-footed mouse, red-backed vole, porcupine, red squirrel, and chipmunk. Coyotes also fed upon grouse, duck, and wood-chuck. "Wild fruits were consumed as soon as they ripened and continued to be eaten until snow covered the ground.... Blueberries, raspberries and blackberries also occurred regularly during summer and fall." Wild fruit may play an ecologically significant role by relieving pressure on prey species during periods of high vulnerability. In the Great Lakes region with an ample and "diverse food base, with no prey species dominating the food habits, availability may be obscured by density-independent factors (primarily winter weather) that increases the vulnerability of certain portions of the prey population."[10]

These early studies could find no relationship between changes in abundance of coyotes and of prey. Reductions in one prey species appeared to be offset by increases in another, and numbers of coyotes in northern Wisconsin did not seem to vary with changes in the density of a single prey species. Biologists believed that coyotes in northern Wisconsin would ultimately be controlled by winter weather.

NORTHEAST

"Over the past 30 years ... there has become established in the Adirondack region of New York a population of animals that fit the general description of the eastern coyote. Information on the food habits of these animals is of interest".[11]

One of the first studies of coyote foods in the northeast examined 1,500 scats collected in the Adirondack region of New York from 1956 to 1961.

"... These data show the snowshoe hare to have been the primary prey species of the coyote in the Adirondacks throughout the year. There was a high incidence of deer remains in the scats examined, particularly those representing the late fall, winter, and spring seasons. However, it is felt that to a large degree this reflected scavenging on carcasses of hunter-killed and winter-killed deer rather than direct predation. A variety of other small mammals were taken, especially during the warmer months, and a few birds, amphibians and reptiles were recorded. From mid-summer to early fall, fruit provided a substantial share of the diet." [12]

Although the occurrence of deer in summer scats was less than one-half of those in winter (39% occurrence in winter to 17% in summer), snowshoe hare remained high in both seasons (winter, 33%; summer, 39%). Other mammals eaten in winter included the red squirrel, field mouse, muskrat, short-tailed shrew, chipmunk, flying squirrel, jumping mouse, and gray squirrel, although most were of minor importance compared to deer and hare. (Red squirrel was the third most important prey item in winter and summer.) A greater variety of mammals were eaten in summer including beaver, red fox, porcupine, woodchuck and red-backed vole. Common fruits eaten in late summer and fall were raspberry, blackberry, blueberry, wild cherry, shadberry, and apple, and fruit was ranked second in importance only to snowshoe hare.

Gary Brundige, a graduate student at the State University of New York College of Environmental Science and Forestry at Syracuse, New York, recently completed another study of the feeding habits of coyotes in the Adirondack Mountains. This study supported the conclusion that

"The coyote can and does kill deer especially on the northern fringes of its range in northeastern, midwestern, and northwestern North America. The coyote's propensity to prey on deer in the Adirondack region confirms its great adaptability—in this case, to harsh winters, deep snow, and a shortage of smaller prey in winter." [13]

By examining the contents of over 1,000 coyote scats, Brundige estimated that "white-tailed deer make up in excess of 80 percent of the coyote's diet in winter, and a significant, although lower, percentage in spring and summer."[14]

The recent research in the Adirondack Mountains confirmed the wide diversity of

White-tailed deer represent an important component of the winter diet of coyotes in the Adironadack Mountains of New York, northern Maine, southeastern Quebec, and throughout much of New Brunswick and Nova Scotia (G. Parker).

mammals eaten in summer, including beaver, hare, red squirrel, chipmunk, voles, and mice and the importance of fruit and berries in the fall. One of the more interesting observations from the Adirondack study is a comparison of consumption rates of deer by coyotes in winter to rates documented from 2 earlier studies of coyotes in the Adirondacks, one in 1956-61 (referred to earlier) and the other in 1975-80. [15]

> "...Since the 1950s, coyotes in the Adirondacks have been eating more and more deer.... Winter consumption of deer rose from about 40 percent of the diet in the fifties to nearly 90 percent in the seventies and more than 90 percent in the last decade. Summer consumption also went up significantly. During the same period, the percentage of small prey in the diet declined, in both winter and summer.... Significantly, coyote consumption of deer went up independent of deer density. The 1950s—when coyotes killed relatively few deer—saw the highest deer population densities ever recorded in the area: about 25 deer per square mile. Deer numbers subsequently declined to about 5 per square mile in the 1970s following severe winters; yet, at the same time, coyotes increased their consumption of deer to approximately the present high levels. By the mid-1980s, deer numbers were back up again, to about 20 per square mile.... What then accounts for this trend in the coyote's eating habits?... Up until the '70s, coyotes were sparsely distributed in the Adirondacks, and ... probably hunted alone or in pairs. In turn, this may explain the low proportion of deer in the diet during this period, for bringing down a deer alone is hard work, even for the big eastern coyote.... We calculate central Adirondack coyote densities at about one animal per every nine square miles.... In summer more than three-quarters [of tracks in dirt] were of solitary animals, while in winter (when deer make up the bulk of the diet) about 70 percent represented pairs or packs.... In the central Adirondacks, we found that coyote pack life revolves around a dominant male and female, the breeding pair. Young of the year remain with their parents, hunting with them in winter.... The packs, which resemble those of wolves, operate essentially as a territorial family unit. Over the course of the last 30 years, the coyotes in these packs may have developed a tradition of pack hunting, a sort of deer-hunting culture."[16]

Moving north into Maine we find a number of recent studies on the ecology of coyotes, especially studies of feeding habits and interactions with deer. This preoccupation in the northeast with the interactions of coyotes and white-tailed deer resulted largely from public concern over dwindling deer herds and increasing numbers of coyotes. Add to this the frequent encounters by the public with dead deer in the winter, apparently killed by coyotes, and coyotes seen chasing and occasionally killing deer, and the urgency by Game Department officials to obtain unbiased and quantitative information on the impact of coyotes on deer becomes clear.

Although carcasses of wild canids were occasionally submitted to the University of Maine from 1939 to 1967, reports of coyotes in that state were scarce prior to 1968. [17] The number of carcasses received by the Maine Cooperative Wildlife Research Unit increased significantly from 1968 to 1973. Food items were identified in 51 stomachs from coyotes killed in the fall and winter. Snowshoe hare and white-tailed deer were found in only 20% and 16% of the samples respectively. Most samples, however, were collected in the autumn prior to snow cover. This study concluded that

"eastern coyotes do not seem to rely on two or three major foods during this [Aug-Nov] period.... There is no evidence ... that deer meat is a staple food.... There is no evidence that wolves and coyotes make the same demands on the same resources. Wolves are highly social animals which primarily hunt and kill the large cervids, whereas eastern coyotes appear to be mainly lone or paired scavengers with an opportunistic tendency for small or disadvantaged prey."[18]

Conclusions from this study on the diet of colonizing coyotes in Maine sound very similar to those from earlier studies in Michigan, Wisconsin, and the Adirondack region of New York. However, coyote carcasses from Maine were not collected in late winter, a period of the year when predation on deer may be especially significant. Henry Hilton of the Maine Department of Fisheries and Wildlife continued studies of coyotes in that state, analysing carcasses received during 1973-75 and tracking coyote trails in the snow during the winter of 1974-75.

"Analysis of 112 coyotes and 414 scats indicated that the diet consisted of any readily available food, including refuse, small mammals and vegetation in agricultural areas. In winter, coyotes relied heavily on snowshoe hare and deer in wilderness areas. Moose, beaver and grouse were not significant items in the diet.... Coyotes were not found to travel or hunt appreciably in packs."[19]

"...Single coyotes were not successful in killing deer; paired coyotes were responsible for 73% of the kills and multiple coyotes the remainder.... It is ... significant that of all the deer kills examined, all fawns were below the mean fall weight, and 9 of 14 adults were either old (greater than 5 yrs) or exhibited abnormalities."[20]

Coyotes killed more deer as the winter progressed with over half the kills located after 1 March. Hilton suggested that coyotes were selecting for inferior animals and, because of that, most mortality from predation would be compensatory. But more recent collections of much larger samples of deer killed by coyotes, both in Maine and New Brunswick, have shown different results.

Dan Harrison examined scats from pups and adult coyotes at or near the vicinity of active coyote dens in Maine from May to October, 1981. Both adults and pups relied heavily on white-tailed deer during the denning period. The occurrences of deer in scats of adult breeding coyotes in May, June, and July were 50%, 69%, and 43%, while snowshoe hare was found in 44%, 19%, and 7% of those samples. In summer and fall, when both adults and pups began to travel more, blueberries became the dominant food item. Overall the most common foods in those summer-autumn samples were blueberry (68%), white-tailed deer (43%), and snowshoe hare (30%). Harrison noted the higher occurrence of deer in his samples than in earlier studies of coyotes in Maine, although he attributed that to the exclusiveness of samples from adults and pups at or near den sites.

"...We believe that it was energetically and/or nutritionally less efficient for coyotes to catch and transport sufficient quantities of small prey items to sustain their litters than to prey upon and transport deer fawns. This probably caused adult coyotes attending pups to kill proportionately more deer during June and July than did nonreproductive coyotes.... The incidence of deer observed in the feces during May-July was probably the result of feeding on newborn fawns.... The high incidence of deer remains in feces observed during the study may have partly resulted from the forested nature of the habitat." [21]

A comprehensive study of coyotes, bobcats and red foxes was conducted in western Maine from 1979 through 1982 by the Maine Cooperative Wildlife Research Unit in Orono, Maine.[22] This study was prompted by growing concern over the effects of coyotes on other predators and white-tailed deer and included radio-telemetry, winter tracking, and scat analysis. The occurrences of prey in scats were similar to earlier food habit studies in the northeast. White-tailed deer were found in 10%, 24%, 58%, and 41% of the summer, fall, winter, and spring samples respectively. Respective values for snowshoe hare were 69%, 67%, 37%, and 40%. Although snowshoe hare was important to the coyote throughout the year, especially in summer and fall, deer was important in winter. Mice, voles, beaver, muskrat, red squirrel, and other mammals were of minor importance in summer, and near absent in winter. It is no surprise that raspberry was second in importance in summer samples. The importance of deer to coyotes in winter and spring was related to winter severity. Eleven of 17 deer found dead were believed to have been killed by predators (coyotes or bobcats). Fat in the bone marrow (indicative of condition) of only 1 of 9 deer carcasses suggested malnutrition.

The coyote-bobcat-red fox study by the Maine Cooperative Wildlife Research Unit was updated in 1990, and included over 2,000 more coyote scats collected from 1979 to 1983.[23] This new information was examined for differences between regions of collection: inland forested (wilderness-severe winters), and coastal lowlands (forested agricultural-moderate winters). Coyotes in both regions depended extensively upon snowshoe hare at all seasons, while deer was more important to coyotes during winter in the interior forested wilderness area. Not unexpectedly, fruit and berries (apples, beech nuts, blueberry, raspberry, serviceberry) were important in summer and fall in both areas, although more so on the coast where farms and fields were most common. Coyotes fed more on mice and voles near the coast (greater variety and availability) and that food source increased in importance to coyotes from winter through summer and fall. No attempt was made to estimate the effects of predation on deer, nor how many deer might have been lost to predation during the study. However, a model of the population dynamics of white-tailed deer in Maine was referred to, and it suggested that predation was second in importance only to hunting in determining population size.

The most common foods of coyotes on Mount Desert Island in eastern Maine were white-tailed deer, raccoons, small mammals and fruits. Almost one-half of autumn scats contained remains of raccoons; the authors attributed this to the low abundance of more preferred food, such as snowshoe hare, and suggested that this was another example of how coyotes are capable of adjusting their diet to the available food supply.[24] The killing of raccoons by coyotes has also been observed in forested agricultural land of southeastern Quebec[25] and by red wolves recently reintroduced on the Alligator River National Wildlife Refuge in northeastern North Carolina.[26]

At the symposium on the eastern coyote held in Fredericton, New Brunswick, in 1991, Gerry Lavigne, deer biologist for the Maine Department of Inland Fisheries and Wildlife, presented the most recent data on the sex and age structure and nutritional condition of deer killed by coyotes during winter in that state.

In northern forested regions the snowshoe hare is often the most common food of the coyote (G. Parker).

"Although early reports on coyote food habits in Maine confirmed that white-tailed deer constituted a significant proportion of the late autumn and winter coyote diets, the source of this diet component was assumed to be largely carrion from hunting season and winter starvation.... However the initial characterization of the eastern coyote as primarily a scavenger was based less upon field observation of coyotes in Maine than upon published reports of coyote food habits elsewhere [and reviewed earlier here].... Gradually, it became apparant to the public and to resource managers in Maine that coyotes were indeed capable of killing deer in winter ... and at other times of the year.... During the 1970s and 1980s deer fecundity [number born] was high, but recruitment [number of deer added to the population] to age 6 months appeared to have declined relative to pre-coyote times.... During the 1970s, overall deer losses frequently exceeded recruitment, thereby causing regional declines in Maine's deer herd. Whether or not coyote predation was contributing to this decline became a controversial topic among hunters, legislators, and biologists. Prior to 1978, little data were available to evaluate possible prey selection in coyote-killed deer. If coyotes selected primarily the old, sick, or starving

individuals, such mortality would be considered compensatory, and hence would exert little influence on herd dynamics. Alternately, mortality would be considered additive if coyote predation included individual deer that, in the absence of predation, would likely have survived the winter to contribute to future reproduction and/or hunter harvest." [27]

"Eight hundred and sixty three coyote-killed deer were examined in a statewide winter mortality study in Maine from 1977-78 to 1988-89. When possible, the sex and age of coyote-kills were determined, and a femur was extracted to assess physical condition. Annual sample size [indication of the number of deer killed] was positively related to winter severity, while mean femur marrow fat (FMF) [indication of nutritional condition] among coyote-killed deer was inversely related. Coyotes killed significantly more doe fawns and old deer of both sexes, but killed buck fawns, mature bucks and does in the same proportion as they occurred in the wintering herd. Mean FMF values of coyote-killed deer declined monthly from December through April. Mature does consistently had the highest mean FMF levels; fawns were lowest, while yearling does and bucks older than fawns were intermediate. During all months except April, FMF levels among coyote-kills did not differ from road-kills. The physical condition of coyote-killed deer was classified as good, marginal, or malnourished, based on relative FMF levels. Depending upon sex/age class, 50-70 percent of deer killed by coyotes contained high FMF levels indicative of good physical condition. Correspondingly, only 10-23 percent of coyote-killed deer were considered malnourished, and 20-47 percent were in marginal condition. Hence, most deer killed by coyotes in winter in this study would likely have survived to contribute to future reproduction and/or harvest. When the deer population is held in balance with carrying capacity, most predation on deer by coyotes during winter in Maine must be considered additive with other traumatic losses such as hunting, illegal kills, road-kills etc. Consequently, deer managers in Maine must account for these losses in relation to prevailing habitat quality and herd recruitment when determining an allowable harvest." [28]

ATLANTIC CANADA

Our journey, and that of the eastern coyote, finally brings us to Atlantic Canada. We have reviewed the wide variety of foods eaten by the coyote across its range in continental United States and seen how this remarkable predator adapts its diet to those foods most readily available. The coyote evolved, both physically and behaviourally, to feed on the abundant populations of rodents in the open prairies, grasslands and deserts of mid-western North America. It was relatively small physically, a medium-sized predator well suited for preying on the ground squirrels and rabbits of the open plains. It was quite capable of making a living by itself, and family groups quickly dispersed in autumn.

Always an opportunist, whenever a change in menu became available, such as newly born deer and antelope, or free-ranging and vulnerable sheep, the coyote was quick to respond. As it began to expand its range east, taking advantage of a changing landscape with new sources of food and the absence of the wolf, the coyote adjusted to each new set of environmental rules. It remained a medium-sized predator, and whenever possible, continued to feed on small and medium-sized prey. The cottontail rabbit replaced the jackrabbit while the woodrat and muskrat replaced the ground squirrel. White-tailed deer replaced antelope and mule deer, and pigs and chickens replaced sheep and cattle (or supplemented them). The coyote ate watermelons, porcupines, domestic cats, and garbage. It continued northeast and, in the process, again confronted its old nemesis, the timber wolf. However, at the limits of their ranges, both wolf and coyote occasionally found it difficult to rendez-vous with the opposite sex when courting time arrived. In such situations, it appears, breeding between coyotes and wolves did occur, however reluctantly, and in the process, the coyote inherited traits natural to the wolf. Perhaps most important to our interests here was a consequent larger body size and increased sociality.

Bill McCue, New Brunswick Department of Natural Resources and Energy, examines a white-tailed deer killed by coyotes in northern New Brunswick in late winter 1983. Predation in winter by recently established coyotes may have contributed to declining numbers of white-tailed deer in New Brunswick and Nova Scotia during the late 1980s (G. Parker).

This new variety of wild canid continued to breed true, and, you might say, took the best features of both progenitors. The increase in body size allowed it to feed on larger prey, and increased sociality resulted in a more prolonged family group. The pups often remained with the female through the winter and developed pack-hunting skills favourable for preying on deer. Increased body size, of course, created a greater energy demand, and the most efficient means to satisfy that requirement was a greater reliance on larger prey, i.e. white-tailed deer. This switch from small- and medium-sized prey to medium- and large-sized prey was not instantaneous, nor was it likely consistent between regions, or even between family groups or individuals. Hunting behaviour and prey selection, is part genetic and part learned. Pups that are fed deer will probably search out and feed their pups deer. Pups which remain and hunt with their mother over winter will probably tolerate, or encourage, their pups to do the same. Pups which learn to bring down deer in the winter will probably continue to do so.

Thus, having followed the development of coyote behaviour and feeding habits from the open prairies to the closed wilderness forests of northern Maine, we should not be surprised that results of studies in New Brunswick and Nova Scotia are similar to those from the northeastern states. Actually, knowing what we do after 50+ years of studying the development and adaptive strategies of the eastern coyote, it would have been surprising to find otherwise, given the similarity in landscape (forested-wilderness and forested-agricultural), environmental stress (cold winter and prolonged deep snow cover), and food base (diversified prey in summer; deer and hare in winter).

A few coyotes were shot and trapped in New Brunswick between 1958 and 1973, but it was not until the mid-1970s that they became common. By 1977 they had reached Nova Scotia, and by 1981 coyotes were distributed throughout New Brunswick and Nova Scotia. The first study of this new predator, however, did not appear until 1985 when Dr. Louis LaPierre, a biology professor at the University of Moncton, reported on the diet of coyotes collected in southeastern New Brunswick from 1979 to 1982.[29] Food items were identified in stomach samples of coyotes "recently shot" in fall and early winter. Not surprising, snowshoe hare was the most common food item (52% occurrence) followed by the meadow vole (44%), white-tailed deer (31%) and red-backed vole (24%). Rodents were probably most common in stomachs from coyotes collected prior to deep snow cover. Other items of lesser importance were beaver, muskrat, porcupine, grouse, racoon, poultry, sheep, and cattle.

About the same time, Gary Moore, then a student at the University of Western Ontario, examined coyotes collected by trappers and hunters in New Brunswick and

Forest rangers Ken Johnstone, left, and Francois Chiasson say the coyote population in northern N.B. is getting out of hand.

MARC BELLIVEAU PHOTO

Ken Johnstone and François Chaisson with coyotes trapped in the Bathurst area of New Brunswick in 1990-91 (M. Belliveau).

Nova Scotia during October through January from 1979-80 to 1980-81.[30] He analysed the contents of 258 stomachs from New Brunswick and 7 from Nova Scotia. Again no surprise. Snowshoe hare was eaten most often (32% occurrence) followed by white-tailed deer (25%), vegetation (20%) and small mammals (14%). Moore also identified a variety of other food items, including chicken, grouse, porcupine, and cattle.

We now know, from winter scat collections and snow-tracking studies, that predation by coyotes on deer increases from early through late winter (December-March). Thus, the occurrence of deer in stomachs of carcasses collected by hunters and trappers from October through January would be lower than if carcasses had been collected in February and March. Based on what we have learned from studies in Michigan, Wisconsin, New York, and Maine, the variety and proportional representation of food items in the fall-early winter samples from the Maritimes collected by LaPierre and Moore is what should be expected.

I conducted a study of coyotes in northern New Brunswick from May 1983 through March 1984. Coyotes were then well established throughout New Brunswick and were colonizing most of Nova Scotia, while deer populations throughout the Maritimes were reaching all-time highs. In my area of study snowshoe hare were abundant, especially in the numerous spruce and pine plantations on this large tract of managed forests. Coyote scats were collected throughout the year, and hares were the most common food item at all seasons.[31] White-tailed deer, also common in the area, was second in importance through the winter but of minor importance in the summer and fall. As expected, raspberry was important in the summer and, surprisingly, groundhog in the spring. The lack of deer hair in early summer samples led me to believe that predation on fawns was insignificant. My colleagues and I also followed coyote trails in the winter of 1983-84.[32] Those tracking studies confirmed a dependency by coyotes on hare and deer in winter. Coyotes "switched" from hares to deer as the winter progressed, confirming earlier observations from New York and Maine. The number of recorded kills of hares declined from 13 to 6 to 4 in January, February, and March, while deer kills increased from 0 to 3 to 7. We followed a radio-marked female and her two pups through the winter. The predation rate by that family group on deer increased from 0 in January to one per 7 days in February to one per 2 days in March. During snow tracking studies, we found 17 deer which had been killed by coyotes and not one was killed by a smaller group than 3 coyotes. The nutritional condition (fat content in bone marrow) of deer killed by coyotes was good. We suggested that predation by coyotes on deer in winter in northern New Brunswick could be significant and that much of that mortality appeared to be additive (in agreement with later studies in New York and Maine).

At the same time as my studies in northern New Brunswick, Dale Morton, then a graduate student at the University of New Brunswick, studied coyotes in Fundy National Park in southeastern New Brunswick during the winters of 1983-84 and 1984-85.[33] Analysis of scats further confirmed that white-tailed deer (66% occurrence) and snowshoe hare (49% occurrence) were the 2 most important prey species by coyotes in winter. Other food items of minor importance were meadow vole, moose carrion, red squirrel, ruffed grouse, flying squirrel, and porcupine. Morton also followed coyote trails in winter and found 11 deer and 6 snowshoe hare kills. Other species preyed upon included ruffed grouse, common shrew, short-tailed shrew, and red-backed vole. Fat content of the marrow in leg bones of deer killed by coyotes confirmed that most were not malnourished.

In Nova Scotia there have been several summer collections of coyote scats by students at Acadia University. Snowshoe hare was the most frequent food item (60% occurrence) in 112 scats collected from May through October, 1989, followed in importance by adult white-tailed deer (19%), porcupine, red squirrel, fawn white-tailed deer, and meadow vole.[34] A second study of scats collected May-July, 1990, in northern Nova Scotia (Pictou County) found snowshoe hare (52% occurrence) and white-tailed deer (47%) to be the most frequent prey, followed by red squirrel (30%) and birds (9%). Animals of lesser importance included the meadow vole, woodchuck, porcupine, and muskrat.[35] Brent Patterson, a graduate student at Acadia University, has been studying coyotes in Kejimkujik National Park in southwestern Nova Scotia since 1992. He analysed 564 scats collected from July 1992 through June 1994 and found deer to be more frequent than snowshoe hares in scats at all seasons of the year.[36] Surprisingly, and in contrast to most other studies of coyotes in the northeast, deer remains appeared in over 80% of scats collected in May and June, dropping to 50%-60% in July and August, but still considerably greater than the occurrence of snowshoe hare. Fawns composed much of the deer remains in summer scats. Deer was found in over 84% of scats collected in the months of December, January, and February suggesting a year-round dependency by coyotes on deer in that park during the time of study. Other food items frequently found in scats were red squirrel, porcupine, berries and fruit, small mammals and vegetation. Patterson also followed 114 km of coyote trails in the snow and tracked radio-collared coyotes from October 1992 through March 1994 during which time he found 30 dead deer, 16 of which were confirmed kills while the exact cause of death for the remaining 14 was uncertain.

Ross Hall of the Nova Scotia Wildlife Division found 2 deer, 11 snowshoe hares and 2 ruffed grouse killed by coyotes in 79 km of trail followed in February and March 1983-85.[37] Coyotes also fed on found carcasses of 6 deer (2 of which were thought to have been killed by coyotes) and 2 moose, and they chased 2 deer unsuccessfully. Snowshoe hare and white-tailed deer occurred most often in scats collected during the tracking. During the tracking of coyote trails in the winters of 1988-89 and 1989-90, coyotes killed 18 snowshoe hare, 4 deer, 6 squirrel, 19 small mammals, and 3 ruffed grouse.[38] Surprisingly, 3 of the 4 deer were killed by single coyotes; the fourth was killed by a group of 5 coyotes. There are few published accounts of single coyotes successfully killing deer in winter. All deer were in good physical condition. The Nova Scotia tracking data was updated through 1992 to include over 1,300 km of coyote trails (all group sizes).[39] Fifty-two percent of the trails were of single coyotes and 32% were of groups of 2. Of 184 chases of prey, 87 were of snowshoe hare (47%) and 30 (16%) were of white-tailed deer. The remainder of chases included small mammals (21%), squirrel (9%), ruffed grouse (3%), and otter, porcupine and unidentified birds (4%). Coyotes were successful on 39 of the 87 chases of hares (45% success) and 6 of the 30 chases of deer (20% success). Coyotes also fed on carrion (mostly deer) 93

Predation by coyotes on sheep in winter may be significant in the western United States, where large flocks are left outside (G. Connolly).

times. Cause of death for most carrion was not determined, but some of the animals were most certainly killed earlier by coyotes. Twenty-six deer carcasses were examined for levels of fat in bone marrow of which 15 (58%) were in excellent condition, 9 (35%) were in fair to good condition, and only 2 (7%) were in poor condition. Eleven (42%) of the carcasses were fawns, 3 (12%) were yearlings, and 12 (46%) were adults.

I referred earlier to a study in Maine by Gerry Lavigne which showed that a sample of deer killed by coyotes was similar in sex and age structure and body condition, to the population at large (as determined from automobile kills and hunter harvest). Lavigne interpreted those data to mean that some mortality of deer from coyote predation was additive, and that those losses should be considered in white-tailed deer management plans.

A similar study was conducted in Northumberland County, New Brunswick. Sex and age structure and condition of 65 deer killed by coyotes (December-April 1984-85 and 1985-86) were compared to similar measurements from 101 non-coyote killed deer (includes poached, starved, dog-killed and road-killed) and 973 deer killed by hunters during the same time period. [40]

"*Ages of deer killed in Autumn by hunters, and deer killed by all other means (except coyote predation) in Northumberland County of New Brunswick (1984-1985; 1985-1986) were used as two indices of age distribution of living deer. Comparing these to age distribution of coyote-killed deer showed no difference. Nutrition level as indicated by percent femur fat [the amount of fat in the marrow of a leg bone, usually the thigh bone] was not different among non-coyote-killed-deer and coyote-killed-deer. Results indicate coyotes were not selecting deer of certain ages or physical condition. Other similar studies have shown that coyotes often select young, old and (or) poorly nourished deer. The author suspects a higher ratio of coyotes to prey species in Northumberland County as compared to areas where coyotes prey selectively upon deer.*" [41]

Although coyotes have only been reported from Newfoundland since 1987 several carcasses and a small collection of scats have been examined for food item identification. [42] Common foods in five carcasses and eleven scats (autumn collections) included beaver, snowshoe hare, red squirrel, moose, ruffed grouse, and common shrew.

5 REPRODUCTION

"It is a natural law that all animals attempt to reproduce at the maximum increase rate permitted by their physical endowments. It is an equally valid law that this maximum reproductive rate is always defeated in part."[1]

The ability of an animal to reproduce and recruit young into a population to replace those that die is the evolutionary measure of success or failure of all wildlife species. Fossil records provide ample evidence of species which, for one reason or another, failed to compensate through reproduction for those losses to mortality. Today the earth is losing species at a rate perhaps greater than at any time in biological history, and much of that is due to habitat loss and environmental change. The "reproductive potential" of a species, often measured in terms of numbers of young born, is not always a good measure of evolutionary success. The number born and the number of juveniles that survive until they breed, (a measure of population recruitment), combined with rates of adult mortality, are required to properly measure population trends.

The annual process of replacing individuals lost to mortality through juvenile recruitment is, of course, never completely in balance. The numbers of individuals change each year; the direction and intensity of that change is influenced by many factors which combine to influence the dynamic state of each population. Most animal populations experience short-term changes in numbers and those changes can be subtle or dramatic. Real population change, however, can only be recognized and measured through long-term monitoring, or tracking of numbers, or indices of numbers, for a particular population or species. Changes in the rates of reproduction and recruitment are symptoms of, and responses to, environmental stress. These annual variations in rates of reproduction and survival influence the highs and lows of population change. The two factors that influence the reproduction and productivity of mammalian predators most are the density of the predators and the abundance and availability of food.

Some predators are so dependent upon a single prey species that population changes can be quite robust, and, as in the relationship between the Canada lynx and snowshoe hare, quite predictable and cyclical. Charles Elton first showed this rythmic pattern in lynx populations of northern Canada by tracking fur returns from records of the Hudson's Bay Company.[2] Since then other studies have documented the clear dependency of lynx upon snowshoe hare.[3] The evidence of lynx cycles from Hudson's Bay Company fur records, the well-documented cyclical changes in hare abundance and the near total dependence of lynx upon snowshoe hare throughout its range clearly established the link between population changes in hares and lynxes.

Although studies of feeding habits and reproductive biology of coyotes have been conducted for over 50 years, and as we shall see, a range in coyote pregnancy rates and litter sizes has been documented, it is only recently that studies have established correlations between fluctuating food availability, noteably snowshoe hare, and coyote reproduction and recruitment. This dependency by coyotes on a single food source appears to increase with latitude, and that trend corresponds to decreased diversity and abundance in the available food base and increased environmental stress, particularly during winter. Thus, as the coyote approached or entered into the northern environment which drives the lynx-hare cycle, it too responded to increased environmental stress by adjustments to reproduction similar to those of the lynx. We will pursue this interesting adjustment in coyote population dynamics later.

Here we review selected studies from across North America to illustrate the range in measures of coyote reproduction and examine those data for evidence of reproductive uniqueness in the eastern coyote. We will also examine other characteristics of coyote reproduction, including geographic synchrony of breeding behaviour and biology, den site characteristics, adult attendance and care of pups, and pup development and dispersal. Four seasons in the reproductive cycle of coyotes have been recognized, and I have chosen to use those here.[4] Although there may be variation in measurements of reproductive performance, especially rates of ovulation and pregnancy in juvenile and adult females, the chronology and scheduling is fairly uniform throughout, especially in the northeast.

Most information on rates of ovulation and pregnancy come from examining reproductive organs and tracts of coyote carcasses collected by hunters and trappers. Much of the earlier data from the western United States came from coyotes removed during programs of control. The reader should be aware that many studies are based on relatively small samples, and resulting data on reproductive performance may be biased. That bias may be a direct result of low sampling of the population, or a more subtle artifact of trapping susceptibility by female coyotes of certain age classes or reproductive condition (e.g., non-breeding females without territories may be more prone to being trapped).

PAIR BONDING AND MATING (JANUARY-FEBRUARY)

Stanley Young and Hartley Jackson, in their book *The Clever Coyote*, described the reproductive biology and behaviour of western coyotes in detail. Later studies often refer to this book and frequently use it as a benchmark to compare ecological measurements of various regional populations of coyotes.

"As a rule coyotes do not mate for life. Some pairs may remain together for a number of years, however ... [I]n the mating season coyotes may be heard yelping much more than usual, and packs of three to a dozen animals may be seen. Later the breeding animals pair off.... The whelping season in the United States varies with latitude. In general, according to studies of a large number of

embryos ... the season in the northern tier of states seems somewhat earlier than farther south. In Montana ... breeding begins about February 1 and lasts throughout the month, the height of the season being about February 15. In Texas, breeding apparently begins somewhat later, although data are inadequate for definite conclusions. In some States [there may be] a variation of at least 2 months in the time of breeding, probably because of great diversity in altitude and other environmental factors."[5]

The results of a comprehensive study of coyotes in Kansas by H.T. Gier was published in 1957 and it, like the publication by Young and Jackson several years earlier, represents a classic reference for the general ecology and control of the western coyote. That study included biological data from 1,733 coyote carcasses collected "from sportsmen, game protectors, and country agents throughout the state [of Kansas] during January, February, and March, 1948 through 1951."[6]

"Pregnant female coyotes were encountered from early February to May. By determining the age of a set of embryos the time of breeding could be estimated within a few days, and the breeding pattern for any one year established. The earliest ovulation time among pregnant coyotes examined was February 2, and the latest was March 26. The range of breeding times varied from year to year, but no factor responsible for this variation was found.... Breeding season of the male coyote corresponds to that of the female but is a little longer. Old males are capable of mating by early January and continue in breeding condition until early March; young males can breed from late January to mid-March.... Only 14 males [of 908 carcasses examined] were found during the breeding season that by the condition of the testes, could be considered to be nonbreeders."[7]

In Kansas, at least, most males, regardless of age, come into breeding condition.
H.T. Gier provides a more detailed account of the breeding behaviour of coyotes in his contribution to the book *The Wild Canids*.

"It appears that the social unit among coyotes is the family, revolving around a reproductive female.... Nonfamily coyotes are loners that occasionally join forces for companionship or for killing prey too large for one coyote.... A coyote family has its inception in midwinter when a female comes into estrous and attracts one or more sexually active males. Normally over 90% of the females 20 months or older become sexually active and emit the sex attractrant by the end of January; a smaller proportion (0-60%) of the 9-to-10-month old females by mid-February. It appears that all the reactive, unattached males within an attractive female's territory join the parade and follow that female for days. I have seen as many as 7 males following 1 estrous female. Copulation between old males and old females may occur (in central Kansas) as early as January 12, but the earliest record of ovulation that I have from 20 years of study is January 31. The males follow the estrous female for as much as 4 weeks. Copulation is frequent and involves more than a single male although

observations from distances sufficient not to disturb the activities do not allow definite identification of individual males....

As the breeding season progresses, other bitches in the area become attractive, and one by one, the male entourage of the earlier female drift to new females until a single male is left with that particular female and the 'wedding' is consummated, with the female and her selected mate having the last few days of her estrous period alone. Ovulation occurs 2 or 3 days before the end of receptivity, so in most cases, elimination of the suitors, either by discouragement by stronger males, dissipation of stamina, or rejection by the bitch, has been effective in limiting the sire of the pups to the strongest, most cunning male available.... Old females in Kansas ovulate between January 31 and February 20. Old males mate with old females, and most of the old males will find a mate. Estrous of the earlier maturing young females (those born in April) overlaps that of the late-breeding old females so the last of the unmated old males may proceed on down the line to follow and mate with the young females, if their stamina holds. Males of the year enter the breeding pool in late January or early February, so there is little reduction in the number of available males when the last females select their mates in mid-March. Old males are reproductively active from late December to early April; males of the year from late January into May.... At the end of the breeding season, there will be unmated males to the extent of noncompetitive old males plus young males equivalent in numbers to the nonbreeding females. The bachelor males disperse, possibly maintaining a loose association with others of their kind, wandering and trying to survive until the next breeding season. Unmated females seem to have other possibilities, such as serving as nursemaid and 'baby-sitter' for mother or sister, or teaming up with an unmated sister or brother until 'next year.' "[8]

Whether observations on the breeding behaviour of coyotes in Kansas apply to the eastern coyote is uncertain, although as we will see, one of the characteristics which appears to be most universal among North American coyotes is synchrony of breeding. It should be remembered, as we review breeding behaviour studies of coyotes from more established western prairie ranges, that densities can be much higher there than for eastern populations, and interactions among eastern coyotes may be more like behavioural patterns of wolves. This is even more probable given the assumed genetic linkage between wolves and eastern coyotes. Thus, the groups of male suitors drifting from one receptive female to another, as described for coyotes in Kansas, may not apply to coyotes in the northeast, or within forested habitats in general. Male-female bonding may be stronger and more permanent and adult territoriality more developed in eastern coyote populations.

James Kennelly of the Massachusetts Cooperative Wildlife Research Unit summarized recent studies on coyote reproduction across its range in North America:

"...males frequently attain sexual maturity during their first breeding season following birth and are capable of impregnating females.... The proportion of juvenile males (less than 1 yr old) breeding in natural populations each season

is unknown.... The onset of breeding condition in adult males varies from year to year both within one geographic region and from one to another.... In a series of reproductive tracts collected from 13 western States, the first sign of breeding onset ... occurred in November [and]. . . the breeding season was in 'full-swing' by February.... Studies with coyotes from Arkansas..., Oklahoma..., and Colorado, however, indicate ... full breeding condition is attained in December.... Regression of the adult testes begins in March."[9]

Kennelly continues by describing female coyote reproduction.

"The coyote is seasonally monestrous [i.e., the female only comes into breeding condition once each year].... Contrary to earlier beliefs, juveniles may cycle and reproduce the first breeding season following birth but the proportion depends upon environmental conditions ... and control intensity....Proestrous [vulval enlargement and bleeding] is first evident in adult coyotes 2-3 months before estrous onset.... These two indicators of sexual maturity are not always evident in juveniles but in those that show them, the changes vary in intensity and duration compared with adults.... Date of estrous onset and duration of breeding season varies geographically.... and by season within a particular region.... Based on over 2900 records [carcasses] from 13 western states, ... breeding generally begins in February and most females bred within a month.... The early literature relating to estrous onset, much of it primarily based on trappers' accounts, clearly showed January through March as the general breeding season.... The duration of estrous for 41 females was 10.2 days (range 4-15 days) with age having no significant effect on either onset or duration."[10]

A radio-marked male coyote in southeastern Colorado continued to breed at 12-13 years of age.[11] The most recent information on reproduction in coyotes, especially the eastern coyote, was a paper presented by Robert Chambers at the symposium on the eastern coyote held at Fredericton, New Brunswick, in November 1991.

"Data on breeding patterns and success of eastern male coyotes are extremely minimal. Silver and Silver ... indicated a lack of testicular development in captive males until the age of 19-20 months. Hamilton ... reported on a single male specimen from New York that evidenced incipient enlargement of testes in December and maximum development in late January. Moore ... assigned breeding status based on testes and epididymis weights to 20.6 percent (⁷/₃₄) of males from what he described as "longer established" populations from western New Brunswick and to 0.0 percent (%) of males from "recently colonized" areas in eastern New Brunswick and Nova Scotia. Several authors [previously noted] have reported that at least some western male coyotes are capable of breeding in their first year.... Gier ... reports that males of the year enter the breeding pool in late January or early February and are active into May; older males were active from late December until early April."[12]

Mating in wild eastern coyotes has been reported as early as late January in New York and early February in Maine.[13] In Kejimkujik National Park, Nova Scotia a radio-marked adult male coyote mated on January 31, 1993, and January 24, 1994, while an adult female on an adjacent territory copulated frequently on the night of February 24, 1993.[14] The peak of mating is believed to occur in mid-February, with most young being born in mid-April. Length of pregnancy (gestation) in captive eastern coyotes from New Hampshire was 61-66 days, similar to 60-63 days reported for western coyotes.[15] Studies of coyotes in Connecticut and Quebec indicate that significant proportions of female coyote pups ovulate just prior to their first birthday.[16] For all ages combined, 57% of female coyotes from Quebec and 64% from Connecticut had ovulated. Gary Moore assigned breeding status based on ovarian weight to 2.6% of the pups and 61.5% of the yearlings and adults in his samples from New Brunswick and Nova Scotia. He further reported a higher occurrence of breeding from earlier established populations (75%) than from more recently colonized areas (50%).[17]

In summary, reproductively active mature female eastern coyotes are probably on established territories year-round, having a loose bond with one or more adult males during the autumn and early winter when the female is with that year's pups. By late January, adult males enter breeding condition and begin to seek out and associate with adult females. My observations during winter tracking of an adult female and her two pups in northern New Brunswick showed that at least one male occasionally travelled with the female by February, at which time the pups frequently travelled alone. Copulation is frequent and conception probably occurs from late January through February, with a peak in the first two weeks of February. I found a litter of pups in northern New Brunswick on May 24, 1984, which I aged at approximately 7 weeks. That litter would have been born in early April and, with a gestation period of 63 days, conception would have occurred the first week of February. A litter found on April 29 in Maine was aged as 12-15 days old, giving a birth date of April 14-17.[18]

Most adult males are reproductively active, although the proportion of juvenile males which enter breeding condition their first year is less certain. There are probably sufficient males available to service all receptive females, certainly those females on established territories. Although food, environmental stress and coyote densities all influence rates of ovulation and pregnancy in juvenile and adult coyotes, it appears that, in general, 60-80% of adult female eastern coyotes normally breed and bear young each year. Many of those that fail to breed successfully may not have established territories. The extent to which juveniles become established on territories (density dependent), in addition to food and environmental stress, also serves to influence the proportion of juvenile females which breed. The proportion of juvenile females breeding may vary from 0%-50%, and probably averages around 20-25%.

DENNING / GESTATION / BIRTH (MARCH-APRIL)

Once conception occurs and the female is no longer receptive to advances by her male companion, the pair begin to spend time investigating prospective sites for whelping. Stanley Young provides this early account of denning activities by western coyotes.

"...Coyotes generally use a den when bringing forth and rearing their young, though there are exceptions to this general rule, such as the choosing of cover *beneath sagebrush and giving birth to the litter above ground.... Dens may be found in a canyon, washout or coulee, on a bank or hillside, in a rock bluff, or even on level ground, as in a wheatfield, stubblefield, or plowed field. They have been discovered under deserted homestead shacks in the desert, under grain bins, in a drainage pipe, in a dry culvert under railway tracks, in a hollow log, in a thicket, and under a clump of thistles that had blown into a canyon.... As a rule, instead of digging entirely new dens, coyotes will enlarge abandoned badger or rabbit holes or use deserted porcupine dens in rocky promontories or canyon walls. Usually they start cleaning out holes several weeks prior to whelping. They generally claw out the dirt in one direction from the mouth of the den, where it piles up into a mound, although some dens have no such mound.... The female continues digging and cleaning out den holes, sometimes a dozen or more, until the young are born. Then, if one den is disturbed the family moves to another. Sometimes the animals move only a few hundred yards, apparently just to have a cleaner home, leaving many fleas behind."[19]*

Gier provides the following description of breeding and denning activities of coyotes in Kansas.

"The pair, consisting of a pregnant female and compatible male, select a territory, clean out old badger, marmot, or skunk dens within their territory or dig a new den, and otherwise prepare for their family responsibilities. They hunt together, sleep near each other, and in late pregnancy, the male frequently hunts alone and brings food to his heavy mate. Possibly as a means of strengthening the tie between mates, there is another round of copulation in the last 10 days of pregnancy. How frequently preparturition copulation occurs, I do not know, but I have seen it 2 times in the wild and with 3 out of 4 pregnant coyote bitches in the laboratory.... We have been told ... that the male coyote is excluded from the den before, during, and after parturition. I consider this idea to be more folklore than fact, as I have observed both male and female entering the den in which there were young pups, and on some occasions, both male and female were taken with the pups when the den was dug out."[20]

In Kansas coyotes may give birth in a den, a hollow tree, or under a ledge or other protection. Some females prepare a grass- or leaf-lined nest while others deposit the young on the bare floor. Some females pull fur off their bellies for bedding much as rabbits do and completely bare the nipples.[21]

"Coyote dens or nests may be any place that gives the coyotes a sense of security. Most pairs of coyotes go 'house hunting' during or shortly after the breeding season so that by whelping time several possible dens have been cleaned out or other suitable spots located. Favorite sites include brush-covered slopes, steep banks with or without brush, nearly level areas with thickets partially surrounding openings, knolls or slopes in open prairie, fence rows, rock ledges, hollow logs, or even under granaries or log piles.... Some coyotes [may never] have dens, as many pups are found in thickets or under brush piles.... Dens vary greatly in construction and depth. Some dens extend straight back in a bank; others go

straight down 2 or 3 feet, then level off, while others descend at an angle for variable depths before leveling off to the nest. Some dens are only a few feet long, others extend far into the earth and may be branched. The length seems to depend to a large extent on the ease with which the earth can be removed.... Most of the dens observed were on south slopes or in a bank facing south, or if on the level, were open to the south. Less frequently, dens opened to the west, and only a few were seen opening to the east. Some of the dens used by coyotes are undoubtedly dug by other animals and are only cleaned out and possibly enlarged by coyotes. Other coyotes certainly dig their own dens."[22]

Coyote den sites in South Dakota are most frequently in a sunny area, with the primary or natal den having a single entrance, usually facing south.[23] Here, coyotes seldom dig their own dens, but enlarge existing holes dug by other animals. Den entrances are elongated vertically and quite distinguishable. Secondary dens may be a series of holes with several entrances.

"Any disturbance of the surroundings, or signs that a man has been near the den or nest after whelping time, usually results in the pups being moved to a new location. Even if the den is not disturbed, it appears likely that in most cases the pups are moved to a new location at intervals. There seldom are excessive tracks or any large accumulation of food remains around a den as would be expected if the den were used several weeks. At any rate, the pups probably do not stay in the dens much longer than a month."[24]

Disturbed adults in Nebraska moved young over 1 km from primary to secondary den sites.[25] Adults progressively increased their time at dens from the breeding season through pregnancy and nursing. Protected den sites in Tennessee have been described as steep banks, rock ledges, brush-covered slopes, thickets and hollow logs as well as dens of other animals.[26] In Wisconsin coyote dens are often burrows consisting of 2 or more tunnels leading to a deep hole 1m or more in the ground.[27] Coyotes may enlarge abandoned dens of badger, woodchuck, fox, or skunk or other old coyote dens but will occasionally dig a new den. Den entrances average 25 cm wide and 33 cm high. Unlike foxes, coyotes remove bones, scats and other debris from the den site. Females prepare more than one den so young can be moved if disturbed or if fleas become too bothersome.

Closer to home, 5 of 7 coyote dens found in Maine were in young hardwoods, 2 of which had been previously occupied by porcupines. Den opening widths averaged 37 cm (similar to the average of 32 cm for dens in Nebraska) and most were in sandy loam with one opening. Most dens were on a knoll or hummock and in a sunny location (south facing). Dens varied from above ground shallow depressions under spruce branches to multi-chambered burrows 8 m in length and 1-2 m below the surface. Above-surface dens were often associated with poor drainage sites. Active dens were devoid of prey remains and adult scats, similar to observations in Missouri. One adult relocated pups to new den sites 6 times, another 3 times, usually after disturbance, although undisturbed litters were also relocated to secondary den sites. Dens were normally abandoned 8-10 weeks after birth (June 14-July 3). Denning

Coyotes in the northeast often use hollow logs as den sites. Here, Mike Boudreau, Nova Scotia Department of Natural Resources, holds a young pup found at a den site in spring 1994 (B. Patterson).

coyotes in Ontario often enlarge groundhog or fox burrows in secluded locations along stream banks, ravines or on sandy ridges.[28]

The one natal den that I found in northern New Brunswick was an abandoned porcupine lair in a hollow log within an immature hardwood stand, very similar to several of the dens described in Maine. The litter (7 wks old) was found in a second hollow log approximately 164 feet (50 m) from the natal den. Two of three coyote dens in Nova Scotia were in rocky caves while the third was in a hollow log.[29] To summarize, coyote pairs begin searching for potential denning sites at least several weeks before the female gives birth. In the northeast, coyotes often den in sunny locations within young hardwood stands and prefer to occupy and enlarge dens or lairs of other animals. Here, with fewer kinds of animals using dens than in the west, coyotes prefer dens, or lairs of porcupines and foxes. In the west, coyotes often use abandoned dens of badgers and woodchucks. Of course, as the literature suggests, and in keeping with the generalized habits of the creature under study, coyote dens can be located in a wide variety of forested and agricultural habitat and can be above or below the ground surface. In all instances, however, locations are usually secretive, and the disturbance is minimal. Birth of eastern coyotes usually occurs during the month of April. Juvenile females enter breeding condition later than adults, so litters born in late April are probably from younger females. There are few observations of coyotes giving birth, but it is reasonable to assume that the female seeks the seclusion of its den and birth follows the pattern documented for domestic dogs and wolves.

Let us now review information on the number of young in coyote litters as reported in selected studies from across North America. This is important in order to assess the uniqueness of the eastern coyote, or how much it is like its western relatives. The number of young born is dependent upon many factors. Availability of food and the subsequent ability of females to successfully ovulate, conceive, and give birth, is of major importance. Food availability, or nutritional intake, can influence the proportion of juvenile females breeding their first year, and to a lesser extent the proportion of adults which breed. Food availability can also influence litter size and subsequent survival of the young coyotes. It is generally recognized, however, that *the one factor which most influences population change is the proportion of females which successfully breed and give birth their first year.* We will examine these mechanisms for "population control" in more detail under "Population Dynamics."

Early studies established that a litter of western coyotes averaged 5-7 young. Of 120 female coyotes killed by government hunters in New Mexico during the years of 1928-31, litters of 5 were most common. The average number of unborn young per female was 5.5, and 77% of all the females carried from 4-7 young. Of 396 litters of unborn coyotes killed in Arizona from 1942 to 1945, the average litter size was 5.0. The range in sizes of litters can be large and it has long been thought that litter size is most likely influenced by food availability, and that in time of plenty (at least in the western states) litters of 9-12 are not uncommon. Some females were known to have as many as 17 to 19 pups although these were exceptions.[30]

Dens examined in the west occasionally contained 2 litters of obvious age difference. Double litters have been attributed to a young female, not having suitable denning territory, taking up quarters with the mother. In the forested northeast, where densities are lower, food is less available and environmental stress greater, it is doubtful that the extremes in litter sizes and double litters occur as frequently, if they occur at all.

Litters of coyotes in Kansas can vary from 2 to 12, and dens containing over 12 young always have 2 litters.

"Of 27 extra large litters I have personally examined, 15 had 2 sets of pups 5-15 days difference in age; the others were more nearly alike. In central Kansas, approximately 10 percent of all litters dug from dens consist of 2 age groups. Two sets of pups in a single den may be explained by 2 bitches using the same den, either from a mother-daughter or sister-sister relationship, or by 2 bitches having been won by a single male, or it is possible that the mother has adopted the pups of another bitch that had been killed or was away from home when visited. I have no records of 2 bitches and a male sharing a den, although I do have records of 2 bitches being killed in a den with a double litter and of a male and female in a den with a double litter. Double litters cannot be explained by consecutive births from 1 female. There are no records of any canid giving birth to young over a period exceeding a few hours. Spaced ovulation may result in different aged pups within the uterus by as much as 2 days, but they are always born as one litter."[31]

Adult female coyotes spend considerable time at the den site with young pups, while the adult male hunts for food (M. Bekoff, 1978).

In Texas several studies have found coyote litters to average between 5 and 7 pups. Other collections in Texas showed average uterine swellings per female to range from 5.1 to 6.9. Studies in Texas provided convincing evidence of an inverse relationship between coyote density and litter size. Litters averaged 4.3 where control was absent and coyotes were common but 6.9 where control was in effect and coyote densities were low. Coyote litter size was also found to be density dependent in Wyoming. In 3 years of experimental removal, mean litter sizes ranged from 6.0 to 8.0, whereas on a site with no removal (control), litters ranged from 3.7 to 4.0. Litters of female carcasses collected near the Utah-Idaho border from 1966 to 1970 ranged from 5.9 to 7.6, and averaged 6.7. Reproductive performance was dependent on availability of jackrabbits. In Colorado the average number of placental scars (attachment sites for embryos in the uterus indicating that the animal had given birth that year) in 10 pregnant females was 3.4, and litters averaged 3.2 pups. Litter sizes in Illinois have varied from 4.3 to 6.8, from 5 to 7 in Wisconsin and averaged 5.0 in Tennessee. Only 7 of 51 reproductive tracts from female coyotes collected in 1968-69 from trappers in Minnesota showed signs of having given birth and placental scars averaged 5.1 in those that did. In the Lower Fraser Valley, British Columbia, the mean litter size of 20 carcasses and 2 free-ranging litters was 5.4.[32]

Perhaps the most convincing studies illustrating the dependency of coyote reproduction on availablity of food resources have been in Alberta. (We will review those studies in greater detail under "Population Dynamics.") Coyote carcasses collected from 1964 to 1968 showed placental scars averaged 6.0 per adult breeding female and 5.2 per yearling breeding female. A later and much larger collection of coyote carcasses from 1972-73 through 1974-75 in the forested regions of Alberta (n=1135) showed *in uteri* (unborn) litter sizes of 4.9 for adults when hares were abundant and 4.0 when hares were scarce.[33]

How does productivity of coyotes in eastern North America compare to productivity of coyotes on traditional western ranges? Let us examine reproductive data which is only now accumulating from newly established populations in the northeast. Only 6 of 27 (22%) female reproductive tracts collected in Connecticut from May 1985 through April 1986 had placental scars, although the average number of scars per breeding female was 8.2. Dan Harrison, Associate Professor of Wildlife Ecology at the University of Maine, summarized his extensive studies of coyotes in that state and suggested the average litter size was 5-9 pups. The average litter size of 43 female coyotes collected from southern Quebec from 1977 to 1979 was 7.1 and increased from 5.3 for juveniles, to 6.7 for subadults and to 7.7 for adults. The mean number of uterine scars in a sample of 8 female carcasses from New Brunswick and Nova Scotia was 5.9.[34]

Nova Scotia introduced a bounty on coyotes in 1982. (The first coyote was trapped in that province in 1977.) This was a political rather than a biological response to increasing numbers of coyotes in the province. The ineffectiveness of the bounty in deterring growth in the provincial coyote population soon became apparant to all but the most ardent of bounty enthusiasts, and the program was terminated in 1986. However, the program did result in a considerable number of carcasses being submitted to the Nova Scotia Wildlife Branch (in return for a $50 bounty) from which data were taken on reproduction and sex and age structure of the sample.[35]

Reproductive data from the 1982-85 sample of coyotes from Nova Scotia confirms the higher rate of breeding, and larger litter sizes, in adult (2.5 years+) than in juvenile (1.5 years) females (Table 2). Only 30% of the juveniles bred, compared to 44% of the adults. The average litter size of those adults was 6.3 compared to only 2.9 for juveniles. The 4-year sample shows that adult female pregnancy rates (% females with placental scars) declined from 100% to 71% to 39% to 36% from 1982-83 through 1985-86. Pregnancy rates for juvenile females, however, showed no such trend. Although sample sizes of adults are small, especially for the first two years, it does suggest that as densities of coyotes increased throughout the province, average productivity declined.

Coyote carcasses were again collected from trappers in Nova Scotia during the trapping season of 1992-93. Only 1 of 32 (3%) yearling (1.5 years) females had given birth that year with a litter size (placental scar count) of 3.0. One-half (29 of 58) of the adult (more than1.5 years) females had given birth with a mean litter size of 5.4. The Nova Scotia data suggest that, as coyotes became established there, concurrent with a decline in the provincial deer population, the rate of breeding in subadult females also declined. Although adult females also showed declines in pregnancy rates and litter sizes over the same time span, those changes were less pronounced. Brent Patterson suggests that high numbers of coyotes during the early

Table 2: Pregnancy rates (placental scar counts) and litter sizes of female coyotes submitted for bounty in Nova Scotia, 1982-83 through 1985-86 (from Anderson 1988).

| Juveniles (1.5 years) | Females | | Percent | Placental Scars | |
Year	Total	With Scars	pregnant	Total	Average
1982-83	19	2	10.5	11	5.5
1983-84	34	13	38.2	35	2.7
1984-85	30	4	13.3	16	4.0
1985-86	32	15	46.9	37	2.5
Totals	115	34	29.6	99	2.9
Adults (2.5 years+)					
1982-83	2	2	100.0	14	7.0
1983-84	7	5	71.4	38	7.6
1984-85	18	7	38.9	42	6.0
1985-86	25	9	36.0	52	5.8
Totals	52	23	44.2	146	6.3

years of colonization in Nova Scotia, and prior to the establishment of traditionally defended territories and development of social hierarchies, might explain the higher rates of breeding in younger female coyotes at that time (a sort of "social chaos" during early colonization).[36]

In summary, the literature contains numerous references to average litter sizes for coyotes throughout its range in North America. Litter sizes vary, as do the proportions of juveniles and adults breeding, and much of that variation is a result of the influence of food availability and coyote density on reproductive performance. Because of that relationship, it is not possible to assume standard measurements of reproduction for all populations, or for any one population through time. It does appear, however, that litters of 4-6 are common in the northeast, and throughout coyote range in general, with extremes at either end dependent upon extremes in food availability and coyote densities.

DEN ATTENDANCE AND PUP DEVELOPMENT (MAY-JUNE)

Adult coyotes spend increasingly more time at or near den sites from the period of breeding through pregnancy, nursing and pup training. In Maine the nursing period lasts for about 6 weeks, during which the adult females usually remain near their dens. Coyotes often move to new dens during this period, especially if a den is disturbed. After weaning, adults travel more and pups leave den sites at 8-10 weeks of age.

A radio-telemetry study of breeding coyotes in Maine found that adults were located more than 300 m from their den at all times of the day during nursing and weaning periods combined. The Maine study also found that radio-marked adult males and females increased their daily travel (as measured by distance between independent relocations) from 1.5, 2.4 to 2.7 km during the three biological phases of nursing, weaning and pup independence.[37]

Coyotes in the northeast normally mate in mid-February. Pups are born 60 days later. Here, the author holds 3 coyote pups found in northern New Brunswick in May 1983 (G. Parker).

"...Females were more restricted than males during pup rearing because of nursing responsibilities. Pups probably continued to nurse occasionally after the time that they began eating meat, accounting for smaller ranges of females into the weaning period. Males restricted their movements during nursing to supply food for mates, and during the weaning period to provide food and protection for the pups." [38]

Coyotes in Nebraska increased their home ranges after the denning season. Mean home range size for breeding females increased from 9.3 km² (nursing), to 23.1 km² (weaning) to 40.1 km² (pup independence). Respective home range sizes for adult males were 14.0, 8.6, and 30.5 km². Female coyotes in South Dakota remained in the den during the first few days after pups were born, and males did not feed them during this sedentary period of pup attendance and convalescence. [39]

Weights of new born eastern coyote pups from 7 litters raised in captivity in New Hampshire averaged 283-396 g for males and 320-442 g for females, considerably greater than the weight for one male (170 g) and one female (198 g) new-born western (Colorado) coyotes also raised in the New Hampshire study. [40] Newborn western coyotes normally weigh 200-250 gm at birth, depending upon the number in the litter. [41] These limited data suggest that eastern coyotes are considerably heavier at birth than their western cousins, which is compatible with the general agreement that adult eastern coyotes are also substantially larger than adult western coyotes.

The development of young pups has been described in detail from several studies of captive western coyotes. Especially descriptive is this study from Wyoming.

"Their fur [at birth] was dark, tawny brown, darker areas being present on their backs, ears, faces, and tails. The head was blunt, the ears rounded and flat against the head. The pads of the feet were pink. An umbilical cord approximately three inches in length was present. This umbilical cord was gone by the third day, leaving a small clean scar. The fur changed from a soft, pliable texture, becoming somewhat stiffer, but still was softer and more pliable than that of the adults.... At the age of ten days the points of the milk teeth could be felt beneath the surface of the skin. At this time also the pads of the feet had turned black. The feces had changed from yellow to brown.... The inside corner of the eyes began to open at 10-13 days and all pups had their eyes completely open by 14-17 days.... The most prominant types of behavior up to the time that the pups can see are ingestive, eliminative, contactual, and care-seeking. Suckling was most strongly developed up to the time of weaning, the latter process beginning when the pups were about three weeks old and appearing to be completed when the pups were four to five weeks old. When the pups attempted to nurse, the female growled and walked away, the intensity of the growling and the abruptness of moving away increasing as the time for total weaning neared.... By the age of four weeks the pups were taking solid food.... The mother ... was first observed regurgitating food to her pups when they were five weeks old. The general pattern was that [the female] would eat some food, then begin whining. Upon hearing this the pups would run over to her, wagging their

tails and sometimes pawing at her mouth. [The female] would then undergo a few convulsive heaves and regurgitate. The pups would consume what she brought up.... For the first three weeks that the pups were fed regurgitated food they were not observed to eat anything else.... Eliminative behavior undergoes some changes with maturation. For the first few days, urination and defecation were stimulated by the pressure of the mother's tongue as she licked their bellies and licked up the waste products. By the age of ten days they were able to urinate and defecate without the mother's stimulation; in the case of the hand-raised pups, proper stimulation by the author was necessary until this same age. Both males and females squat when urinating.... Contactual behavior is most strongly developed during the neonatal period and diminishes after the pups' eyes have opened. When in contact with its littermates, a pup would be relatively quiet. When a pup is isolated, vocalization increased in varying degrees depending on the length of time it was separated. The hand-raised pup whined, yelped, and howled when left alone, the type of vocalization depending on the age of the pup. Once the eyes were open, contactual behavior decreased by degrees."

An interesting observation in this study was the relationship of the "aunt" (unmated sister to the mother of the litter) to the adult pair and the litter.

"In a normal situation a coyote family consists of the mated male and female, plus the pups of the year. In this situation a female was present that otherwise would not have been. The male... became agonistic in behavior towards [the unmated female] in February when both females were in heat. This situation has not changed.... The first time that their mother was observed regurgitating to the pups, [the aunt] also exhibited the same behavior. The pups would respond readily to either female when the female called them.[The aunt] would feed the pups as often as, if not more frequently than, their mother. It was [the aunt] who played more often with the pups. Their mother did not try to keep [the aunt] away from the pups when [the aunt] was put in the same pen. At this time the pups were a month old. [The aunt] never made any attempts to hurt or kill a pup."[42]

Henry Hilton described the colouration of juvenile eastern coyotes in Maine.

"At birth, pups are dark gray, but by 2 weeks the head is distinctly reddish brown with white marks becoming distinct on the chest. By 6 weeks, individual variation is apparant, and by the third month, adult markings are conspicuous."[43]

The very thorough study of hand-reared and captive bred western coyotes and wild canids (dug from a den in New Hampshire in 1960 and presumed to be eastern coyotes) in New Hampshire provides us with an early detailed account of the appearance and developmental biology and behaviour of the eastern coyote.

"Females removed hair from their bellies ... shortly before whelping but there was no evidence that it was used to line nests. Removal of hair may well have facilitated nursing since nipples ordinarily were difficult to locate in the otherwise dense fur.... As soon as a pup was born, the mother began licking it and

*consuming the birth membranes.... Whelping was completed in 3 to 10 hours....
While the female was giving birth, the male stood guard in the far end of the pen
or paced nervously back and forth. Before the pups were old enough to leave the
nest and if the bitch was away, the male stood guard or lay near the entrance of
the den, frequently looking inside but not entering.... There were two pairs in
the same pen during the birth of the F2 [second generation] litter.... The second
female ... entered repeatedly and attempted to take over care of the pups; this
precipitated violent fighting between the females.... Two of the F1 [first
generation] litters were moved by the bitch when they were 2 and 3 days old,
respectively."[44]*

The eyes of 25 wild canid pups in the New Hampshire study opened between 12-16
days, the pups walked between 16-21 days and ran 18-23 days after birth.

*"All incisors in one jaw were cut the same day, usually the 17th. Canines
frequently erupted on the same day as the incisors, but never earlier. Teeth
appeared on the upper jaw first in most cases, but in four males the order was
reversed.... Permanent incisors and canines and the first and second premolars
were cut by 19 weeks, although the canines were not full length. At 23 weeks,
all permanent teeth were present.... Pups were nearly black at birth.... A dark,
vertical stripe down the foreleg, barely visible in some pups by the 3rd week,
became more conspicuous.... For the first 2 weeks, our pups did little except
eat, sleep, crawl in seemingly aimless fashion, and squeak when they were cold
or hungry, or became separated from each other. If their discomfort was not
relieved, the squeaks became shrieks. As soon as the newborn pups were cleaned
and dried, they found their way up along the mother's body, assisted by her
licking and nuzzling, and started to nurse.... Weaning was essentially completed
by the end of the 6th week.... The male spent much time playing with the pups...,
and as they grew older he led them in hunting birds and butterflies that flew into
the pens.... The male was never observed to regurgitate. The female started to
regurgitate food for the pups about the middle of the 3rd week.... Care-soliciting
behavior of very young pups was limited to squeaking or shrieking when they
were uncomfortable. Yelping was rare in wild canids of any age.... We were
able to tape one individual vocalization (a true howl) from a 15-day-old pup....
Pups were 2 months old before they began to howl in unison."[45]*

Gier observed captive western coyotes in Kansas and found that for the first 10
days pups are fed milk at intervals of 2 to 12 hours.

*"The pups' incisors appear at about 12 days, canines at 16, and second premolars
at 21. Their teeth are of little use for tearing or cutting for at least 6 weeks, so
milk continues to be the stable food for nearly 2 months. The eyes open on the
10th day, and at that time the pups can move around to some extent, becoming
progressively more mobile until they can walk quite well by 20 days and can
run before they are 6 weeks old."[46]*

Western coyotes begin supplementary feeding of pups at 12-15 days of age, and
pups soon learn to stand on their hind legs and claw at the sides of the parent's mouth

to stimulate regurgitation. Feeding by regurgitation provides a convenient means of carrying and delivering food to the pups.

> *"When the pups are 4 to 6 weeks old and their milk teeth are functional, the parents bring in small food items such as mice, then rabbits ... so by the time the pups are 3 to 3.5 months old, they have been effectively transferred from milk and regurgitate, to regurgitate and fresh items, to fresh items only. Lactation is progressively reduced after 2 months, but may be continued to 4 months.... The male is an integral part of the family throughout the denning period, helping with the grooming and feeding, and moving the pups to a new den if necessary. He stands guard usually within sight of the den.... If the den or nest area is disturbed by man, the parent coyotes move the pups to another shelter 50 m to 2 km away, carrying them one by one if they are too small to walk.... Sometimes the pups are moved without apparent reason, maybe to get away from their fleas."[47]*

WEANING / PUP INDEPENDENCE (JULY-SEPTEMBER)

Western coyote pups emerge from the den when about 3 weeks old and after about 8-10 weeks the dens are abandoned, and the entire family moves about, remaining together until early fall.

> *"Occasionally the mother coyote will take her pups to an area a short distance from the den which is used as a sunning place, when weather permits, after which they return to the den.... [B]oth parent coyotes will at times gorge on the meat, return to the den and disgorge portions of the food around the entrance to the den for the pups to feed upon. The disgorged meat is often mixed with a whitish fluid which in appearance and viscosity resembles pigeon milk. The habit of disgorging food, which is also done by the large wolves, begins about a month after the puppies are born and the mother's milk is disappearing. At that time also, pieces of meat and bones will be carried to the den."[48]*

Young coyotes in Kansas leave the natal den by late June or early July (8-10 wks old) at which time adults begin giving the pups "survival" training.[49] In Ontario coyote pups are able to leave the den when only 3-4 weeks old, but that most often occurs when adults chose to move the litter to alternate (secondary) den sites. By July, coyote families in Ontario often use rendez-vous sites, similar to family behaviour documented for wolves. Such sites provide water, shade, activity areas for pups, visibility of intruders, and nearby escape cover. Adults make nightly excursions from these locations, and by late August pups are becoming familiar with the surrounding country. They still often travel together in small groups or with the adults.[50]

From July through August, pups become free of the natal or secondary dens and assume more independence at selected rendez-vous sites. Pups are often left at rendezvous sites during the day while adults take a break and rest a short distance away. At such sites in mid- to late-summer most pup activity consists of rest, play and "short" exploratory excursions. In early evening, near dusk, the adult female returns to the rendez-vous site, often announcing her arrival to the pups with a brief howl. This creates a great commotion among the pups, and a chorus of howls, yips, yaps and barks break up the evening solitude. Late summer-early autumn is when evening choruses are most frequent and these "evening songs" most often represent a family greeting between the juveniles and adult female. An occasional deeper, more resonant howl is that of the adult male who may or may not choose to join the daily rendezvous. In July and August the adults may bring food to the young but gradually the juveniles join the adults in the evening hunt, and their home range expands.

In Kejimkujik National Park, 2 juveniles from separate litters used less than one-half of the home range of the adult females up to dispersal in October-November. A third juvenile remained with its mother at least until March but never used the entire home range of the adult female. It is here that some uncertainty has developed about when, and to what extent, dispersal of young coyotes takes place.[51]

PUP DISPERSAL (OCTOBER-FEBRUARY)

Many factors may combine to influence the timing and extent of pup dispersal among coyote populations across its range. The need, of course, is to leave the occupied territory of the parental pair and search for suitable unoccupied range to establish a new territory, find a mate, and successfully raise a new litter. Dispersion of the young ensures genetic mixing and occupation of all suitable habitat and is common to most species of wildlife.

In western coyote populations dispersal of juveniles occurs as early as August, but it may occur later in eastern populations. Most young coyotes in western populations, however, are thought to disperse in November and December.[52] Radio-marked juveniles in Minnesota dispersed in October-November, for distances of 16-68 km with an average of 48 km, although some did not disperse until January. Dispersal in Minnesota was generally in a southeast to southwest direction, and prior to dispersal juvenile home ranges averaged only 5-8 km². The rate of movement averaged 11 km per week. Singles, pairs and groups of 3+ coyotes represented 60%, 34%, and 6% respectively of group sizes in winter from snow tracking studies. Aerial observations of coyote groups supported the observations from snow tracking. The authors were uncertain, however, what role dispersal of juveniles played in regulating population densities of coyotes in northern Minnesota.[53]

Young pups were ear-tagged during a study of the population dynamics of coyotes in Alberta from 1965 through 1968.[54] All relocations of pups through September were within 3-4 km of the rearing den. Dispersal of juveniles began in October although the earliest recovery of a pup from over 16 km was on October 27. Direction of movement was random, in contrast to the "southerly" direction of dispersal reported for Minnesota. Some coyotes did not disperse until late in their first year or until their second year. Dates for dispersion of pups from other regions include early October in Yellowstone Park, October in Texas and late October in Iowa.[55] Juvenile females appear to disperse farther than juvenile males.[56]

Eleven of 13 radio-marked coyotes in southeastern Colorado, which dispersed a mean distance of 59 km, were juveniles.[57] In that study only 4 juveniles remained in their natal home range for more than 1 year and 10 of the 13 dispersers were killed less than 1 year after leaving their natal home range. Most of the dispersal there occurred from October through January.

"Prior to dispersal, the home ranges of juveniles are small and within the boundaries of their mother's home range. As pups grow and become more active, their home range increases in size. Reported home range sizes of juveniles have varied from less than 5 sq km (2 sq. mi.) in Oklahoma and Quebec to 5-8 sq km (2-3 sq. mi.) in Minnesota and Ontario to 54 sq km (20 sq. mi.) in Washington.... Dispersal movements of juveniles and subadult coyotes are generally linear, making it difficult to determine home ranges. Dispersal directions may be random or unidirectional. Coyotes usually begin dispersing after age 5 months and continue to disperse throughout the winter. Dispersal may be delayed in saturated populations, and some individuals may not disperse until their second year.... Juveniles usually disperse alone. Dispersal distances of males were greater than those of females in Minnesota, less in California and Alberta and similar in Iowa. Juveniles dispersed 28-31 km (17-19 miles) in Alberta, 7 km (4 miles) in Arkansas, 5-6 km (3-4 miles) in California, and 48 km (30 miles) in Minnesota. Dispersal distances may be greater from exploited than from unexploited populations. Maximum dispersal distances are often greater than 100 km (60 miles) and can exceed 500 km (300 miles)."[58]

Two juvenile coyotes radio-marked in Vermont dispersed 38 km (male) and 91 km (female) from their point of release.[59] Dispersal of pups in Maine begins in September, with peaks during October-November and February-March. The cummulative dispersal rate in the first year for 36 coyote pups radio-marked in Maine from 1981 through 1984 was 87%. In the first 12 months juvenile females dispersed at a greater rate than juvenile males, all juveniles had dispersed by 19 months of age and most dispersal was to the northeast and northwest.

"Overall, 53%, 33%, and 14% of juvenile coyotes emigrated during autumn, late winter and delayed dispersal periods, respectively.... The annual rate of man-induced mortality for dispersers (0.40) was nearly twice that for residents (0.22)."[60]

"Minimum distances dispersed averaged 94 km for 11 juvenile female coyotes and 113 km for 9 juvenile males. There were no differences ... between sexes in the first -year dispersal rate or in the proportion, age, or distance of dispersal. Low food densities may preclude delayed dispersal and pack formation in this population. Juvenile dispersal probably confounds attempts to manage coyote populations intensively in localized areas."[61]

A male coyote pup captured and radio-tagged by Dale Morton in Fundy National Park during the fall of 1984 left the park and was shot one year later 18 km north of the capture site.[62] A second male pup also marked by Morton was shot 6.5 years later 125 km northeast of the point of capture.[63] A juvenile female coyote which I radio-marked near St. Leonard in northern New Brunswick on October 7, 1983, was killed by a truck 70 km south of the point of release in late November of that year. A second female radio-collared near St. Leonard on October 7, 1983, and which raised a litter of pups on our study area in summer 1984 was trapped near Escuminac, Quebec, in the fall of 1992 (9 years after capture), approximately 110 km to the northeast of the point of release. This is unusual, as adult females with established home ranges are normally not associated with long-range dispersal. In Nova Scotia Brent Patterson told me of an unusual movement of an adult male coyote captured and radio-marked in Kejimkujik National Park in the autumn of 1992. That animal, described by Brent as a "non-breeding helper" to another established pair, remained with that family until July 1993. On July 6 the unmated male left the park and 9 days later was killed on the highway approximately 130 km to the northeast near the city of Halifax.

Dan Harrison of Maine has suggested that the social organization of coyotes in the northeast may differ from that of western coyotes because of their recent colonization into previously unoccupied habitats, larger body size, questionable taxonomic status, and high use of large prey such as white-tailed deer as a food source. He found that the sizes of home ranges of northeastern coyotes were generally larger than home ranges of coyotes on traditional pre-1900 ranges and that lower food availability in the northeast might be responsible.[64] This would lead to lower coyote densities in the northeast, at least in areas where coyotes have become established. Ranier Brocke of Syracuse University, New York, has postulated that coyotes in the Adirondack Mountains of New York appear to have changed certain behavioural patterns over the past 20 years. He speculates that, as a behavioural adaptation to increased predation on white-tailed deer, family groups may be remaining together longer through the winter.

Obviously there are uncertainties as to just what social and behavioural changes the eastern coyote may be adopting and just how such changes might be influencing the structure and cohesiveness of family groups and affecting white-tailed deer populations.

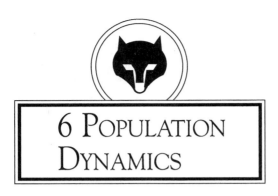

6 POPULATION DYNAMICS

"...Game at any one time is either increasing or it is decreasing. Even under apparantly static conditions, the species increases at the time of birth, ... then decreases for the remainder of the annual cycle.... The actual net change in population figure for most wild animal populations is seldom the same for any extended number of years. The usual behavior is for the net change toward either increase or decrease to maintain more or less a constant course for several successive years, followed by reversal for several years."[1]

DENSITY

The abundance of wildlife populations is often expressed in terms of density, i.e., the number of animals per unit of area. For larger carnivores, such as the coyote, with relatively large home ranges, density is often given in numbers per square kilometre (km²) or per square mile (sq. mi.). The numbers of animals in all wild populations are in constant change (dynamic state), with the lowest numbers usually just prior to the production of young which, for most large northern mammals, is in the spring before giving birth. Those animals which survive the winter are the breeding core of the population, and estimates of spring populations are most useful for assessing long-term trends and relationships between animals and their habitat and food supply. The coyote now occupies much of temperate North America, and is found within most habitats, from the deserts and prairies of the southwestern United States to the spruce-pine boreal forests and taiga of Alaska and Newfoundland. Each region has certain food resources and environmental stresses, and it may not be wise to assume that measurements of populations remain constant from one region to another. Even within regions a population is in a constant state of change, depending upon the season of the year. There is also reason to believe that densities of coyotes may increase from north to south,[2] probably due to an increase in food availability and a decrease in environmental stress.

However, even with all these considerations, the public is often interested in knowing how many coyotes, deer, or moose there are in a certain region. The biologist, understanding the dynamics and uncertainties of populations and the risks when providing absolute numbers or densities, must still oblige and provide a "best guesstimate" with the information available for specific regional populations. These data are often useful when preparing models used in the management of wildlife resources. With this in mind, I have summarized data on coyote densities from a selection of studies across its range in North America (*Table 3*). The lack of data from the northeast is apparent.

Table 3: Estimated coyote densities for various regions of its range across North America (coyotes per km^2).

Region	Season	Density	Source
Wyoming	Prewhelping	0.53	Camenzind (1978)
	Postwhelping	1.37	
	Winter	0.57-0.98	
Wyoming	Prewhelping	0.23-0.32	Weaver (1977)
Wyoming	Prewhelping	0.01	Springer and Wenger (1981)
Colorado	Prewhelping	0.29	Gese et al. (1989)
Texas	Prewhelping	0.90 (Max)	Knowlton (1972)
		0.30 (Av)	
Texas	Prewhelping	0.80-0.90	Andelt (1985)
	Autumn	0.90-1.00	
Nebraska		0.30-0.52	Fichter et al. (1955)
Kansas	Prewhelping	0.31	Gier (1957)
	Postwhelping	0.94	
Kansas/Colorado	Prewhelping	3.00 (Max)	Gier (1975)
		0.50 (Av)	
Utah/Idaho	Postwhelping	0.10-0.30	Clark (1972)
Utah/Idaho	Postwhelping	0.17 (Max)	Wagner and Stoddart (1972)
		0.11 (Min)	
Montana	Prewhelping	0.15	Pyrah (1984)
	Postwhelping	0.39	
Missouri		0.26	Bennitt (1948) in Gier (1957)
Tennessee	Winter	0.35	Babb and Kennedy (1989)

Minnesota	Winter	0.20	Berg and Kuehn (1986) in Voigt and Berg (1987)
Alberta	Postwhelping	0.20-0.40	Bowen (1982) in Voigt and Berg (1987)
Alberta	Winter	0.44 (Max) 0.07 (Min) 0.30 (Av)	Todd et al. (1981)
Alberta	Winter	0.42 (Av)	Nellis and Keith (1976)
Ontario	Winter	0.10	Voigt and Berg (1987)
New York (Adirondacks)	Winter	0.05	Brocke (1992)
Maine	Winter	0.57	Hilton (1986)

The wide range in regional and seasonal density estimates reaffirms the dangers of even cautious generalizations. There are, however, several points to be made. First, there appears to be a trend of higher densities in the south (Texas) and lower densities in the north (Montana, Minnesota, Ontario). A quick study of Table 3, however, also shows considerable variation in that trend (e.g., Wyoming: prewhelping = 0.01 km^2; Maine: winter = 0.57 km^2) but each estimate is restricted to a specific time and place, and each study is subjected to a certain margin of error. Second, coyote densities are lowest at prewhelping, highest immediately after whelping followed by a continued decline to the next whelping season. The order of change between pre- and postwhelping can be substantial. Third, coyote densities can be strongly influenced by prey availability. In Utah/Idaho, postwhelping densities ranged from 0.11/ km^2 when hares were scarce to 0.17/ km^2 when hares were abundant. In Alberta coyote densities in winter changed from 0.07/ km^2 when snowshoe hares were scarce to 0.44/ km^2 when hares were abundant. We will pursue this interesting relationship between coyotes and their prey at greater length in a subsequent section.

On certain western ranges, declines in populations of jackrabbits can cause densities of coyotes to decline to only 14%-15% of densities when jackrabbits are abundant.[3] The density of jackrabbits appears to operate either through the coyote reproductive or mortality rate, or both, to influence the rate of population change. This predator-prey relationship becomes more pronounced as the predator increases its dependency upon one specific prey (from generalist to specialist), a situation increasingly common in northern latitudes where the potential prey base is limited (eg., snowshoe hare) and often locked into cyclical and frequently robust patterns of population change. The association between densities of snowshoe hares and coyotes has been studied extensively in Alberta.

To summarize, coyote populations which are dependent upon cyclical prey, such as jackrabbits and snowshoe hare, have the potential to experience changes in density as high as the order of magnitude of 7, and these changes may occur over a period of several years. Coyote densities can also vary between seasons, and, in certain situations of abundant food, or high rates of mortality, numbers may triple during the whelping season. Whether such seasonal increases contribute to actual between-year population gain depends upon continued availability of food resources and rates of mortality.

Most estimates of coyote densities are from pre-1900 ranges (prior to substantial range expansion), i.e., west of the Mississippi River. How relevant are those data to post-1900 ranges, especially in the northeast? We have already noted a trend of reduced densities with increased latitude. There are several studies from which we might draw some assumptions. Winter estimates for Minnesota (0.20/km²), Alberta (8-year mean=0.30/km²) and Ontario (0.10/km²) might be considered "compatible" with the prey base and environmental stresses which coyotes must cope with in much of the northeastern United States and Atlantic Canada. These data would suggest, then, that a reasonable estimate of coyote densities in winter over much of the northeast, given adequate availability of snowshoe hare (and white-tailed deer in certain regions), would be in the range of 0.20-0.40/km². That, incidentally, has been a general estimate suggested for coyote densities throughout much of its range.[4] However, given the extreme environmental limits of coyote range in much of northeastern United States and Atlantic Canada, that estimate might well be somewhat high. I suggest that a more realistic overall density for the northeast might be 0.10-0.20 coyotes/km². The average of 0.15 coyotes/km² provides provincial population estimates in winter of 8,000-9,000 coyotes for Nova Scotia and 11,000-12,000 coyotes for New Brunswick. Prince Edward Island, where coyotes are presently colonizing and should soon reach relative stability, might expect winter populations of 800-900 coyotes. As coyotes are still colonizing several provinces (e.g., Newfoundland) and states (e.g., North Carolina), populations there would not yet have stabilized, and densities would not represent subsequent long-term levels.

How do population estimates from other regions relate to a density of 0.15 coyotes/km²? The population of coyotes in Maine during winter has been estimated at 10,000-16,000, for a statewide density of 0.14 to 0.22/km², and very similar to the density of 0.15/km² suggested for New Brunswick and Nova Scota. Given the more southerly location of Maine relative to Atlantic Canada, a slightly higher density of coyotes should be expected. Coyote numbers in Illinois have been estimated at 20,000-30,000, for a statewide density of 0.16-0.25/km², similar to the density estimated for Maine. The estimated population of coyotes in Wisconsin is 14,000 for a density of 0.11/km².[5]

The state of Mississippi must hold the current record for coyote harvest and density. In 1988, 40,000 coyotes were harvested and the state population was estimated at 400,000 (3.93/km²).[6] In 1988 hunters and trappers in Mississippi harvested

81

over 5 times the total population estimate for the province of Nova Scotia, even though Mississippi is only twice as large! This certainly supports the theory of a north-south increase in coyote densities. Such densities could only be reached in the absence of "winter stress" and in the presence of a wide diversity and great abundance of food.

Winter coyote populations in Maine have been forecast to continue to fluctuate between 10,000 and 16,000, depending upon the availability of white-tailed deer and snowshoe hare and prevailing winter severity.[7] Populations in Nova Scotia and New Brunswick may stabilize at densities below those estimated for Maine. Given the sequence of colonization, densities may now be reaching stability in New Brunswick (or declining in response to declines in white-tailed deer) and can be expected to do so soon in Nova Scotia for similar reasons. The extensive agricultural landscape and absence of deer on Prince Edward Island makes forecasts of coyote densities there less clear.

We can only guess at long-term densities and population levels for coyotes in Newfoundland. The severity of winter weather, absence of white-tailed deer, and limited variety and abundance of small mammals suggests that coyote densities there will not reach those estimated for Nova Scotia, New Brunswick, and Maine. Snowshoe hare will be the main source of food for coyotes in Newfoundland, especially in winter. However, there are moose and caribou on the island, and with the possibility that wild canids may evolve physically in response to size of prey (larger prey = larger predator), coyotes in Newfoundland may develop modifications in body size and behaviour to take advantage of food sources available. The situation certainly provides the opportunity to test several predator-prey hypotheses.

AGE STRUCTURE

The numerical or proportional representation of animals of specific age, usually estimated from samples collected in as random or representative fashion as possible, is referred to as the age structure of a population. With game species, such as the coyote, samples usually represent animals collected during the fall hunting and trapping seasons. Carcasses are often collected from hunters and trappers from specific regions, states or provinces. As part of long-term predator control programs in the United States, coyotes have been shot, trapped and poisoned in many western states and large samples of carcasses have been obtained in that manner.

The most reliable and frequently used method for determining the age of coyotes is by extraction and processing of a canine tooth.[8] Juveniles collected in October-December of their first year normally have an open root canal (tip of the root). Teeth with a closed root canal are decalcified, sectioned, mounted on slides, and stained. Tooth sections are examined for dark lines (like rings on a tree) in the cementum, a deposit on the outside of the root. A line, or annulus appears at about 20 months of age, and one each year thereafter. Thus, a coyote (caught in the fall) with a closed root canal, but no annuli would be 1.5 years old, with one annulus 2.5 years old, and so on.

Table 4: The age structure (% of sample) of coyote populations sampled from various regions throughout North America (expanded on from Jean and Bergeron 1984).

Location (≤ 1 yr)	Source	Juveniles (1–2 yrs)	Subadults	Adults (≥ 2 yrs)	Population (≤ 3 yrs)
New Mexico; Arizona; Texas	Knowlton 1972	50	15	35	77
Texas	Meinzer 1975 et. al.	25	28	47	87
Nebraska	Adams 1978	34	31	35	87
Wyoming	Springer & Wenger 1981	51	22	27	86
Wyoming	Crowe & Strickland 1975	62	17	21	92
Colorado	Gese et. al. 1989	23	18	59	–
New Mexico	Rogers 1965	53	27	20	90
Montana	Schladweiler 1977	43	32	25	87
Kansas	Gier 1957	50	30	20	80
Illinois	Mahan & Gier 1977	17	28	55	70
Iowa	Mathwig 1973	64	15	21	93
Iowa	Andrews & Boggess 1978	56	14	30	80
Utah	Knudson 1976	42–56	14–17	30–41	74–89
Minnesota	Longley 1970	45	35	20	90
Minnesota	Berg & Chesness 1978	47	15	38	74
Alberta	Nellis & Keith 1976	72	17	11	95
Alberta	Todd & Keith	49	30	21	90
Alberta	Todd 1985 Forest	46	31	23	86
	Agriculture	61	25	14	93
Manitoba	Pastuck 1974	31	25	44	69
Quebec	Jean & Bergeron 1984	63	14	23	84
Vermont; Massachusetts	Lorenz 1978	38	35	27	86
New Brunswick	Moore 1981				
	1973–81	67	13	20	90
	1979–81	71	10	19	–
Nova Scotia	Anderson 1988	43	38	19	–
Nova Scotia	Mills 1993	56	10	34	–

There are errors with this approach to aging coyotes and inferring that age struc-ture to the total population. The most obvious is the process itself, i.e., although *most* juveniles have an open root canal at 6-8 months, some are closed, and although *most* 1.5 year old coyotes do not show an annulus, some do. Although annuli are quite distinct and easily counted on many tooth sections, they can be quite confusing on others. Thus, there is always a margin of error. Perhaps a greater source of error, however, is the sample and how representative it may be of the general population. Juveniles are almost certainly overrepresented in most autumn samples simply because they are inexperienced and more easily trapped or shot. Many are dispersers which are travelling through unfamiliar territory and are susceptible to mortality from humans and other natural sources. However, given the recognized limitations, the age structure of a sample of coyotes can be very useful when assessing the dynamic state of a population, i.e., the relationship of the population with its environment and whether it is expanding (high representation of juveniles-high productivity) or declining (low representation of juveniles-low productivity).

A selection of studies from across North America which illustrate the range of juvenile and adult representation in various populations is shown in Table 4. Perhaps the most interesting column is that showing the proportion of each sample under 3 years of age. In 8 of the 21 studies, coyotes 3 years old or less represented more than 90% of the samples. Many studies have associated high proportions of juveniles with either expanding or heavily exploited (high rates of mortality) populations.[9] Low representation of juveniles is often associated with declining populations.[10] The age structure, of course, is influenced by reproductive success and mortality. The repro-ductive success of a population is influenced by the proportion of females in each age class which breed successfully (particularly the juvenile and subadult cohorts) and litter size, and is strongly influenced by population density and food availability.

The response of a predator to changes in prey availability can be of two types: *numerical*, i.e., changes in the numbers of the predator, and *functional*, i.e., changes in the kill rate of the predator. A decreasing functional response to declines in prey can result in suppressed reproductive success (especially reduced productivity by juveniles), lower survival, and changes in spatial distribution and/or unusual move-ments. The functional response to changing densities of prey drives the numerical response.

The influence of food availability and coyote densities upon reproductive perform-ance and age structure has important implications for efforts to control coyotes through population reductions. Most coyotes removed in autumn and early winter are juveniles, usually the most expendable segment of a population. Most juveniles are dispersers, do not have established territories and experience a high rate of natural mortality. Removing juveniles is often compensatory to natural mortality factors, i.e., many would not have survived the winter anyway. Thus, the removal of surplus juveniles in the autumn merely decreases overall density and reduces total predation, both factors contributing to sustained or enhanced reproductive performance by the older and established segment of the population.

Most studies have related low numbers of juveniles to declining populations (i.e., low reproductive success), and most represent established populations with little or no exploitation. In the absence of organized programs of control (as throughout most of the range of the eastern coyote) more than 70% of prewhelping populations are 3 years old or less, while less than 5% are over 7 years of age. In the autumn more than 80% of coyotes can be expected to be under 3 years old. Mortality rates are highest on juveniles and subadults, and mortality appears to progressively decline with age of the coyote. In western populations juveniles normally comprise about one-half the autumn population. However, there may be considerable variation around that average.[11]

Studies in Alberta and Utah have convincingly related coyote productivity, survival, and representation of juveniles in a population to changes in food availability, which is often a function of the dynamic state of prey populations (especially rabbits, hares, mice, and voles) or spatial distribution of coyotes among habitats (forested vs agriculture).[12] In Alberta, the proportion of juveniles decreased from 64% when hares were abundant to 41%-44% when hares were scarce, and within a span of only 3-4 years.[13] The mean age of coyotes from samples in that Alberta study increased from 1.5 years when hares were abundant to 2.1 years when hares were scarce. In Ontario 65% of coyotes taken by hunting and trapping in the autumn were young of the year.[14]

The age structure of coyote samples from the northeast (e.g., Quebec, Vermont, Massachusetts, New Brunswick, and Nova Scotia) are quite similar to studies from western North America. The New Brunswick data were from a colonizing population of coyotes at a time when deer numbers were high (prior to the declines of the late 1980s) and food was abundant. A high representation of juveniles, especially in the earlier years, indicated an expanding and highly productive population.

Subadults (under 2 years old) represented 81% of 646 coyotes bountied in Nova Scotia from 1982-83 through 1985-86, a time of early coyote colonization and high numbers of white-tailed deer.[15] The age structure of 504 coyotes trapped in Nova Scotia in 1992-93 showed a lower representation of subadults (66%) and a higher representation of adults (34%) than the bountied sample 6-10 years earlier.[16] White-tailed deer had declined during that interval and coyotes had become established throughout the province. The apparant decline in the productivity of coyotes in Nova Scotia is further evidence of the influence of food availability, and coyote densities, on the population dynamics of predators.

Coyotes do not have a long life expectancy. Only 6% of a sample of coyotes from an unexploited population in Colorado were over 6 years old, and the mean age for that sample was 3.4 years. The oldest coyote in a sample of 321 killed by hunters in Nebraska was 9 years old, while in Texas only 1 of 67 coyotes was over 8 years old. The oldest coyote in a sample of 1,558 carcasses collected from hunters and trappers in Minnesota from 1968-1976 was an 11-year-old female while the oldest in a sample of 548 carcasses collected in Alberta from 1964-76 were a 11.5-year-old female and a 13.5-year-old male.[17] Several longevity records of western coyotes include 14.5-year-old female from western Colorado and a 13.5-year-old male from Texas.[18] A captive male coyote in Michigan lived for 15 years.[19]

SEX RATIOS

The proportion of males to females is referred to as the sex ratio of a population. This measure, combined with population age structure, reproductive performance and rates of mortality can be used to develop models for study of population dynamics and to develop strategies for population management. If only the real world was so simple and straightforward! Sex ratios, similar to rates of reproduction, can and often do vary by age class and by the extent of exploitation (mortality), subsequent rates of reproduction and survival, and numerical trends of a population. While some animal populations have highly unbalanced sex ratios, studies suggest that, in general, there are near equal numbers of males and females in most established populations of coyotes. Having said that, we will now look at the results from some of those studies and touch on the exceptions to the theory of equal sex ratios.

Similar to measurements of age structure and reproductive performance, most information on sex ratios in coyote populations comes from the examination of samples, and most samples represent coyotes which have been harvested in the autumn. Most samples, however, are from the western United States during the era (early 1900s) of wide-scale and intensive programs of coyote control.

The "Cooperative Hunting Force" of the United States Fish and Wildlife Service killed 56,595 coyotes in Arizona between 1919 and 1946. The overall sex ratio (male:female) of that extremely large sample was 52:48. The annual sex ratios over that 27-year period usually favoured males (22 of 27 years). It was thought that, because many coyotes were taken in traps baited by scent and lure, males would be trapped more frequently than females. However, when records of coyotes killed by poison (assuming an unbiased sample) were examined, the ratios were similar to those from samples collected by traps. Another large sample of coyotes was collected in Oklahoma in 1943-1947. The sex ratio of 6,494 coyotes was 3,229 males and 3,265 females and, although slightly favouring females, was virtually equal.[20]

More recent studies from the western United States also suggest an overall balanced sex ratio. The sex ratio in a sample of 67 coyotes collected in Texas in 1972-73 was 54:46.[21] In Texas the sex ratio of coyotes in spring (prewhelping) was near 50:50, although there were substantial differences between samples from regions subjected to light (ratio = 50:50) and intensive (ratio = 40:60) programs of coyote control.[22] Coyotes may compensate for increased mortality by producing more females than males.[23] The production of more females, combined with an increased productivity of females (higher rates of pregnancy and larger litters), especially in the younger age cohorts, when exploitation (mortality) is high, certainly helps to explain a great deal of the mystery for the success of the coyote in North America *in spite* of extensive efforts of population control by humans.

The suspected correlation between increasing rates of exploitation and decreasing male:female sex ratios (i.e., more females) was supported by a study in Alberta.[24] However, rather than an actual functional response by coyotes to increased mortality (compensation) the change was attributed to greater mobility of females; i.e., juvenile females are more mobile than the juvenile males (see "Home Range and Movements") and would be expected to infiltrate such "vacuum areas" in greater numbers. More recent collections of coyotes in Alberta confirmed a significant preponderance of males (59%) at intermediate levels of snowshoe hares but more balanced (51-53% males) sex ratios during periods of hare abundance and hare scarcity.[25] Again, rather than relating differences through time to changes in food availability, the authors suggested a more likely explanation would be sex-specific sampling biases, and they cited examples of male coyotes using carrion sources more frequently than females (increased susceptibility to being trapped). A preponderance of females in hunted samples from Alberta might have resulted from a less effective escape response in females when pursued by snowmobiles and dogs.[26] Female coyotes in Alberta were found to be about 1.5 times more prone to aerial observation than males due to differences in habitat selection and perhaps flight response.[27] However, the studies in Alberta concluded that sex ratios in canid populations can be influenced by densities of the predator and availability of food.[28] his agrees with studies of other wild canids which suggest that sex ratios favouring males may be a "physiological response" to declining numbers in a saturated habitat (and low food availability) rather than just trappability or postnatal mortality (which, however, may also play a role).[29]

The few data available on sex ratios of coyotes in the northeast come from small samples subject to error associated with sampling bias. A preponderance of males (66%) in a sample of 87 coyotes from Massachusetts and Vermont was attributed to the greater mobility of males and a consequent higher probability of being trapped.[30] (In contrast to other studies which have suggested that juvenile females are more mobile and more likely to be trapped during times of heavy exploitation.) A larger sample (n = 292) of eastern coyotes from New Brunswick and Nova Scotia collected from trappers in 1979-81 did not support the results from Massachusetts and Vermont and, although males predominated in most samples, sex ratios during the study were near equal.[31] In 2 small samples from colonizing populations of coyotes in Nova Scotia the sex ratio favoured males in 1977-81 (53:47) and females in 1981-82 (42:58).[32] The author noted the various reasons which might explain skewed sex ratios (reviewed earlier here) and suggested that, as determined in other mammalian dispersal studies, an overrepresentation of females is normally associated with colonizing populations. The overall male:female ratio of 756 coyotes collected in Nova Scotia from 1982-83 through 1985-86 was 57:50[33] (Table 5). More interesting, perhaps, was the progressive change in the ratio from 41:50 in 1982-83 (early colonization) to 61:50 by 1985-86 (complete colonization). If this change was real, and not an artifact of sampling bias, it is further evidence of density dependent changes (e..g., sex ratios at birth, age specific pregnency rates, juvenile survival) which serve as self-regulating mechanisms for population growth. In this example, a change in sex ratio at birth favouring males, in response to increasing densities, would serve to limit the rate of population increase (i.e., fewer females). A more recent (1992-93) sample of 563 coyotes trapped in Nova Scotia suggested a fairly even overall male:female sex ratio of 54:50,[34] very similar to collections from that province in 1982-85. However, the sex ratio in the 1992-93 sample varied with age, favouring females in subadult (43:50)

Table 5: Sex and age structure of coyotes submitted for bounty in Nova Scotia, 1982-83 through 1985-86 (from Anderson 1988).

Year	0.5 Years				1.5 Years				2.5 Years+				Totals			Male:Female Ratio
	M	F	T	%	M	F	T	%	M	F	T	%	M	F	T	
1982-83	13	11	24	41	11	19	30	52	2	2	4	7	26	32	58	41:50
1983-84	16	15	31	27	35	34	69	59	2	7	17	15	61	56	117	54:50
1984-85	56	64	120	50	41	30	71	30	30	18	48	20	127	112	239	57:50
1985-86	119	97	216	63	41	32	73	21	28	25	53	16	188	154	342	61:50
Totals	204	187	391	52	128	115	243	32	62	52	122	16	402	354	756	57:50

and males in adult (95:50) age classes. As noted earlier uneven sex ratios might be due to greater mobility of one sex over the other and thus greater vulnerability to capture, uneven sex ratios at birth, and/or higher sex-specific mortality from other sources. The sex ratio of 103 coyotes killed on Prince Edward Island from 1990-91 through 1992-93 was 50:50, although it changed from 62:38, to 52:48 to 44:56 over that 3-year period. The observed change may have been from low sample sizes, especially in the first two years.

This short review illustrates the great variation in measurements of sex and age structure which can be expected from samples, and how each sample can be influenced by the manner of collection and the dynamic state of the population. It is probably realistic to assume a fairly even sex ratio in most age classes of eastern coyotes throughout its range. However, realizing the dynamic state of all populations, and the very real possibility of sex ratios being influenced by food availability and coyote densities, a fairly wide range in ratios should be expected, especially with small samples.

MORTALITY/SURVIVAL

The mortality rate of a population is simply that proportion of individuals which dies during a specified period of time. Mortality rates may be calculated annually (usually from birth to the following spring), or by season, such as for adults through winter, or for pups from birth to dispersal. The survival rate is that proportion of a population, or population age class, which survives a specific period of time, i.e., 1.0 minus the rate of mortality. A mortality rate of 0.60 for coyote pups from birth to dispersal means a survival rate of 0.40. Mortality and survival rates vary with age, i.e., the chance of a juvenile dying in its first year is greater than the chance of an older animal dying during the same time interval. Thus mortality rates are often calculated for juveniles and adults separately.

As with other measures of population dynamics, information used for calculating rates of mortality are usually obtained from samples, and these rates are then inferred to the general population. Mortality rates can also be calculated from ear-tagging and radio telemetry studies. Perhaps the most difficult time interval for calculating rates of mortality in coyote populations is from whelping to autumn. In many of the western states, where coyote dens are frequently found, extensive ear-tagging studies have provided useful information on early pup mortality there, but that approach is hardly feasible in the forested regions of the northeast, where coyote dens are found more by chance than design.

Mortality of pups can be high. In Alberta less than 10% of pups died from birth to 40 days but 68% died from 40 days to 1 year. Loss of pups from birth to July was estimated at 50% in Kansas, 56% from spring to fall in Missouri, and between 41% (1974) and 72% (1973) from birth to December in Utah. The study in Utah found that mortality of pups from 4-6 weeks of age (at time of tagging) to autumn was only 10%, suggesting a fairly high loss of pups during the first month of life. Observations of captive coyotes have shown that the loss of entire litters might occur immediately after whelping, primarily among females which are nutritionally or socially stressed.[35]

Recent studies in Kansas and Alberta suggest annual mortality rates of 40%-60%, and annual mortality rates of 25%-45% appear common, with 65%-75% not uncommon in areas such as the northern forested region of Alberta.[36] Two hundred and five of 437 (47%) radio-equipped coyotes in four research studies in Texas, Wyoming, Idaho and Utah died during the period of study (range of 19%-100%), and most mortalities were human related.[37]

Hunting with snowmobiles selected for juvenile coyotes in Alberta.[38] In Utah more coyotes were killed (predominantly by hunting) outside of their home range than along the periphery and no residents were killed within their respective home ranges.[39] Young dispersing coyotes are more susceptible to hunting than resident coyotes because they are away from familiar territory. But vulnerability to hunting may be a result of lack of experience rather than unfamiliarity with the surrounding territory. These findings have important management implications, e.g., preventive control during March-May would be more efficient because resident coyotes would be those most likely to be removed.

The age structure of coyotes from western ranges implies that mortality rates of coyotes greater than one year old might exceed 40% annually even when populations are not exploited.[40] The decreasing annual mortality rate noted for successively older coyotes suggests that experience, learning, or accepted social positions may be factors which influence coyote survival, at least through 8 years of age (probable maximum life expectancy). Assuming a 40% mortality of adults on an annual basis, a net survival of 33% of the young to 1 year of age is sufficient to maintain a stable population.[41] A 33% survival of juveniles their first year does not seem unreasonable, given autumn estimates of population structure and an assumed small mortality among very young pups.

Annual (autumn-to-autumn) survival rates of adult coyotes varied from 0.54 to 0.84 during a 4-year study in southern Texas.[42] Comparable rates for juveniles (0.5-1.5 years) ranged from 0.37 to 0.60. Overall annual survival for adults (0.70) was significantly higher than for juveniles (0.42). Estimates of survival for adults and juveniles in that study were both higher than comparable estimates in northern Utah (adult, 0.47; juvenile, 0.23) and southern Idaho (adult, 0.51; juvenile, 0.45). Mortality was highest for radio-equipped coyotes during winter in Idaho, Utah, and Wyoming.[43]

Annual survival rates for 88 radio-collared coyotes (all ages) during a 4-year study (1983-1986) in Colorado were 0.78, 0.80, 0.75 and 0.72. Seasonal survival estimates for spring, summer, fall and winter were 0.95, 0.94, 0.89 and 0.84, respectively. Annual survival for males and females was identical (0.72). However, age and status of coyotes influenced survival. Annual survival rates for adults, yearlings and pups were 0.87, 0.52 and 0.51 and for residents, transients and dispersers were 0.87, 0.61 and 0.39. Survival of coyotes was lower in autumn and winter than in spring and summer because of increased pup dispersal and the presence of hunters and trappers, which agrees with studies elsewhere. Adult residents that remained on the study area had the highest survival. This agrees with a study in Texas where survival of transient and resident coyotes in a lightly exploited population was estimated to be 51% and 82%, respectively.[44]

Estimated mortality rates for marked coyotes in a mixed farming-boreal forest ecosystem in central Alberta were 0.71 for juveniles and 0.36-0.42 for adults[45] and mortality was similar between sexes. The higher rate for younger animals calculated from trapped samples probably reflects the greater vulnerability of juveniles to human related mortalities.

Closer to home the estimated survival of pups (to 12 months) from a sample of coyotes collected in Maine from 1973 to 1975 (trappers, hunters, and highway kills) was only 4-7%.[46] This was substantially lower than first-year survival rates of 30-35% estimated for coyote populations on western ranges. The sample in Maine was obtained from human-related mortalities and from an expanding or colonizing population, both factors contributing to samples skewed towards juvenile coyotes and providing unreasonably low estimates of juvenile survival. Established populations of eastern coyotes probably experience survival rates more comparable to those estimated for many western populations, such as in Alberta, i.e., 30-40% for juveniles (0-1 year) and 50-60% for older age classes.

Many coyote mortalities are human related.[47] In a Colorado study 35% of radio-collared coyotes died; 16 were shot by ranchers, 6 died of disease or starvation, 4 were hit by vehicles, 3 were trapped, and 2 were poisoned.[48] In south Texas 51% of 35 radio-equipped coyotes which died within 1 year following marking (18 adults and 17 juveniles) were shot, trapped or killed by vehicles.[49] The percentage of human-caused mortality for adults and juveniles did not differ; i.e., although juveniles died at a greater rate than adults, the proportions of both age groups which died from human causes were similar. Other studies have reported even higher rates of human-related mortalities e.g., Utah- 92% of 52 mortalities; Wyoming- 93% of 41 mortalities.[50] In Montana 91% of the mortality of radio-instrumented coyotes was human-related (hunters and trappers) and of the total sample of radioed coyotes, 79% of juveniles and 39% of adults were known to have been shot or trapped.[51]

All but one of 51 returns from dead coyotes ear-tagged during spring and summer in Utah-Idaho were human related – 20 from winter aerial hunting, 17 shot by hunters and ranchers, 2 by poison, 1 by a coyote getter (cyanide gun), 6 by steel traps, and 1 by unknown causes.[52] However, these were ear-tagged coyotes, and most if not all returns would be expected to come from coyotes killed by humans. Another 25-45% of the marked sample which was estimated to have also died during the same period probably succumed to other non-human related causes. The following causes of mortality were determined for 63 of 250 juvenile coyotes ear-marked in Iowa: shot- 54%; trapped- 30%; roadkilled- 8%; killed by dogs- 7%; snared- 1%.[53]

Eleven of 47 coyote pups captured, radio-equipped and released in Maine from 1981 through 1984 were known to have died.[54] The annual mortality rate for dispersing juveniles (0.53) was higher than for juveniles which remained within their natal home ranges (0.26). The annual rate of human-caused mortality for dispersers (0.40) was nearly twice that of residents (0.22).

To illustrate the intensity of control efforts and human-induced mortalities of coyotes in the United States, 295,456 coyotes were estimated to have been harvested in 17 western states in 1974 alone.[55] It is interesting that the estimate of coyotes killed

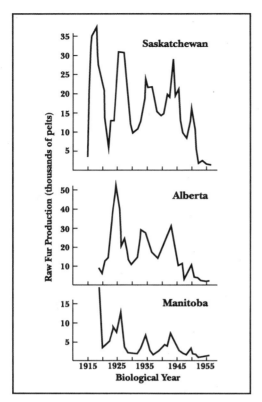

Figure 7: Fur returns from the Prairie Provinces of Canada show that coyote populations in northern regions have cycles of abundance similar to the Canada lynx, and they are most likely a response to cyclical changes in the abundance of snowshoe hares (Keith 1963).

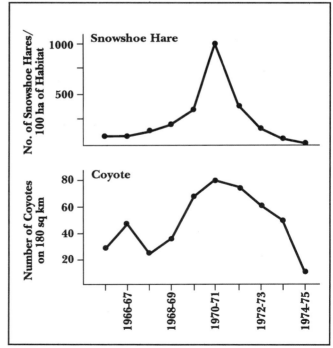

Figure 8: The close relationship between numbers of coyotes and snowshoe hares was demonstrated by a study in Alberta from 1965-66 through 1974-75 (Todd et al. 1981).

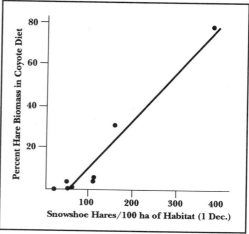

Figure 9: The study at Rochester, Alberta, showed a close relationship between the abundance of snowshoe hares in winter and the number of hares eaten by coyotes (Todd et al. 1981).

in those states in 1946 was 294,400. Did 28 years of control efforts prevent coyote populations from reaching even greater numbers, or is this an example of increasing coyote productivity through sustained harvest?

Finally, a story out of West Virginia to illustrate the wariness of certain "educated coyotes" and to further illustrate why the coyote has been so successful in colonizing most of the United States and much of southern Canada.[56] In 1968, before coyotes became common in West Virginia, a wild canid, identified by some as an escaped coyote probably brought in from some western state, began to terrorize local sheep farmers. Traps were used early in the hunt, but to no avail. A more intensive effort was mounted and hunters combed the area alone and in pairs, hoping to surprise the coyote while at rest or asleep, but with equal futility. Tracking dogs, primarily foxhounds, joined the hunt, but the coyote would leave a trail behind fresh deer tracks or would use some other equally effective ploy to confuse the hounds and allow escape. Uncoordinated hunting with dogs was discontinued after 21 prized hounds had been dispatched by farmers who mistook them for the troublesome coyote.

A year passed and sheep kills mounted. A study of tracks convinced the hunters that they were pursuing one old male coyote. As sheep losses continued, state assistance was sought. With the return of snow in January, 1970 the hunt for the coyote continued daily. A Kansas rancher brought in 6 Walker hounds specially trained for tracking coyotes. Although eager and able to follow the coyote trail, the rugged hills of West Virginia proved far more formidible to the hounds than the flatlands of Kansas, and the Walkers returned home. Soon an aerial assault was launched against the coyote. The National Guard provided a helicopter and pilot, but in the hills of West Virginia, aerial pursuit proved as futile as the ground assault. Finally, sex, that most powerful of drives that dulls all other senses and which has proven the downfall of many a smart male, was brought into the chase. A female coyote in a cage was used as "bait" surrounded by an array of traps. This proved too much for the old rogue, and with his defences dulled by this "fatal attraction," he fell to the trap and was quickly dispatched.

PREY DEPENDENCY

The forces which drive and direct the dynamics of predator-prey models can be complex. Although similar factors may influence coyote and deer populations in Minnesota and Nova Scotia, for instance, the extent to which each operates and influences the dynamics of both predator and prey can be, and most often are, quite different. Coyote-prey interactions may differ between areas of a specific region, such as southern Nova Scotia and northern New Brunswick.

We will now deal with the real, perceived, and potential interactions between coyotes in the northeast and two important prey species; snowshoe hare and white-tailed deer. To properly assess these relationships, however, it is necessary to examine coyote-prey studies far removed from the spruce-fir forests of Nova Scotia and Maine. It would be preferable, and certainly more precise, to draw upon studies from the northeast, but such studies are just not available. However, those basic principles which apply to coyote-snowshoe hare interactions and populations in the northwest, for example, are probably quite comparable to those operating in similar forested-agricultural habitat in the northeast. For discussion purposes, at least, it is worth our while to review those studies here.

To appreciate the dependency of coyotes on snowshoe hare in northern forested regions of its range we must examine the classic long-term study in Alberta by Lloyd Keith, a professor of wildlife ecology at the University of Wisconsin. Although there are other studies in more southern latitudes which have examined the relationship between coyotes and blacktailed jackrabbits, the study by Keith and his colleagues at the Rochester study area in central Alberta provides the most useful information, and perhaps that most applicable to coyotes in the northeast. They described the functional (diet, reproduction, mortality) and numerical (population change) responses of coyotes to changes in numbers and availability of snowshoe hare. Those changes were measured through time, and represent the most comprehensive coyote-snowshoe hare data set available. It would be convenient to have similar data for coyotes and white-tailed deer, but there are none. We are only now realizing the role of the coyote as a predator on white-tailed deer in the northeast, and for that reason we must review what data are available elsewhere which might serve to measure the importance of deer to coyotes here. There have been many studies of wolf-ungulate relationships in northern ecosystems, including wolf-deer predator-prey systems and I review a selection of those studies as well. I conclude with a summary of what role the eastern coyote may be assuming within the spruce-fir forests of the northeastern United States and eastern Canada. Given the facts at hand, and the knowledge accumulated from scientific studies of coyotes, wolves, ungulates and canid-hare-ungulate interactions in other northern ecosystems, the model which I propose for coyote and white-tailed deer populations in forested-wilderness regions of the northeast stands as the "best reasonable" guess.

The 10-year cycle of certain wildlife species is largely restricted to the northern coniferous forests of North America and it has been popularly identified with snowshoe hare, ruffed grouse and the Canada lynx. Lloyd Keith recognized the existence of nonrandom long-term fluctuations of certain species, but cautioned against the use of "cycle" to suggest strict regularity. What is less commonly understood is that many species of predator other than lynx also show population trends which suggest nonrandom fluctuations. Keith tracked fur returns from the Prairie Provinces and showed "cyclic" patterns of abundance from 1914 through the mid-1950s for several northern predators, including coyotes (*Figure 7*). The numerical response of many predators to nonrandom fluctuations of prey, especially snowshoe hare, encouraged Keith to initiate the Rochester, Alberta, study, and to measure the functional response of predators to prey abundance, i.e., to address how and why predator populations respond as they do.

The Rochester study, which began in 1964, was designed as a long-term investigation of populations and ecology of cyclic vertebrates in a northern forested ecosystem. Keith and his colleagues monitored coyote numbers in winter from 1965-66 through 1974-75. More intensive measurements of coyote populations were taken during 2 periods: 1964-68, from a low to the early recovery of hare populations, and 1971-75, during a hare population decline from a cyclic peak in 1970-71. The numerical response of coyotes to a 10-year change in hare numbers (increase-1964-1969; peak-1970-1971; decline-1972-1975) was striking (*Figure 8*) and supported earlier coyote-snowshoe hare data from fur returns and Hudson's Bay records. However, what functional changes to coyote populations were responsible for the numerical correlations with hare abundance? By examining food items and biomass in stomachs from coyotes collected from trappers they demonstrated a dramatic change in the amount of hare in the winter diet of coyotes, from 0% in time of hare scarcity to 77% during the peak in hare abundance (*Figure 9*).[57] Other studies had demonstrated functional responses of coyotes to changes in abundance of microtines (mice and voles) and jackrabbits in more southern latitudes.[58] But the Rochester study was the first to relate similar changes in coyotes in northern forested ecosystems to changes in abundance of snowshoe hares. The Rochester study documented responses by coyotes to changing hare densities other than dietary. Measures of body fat in winter declined concurrent with decreased hare consumption (and availability) suggesting a negative energy balance during winters of hare scarcity. Reduced body nutrition of coyotes resulted in a decrease in the finite rate of reproduction of 33%, a consequence of reduced pregnancy rates and litter sizes. They concluded that declines in body condition of Alberta coyotes during times of hare scarcity pointed to food supply as a key determinant of coyote populations in boreal forests.

Other studies have documented a lag or delay between declines in prey and predator. At Rochester, Alberta, the initial decline (1970-71 to 1972-73) in hares was precipitous (80%) but much less so for coyotes (25%). Major changes in coyote populations (e.g., food habits, consumption rates, body condition, reproduction, age structure) did not occur until snowshoe hares declined below intermediate levels. The most obvious explanation for this lag in predator response to declining prey is that hare populations provide food far in excess of coyote needs and hence must decrease markedly before coyotes are adversely affected.[59] Implicit in this assumption is that peak densities of snowshoe hares are controlled by factors other than predation, a factor we will comment on further as it may relate to snowshoe hare and white-tailed deer populations in the northeast.

The Rochester study also showed that coyotes in forested and agricultural habitats in central Alberta responded differently to changes in hare abundance.[60] Coyotes in agricultural habitats relied more on mice, voles, and agricultural carrion, and occurrence of hare in the diet was only one-half of that for coyotes in the forests. Not surprisingly, differences in the winter diet between coyotes in forested and agricultural habitats was attributed to differences in food availability. Whereas rates of food consumption by coyotes in forested habitat declined with decreasing hare abundance, consumption rates by coyotes in agricultural habitats did not. As well, overwinter weight loss by agricultural coyotes was generally less than by forest coyotes, and fat deposits were greater. Pregnancy rates for adult and yearling coyotes tended to be lower and vary more between years in forested habitats. There was also evidence of winter movements of coyotes from forest to farming areas and of such movements in response to changing hare abundance.[61] Coyotes in agricultural habitats depended on small mammals more and upon hares less, especially in winters of severe weather and low numbers of hares.

> *"Relative stability in numbers, physical condition, breeding rates, and age and sex structure of coyotes in agricultural habitat is attributed to more favourable environmental conditions there, where farm carrion provides a continuing, accessible food supply in winter, and snow conditions are less adverse."*[62]

Important to our interest in coyotes of the northeastern forests was the importance of deer to the winter diet of forest and agriculture coyotes in times of hare scarcity and abundance. Although deer were not abundant on the central Alberta study area, and snow seldom reached depths that severely restricted deer mobility, there were notable changes in deer consumption relative to hare abundance and type of habitat occupied. As hares began to decline, the occurrence of deer in the stomachs of forest coyotes was 7%. After hares had been declining for 4 years and had reached a 10-year low, the occurrence of deer in coyote stomachs was 24%. The volume of deer in coyote diets from forested habitats for those same time intervals changed from 6% to 33%. Deer remained a small component (3-5%) in the diet of coyotes on agricultural habitat during the same period. In times of hare scarcity, coyotes in forested habitats increased their consumption of white-tailed deer in winter while coyotes in agricultural habitats increased their consumption of agricultural carrion and small mammals. Use of deer by forest coyotes increased significantly over that 3-year period. Although some of the increase in the use of deer by forest coyotes may have resulted from increased scavenging on winter-killed deer, it most likely reflected increased predation by coyotes on deer.[63] Deer in the study area were unusually vulnerable to coyotes in March 1975, when snows were deep and thickly crusted.

As mentioned earlier, there are other studies which have measured the responses of coyotes to changes in densities of prey, and most support the "food dependency" model described for coyotes and snowshoe hare in central Alberta. Coyote predation was a major source of mortality on black-tailed jackrabbits on a study area in Utah and may have been responsible for a decline in the jackrabbit populations there.[64] However, although other studies related increasing rates of consumption with increasing populations of hares and rabbits, most did not identify predation by coyotes as the primary factor initiating declines in those prey.

A 5-year study of black-tailed jackrabbits and coyotes on a 700 sq. mi. (1,812 km²) area at the Utah-Idaho border provides data supportive of the Alberta study. The density of jackrabbits appeared to be one independent variable operating, through either the coyote reproduction or mortality rate or both, to influence the rate of population change. Both coyote litter size and percentage of females pregnant were positively related to relative densities of jackrabbits.

> "Whatever the link may be, the reproductive rate and changes in coyote populations seem to have varied with the food base, and that base depends importantly in this area on the jackrabbit population density.... Hence, the food level plays at least some role in determining the long-term mean coyote density."[65]

A long-term 14-year study in the Curlew Valley area of Utah-Idaho (which includes the study referred to earlier) also showed that coyote abundance was positively correlated with populations of black-tailed jackrabbits. Results from that study implied that coyotes may have been a causal factor *in initiating* the sharp decline in jackrabbit numbers as well as a depressant upon the population during the latter stages of the decline. This was interpreted as representing a servomechanism whereby coyotes influence their own density through their impact upon a primary food item. If the abundance of coyotes is a function of winter food, coyote densities should increase from north to south as food supplies become less restrictive. This is supported by coyote

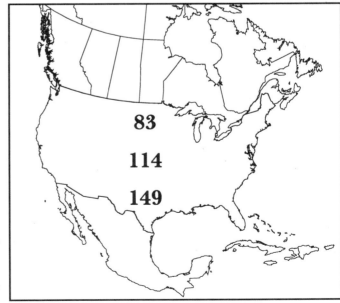

Figure 10: Predator abundance indices from the western United States suggest that densities of coyotes increase from north to south (Knowlton and Stoddart 1983).

population indices obtained from the Survey of Predator Abundance in the western United States (*Figure 10*). Social intolerance dictated by the abundance and availability of food may be a primary determinant of coyote density.[66]

The general increase in coyote densities from north to south is most likely a response to a greater variety, abundance, and availability of prey. In the forests of the Gaspé Peninsula, Quebec, the Adirondack Mountains of New York, and most of Maine, Nova Scotia and New Brunswick, the dominant food base of coyotes, especially in winter, is snowshoe hare and white-tailed deer. There is every reason to expect that coyote populations in northeastern forested habitats are driven by the abundance and availability of those 2 food sources, especially in winter. It is also reasonable to assume that the numerical and functional responses of the coyote in the northeast to prey availability is quite comparable to that described for central Alberta. Having said that, however, the situation in the northeast must be assessed relative to 3 important factors: 1 / the genetic, morphologic and behavioural uniqueness of the eastern coyote, 2 / the presence of "predator free" populations of white-tailed deer prior to colonization by the eastern coyote and 3 / winter severity, especially the depth and duration of winter snow.

7 HOME RANGE AND MOVEMENTS

"No wild animal roams at random over the country: each has a home region, even if it has not an actual home. The size of this home region corresponds somewhat with the size of the animal. Flesh-eaters as a class have a larger home region than herb-eaters."[1]

It is important to understand the difference between the home range and the territory of an animal.

"A home range has a flexible, undefended boundary, so that the home ranges of different individuals or groups may overlap considerably. A territory, on the other hand, is defined as the area that an individual or group occupies to the almost complete exclusion of other animals of the same species and that it will actively defend against them. In some geographical areas coyotes clearly defend their territory against other animals, but in other areas there is no evidence that they are territorial. Our own findings indicate it is only coyotes in packs that are territorial; individuals with a fixed home range but living alone or in mated pairs are not."[2]

Studies of coyote home ranges and activities are only surpassed in number by studies of coyote diet and feeding habits. Measurements of patterns of daily and seasonal activity over time and space (activity budgets) were greatly facilitated by the development of remote sensing technology, especially the refinement and application of radio telemetry within the past 25 years. In a radio telemetry study, coyotes are live-trapped, immobilized, fitted with transmittors (often attached by a collar) and released. Subsequent locations of marked coyotes can be followed using a radio receiver and directional antennae. Plotting the direction of a transmittor from several locations allows an approximation of the animal's location. A sample of locations through time allows calculation of home range boundaries, core areas of preferred use, and daily and seasonal rhythms of activity (See *Figure 11.*)

As with any "tool" used to obtain new information, results from radio telemetry studies have been misused and misinterpreted. Most problems result from inadequate sampling and misleading or inaccurate interpretation of data. Radio telemetry studies should answer how, why, and when an animal is using an area, not just how large an

Brent Patterson sets a padded trap to live-capture coyotes for a research study in Nova Scotia (B. Patterson).

A radio transmitter tracks the movement of a coyote. This coyote captured near St. Leonard in northern New Brunswick in 1983, was caught by a trapper 9 years later near Escuminac, Quebec, 110 km from where it was released (G. Parker).

area is used.[3] Use should be related to measurements of food abundance and distribution, and to habitat characteristics of the home range. This information can then be interpreted relative to the behaviour and social status of the coyote.

Dan Harrison examined home range estimates for coyotes on historic (pre-1900) and recently colonized (post-1900) ranges. He concluded that coyotes in northeastern North America have larger home ranges than coyotes on historic ranges. He attributed larger home ranges in the northeast to lower food productivity there than in western North America where the variety and numbers of small rodents, hares, and rabbits are high. (Coyotes in the northeast must travel farther to secure adequate food.)[4] These differences in available prey between the northeast and more southern and western ranges appear to influence other measured characteristics of coyotes in the northeast, such as diet (larger prey), body size (larger), densities (lower), social organization (delayed juvenile dispersal resulting in larger groups in winter, which enhances ability to catch larger prey), and interactions with humans (competition with hunters for white-tailed deer; predation on domestic animals).

"...Use of white-tailed deer as a winter food may ... contribute to larger home ranges of coyotes in the northeast.... Higher winter use of white-tailed deer by coyotes in the northeast is evident; 5 of 6 northeastern studies documented [more than] 50 percent occurrence of white-tailed deer in winter coyote diets ... compared with 1 of 10 studies with [more than] 35 percent occurrence of ungulates from the historic range.... The only northeastern study with [less than] 40 percent occurrence of white-tailed deer in coyote stomachs during winter was conducted in an area of Vermont characterized by extensive dairy farming.[5] The use of deer during winter may have been buffered by the availability of livestock carcasses during this study; 41 percent of winter scats contained remains of cattle and deer, and 40 percent of spring scats contained deer."[6]

A coyote pack has been defined as a territorial group, probably of genetically related coyotes; a resident pair, as a territorial or non-territorial breeding unit; and an individual coyote, as likely nomadic. Coyotes of different social status often show different patterns of behaviour. These behavioural differences, although often subtle, can influence patterns of daily and seasonal activity and home range characteristics and use. Several studies have related patterns of spatial use to social groupings of coyotes.[7]

Thus, forested range occupied by coyotes in the northeast often resembles a mosaic of fairly well defined home ranges, each home range occupied by a dominant adult pair (the core of most social units), and each social unit being numerically flexible and dependent upon the reproductive status of the dominant pair (pups present or absent; age of pups). Other factors influencing size and use of home range include the abundance and distribution of food resources and the "environmental stresses," including disturbance and mortality from humans. Superimposed upon this relatively stable spatial distribution of resident coyote pairs and family units are the nomadic wanderings of dispersing juveniles, subordinate and unmated adults, and other coyotes which have been displaced for various reasons and forced to wander and search for an area within which to live. This dynamic dimension to patterns of coyote distribution ensures a measurable amount of social interaction and variability in home range sizes and patterns of use. It also ensures that, even in a region supporting moderate coyote densities and rates of productivity, home ranges are soon reoccupied following the removal or loss of a resident pair, and that adult residents which lose their mates are not long without a partner.

Occupation and defence of a defined home range might be considered a form of population control by many species of territorial animals. In coyote populations, young often disperse from parental home ranges in autumn or winter (see "Reproduction"). Dispersal appears to be delayed in the northeast, where winter survival can be enhanced through cooperative hunting of larger prey by the family unit. However, dispersal by juveniles normally does occur, and as far as the population is concerned, dispersal of juveniles is functionally the same as death. Loss of those dispersers is not critical to the welfare of the population so long as the adult resident pair remains to reproduce again. If the dispersers survive to find a suitable area and reproduce, the population benefits. If no suitable space is vacant, and the dispersers perish, the population remains in balance with the prevailing environmental limits.

> "...Dispersal would occur when that action increased an animal's chance of surviving and breeding. Dispersal may be enhanced by abundant food and inhibited or delayed by food shortage. Survival of juveniles may be extended if they can depend upon adults to some extent when food is scarce. Thus, during food shortage, juveniles may remain with their parents or den adults."[8]

Coyote movements, spatial distribution and survival is influenced by the social status of each coyote.

> "Adult coyotes in the Missouri River Breaks [Montana] have four social [positions]: den breeders, den [extras], nomads, and dispersers. Most juveniles ... become nonbreeding den [extras], nomads, or dispersers.... Den breeders have apparent low mortality.... Mortality for dispersers in low security habitat was exceptionally high. Population regulation appeared to be accomplished by: density restrictions imposed through spacing of den areas; dispersal of young plus infirm and [extra] adults; and finally, by food abundance.... Den areas are traditional, both from the aspect of coyote behavior and geographical areas occupied. Coyotes occupying den areas during summer account for most of the coyotes on a particular area of land."[9]

Resident coyotes in Colorado remained within well-defined home ranges, with little or no overlap between adjacent home ranges.[10] Transient coyotes also had home ranges, but they overlapped home ranges of residents and other transients. Although home range sizes changed slightly with changing seasons, the area of occupation remained relatively stable. Seven marked coyotes used the same home range all four years of the study. Resident coyotes had the highest annual survival and most radio-marked dispersers were killed by humans after leaving their natal home range. Long-term occupancy of the same territory has been documented from Wyoming and Nebraska and occupancy of territories in Texas was sustained even when membership changed.[11]

"*The presence of a reservoir of transient animals available to occupy vacant territories emphasizes logistical problems associated with resolving coyote depredation problems through population reduction, especially on small areas. Alternatively, where depredations are temporary or local, efforts might be focused on selective removal of territorial adult coyotes.... Territorial coyotes might be more vulnerable to some removal techniques than others.*"[12]

The following short review will give the reader an appreciation of home range sizes from across coyote range, and confirm that home ranges are usually largest in the northern spruce-fir forests during winter.

Coyotes in Texas appear to have some of the smallest home ranges, and those of resident females are smaller (2-4 km^2) than transients (greater than 11 km^2).[13] Resident females were adults and most transients were juveniles. Only 34% of transients had home ranges and transients tended to wander off their home ranges more than residents. Home ranges in Texas could be divided into core and peripheral zones, depending upon degree of use. The authors of that study commented on how spatial patterns of coyote distribution might influence control efforts. Colonizing coyotes in Georgia occupy home ranges of between 10 and 12 km^2 and home ranges are smallest during pregnancy. Coyotes in Georgia were more prone to trapping (mortality) outside the core area, confirming the susceptibility of juvenile dispersers to mortality from humans, and the questionable utility of control programs in the autumn and early winter.[14]

Core areas were also identified within coyote home ranges in Washington. These core areas represented only 7% of the home range, but they included 83% of all locations of 10 radio-marked coyotes. Home ranges were very large and were greatest in winter (143 km^2), least in summer (55 km^2); they averaged 92 km^2. Much of the Washington study area was protected land, and the author of that study speculated on how the low levels of exploitation might have influenced home range sizes.[15]

In a study in Mississippi and Alabama, the mean home range size of adult females (41 km^2) was twice the size of adult males (20 km^2) and 4 times the size of juveniles (11 km^2). In North Dakota, home ranges of coyote families were also large (61 km^2), and relatively exclusive. Home ranges in Idaho were usually elongated in shape and varied from 21 to 114 km^2; within those core areas were also identified. On Nebraska farmlands home ranges of adult males and females were 28 km^2 and 24 km^2, respectively, while in Colorado the mean annual home range size for radio-collared coyotes was 11 km^2 for residents and 106 km^2 for transients.[16]

Most transients in the Colorado study were either juveniles or very old coyotes. Resident coyotes there made up 78% of the population; transient coyotes, 22%. Transients most likely serve as a reservoir from which animals are recruited into the resident reproductive segment of the population. Radio-marked coyote families in Nebraska occupied largely non-overlapping contiguous home ranges where scent-marking and vocalization were important in territorial maintenance and avoidance of physical confrontations.[17] Coyotes occupied with pup rearing in Oklahoma had smaller home ranges than did unmated coyotes, and home ranges of adjacent females and established pairs often overlapped.[18] The extent of home range overlap varied, from complete inclusion of a small home range within a larger one to slight boundary overlap.

An extensive study of the behavioural ecology of coyotes on the Welder Wildlife Refuge in southern Texas included over 17,000 telemetry locations of 63 radio-collared coyotes and more than 800 visual observations of collared and non-collared coyotes from January 1978 through February 1982.[19] Coyotes were classified as resident groups, resident pairs, and transients. Composite home ranges of adult males and adult females were similar (4-5 km²). The difference in size between resident adult home ranges in this Texas study and those from Washington, Nebraska, and Idaho (mentioned earlier) is striking, and illustrates the importance of physical and biological factors which influence size and configuration of coyote home ranges. Home ranges of resident adult males and females did not differ within or among seasons. Home ranges of transient males and females averaged 43 km² and 31 km², respectively. Home ranges of pups increased as they matured and adult coyote home range sizes were not related to group size.

It must be remembered when reviewing home range sizes of coyotes that size and use may be influenced by geographical region, topography, variety and availability of food, season, sex and age of the coyote, and the means used to collect and analyse the descriptive information. With that in mind, how do home range sizes and movements of coyotes on traditional western ranges compare to those for eastern populations?

The mean home range size for adult females in northcentral Minnesota was 28 km2, substantially smaller than home ranges of 94-130 km² estimated from winter snow tracking studies of coyotes in Michigan. Studies have since shown that home ranges can be substantially larger in winter than in summer, especially in northern forested wilderness habitats. Female coyotes occupied well-defined and non-over-lapping home ranges. Pre-denning, denning, and post-denning home ranges averaged 13, 5.3, and 14.8 km² respectively. A radio-marked adult female in Ontario stayed within a home range of 20 km² and showed no predictability in her movement patterns.[20]

Although there have been far fewer studies of coyotes in the northeast than in the west, there is some information on home range sizes and movements. Home range sizes of 7 radio-collared male and female coyotes in Maine averaged 52 km² and 48 km², respectively and core areas were identified within each home range.[21] Home ranges of males and females during pair bonding and initial breeding (January-February) averaged 11 km² and 10 km² respectively. During pregnancy (March-April) home ranges of males increased to 18 km² but decreased to 8 km² for females. Although adult pairs increased their home ranges to 30 km² during nursing in May-June, home ranges progressively decreased from July through December. Like the coyotes studied in other areas, coyotes in Maine were more active in early morning than late afternoon and evening. During mid-day coyotes often rested for up to 4 hours. In western Maine coyotes occupied home ranges of approximately 43 km² and in winter preferred forest stands of predominantly coniferous overstory.[22] In 1983-84 I studied the seasonal home ranges and movements of radio-collared coyotes in northern New Brunswick. The home range of an adult female was smallest (9 km²) in May-June, when she attended young pups at the natal den and largest (41 km²) in winter (January-March), when she travelled and hunted with 2 of her pups. The pups had not dispersed by early March, although they spent progressively less time with the female.[23]

A number of studies have related food abundance and the use of space by animals. We have seen that home ranges for coyotes can show great variation. That variation may be related to food availability or to behavioural differences and social and reproductive status. A study of spatial use of coyotes and the abundance and distribution of black-tailed jackrabbits in the Great Basin of northern Utah and southern Idaho concluded that prey abundance alone was not adequate to predict changes in coyote spatial use.[24] Results of that study suggested that examination of the dynamics of space use in relation to changing food abundance should include consideration of mortality patterns, as well as interactions between transient and territorial animals.

Studies of western coyotes suggest that food may overshadow coyote density as an influence on home range size.[25] Larger home ranges in winter can be attributed to decreased abundance and/or availability of food. Marc Bekoff, University of Colorado, studied the social ecology of coyotes in Grand Teton National Park, Wyoming, and offered these comments on the influence of food and the sex and age structure of the coyote population on pack size and territoriality.

"The sizes of coyotes' home ranges and territories vary markedly, although not consistently, with the locale, the season and the year and also with the age and the sex of the individuals. When we measured the home ranges of 10 adults in the Blacktail Butte area, we found that the average size was 21.1 square kilometers, with no discernible differences according to sex. When we classified the home-range sizes according to the coyotes' social groupings, however, we found that solitary individuals and mated pairs, which are excluded from carrion in winter, have a larger home range, with an average size of 30.1 square kilometers. Pack members, which defend a food resource in winter and tend to remain in their own territory, have an average home range of only 14.3 square kilometers. The sizes of pack members' home ranges also show considerably less variation, probably because of the clumped distribution of ungulate carrion."[26]

The activities and movements of coyotes can be either those of adults within well-defined home ranges, which are therefore restricted in linear distance, or those of dispersing juveniles and transient adults, which may be substantial. An early (1931-1949) ear-tagging study of 616 coyotes in several western states provided information on distance travelled between tagging and recovery. The mean distance of 301 recoveries was 14 miles (22.5 km), and the maximum measured coyote movement was 115 miles (185 km).[27] Another ear-tagging study of 98 coyotes in California found the longest known distance between tagging and recovery was 87 miles (139 km), by a juvenile male.[28] Theaverage movement for adults was 4 miles (6 km) for males and 4 ¾ miles (7.6 km) for females. The average distances between tagging and recovery for juvenile males and females [excluding the 87-mile (140-km) transient] were 3 ¼ miles (5.2 km) and 4 miles (6 km) respectively.

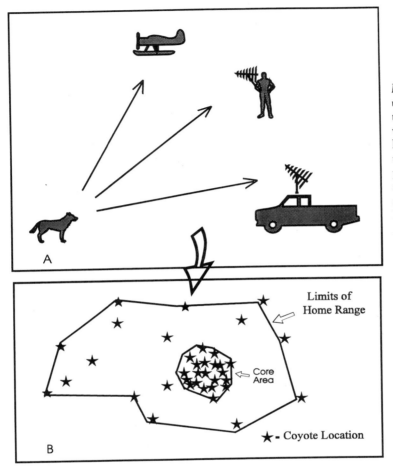

Figure 11. The use of radio telemetry in wildlife research has increased our understanding of patterns of animal activity and definition of home ranges: **A**. A coyote is live-trapped, fitted with a radio transmitter, released, and subsequent locations monitored by foot, truck or aircraft. **B**. The plotting of locations on maps allows the calculation of home range size and core areas of intensive use.

A study of 13 radio-marked coyotes in Mississippi and Alabama (1982-84) found that coyotes were most active and traveled the greatest distances between 6 p.m. and 6 a.m. and that the highest rates of travel were near sunset and sunrise.[29] Distances travelled per day (full-night periods) were greatest for adult females (9 km) followed by adult males (8 km) and juveniles (5 km). The average daily distance travelled was least in autumn (5 km) and greatest in winter (12 km). One juvenile dispersed 140 km between November and January. A second juvenile and an adult each dispersed 20 km during the same time period.

> "...It seems reasonable that a coyote moving about an area populated by relatives and other long-standing acquaintances might have fewer ...[stressful encounters with other coyotes]... than a coyote in an area populated by strange individuals, the result of rapid and high dispersal rates in response to heavy exploitation rates. Social stability should produce stable territory boundaries, which could

be established among family units as with wolves."[30]

Straight-line distances travelled by coyotes during 24-hour tracking shifts in Nebraska averaged 11 km.[31] Daily movements there were greatest during the breeding period (February), which is similar to studies of eastern coyotes in Maine and New Brunswick. Adult females travelled greater average daily distances than adult males at all seasons. Not surprisingly, activity was greatest at night and early morning. Distances measured during 24-hour monitoring sessions of adults during pup rearing in Oklahoma averaged 6.0 km for adult females and 6.3 km for adult males.[32] Coyotes in Texas were most active at night, and activity patterns were similar for adult males and females, for residents and transients, and among seasons.[33] Distances moved in 24 hours were similar for adult males and adult females (7-8 km). Distances moved by pups increased as they matured (similar to home range size) and were like those of adults by November-December. In northern New Brunswick distances between consecutive daily radio locations (minimum daily cruising distance) varied with home range size and were lowest in early summer (1.3 km) and highest in late winter (6.1 km). The actual distance travelled during a 24-hour period would be somewhat greater than the minimum daily cruising distance.[34] Bekoff and Wells related activity of western coyotes with availability and accessibility of food.

"*Coyotes typically are active in the early morning and early evening, but when we compared the time 50 coyotes (35 of them marked) devoted to hunting and resting, we found that in winter, when carrion is available but the food supply is usually low, much less time is spent hunting and considerably more is spent resting than is the case in summer, when small rodents are readily available but must be found, caught and killed. The higher ratio of resting time to hunting time may be generally beneficial for pregnant females, which must conserve energy for the nutritional demands placed on them during the nine-week gestation period and afterward.... Our findings about the pack-living adaptation of coyotes are supported by data gathered for golden jackals and hyenas, and we have been able to draw some general conclusions that should be tested with other species of carnivores. We have found that in situations where there are "haves" and have-nots" with respect to the winter food supply... the halves 1) are more social and cohesive than the have-nots, 2) are territorial and will defend the food resources, 3) have a more compressed home range, 4) are subject to higher rates of intrusion by members of the same species on the areas where the food is clumped and 5) in winter are able to travel less and so rest more...[Advantages] of pack living can include any of the following: 1)food can be more successfully defended, particularly in winter; 2) food items can be more readily located; 3) individuals, particularly sexually mature females, can conserve energy needed for reproduction and care of the young, and 4) help, in the form of feeding and protection, can be provided for the young by individuals other than parents (most likely older siblings). Whether pack living confers an advantage in the acquisition of large prey remains an open question.*"[35]

In the west the traditional prairie coyote is more scavenger than direct predator of big game. For that reason, differences in pack social structure and territoriality between "haves" and "have-nots" may not apply to coyotes of northeastern forested habitat where prey is less abundant and diverse (see "Food Habits"). This is especially relevant when assessing the advantages of pack living for increasing predation success on big game. As discussed earlier, delayed juvenile dispersal appears to be a functional response of coyotes in the northeast to greater dependency upon white-tailed deer in the winter.

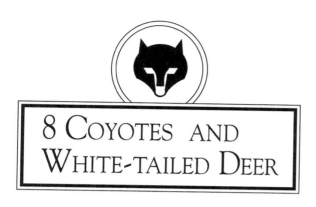

8 COYOTES AND WHITE-TAILED DEER

"No one seems to approve of predation but, like sin, it is not often that anyone succeeds in stopping it for an appreciable length of time."[1]

We now leave the general review of coyotes and their prey and examine in greater detail the real, potential, and perceived but perhaps unreal impact of coyotes upon white-tailed deer. We will review studies, some already referred to, which have measured or estimated the importance of deer in the seasonal diets of coyotes across its range. We will assess the results of studies which measured the response of deer populations to changes in densities of coyotes, and we will look at studies of the relationship between deer and wolves, a comparison perhaps not inappropriate given the suspected genetic makeup of the eastern coyote and apparent adaptation of behavioural and hunting strategies by coyotes to more efficiently and effectively prey on white-tailed deer. The reader is given background information on the history of white-tailed deer in the region: the changes to continental deer populations initiated by early settlement, landscape change, market hunting, and extirpation of the wolf from most of the continental United States (excluding Alaska) and Atlantic Canada. By understanding these historical developments and changes, the reader should develop a greater understanding of how the coyote has become established as the dominant canid predator throughout the eastern United States, southern Ontario and Quebec, and the Atlantic Provinces. The reader may also appreciate the long-term implications to other resident wildlife, and the adjustments that may be required in human behaviour and values to develop a rational philosophy towards our forested ecosystem which includes the eastern coyote.

The herbivores (plant-eaters) and carnivores (meat-eaters) have evolved together through the mists of time. The herbivores continue to develop means to avoid capture such as running faster and hiding, while the carnivores in turn improve their skills of detection, stalking, hunting, and killing. Among predator and prey, the species which are most successful continue to survive and evolve, while the less successful fall by the wayside and become extinct. This process of trial and error, success and failure, has contributed to the profusion and diversity of life forms that exist on the planet today. There is no question that the process has proven successful in primative times; the problem is how successful can it continue to be in a world ravaged by the increasingly insatiable demands of humans.

History is filled with attempts to exclude predators, including the coyote, from a landscape which humans have altered and changed (not always for the better) for their benefit, pleasure, and use. The coyote is a competitor with humans, and a very efficient one at that. That, however, is no reason to feel threatened by, or hostile towards, the coyote. Rather, it is more reason to respect and admire this marvellous creature. Surely there is a lesson to be learned from this story. In the ever-changing biological world, the species that survives is the one which adapts best to changed conditions and in time benefits from the changes. We would do well to learn from this amazing story of the eastern coyote, truly a species which survives and flourishes through adaptation and improvization.

White-tailed Deer: early history

The historic range of the white-tailed deer in eastern North America was expansive; early records suggest that the species was found in all states east of the Mississippi River, throughout the midwestern states and north into the southern Prairie Provinces and British Columbia.[2] In the east, populations are believed to have been as far north as southern Ontario and extreme southern Quebec, but not into northern Maine or Atlantic Canada (*Figure 12*). This is very important for understanding what factors may now be in operation between deer and the newly established populations of coyotes in the northeastern United States and eastern Canada. Prior to European colonization coyotes were largely restricted to the open prairies and grasslands west of the Mississippi River, and the timber (or gray) wolf was the only large wild canid predator east of the Mississippi River (*Figure 13*). Timber wolves occupied most of the early range of white-tailed deer north of the Carolinas, Alabama, Georgia, and Louisiana. It is most likely that the interactions between wolves and deer were dynamic and that populations of both predator and prey experienced both short- and long-term numerical changes. Some early authorities have estimated as many as 40 million white-tailed deer may have occupied early pre-European North American range.[3]

Helenette Silver provides this enlightening image of early white-tailed deer populations in New Hampshire:

> "*Under the amply documented conditions which existed at the time of settlement [1623] deer populations must have varied widely between areas, and were likely subject to violent fluctuations from year to year. In the absence of any evidence of range damage, it must be concluded that, predation, coupled with hunting in the south, and with severe winter in the north, kept deer populations below carrying capacity.... [Wolves] may have been cyclic. Certainly their wanderings gave the appearance of periodicity. The extent of their depredations on domestic stock, and probably also on deer was related to the severity of the winter.*"[4]

[Important in context of coyotes and white-tailed deer in the northeast]

Early clearing of the forests, settlement, and agriculture initially improved habitat

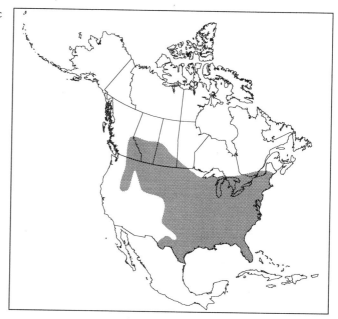

Figure 12: The early historic range of the white-tailed deer did not extend far into eastern Canada, and when settlers first arrived in the northeast, deer were not found north of Maine.

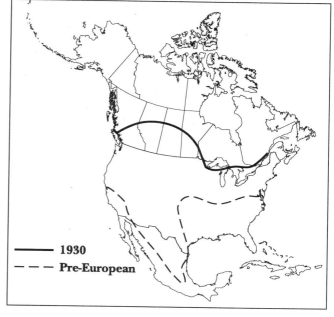

Figure 13: The pre-European distribution of the gray wolf was expansive, but by 1930 wolves had been eliminated from most of the continental United States (excluding Alaska) and all of Atlantic Canada (Nowak 1983).

for white-tailed deer, and the "war" waged by early colonists and settlers on wolves would have helped to release herd productivity and contribute to population growth. Initial growth of white-tailed deer populations from improved habitat and decreased predators was short-lived.

"The ... habitat improvement following farm abandonment [late 1800s] paved the way for the resurgence of deer when they were finally afforded adequate protection in the [1890s].... Deer were not hunted at first in the northern settlements because of their rarity. Wolves, on the other hand, were common, and every effort was made to exterminate them. By 1810 they [the wolves] were under control, but as deer increased, reaching peak by 1830, wolves again became numerous. Farmers—with perhaps some justification—believed that deer attracted them. In the interests of eradicating wolves, the citizens undertook to destroy deer as well. Deer were run with dogs, knifed in the winter yards, jacked and taken in the water. There were no closed seasons, and some hunters took from 20-100 a year. Lumber camps, which were constantly increasing, employed men and kept dogs to supply them with venison.... Over a quarter century of persecution, deer became progressively scarcer. Once the decline ... had started, it progressed without interruption. Lumbering was in its infancy at the time of the slaughter in 1830.... The peak of agriculture was far in the future. Improvement of habitat, which must have been in progress all through the period of decline, never succeeded in accomplishing an improvement in the status of deer."[5]

From the 1840s through the 1870s, large-scale lumbering opened up the northern forests. Improved deer habitat was offset by a wave of commercial market hunters and, with improved living conditions and greater leisure, sportsmen. State deer herds, already depleted by virtually uncontrolled harvests reached an all-time low following 6 years of unusually heavy snowfall and cold temperatures between 1873 and 1879. At this time (1877) the New Hampshire Fish and Game Department was organized, and state regulations came into effect. Deer numbers responded and populations were increasing by 1900. The rate and degree of deer population changes were strongly influenced by 2 man-made factors: land use and regulation of hunting.

This development of pioneer settlers, lumbermen, and market hunters opening up the forests of New Hampshire and the consequent exploitation of white-tailed deer was typical of what happened in most of the eastern forested United States during the era of early colonization and settlement.

In West Virginia Indians burned forests to improve range and increase game, as well as to facilitate travel, and deer thrived on the abundance of forage which grew rapidly in these forest openings. Settlers in the early 1700s found deer common and a ready source of food. As the forests fell before the wave of settlement into the west, wide-scale market hunting, use of dogs, poaching, and possibly climatic change caused the numbers of deer to decline dramatically and approach extirpation in that state by 1910. Deer were introduced in the 1920s and, with harvest regulations and enforcement, populations began to rebound.[6]

Changes to the forests from early logging, settlement, and fires combined with a harsh war waged by the market hunters considerably altered Wisconsin's wildlife picture, including that for deer. A brief increase in deer between 1850 and 1900 in response to improved habitat from logging and settlement ceased abruptly due to market hunting and uncontrolled forest fires. Deer in Wisconsin reached an all-time

Early timber operations relied on sleds and wagons drawn by oxen or horses (Benson and Dodds, 1977).

low around 1910. By 1915 the establishment of law enforcement, predator control, forest fire protection, limited hunting seasons, and bag limits saw a slow regrowth of the deer population, until by 1930 the first sign of over-browsed range began to appear.[7] To the west as far as Kansas, where white-tailed deer were common through the early- and mid-1800s, uncontrolled market hunting led to state-wide eradication by 1930.[8] Reintroductions and natural ingress, combined with hunting restrictions helped re-establish deer in that state.

The reader should not confuse the well-regulated harvests of white-tailed deer throughout its range today with the absolute uncontrolled, and actually promoted, market hunting which prospered in the United States during the mid- and late-1800s. Construction of the railway west during that era provided the means for shipping venison to the rich New England markets.

> "Trains that ran on the labyrinth of tracks across whitetail range were important vehicles, both figuratively and literally, in the species' nearly total demise. By rail, millions of immigrants flooded the continent's interior, and millions of pounds of deer hides and venison were drained out. ...
>
> The concept that civilization pushed back the American frontier, sweeping wildlife before it, is misleading. Repeatedly species by species, it became obvious that wildlife, including whitetails, were not retreating to habitats 'somewhere else,' they simply were being overrun. ...
>
> Not until the federal [U.S.] Lacey Act of 1900 – which prohibited interstate traffic in wild game taken in violation of state law – was market hunting and the decimation of wildlife for commercial gain effectively ended."[9]

The whitetail count for all of North America at the turn of the century was estimated at about 500,000.[10] This is a far cry from the estimated 40 million estimated at the outset of American colonization!

> "...The laws restricting commercial harvests, and in addition the relatively sudden realization by sportsmen that wildlife was an exhaustible and exhausted

resource, helped to give pause to the decline. The history of the white-tailed deer helped to stimulate the concern that was the origin of modern wildlife management, initially as a political process of trial and error and eventually a scientific discipline."[11]

The history of white-tailed deer in Atlantic Canada was different from that of much of the continental United States. At the beginning of European colonization, the northeastern limit of white-tailed deer was the southern limit of the spruce-fir forests in Maine. Archaelogical excavations in Nova Scotia indicate that white-tailed deer were once common in that province, and probably throughout New Brunswick as well.[12] Excavations of early native shell heaps in Nova Scotia found remains of white-tailed deer to be common prior to approximately 1100 A.D., at which time the climate appears to have cooled and caused a gradual change in the native fauna.[13] Deer subsequently declined, perhaps died out, and climatic change was most likely responsible for the northern limit of white-tailed deer lying to the south of New Brunswick by early European settlement [17th century]. It is interesting to note, from early native middens, that coincident with the cooling trend and decline in deer, was the appearance and increase of snowshoe hare and caribou. Perhaps most important to our interest, however, was a corresponding decline in the presence of wolves. This suggests that white-tailed deer were probably the main prey of wolves in those early times, and as deer declined and range limits shifted south, numbers of wolves responded accordingly. The presence of caribou and moose would have continued to support wolves following the decline and demise of deer, but probably in reduced numbers.

Deer expanded their range north into New Brunswick during the early years of European settlement. The presence of moose and caribou and the scarcity of deer probably spared the pioneering populations of deer the heavy exploitation which occurred in the United States. By 1900, deer were well established throughout New Brunswick.

Over the last 20 years, large clearcuts have changed the face of much of the forested landscape in the northeast. As a result, deer and predators have been concentrated in smaller areas in winter, increasing the predator-prey ratio and the rate of predation by coyotes on deer (G. Parker).

Deer were reintroduced to Nova Scotia near the turn of the century. One of the earliest introductions included 11 deer from New Brunswick released near Lake Jolly in Digby County in 1894 (referred to as Daley's deer). Other releases and the natural ingress into the northern portion of the province from New Brunswick saw deer become established throughout the mainland by 1904, and on Cape Breton Island by 1911. The increase in the provincial herd was remarkable, and an open season was declared in 1916. By 1935 deer had increased to the level that winter mortality was being reported, and they probably reached maximum numbers between 1944 and 1956. Peak populations may have reached 250,000.[14] A province-wide decline then began, which continued through 1970 and was followed by another increase through the mid-1980s. Deer populations in New Brunswick followed much the same pattern.

I have reviewed some of the history of white-tailed deer in the northeast and the impacts of early settlement and exploitation on deer populations to help the reader understand the recent changes to deer in the region and the possible consequences of interactions between deer and colonizing eastern coyotes. Now a few words on the wolf.

Historically the timber wolf was the only widespread large canid predator in eastern North America.[15] However, the battle lines were drawn early between the settler and the wolf. J. A. Allen left us with these 1876 comments on wolves in New England.

> *"In early days the gray wolf was abundant everywhere, and as early as 1630 became an outlaw in the Plymouth Colony. In that year the court ordered that any Englishman who killed a wolf should have one penny for each horse and cow, and one farthing for each sheep and swine, owned in the colony. In 1698 the town of Lynn voted to allow a premium of twenty shillings for every wolf destroyed in the town. ...*
>
> *It is now [1876] many years since the last wolf was seen in New England east of the Connecticut and south of New Hampshire, but as late as the beginning of the present century it was abundant in Southern Maine as well as in Southern Vermont and New Hampshire, and was of rather frequent occurrence in the mountainous portions of Western Maine and the White Mountains."*[16]

Native shell heap excavations in Nova Scotia (referred to earlier) suggest that, with the extirpation of deer from that province sometime prior to European colonization, the wolf also declined. Following settlement in the 18th and early 19th centuries the reappearance of white-tailed deer in New Brunswick seems to have promoted wolf productivity and survival, at least temporarily. A review of historical records by Austin Squires provides insight into the dynamics of certain wildlife populations in New Brunswick during the early years of human settlement.

> *"The wolf was apparently very scarce or absent from this region in the early years of colonization. The early writers, Marc Lescarbot and Samuel de Champlain, from whom we have learned what little is known about the natural history of this region in the early 1600s, did not mention the wolf at all. Neither did Nicolas Denys who in his book ... published in 1672 gave detailed information*

about the animals and birds which he found in this region in the previous forty years....

Rev. W.O. Raymond in his History of the River St. John, A.D. 1604-1784, *published in 1905, was the next author to mention wolves. In a list of furs shipped from the trading post at the mouth of the St. John River between 1764 and 1774 he found listed two skins of the Nova Scotia wolf. No explanation was offered for the use of the words Nova Scotia in this connection....*

Either wolves were much more numerous than these meagre reports suggest, or else they increased rapidly in the next few years, as we find that the government of New Brunswick placed a bounty on the wolf in 1792....

Abraham Gesner in his New Brunswick with Notes for Emigrants *in 1847 made the following partially incorrect but frequently quoted statement: 'The Virginian deer was not seen in New Brunswick prior to 1818, and it is evident that they have been driven into the Province from the southwest by droves of wolves.'...*

Another author writing about his experiences in North America was Captain R.G.A. Levinge who published Echoes of the North Woods *in 1846. His first statement about wolves is very similar to Dr. Gesner's report. 'Wolves are not indigenous to the province but have made their appearance in New Brunswick, following the deer, likewise a stranger, which they have driven before them from the eastern States.'...*

C.L. Hatheway in his book of 1846 [The History of New Brunswick]*... was probably more accurate when he said: 'Within the last seven years they [wolves] have visited us again in quest of the emigrant deer, but so many have been captured and poisoned that we hear little of them lately.'...*

In 1907 Dr. W.F. Ganong tried to find out when the last wolf had been seen in New Brunswick. He found that the last bounty had been paid for three wolves in 1862....

We may conclude then that the wolf was absent from this region or very scarce here in the 1600s and in the 1700s until about 1780. Then so many of them appeared in the province that a large bounty was put on them. As a result they became very scarce in a few years, but about 1840 large numbers appeared in the province again. Whether they came into the province from the west as people apparently believed at that time, or whether there was a natural increase in the wilderness areas which overflowed into the settled part of the province, is impossible to tell today." [17]

That wolves made their appearance in the Maritimes several times in the early 1800s is supported by early descriptions of wildlife in Nova Scotia, such as the following account by J. Bernard Gilpin in 1864.

"I have identified this destructive animal as existing in Nova Scotia. A very large specimen, taken at Windsor, was exhibited in Halifax. I can only mention

Regulated hunting seasons, increased food from timber harvesting, and the elimination of the wolf allowed white-tailed deer populations to increase substantially throughout the 1900s (Benson and Dodds, 1977).

it to observe how very difficult it appears for some large species to find new habitations. In Nova Scotia the cover and the game are alike and equally abundant as in New Brunswick or Newfoundland, yet twice this century a voluntary migration of Wolves has been made and both failed. About seventy years ago [around 1800] Wolves made their appearance, but were soon lost sight of. About 20 years ago [1844] they again appeared simultaneously in every part of the Province. The mail courier had scarcely reported one crouching before his off leader in the gorge of the Cobequid hills, before one was trapped at Yarmouth. They seem to have trotted through the whole Province from north to the extreme south, and to have retreated on their tracks with equal stealth; since for twenty years no word has been heard of them. Their instinct taught them that it was no place to found a race in."[18]

By 1900 the wolf had been extirpated from the eastern half of the United States and Atlantic Canada except for a few in pockets of wilderness which remained in parts of the Appalachian chain and the upper Great Lakes region. Wolves were probably eliminated by human persecution and progressive loss of suitable wilderness habitat from urban and agricultural development. Whatever the case, wolves were absent from most of eastern North America by 1900, although there is speculation by some that relic populations of "wild dogs" of some ancestry may have remained in pockets of wilderness in the northeast, such as the Adirondack Mountains of New York.[19]

The demise of the wolf throughout most of the continental United States and Atlantic Canada during the late 1800s and its absence throughout most of the 20th century (minor exceptions being reintroductions and natural ingress into several northcentral and northwestern states) may represent the first time in the evolutionary development of large mammals in North America that this vast tract of forested

117

landscape did not support at least one large canid predator. The absence of such an important predator link in the ecological food chain has certainly contributed to the geographic and population instability of many wildlife species, especially white-tailed deer. As noted earlier, in the absence of market hunting, and with the establishment of state and provincial game agencies in the late 1800s and laws which regulated game seasons and harvests, deer populations not only recovered but "exploded" throughout most parts of its range.

Deer habitat had been created during early settlement by agriculture and forest harvesting, but deer populations had been suppressed by widespread and uncontrolled market hunting. This abundant but underutilized deer habitat was quickly occupied, and state game authorities soon changed their concern for deer from how to increase populations to how to control them. The legal harvest of deer could not contain the surging productivity and growth of most populations. Restrictive harvest regulations, developed to enhance population growth, soon became antiquated, and when most populations should have been heavily harvested to avoid overuse of habitat, many states were still toying with "buck only" seasons. The science of wildlife management was still in its infancy and the dynamics of wildlife populations were little understood. Throughout this period of deer herd expansion, there was no canid predator to act as a natural population regulator. Without substantive harvests, depleted food supplies and environmental stresses served as the ultimate reaper.

Over the last 50 years, research has provided answers to many of the questions concerning the dynamics of white-tailed deer populations, and deer management has developed into a sophisticated science. It includes data collection and analysis, population modelling, and manipulating population change through flexible and often innovative harvest regulations. Today more people harvest more deer across North America from higher populations than ever before.

As a rule, the science of deer management and the reliability of information used to drive population models for predicting and regulating harvests becomes less precise as habitat quality declines and environmental stresses increase. These conditions assumed greater significance as white-tailed deer moved north into marginal habitat and had to cope with severe winter conditions. Like most wildlife species, white-tailed deer will expand their range to the geographical limits, and those limits were often met and exceeded in the northern spruce-fir forests of the northeastern United States and southeastern Canada. Deer expanded to the northeast because of habitat conditions improved through forestry and agriculture, possibly combined with an ameliorating climate, and an absence of significant predation due to the disappearance of the wolf. Their history here has been one of unpredictable numerical changes and a deer manager's nightmare. A series of favourable winters (moderate temperatures, low snowfall and snow cover) stimulate periodic bursts of productivity, survival, and herd growth. Deer are abundant and hunters are happy. In such times legal harvests probably have little influence on population trends. Then come several consecutive winters of deep and prolonged snow cover, and the grim reaper takes his toll. Deer become fewer and hunters become unhappy. Deer management can often only control the intensity, composition, and spatial distribution of legal harvests. Real

During periods of deep snow, white-tailed deer in the northeast often congregate into deer wintering areas that provide shelter and food (Dahlberg and Guettinger, 1956).

population growth must wait for environmental stress to moderate and release herd productivity and recruitment.

Nature has now added a character to the saga of the delicate balance between deer and its northern environment. Enter the eastern coyote. Like the white-tailed deer, the coyote expanded its range as habitat and food supplies were improved by human disturbance and change to the forested landscape, and as a competing canid predator (i.e., timber wolf) disappeared. The coyote pioneered and colonized new territory as long as conditions allowed, and those conditions have now allowed it to occupy most of continental North America south of the boreal forests. Along with the white-tailed deer, the eastern coyote has expanded its northeastern range to the limit where deep and prolonged winter snow cover and limited food resources impact upon it. Without white-tailed deer, it is doubtful that many coyotes would survive the long arduous winters throughout much of the present northeastern portion of its range. Snowshoe hare is the only other dependable prey in the spruce-fir forests, especially throughout much of northern New Brunswick and the Gaspé region of Quebec.

Thus, when the coyote first arrived in the northeastern states and Atlantic Canada, it found an abundant, and probaby naive, source of food in the white-tailed deer. Under severe winter conditions coyotes are quite capable of killing both juvenile and adult white-tailed deer. The deer killed in winter are often representative of the general population, suggesting that the coyote is an opportunistic predator not necessarily always selecting for old, weak, or diseased animals. On the open northern tundra, arctic wolves frequently harrass herds of caribou and watch for abnormal individual behaviour. Once that stimulus is received, wolves concentrate their attack on that particular animal. Thus, much of the diet of the northern wolf may well be selective and compensatory to other forms of mortality. This does not appear to apply to the eastern coyote and white-tailed deer in the northeast. Successful predation by coyotes on deer is highly influenced by frequency of chance encounters in forested habitat rather than by deliberate harrassment and specific visual stimuli (i.e., abnormal behaviour) prompting the chase.

Given the facts at hand, it is tempting to name the coyote as one of the main reasons for recent declines in white-tailed deer populations throughout parts of New Brunswick, Nova Scotia, southeastern Quebec, and northern New England. Declines were not immediate, but a delayed response by deer populations (as measured by hunter harvest) to increasing predation by coyotes should not be unexpected. A continued drain on fawns in winter (recruitment) and the slower attrition of healthy adult females would be measurable only several years after those losses began. Adult deer would continue to be seen, and shot, although decreasingly so, and fawns would still appear in the harvest because much predation by coyotes on fawns occurs after the fall hunting season. Hunters would require additional effort to kill a deer, and although deer numbers might be declining, this decline would not be immediately apparent in the annual kill statistics. Declining deer populations reach the point, however, when additional hunting effort fails to compensate for reduced availability, and the deer harvest drops rapidly. This appears to have occurred in the late 1980s in New Brunswick and Nova Scotia.

The precise predator-prey model which developed, and may still be developing, between coyotes and white-tailed deer in the northeast is not yet clear, although I propose a general model which suggests that reduced numbers of deer and coyotes may be expected for many forested-wilderness regions of the northeast. The intensity of forces which drive that model probably vary by region, depending upon the abundance of deer and hare, winter severity and, something which we know very little about, the changing social patterns and hunting behaviour of coyotes. As deer decline, coyotes themselves become more stressed in winter, a factor which leads to reduced coyote recruitment, lower populations, and vacant home ranges. As deer populations decline, those that remain adjust their behaviour to cope with this new predator. Deer become more wary and avoid habitats which favour encounters with coyotes. Their normal short flight response to danger prior to the arrival of the coyote become more swift and prolonged. Changes in the response of deer to coyotes have also changed their response to hunting. In forested areas, deer are now less prone to stand and watch the approach of a hunter. Harrassment by coyotes has enforced a stronger sense of awareness to potential danger: the deer which hesitates may soon be feast for coyote, raven, and fox. Such changes in deer behaviour also contribute to declines in hunter success, an index often used to measure the abundance of deer. The relationship between deer abundance and hunting success has probably changed since the arrival of the coyote, and direct comparisons between times of pre- and post-coyote are risky.

Although few things in life are certain, it is very doubtful that coyotes will cause the extirpation of deer in Atlantic Canada. Predator-prey models just don't work that way (usually). In single-prey models, the prey might be reduced to a level that adversely affects recruitment and population levels of the predator. That is most likely the direction that white-tailed deer and coyotes will follow in this region. However, I did say single prey models, such as wolves and caribou or lynx and snowshoe hare. Coyotes are opportunistic, and because of that, it is more difficult to predict population trends of deer or coyotes. Increases in numbers of hares might relieve predation on deer. On the other hand, an increase in an alternate food source might also allow coyotes to maintain productivity and population levels in spite of declining deer, and then in late winter switch to preying on the few deer that remain. Much remains to be learned of the eastern coyote and its ability to adapt to this new environment.

In the early years of white-tailed deer management, harvest regulations were the only tool that managers could directly manipulate in order to influence herd dynamics. Wildlife research had shown that deer populations were normally responding to habitat conditions (prior to the arrival of the coyote). The term "carrying capacity" was coined to describe that upper population limit which could be sustained by available habitat (food supply and cover). As a population surpassed the carrying capacity of its range, annual rates of mortality would surpass rates of survival and the number of deer would subsequently decline. Population trends were influenced by reduced rates of pregnancy, especially in the younger age classes, and the numbers of young born and fawn survival. A reduction in the productivity of a herd was often compounded by increased rates of mortality, the latter quite often the result of reduced food supplies in winter.

Deer herd management, through harvest regulations, is an effort to prevent numbers from surpassing the carrying capacity of a particular range or habitat. In theory, if a herd is prevented from surpassing the carrying capacity of its range, it can continue to have high rates of productivity and maintain an abundance of surplus animals which can then be harvested by hunters. This balancing act, of course, is laden with traps and pitfalls; the most obvious is defining just what, in numbers of deer, the mythical carrying capacity threshold represents. This is no easy task at the best of times, and by definition carrying capacity is a moving target. Food supplies change in response to changes in patterns of habitat and landscape. Forests which are disturbed by fire, disease, or timber harvest begin a path of development back towards maturity. Most mature forests do not support abundant food for deer, so total available food, one measure of carrying capacity, is constantly changing relative to forest age and development. The spatial arrangement of forest stands influences the distribution of food and, in turn, the distribution and total numbers of deer. To complicate the equation even further is the "availability" factor, i.e., even if a fairly precise measure of the amount of food (standing crop) were known for a range at a particular time, how much of it will be available for deer to make use of? The influence of food availability on deer survival increases in direct proportion to the severity of winter weather, and winter severity is influenced most by the depth and duration of winter snowfall. The winter period is often referred to as the "bottleneck" for many northern animal populations, especially those like the white-tailed deer which evolved and adapted for survival in more temperate regions. The reader should now have an appreciation of the task of the deer manager, especially in the northeast. Basically the number one priority is to manage towards a sustained population of deer for a particular region somewhere below the critical threshold level which might surpass range carrying capacity and cause long-term damage to both the deer and its habitat.

121

In theory carrying capacity can be increased by providing more food through controlled manipulation of habitat change. In reality, most forest change (and landscape change) by humans is a product of actions with motives other than improving habitat for deer. Timber harvest operations, although often regulated and advised by government guidelines, are geared towards removing trees in the most cost-effective (profitable) manner possible. Although these operations are becoming more aware of environmental concerns and other "user" interests, the age when timber is managed as one component within a total forest ecosystem (integrated forest management) is still a long way off. Even so, a forest ecosystem managed for a number of resources does not necessarily mean one managed for maximum numbers of white-tailed deer. The importance of maintaining ecological maturity in forest stands and enhancing structural diversity for a wide array of plant and animal life is rapidly becoming recognized. The deer manager must operate within those and a wide variety of other very real limitations. Past experience often influences the deer manager's concept of range carrying capacity; i.e., by examining past records of deer harvests, herd productivity from pregnancy rates and fawn ratios, and snowfalls and depths (a winter severity index is often used and is a more reliable measure of the impact of winter weather than total snowfall and depths alone) the manager can see demographic trends and develop a population model for a particular region, state, or province. The manager refers to earlier harvest statistics to drive this model, from measures of deer abundance and availability (often measured by hunter success) to the sex and age structure of the harvested sample (herd productivity). There are warning signals that the manager looks for in harvest statistics which often indicate the health of the herd and its approach to the "environmental limits" of its range. Fewer fawns in the kill combined with reduced pregnancy rates of does killed by automobiles, and low levels of fat in the bone marrow of deer found dead in late winter indicate an environmentally stressed (food and/or weather) herd, and one which may be approaching the environmental limits of its range. Sometimes herd reduction through increased harvests will alleviate the matter (symptoms are density dependent) while at other times density independent factors (increased environmental stress) are in operation and herd reductions are unavoidable.

So why have I digressed from coyotes to some of the concepts and difficulties in white-tailed deer management? To illustrate the very close relationship between deer and its habitat, the vulnerability of northern deer herds to environmental stress in winter, and the limits of management options to deer managers, especially in the northern regions. Management is often "reactive" rather than "proactive." Harvests are liberalized when populations increase in response to reduced environmental stress, increased access to food, and consequent enhanced survival and herd productivity. Hunting seasons may be reduced, or closed, in response to population declines, although reductions in populations may be, and most often are, driven by factors other than losses to human harvest. However, decreasing the harvest in response to declining populations is natural, and often advisable, especially when addressing public concerns, although it may have few biological implications. The public should be aware that deer herds are seldom controlled, or greatly influenced, by regulated human harvest, and decreasing the harvest in response to herd reduction should not be expected to be rewarded by immediate increases in numbers of deer. This is not to say that reduction of harvest might not lessen the severity of the decline or that harvest reduction in response to population reduction is not a practical and predictable option, but merely that immediate and proportional numerical responses should not always be expected.

Deer herds in the northeastern United States, Atlantic Canada, and southern Quebec and Ontario have not, until recently, been exposed to significant predation by large carnivores since the elimination of the wolf. White-tailed deer range and population expansion in the past 100 years has been controlled largely by food supplies and environmental stress. Humans are not efficient predators, and population loss to hunter kill, especially under the present closely regulated harvests, has seldom served as an effective population check. Changes in levels of harvest cannot, by themselves, explain the volatility of population fluctuations. The history of harvests throughout white-tailed deer range, especially in the northeast, show similar highs and lows, and human kill has seldom been identified as the main factor influencing herd dynamics.

DEER-COYOTE INTERACTIONS

The arrival of the coyote in the northeast would have been heralded with far less fanfare, and certainly less controversy, if deer had not declined concurrent with coyote colonization and population increase. Concidental? Some say yes; a great many others say no. What are the facts as we know them? What have we learned from other areas where coyotes cohabit range with deer? Do the same patterns occur? Have there been scientific studies of coyote-deer interrelationships? What were the results? Are the results similar, or do they vary by region?

First, as we have already seen for New Brunswick and Nova Scotia and alluded to for other areas, harvest records show significant variation in numbers of deer killed through time. Although some of that variation may be explained by changes in regulations and hunting effort, harvest trends are considered a general indicator of population trends. Earlier trends developed in the absence of significant predation, certainly without predation by coyotes, so other factors must have been in force. I have shown how, in an environment free of large predators, deer numbers are most often controlled by food and environmental stress (the winter "bottleneck" scenario) where food abundance is a function of landscape use (forestry, agriculture) and food availability is a function of winter snowfall and depth. If food is abundant but the deer expend more energy getting to the food and maintaining body temperature and condition than they receive from the food that they eat (i.e., a negative energy balance) they must draw upon body fat reserves. If this situation is prolonged, it can lead to malnutrition, weakness, and death.

In all wildlife populations, certain numbers die annually from disease, accidents, old age, predation, malnutrition, and other "natural" causes. These losses are normally replaced through recruitment, and the imbalance between total mortality and recruitment drives the numerical dynamics of a population. Predation, whether from coyotes, wolves, or humans, has often been considered compensatory to other forms of natural mortality. Predators remove animals that would have been lost to other causes, and those losses are therefore "compensated" for by decreases in losses from accidents, disease, etc. It is often stated that predators selectively remove the animals that, for some reason, are prone to predation. This might include older and diseased animals which, if not removed by predators, would have died anyway. This logical, although quite simplistic, approach to predator-prey models is often misused and abused by well-intentioned persons concerned about anti-predator sentiment or by those interested in harvesting animals through hunting. There can be a point when animals lost to predation or hunting adds to total mortality, thus becoming additive to other forms of natural mortality. There are proponents and critics of both the additive and compensatory theories, but there is general agreement that predation is seldom all compensatory or all additive. The lower the levels of predation and hunting, the more likely that all or most of those losses will be compensated for by decreases in mortality from other causes. As losses to predation increase, so does the probability that a proportion of those losses will be additive. The situation is finally reached where predation approaches the limit where its additive input to total mortality results in numerical declines in prey.

It is necessary to understand the dynamic relationship between white-tailed deer and its habitat and the increasing vulnerability of deer to environmental stress as populations expanded into the northeastern states and southern Canada (for reasons given earlier) in order to appreciate how the arrival of the coyote has affected white-tailed deer, especially in Atlantic Canada. It is now necessary to examine what we know about the impact of large carnivores, especially wolves and coyotes, upon deer populations.

In searching the literature it became apparent that many studies have addressed this very concern, and that it is necessary for us to review the conclusions of at least a selected sample (as there have been many). Most studies belong to one of several study types, classified by method of data collection and analysis. Those types of studies have included stomach and scat collections of predators, tracking (radio telemetry, both predator and prey; winter snow tracking), and experimental predator removal.

I described earlier how food habits can be estimated from examining samples of scats and stomachs of coyotes. Coyote trails can also be followed in the snow and information collected on activity and feeding behaviour. The frequency and success of chases of prey within specific habitat types and the rates of consumption can be measured (as described under "Food Habits"). Tracking can also be accomplished by radio-telemetry. Individual coyotes are captured live, fitted with radio transmittors (usually attached by a collar) and released. Radio-tracking coyotes allows distances travelled through time to be measured, and that, combined with information from snow-tracking, can be particularly useful for determining frequencies of chases and kills of different species of prey and the rates at which they are consumed.

Radio transmittors can also be placed on individual prey animals, such as deer fawns, and the proportion of the marked sample killed by predators or lost to other sources of mortality documented. Tracking in the snow, of course, is restricted to the winter period and to the northern sectors of coyote range, but since this is the time when impact upon white-tailed deer is believed to be most severe, these studies have proven very useful and informative. Tracking studies also provide information on hunting success and the amount of utilization of prey.

Control and experimental studies have been used to measure the response of a prey species, usually antelope or deer, to reductions or total removal of resident coyote populations. Monitoring the response of deer and moose to reductions in wolves has also been carried out. Such studies provide especially useful information on the impact of predator upon prey and allow comment on whether predation, in that particular study area, is compensatory or additive to other forms of mortality.

I will present examples of all 3 types of predator-prey studies by regions and review how each addresses the ability of canids to suppress or control ungulate populations, especially coyotes and white-tailed deer.

1) Stomach and/or Scat Collections

Earlier I reviewed studies of the general diet of coyotes by examining contents of stomachs and scats. Here I refer to some of those studies along with others to show specifically the measured, or presumed, impact of coyotes on deer (antelope in some studies). These studies represent all seasons and areas from California to Nova Scotia and as in the overall assessment of diet presented earlier, I show the data regionally to examine for spatial trends.

United States

Western

Most studies from the western United States consider the coyote an insignificant predator on deer. Coyotes scavenge on carrion, and predation on deer, when it does occur, is largely compensatory. Environmental stress is minimal and the food base diverse and available throughout the year. Deer remains were found in 30%-60% of several hundred coyote scats collected throughout the year in California, but also found were 14 species of rodents and 13 species of birds.[20] The coyote in that state has been referred to as a "benign predator and scavenger."[21] Predation on deer, when it does occur, is probably limited to fawns in the spring. In Washington, fawns represented 59% of deer remains in scats and stomachs, and mortality from coyotes was considered compensatory.[22]

Midwest

Studies on the impact of coyotes on deer and antelope populations from scat and stomach analyses have proven variable and equivocal. Deer were present in only 5% of 48 stomachs collected during winter in one study in Oklahoma, while a second study in that state found no trace of deer in winter scats but traces of fawns in 20%-25% of spring and summer samples.[23] A more recent study there found that 20% of summer scats had traces of deer fawns and that 10%-20% of fall-winter samples contained deer remains.[24] Over 63% of scats collected during summer in Wyoming contained remains of mule deer and antelope fawns, while in South Dakota white-tailed deer in scats varied from 37% to 71% in fall-winter and 39% to 48% in spring-summer. Predation by coyotes in that state was considered a significant factor in declines of deer.[25]

In the midwest predation on deer (and perhaps antelope) appears to be significant only in the winter and therefore most important in the northern states. Predation on deer and antelope fawns occurs throughout, although it may be most severe in the south. As we shall see, predator removal experiments have shown that coyotes can suppress deer and antelope populations by reducing recruitment through excessive predation on fawns. In such situations, predation is almost certainly additive to other forms of mortality.

SOUTHCENTRAL

Predation by coyotes has not been shown to significantly influence the overall population dynamics of most deer herds in this region. Deer were present in only 5% of coyote stomachs collected in Arkansas from July to January 1969-1974. In Louisiana deer were found in 18% of coyote stomachs collected in winter, 10% in fall, and 9-29% in spring and summer. Most remains of deer in spring and summer samples were from fawns, although the authors did not comment on the significance of predation on deer herds in that state.[26]

A more recent study (1985-86) of a composite sample of coyote scats and stomachs from Mississippi, Kentucky, Alabama, and Tennessee found fawn remains in 74% of samples collected during fawning and 76% at post-fawning. Those authors concluded that, as coyotes increase (following colonization) they might well exert a negative impact on deer populations.[27]

GREAT LAKES

The presence of deer in over 3,500 coyote scats and stomachs collected in Wisconsin from 1971 to 1973 was lowest in the fall, highest in winter, and intermediate in summer, with an overall occurrence of 27%. That study concluded that there was no relationship between changes in densities of coyotes and deer and that predation on deer was lessened by the availability to coyotes of more accessible species of prey. Those conclusions were supported by a second study in Wisconsin which found deer in 43%-81% of scats collected during the winters of 1975-77. In Michigan deer remains were found in 89%-93% of scats collected during winter from 1956 to 1965, although the authors of that study chose to attribute most of that to coyotes feeding on deer carrion and concluded that coyotes did not control deer numbers in that state.[28]

Although we see an increase in the presence of deer in coyote scats and stomachs collected during winter in this region, early researchers were reluctant to attribute those high rates to direct predation. Rather they preferred to assume that most was from scavenging on carrion, as studies had not yet identified the coyote, especially the rapidly expanding eastern coyote, as an important predator of deer in the northeastern portion of its range.

NORTHEAST

Coyotes did not become established in New England, at least in significant numbers, until the 1950s and 1960s. An early collection of scats from the Adirondack Mountains of New York found white-tailed deer remains in 17% of summer samples and in 39% of winter samples. Predation on deer by coyotes, at that time, was not considered significant. In Connecticut, studies in 1983-86 and 1985-86 found deer in 46% and 60%-75% of fall and winter-trapped coyotes, respectively. Neither study commented on the impact those rates of occurrence might have on deer populations.[29]

Most studies of coyote food habits in the northeastern United States have been in Maine. An early study found deer in 15% of 51 coyotes trapped in fall and early winter from 1968 to 1973. The authors thought most deer were from carrion, and coyotes were not considered important to the total mortality of deer. Henry Hilton examined 80 stomachs of coyotes collected throughout the year from 1973 to 1975 and found 22% contained deer. He also analysed scats and found 41% of those contained deer. By season, Hilton found deer in 62% of the samples taken in winter, 35% in spring, 20% in summer, and 50% in fall. He concluded that deer was an important component of the diet of coyotes during winter in wilderness areas of Maine (severe winters; few alternate prey species). Dan Harrison found deer in 43% of 452 coyote scats collected May-October 1981. He was uncertain about the impact of coyotes upon deer but suggested the impact, if any, would be greatest in heavily forested regions (in agreement with Hilton).[30]

Two other studies in Maine examined scats collected from 1979 through 1982. Seasonal representations of deer were 41% in spring, 10% in summer, 24% in fall, and 58% in winter, and, as in earlier studies, the researchers were uncertain of the impact of coyotes on deer. A fourth study in Maine examined 349 coyote scats collected in winter from inland Maine (forested interior; severe winters) and 288 scats from coastal Maine (forested-agriculture; moderate winters) from 1979-80 through 1982-83.[31]

The 4-year mean representation of deer for the inland samples was 61% and for the coastal samples 52%. The authors concluded that coyote predation on deer could be significant during winter, especially in inland forested wilderness areas, which agreed with earlier conclusions by Hilton and Harrison. Although some of the Maine studies chose not to draw conclusions on the impact of coyotes on deer,[32] it is interesting to note that their data were very similar to results from other studies in which concern was expressed over potential impact of predation on deer in winter. In summary, food habit studies following colonization and establishment of resident coyote populations in Maine found that the occurrence of deer in scats and stomachs during winter varied from 50% to 60%, that the potential for significant impact upon deer populations was real, and that the impact was likely greatest in forested wilderness areas with severe winter weather and few alternate species of prey.

CANADA

QUEBEC

White-tailed deer occurred in 80% of coyote scats collected during winter in 1976-79 in southern Quebec, 50% of those in spring, and 20% in summer. The authors concluded that coyotes could significantly influence fawn survival in spring and both fawn and adult survival in winter.[33] A second study of coyote stomachs from southeastern Quebec (forested farmland) in 1975-77 found no deer in the spring and summer samples, 4% in fall, and 13% in winter. Cattle and hogs appeared in 30% of the samples, and deer on these southern Quebec farmlands were not considered an important prey of coyotes.[34] These two contrasting studies again illustrate the importance of deer to the diet of coyotes in forested wilderness habitats in the northeast, especially in the winter.

ATLANTIC PROVINCES

The first study of coyote feeding habits in Atlantic Canada was by Louis LaPierre at the Université de Moncton who examined contents of stomachs from coyotes collected by trappers in New Brunswick during early winter from 1978 to 1981. The occurrence of deer in this fall-early winter sample was 31%. Although the presence of deer was substantial, LaPierre did not comment on the implications that might have regarding the provincial deer herd.[35] Gary Moore examined 265 stomachs from coyotes trapped in New Brunswick and Nova Scotia during October-January 1978-1981. Deer were present in 24% of those samples; the coyote was considered an opportunistic predator; and the impact of coyotes on deer was uncertain.[36]

During the winters of 1983-85, Dale Morton found deer in 65% of scats collected in Fundy National Park in southern New Brunswick, although he was also uncertain what impact that level of predation might have on the white-tailed deer in the park.[37] I examined scats collected in 1983-84 from northern New Brunswick. The occurrence of deer varied from 4% in summer to 45% in January and I concluded that coyotes could significantly influence overall deer survival during winter (forested wilderness area), especially when snowshoe hares were scarce.[38]

Deer were found in 20% of coyote scats collected in Nova Scotia during the winter of 1982-83.[39] Remains of adult and fawn deer were present in 2% and 18% of scats collected in that province from May to October 1989 and 30% and 13% of scats collected in May-June 1990.[40] None of these authors suggested that coyotes were significantly affecting overall deer survival; samples were small and most were collected during the summer and fall. A much larger collection of scats from Kejimkujik National Park in 1992-94 found the remains of deer in over 80% of scats collected monthly from October through June and between 55% and 62% of scats collected in July and August.[41] Fawn deer hair was common in early summer samples. The high occurrence of deer in summer scats from Kejimkujik National Park was unexpected and unique among food habit studies of coyotes in the northeast.

These selected food habit studies of coyotes suggest several trends, with considerable regional variation, especially through much of the continental United States, where winters can be moderate and the available prey base diverse and abundant. In southern and western states, predation by coyotes on deer is most often restricted to the fawning season, and under certain situations, the impact of that predation upon local or regional populations of deer or antelope can be significant. In the northcentral and northeastern states, the potential for significant impacts upon deer becomes more apparent, especially in forested wilderness areas with severe winters (deep and prolonged snow cover) and fewer species of alternate prey. Studies in Quebec and Atlantic Canada confirm results from northern United States. In much of Nova Scotia and southern New Brunswick, where winters are usually more moderate than in the Gaspé region of Quebec and the northern portions of New Brunswick and Maine, and where settlement and agriculture is quite extensive and alternate prey (e.g., rodents; domestic animals) more available, especially in winter, the impact of coyotes on deer may be measurably less.

2) WINTER TRACKING STUDIES

Tracking in the snow is useful for obtaining information on the winter ecology of large mammals, especially predators such as coyotes and lynx. It can measure habitat use, the frequency of predator behaviour and activities and the frequency of chases of prey species, hunting success and prey use. Knowing the time when tracks were made (often established by following radio-marked individuals) is important when interpreting observations, such as time of kill, time between chases and kills, and number of kills through time. Although this may all sound quite simple and straightforward, tracking can be very difficult and depends upon frequency and duration of favourable weather, as well as snow conditions. Blowing snow can quickly cover tracks, and mild temperatures often make travel and tracking impossible. It can be difficult to accumulate sufficient miles of trails to enable confident conclusions on predator activities to be developed. However, there have been several published accounts of winter tracking studies of coyotes and these will be reviewed by region.

UNITED STATES

NORTHERN MICHIGAN

Coyote trails were followed at 2 study sites from 1956 to 1965. On Beaver Island, in northern Lake Michigan, 322 miles (518 km) of trail were followed and another 505 miles (812 km) of trail on Michigan's Upper Peninsula. During tracking, information was recorded on coyote behaviour, kills, food, and habitat use. The contents of scats collected during tracking is reported elsewhere. These researchers found 52 dead deer during the snowtracking. Only 9, however, were positively attributed to coyote predation. Five had been killed by other predators (some by bobcat), 10 were crippled and lost by hunters, and 28 died from unknown causes (many believed from winter starvation). Eight other deer killed by coyotes were found incidental to the tracking. All but 3 deer were killed in March and April, and deep snows hampered coyotes as much as deer. Coyotes appeared to happen upon deer by chance and gave chase as the surprised deer fled.

Successful chases were short, usually not more than 60 yards (54 m), and the focal point of attack was the throat and head. The authors concluded that coyotes were opportunistic, feeding upon available carrion rather than hunting for elusive game. They suggested that the availability of deer and hare in winter probably determined the distribution and winter habitat selection by coyotes. Coyotes spent more time at deer yards in late winter and spring, and the authors suggested that could be because more carrion was available from starved deer. Deer were most vulnerable during prolonged periods of deep snow, and prey selection was towards the smallest and weakest deer—those which were the least likely to survive the winter anyway. They believed that the coyotes they followed and observed prospered or failed in proportion to food supplies controlled by forces other than predation.[42]

NORTHERN WISCONSIN

Three radio-collared coyotes were tracked 280 km and unmarked coyotes another 124 km from mid-February to April 1976 and from mid-December 1976 to mid-March 1977. In 1976-77 that researcher recorded hunting behaviour and success of coyotes trailed and found the remains of 4 coyote-killed deer. Most deer were killed after mid-February when formation of ice crust favoured the coyote but hindered deer travel. Examination of several fresh kills did not identify wounds to the head and neck as described earlier in Michigan. Rather, wounds were to the rear legs and rump while the neck and head regions were consumed last. In one instance a deer was knocked down and appeared to have died while the coyotes fed on it. The author believed that physical condition and age were important influences on deer vulnerability to coyote predation and that the increased sociality of coyotes following the onset of breeding in February increased hunting success. Pairs and larger groups were thought to be more successful than single coyotes in capturing deer.

Coyotes killed deer only after environmental conditions (spring crusts) gave them an advantage. Also, deer killed by coyotes were not of prime age and would probably have died of other causes, especially during harsh winters with reduced food availability (example of compensatory mortality). The study concluded that coyote predation was not a significant factor influencing the population of deer in that area.[43]

MAINE

Henry Hilton followed coyote trails in winter using methods like those described for the studies in Wisconsin and Michigan. One hundred and nine tracks were followed for 206 km during the winter of 1974-75. Multiple tracks were most common in late winter and spring, supporting the "increased sociality" theory advanced in the Wisconsin study. Single coyote tracks crossed the most deer tracks but rarely pursued deer and made no kills.

Over the 4-month study, coyotes followed 1/3 of the deer tracks they encountered and killed deer on 15% of the trails they followed. Pairs were responsible for 73% of the 15 deer found killed by coyotes. Of 28 deer found killed by coyotes throughout Maine from 1973 through 1976 (includes the 15 from 1974-75) 2 were killed in December, 4 in January, 8 in February, and 14 in March. The preponderance of deer killed in late winter also agrees with studies in Michigan and Wisconsin. Ten of the 14 deer killed from December through February were fawns but only 4 of 14 killed in March were fawns. Hilton thought that the most likely reason for that difference was availability, i.e., fawns are more available in early winter. It might also mean that adults were in better condition in early winter and could escape easier than fawns; in spring adults might be weaker and more susceptible to predation. Nine of 14 adults were either old (more than 5 yr) or exhibited abnormalities. The mean distance of chase was 56 m, very similar to that reported in northern Michigan (60 yds or 55m).

Once physical contact was made, few deer escaped. During the chase, wounds were generally inflicted to the flank, rump, and rib area. Most carcasses exhibited tooth marks in the back of the neck or head, presumably fatal wounds. Feeding began on the exposed flanks and proceeded through the ribs to the body organs.[44]

Canada

New Brunswick

My colleagues and I followed 263 km of coyote trail in a forested wilderness area of northern New Brunswick from January through March 1984. We found 10 deer killed by coyotes during the tracking; 0 in January, 3 in February, and 7 in March, although most tracks were followed in January (106 km) and the least in March (71 km). Kills of hares declined from 13 in January to only 4 in March. We believed this "prey switching" from hares to deer was a function of increased coyote sociality in February and March (similar to previous studies) and easier travel due to snow compaction. Deer were more concentrated in "wintering areas" at that time and energy demands for coyotes were greater. Most coyote-deer encounters were by chance, and chases were short. Deer were brought down from the rear and feeding began at the flank and advanced into the body cavity, like that described in Maine by Hilton. Of 17 deer found killed by coyotes in the study area, 12 (70%) were fawns, and only 1 (6%) was over 3 years old. All deer were in good condition (bone marrow fat: fawns, 57%; yearlings, 63%; 2-year olds, 72%; adults, 92%).[45]

Dale Morton followed 139 km of coyote trails in Fundy National Park in southern New Brunswick during the winters of 1983-84 and 1984-85. He found 11 deer killed by coyotes, and 8 others which he could not directly attribute to predation. Coyotes appeared to "ambush" deer near their beds. Fat in bone marrow from 9 deer killed by coyotes ranged from 9% to 90%, with only 3 suggesting severe malnutrition, prompting Morton to conclude that coyotes are capable of killing healthy deer in winter.[46]

Nova Scotia

Ross Hall, regional biologist for the Nova Scotia Wildlife Division, followed 79 km of coyote trails in the Chignecto Game Sanctuary in northern Nova Scotia during the winters of 1982-83 through 1984-85. Coyotes travelled in groups of 1-4. Only 2 deer were found definitely killed by coyotes, although coyotes fed on 6 additional deer carcasses and 2 moose carcasses. Two of the 6 additional deer were believed also killed by coyotes. Hall also found chases to be short and believed that much predation on deer was compensatory rather than additive. He suggested that when deer herds are high, coyote predation serves to keep populations in balance with range, but when herds are low, coyotes may delay recovery.[47]

Staff of the Nova Scotia Wildlife Branch followed 652 km of coyote trails during the winters of 1989 and 1990.[48] Group sizes varied from 1 (51.4% of total distance) to 6 (0.3% of total distance). Coyotes killed 4 of 19 deer pursued (18% success) and pursuit distances were 40, 45, 117, and 526 m. One unsuccessful chase continued intermittantly for 2 km. These data were updated through the winter of 1991-92 and the results were presented earlier under "Food Habits." [49] Two of the kills were fawns; one was a yearling; and one was an adult. Coyotes appeared to locate prey by sight or possibly by scent when animals were nearby. Coyotes also fed on 44 remains (carrion) of deer, some of which had probably been killed by coyotes earlier. It is interesting that 3 of the 4 kills were by single coyotes, which differs from other tracking studies where chases of deer, and especially kills, were almost exclusively by 2 or more coyotes. In Quebec for instance, a study of winter predation by coyotes on white-tailed deer concluded that:

> "Group living, territorial coyotes were responsible for most of the predation on deer (17 of 18 known cases). We cannot clearly explain why solitary coyotes rarely killed deer. It could be that single coyotes are less capable of catching a deer or that their searching behaviour is oriented to alternative food sources." [50]

Brent Patterson followed 114 km of coyote trail in Kejimkujik National Park during the winters of 1992-93 and 1993-94. He found 30 dead deer, 16 of which were confirmed coyote kills (some of the other 14, many of them older carcasses, may have been killed by coyotes as well). Other animals killed included snowshoe hare (4), ruffed grouse (1), porcupine (3), red squirrel (1), masked shrew (1) and black-capped chickadee (1). [51]

3) PREDATOR REMOVAL STUDIES

Most predator removal studies represent a measured response of prey, often by fawn/ adult doe ratios where fawn mortality is identified as a problem, or by population estimates, following removal of all, or most potential predators. The most useful studies employ control (no predator removal) and experimental (predators removed) study sites, and prey populations are monitored before and after predator removal. These "cause-effect" experiments are useful for measuring the impact of predation on prey, and they avoid many of the biases of estimating the diet of predators from samples of scats and stomachs. Although most such experiments have occurred in western states, and many address the impact on antelope populations from loss of fawns to predation, they are important to our assessment of the potential impact of the eastern coyote on white-tailed deer.

COYOTE-ANTELOPE

OREGON

Pronghorn fawn survival was measured relative to aerial coyote removal from 1985 through 1987 on the Jackass Creek Study Area, Harney County, Oregon. Fawn/doe ratios in August were significantly higher after coyote control (61:100) than before (14:100). The authors suggested that short duration, high intensity coyote removal might be an appropriate management option for pronghorn populations with poor fawn survival during periods of medium to high predator abundance. [52]

UTAH

From 1948 to 1951 four areas were chosen in Utah to study antelope productivity and population response to 1) intensive coyote control (2 sites), 2) periodic control (1 site), and 3) no control (1 site).[53]

> "Antelope fawn losses from summer to winter were greatest in the area with no organized predator control and periodic predator control, while the smallest losses occurred on areas with intensive predator control. Predators ... appear to have been an important factor ... in retarding increase in small antelope herds.... The rabbit ... may have had a decidedly beneficial effect on antelope survival by providing an abundance of food readily available to predators. Periodic predator control was of little value."[54]

More recent research in Utah supported the results of the study conducted 30 years earlier.

> "The rapid increase in the pronghorn herd on Anderson Mesa from 1980 to 1983 was the result of a dramatic rise in the rate of fawn survival and recruitment. High fawn survival was strongly correlated with the removal of coyotes by heliocopter in spring prior to fawning. We conclude that the reduction in coyote numbers during the spring fawning period was directly responsible for the increased fawn survival."[55]

ARIZONA

Coyote control was implemented for a 6-year period on portions of antelope range and not on others. Results of coyote control were measured by the percentage of does with fawns on treated (coyote control) and untreated (no control) ranges.

Table 6: Responses of antelope productivity on sites in Arizona with and without coyote removal (from Arrington and Edwards, 1951, pp. 188-189).

Time of treatment	% does with fawns	
	treated	untreated
1944 - 45	48.3	11.0
1945 - 46	64.0	35.0
1946 - 47	94.3	31.0
1947 - 48	79.0	49.0
1948 - 49	no control - general decline noted	
1949 - 50	86.0	48.0

The authors concluded that antelope fawn crops corresponded closely with the amount and type of predator control work done in each area. To be effective and to avoid ingress from adjacent untreated areas, control must be done over large areas of antelope range.[56]

A second study saw coyotes effectively removed from an area in northcentral Arizona from 1981 through 1983. A rapid increase in the pronghorn herd from 1980 to 1983 was the result of a dramatic rise in the rate of fawn survival and recruitment. High fawn survival was strongly correlated with the removal of coyotes in spring prior to fawning. The authors concluded that the reduction in coyote numbers during the spring fawning period was directly responsible for the increased fawn survival.[57]

NEBRASKA

An aerial coyote control program was conducted in the Box Butte Unit in Nebraska's westcentral Panhandle in May-June 1990 and April-May 1992. Aerial surveys of pronghorns in 1990 showed significantly better fawn:adult female ratios on the coyote kill area in July (70:100) than on the adjoining non-kill area (44:100). Results in 1991 also showed higher ratios on the kill area in both July (76:100 vs 42:100) and August (58:100 vs 35:100).[58]

There are other coyote removal studies across pronghorn antelope range in the American western states and most show similar results. It should be noted, however, that many of these removal studies were initiated *because of* low antelope fawn survival, and populations were low or declining, indicating a problem. This situation is not indicative of antelope populations rangewide, and suppressed fawn survival from high rates of coyote predation is not widespread especially where alternate prey species such as rabbits and hares are abundant. Such situations are normally local or regional in scope. These studies do serve to illustrate that coyotes can adversely affect antelope fawn survival under certain circumstances.

COYOTE-CARIBOU

QUEBEC

In Atlantic Canada Woodland Caribou (*Rangifer tarandus*) once roamed the forests of all four Atlantic Provinces but are now restricted to the province of Newfoundland. Caribou were last reported on Prince Edward Island in 1874, in Nova Scotia in 1925, and in New Brunswick in 1927. In these Maritime Provinces, caribou are believed to have been the casualty of habitat loss and overharvest. The interaction between caribou in Newfoundland and the newly established population of coyotes there may be cause for concern. A small remnant population of Woodland Caribou still remains in Gaspésie Park in southwestern Quebec. In 1987 biologists became alarmed for the future of those caribou when it was determined that although most adult females were giving birth, few calves were surviving their first winter. Radio collars were subsequently attached to 25 calves in 1989 and 1990 to determine their fate and, where relevant, causes of death. Sixteen of the calves died the first summer. Of the 11 dead calves for which the cause of death could be ascertained, 7 were killed by coyotes, 3 by black bears, and 1 by a golden eagle. Following removal of coyotes and black bears from the park and surrounding area between 1990 and 1992, survival of caribou calves increased from approximately 4 per 100 adult females before removal to 10-27 per 100 females after removal. Biologists were reluctant, however, to attribute all or most of the increase in calf survival to removal of predators.[59]

"*While we cannot conclude that the removal of predators caused the increase in recruitment, it is obvious that this removal reduced the mortality rate among [the caribou], at least in the short term."*[60]

Biologists suggested that increased avoidance behaviour by caribou towards coyotes may have also contributed to increased survival of calves.

COYOTE-DEER

WASHINGTON

In 1954 an intensive program of control removed coyotes from an 80,000–acre– study area in western Washington. Subsequent ratios of fawn to doe black-tailed deer increased substantially, whereas no such increase was evident in an area with no coyote control. The authors concluded that "...coyotes may be an important decimating factor on young fawn populations."[61]

TEXAS

A coyote control program was initiated in a 391 ha fenced enclosure on the Welder Wildlife Refuge in south Texas to measure the effects of reducing predation on white-tailed deer.[62] Coyotes were removed from 1973 through 1976 during which time fawn survival increased and the density of deer rose from 34 to 84 per sq km. However, these fenced predator-free deer experienced a decreased reproductive rate and an increase in mortality in the 3-12 month age class. (Coyotes had been killing newborn fawns.) Population growth ceased, but declines did not begin until adult mortality increased 4 or 5 years after predator removal. This study emphasized the need to understand the relationship between deer and its habitat before predator control is initiated. If the deer are already approaching the limits of available habitat, removal of predation allows other factors to control population growth.

A second study in South Texas addressed the impact of predation on productivity of white-tailed deer by removing predators from one area (experimental) and comparing the response of deer there to a second area where predators were not removed (control).[63] A total of 188 coyotes and 120 bobcats were removed from the 2,186 ha experimental area from February through June of 1971 and 1972. Aerial counts in 1971 showed a fawn/doe ratio of 0.47 compared to 0.12 in the control (no predator removal) area. In 1972 these ratios were higher in both areas (more favourable weather and higher productivity) but the fawn/doe ratio on the experimental area remained high (82:100) compared to that on the control area (32:100). Deer populations could be increased with an intensive program of predator removal, but a lack of natural predators would require an increased harvest of deer by hunters to hold populations below levels where starvation, disease, or other factors would begin to take their toll.

Winter weather seldom influences survival and population levels of deer in the southern states. Thus, predation there is more likely to be additive than in northern regions where mortality from predation (to a degree) may be compensated for by declines in other forms of "normal" winter mortality. The extent that predation may be compensatory, of course, continues to be the subject of considerable debate, as is the compensatory nature of hunting.

OKLAHOMA

Coyotes were removed from several areas in Oklahoma and the response of white-tailed deer was measured by fawn/doe ratios.

> "Coyotes were removed from 3 Fort Sill, Oklahoma, white-tailed deer ranges during 1977-80 to determine effects on fawn survival as measured by mid-August to mid-September fawn/doe surveys. Study areas showed increases in fawn/doe ratios of 262%, 92% and 167% the 1st summer following coyote reduction. Prior to coyote reduction in 1976 combined fawn production was 0.37 fawns/doe for the three areas. The 1980 fawn production was 0.94 fawns/doe, an overall study increase of 154%."[64]

Although coyotes significantly impacted deer fawn survival in the Oklahoma study, coyotes had little effect on fawn survival in other areas. Such differences were probably due to available food sources; coyotes feed on the most abundant and available prey, as other coyote-prey studies show. Although removal of coyotes enhanced fawn survival and population growth, the long-term implication for the health of the deer was uncertain due to the potential for overuse of habitat. As shown by the studies in Texas, a surplus of deer often leads to increases in disease and malnutrition and to decreases in herd productivity.

UTAH

Two mule deer winter ranges were studied in northeastern Utah from 1973 to 1976, one with coyote control and one without. At the end of the study, the density of deer on the area with control was 3 times that of the area with no control. In addition, a significantly higher proportion of the fawns entering winter on the area with coyote control survived the winter than on the area without control.[65]

QUEBEC

A small-scale coyote control (removal) study was conducted in a 155 km² area of southern Quebec to measure whether predator removal would enhance white-tailed deer survival and stimulate population growth.[66] Seventeen coyotes were removed from 1979 to 1982, and the frequency of coyote scats on roads indicated a 60% reduction in their numbers during the period of control. Trapping appeared to disrupt family units and decrease the impact of coyote predation on deer survival in winter. Deer numbers had been stable from 1974 to 1979 (500-700 deer). Deer numbers began to increase concurrent with initiation of coyote removal in 1979, and reached 1,700-1,800 (3-fold increase) by 1985. The authors attributed this increase to lower rates of winter mortality but failed to definitely establish that removal of coyotes alone was responsible. However, the evidence suggested that the removal program was certainly a factor in the increase, and the authors did conclude that:

> "Coyote reduction to increase deer numbers appears to be justified on a biological ground."[67]

However, the authors acknowledged the very real limitations of effective coyote removal over large areas, while numerous technical difficulties restrict the practical application of this management option. The study did provide further evidence that on northern deer ranges coyotes can depress populations by high rates of predation in winter.

4) RADIO-TELEMETRY STUDIES

Tracking animals with radio transmitters and monitoring the activities, movements, and often the fates of marked animals by maintaining contact with radio receivers (antennae can be hand-held, mounted on vehicles, or strapped to aircraft) has been used in a number of predator-prey studies. Radio transmittors can be applied to the prey, and the number lost to predation recorded over a specific period of time. Radio marking the predator provides long-term information on home range size and activity patterns and when combined with ground tracking (especially in winter) provides information on the kinds and numbers of prey killed and hunting success (successful vs unsuccessful chases). Such studies have contributed important information on rates of predation and consumption.

OREGON

In southeastern Oregon from 1971 through 1974, predation, mostly by coyotes, was responsible for 55% of 29 mortalities of 106 radio-marked mule deer fawns during their first 45 days of life. Seventy-nine percent of fawn deaths in winter were from predation, mostly by coyotes, and malnutrition was identified as the major predisposing factor. A program of coyote control then removed 755 coyotes. Loss of fawns declined to 13% on the range with coyote control compared to a 65% fawn loss on a comparable range with no control.[68]

OKLAHOMA

Mortality on 35 white-tailed deer fawns radio-marked in 1974 and 1975 was 88%, and 97% of that mortality was from predation by coyotes and bobcats. The author concluded that:

> *"Study results suggest the experimental use of short-term seasonal predator control to allow fawn survival to increase."* [69]

MONTANA

The impact of predation on mule deer fawns was studied on a 250 km² area in north-central Montana from 1976 to 1981. Fawn mortality was related to coyote population levels, availability of alternate prey, and coyote food habits. Mortality of fawns was determined by changes in observed fawn/doe ratios and relocation of radio-collared fawns. The number of coyotes (estimated from howling responses to siren surveys) varied from 34 to 42 throughout the study. Ninety percent of the summer mortality of radio-marked fawns was the result of coyote predation.

> *"…Coyote predation was the major proximal factor influencing mule deer fawn survival on the study area. …*
>
> *Deer population managers should be aware that coyote predation can reduce fawn survival in a nutritionally healthy deer population."* [70]

However, mice, voles, and white-tailed jack rabbits (*Lepus townsendii*) all increased throughout the study. This increased availability of alternate sources of prey to coyotes reduced predation on deer fawns, so that the fawn survival increased to 96% with no detectable decline in coyotes. The authors cautioned that predation rates on fawns can decline, and fawn survival increase, proportionate to the availability of alternate prey species.

> *"Alternate prey population levels and cycle phase should be determined as part of complete evaluations of the effect of coyotes on fawn survival; they should certainly be integrated prior to decisions about whether or not to control coyotes to increase deer populations."*[71]

MASSACHUSETTS

The survival of 37 white-tailed deer fawns marked with radio-transmitters was measured over a 3-year period (1986-88) in western Massachusetts. Deer in Massachusetts increased from 6,000 in the mid-1960s to approximately 40,000 by 1987, even though coyotes had become established there during that time. Fawn survival was among the highest reported from studies using similar radio-telemetry techniques, and the authors concluded that predation on fawns was having little effect on white-tailed deer populations in that state.[72]

TEXAS

A study in south-central Texas measured mortality of 120 radio-equipped white-tailed deer fawns from 1971 through 1973. Loss of fawns averaged 47% during the first several months of life, and predation accounted for 50% of that loss. Although both bobcats and coyotes were present on the study area, most predation was attributed to coyotes. The authors concluded:

> *"There is little doubt that predators can exert a significant effect on white-tailed deer fawns during critical periods."*[73]

The Welder Wildlife Refuge in South Texas has been the site of a long-term study of white-tailed deer and predators. The fate of 81 young fawns marked with radio transmittors was determined in 1965-66. Marked fawns were monitored for 60 days or until death. Seventy-two percent of the fawns died, and predation, mostly by coyotes, accounted for 53% of that mortality.

The authors concluded:

> *...Predation and disease are potentially major causes of mortality of young fawns in this region. ...Coyote predation accounts for the largest loss of young fawns on the Welder Refuge. ...[W]hen evaluating the effects of predation occurring on the Welder Wildlife Refuge, coyotes play a major role in maintaining a stable relationship between this high population of whitetails and their food supply.... However, disease as an independent mortality factor and as a predisposing factor in predation could possibly be even more important as a regulatory force in the population than these data indicate, especially if the coyote populations were diminished."*[74]

A number of distinguished scientists presented a paper at the 56th North

American and Natural Resources Conference on the results of 35 years (1954-1989) of research on white-tailed deer and coyote populations on the Welder Wildlife Foundation Refuge and summarized those results as follows.

"*The immediate response to removal of coyotes was an increase in the deer herd.... The deer herd responded to this treatment [coyote removal] until they began to reduce the food supply [in the enclosure]. When forage became limiting, deer numbers declined, and ... mortality was caused primarily by low food supply.... Increases in density of deer ... were accompanied by increased parasite loads.... [Carcass] weights of yearlings and fawns from inside ... were less than those collected outside.... After the initial decrease ... numbers began to build again much as one would expect when food supplies returned to normal. Coyotes were present [got into the exclosure following earlier removal] during these times and predation probably prevented populations from reaching the high numbers which occurred during the years of predator control. ...*

[We] offer a conclusion short of alleging that coyotes have controlled the deer herd since 1954. We can say unequivocally that coyotes take a large portion of the fawns each year during the first few weeks of life.... Predation and other environmental perturbations acting together are important factors in herd stability. It seems obvious to us that coyotes can be used in management of deer numbers. Control of coyotes need not be a management strategy when numbers are not cropped by hunting or natural means. Conversely, control of coyotes can be a management strategy where there is adequate habitat and deer numbers need to be increased for greater productivity."[75]

One might ask, if the impact of coyotes on deer populations could not be absolutely determined after 35 years of continuous research on one specific study area in southern Texas, can the question ever be adequately resolved? I submit the following as a best-guess scenario of the recent, current, and projected role of the coyote as a dominant predator in the forested ecosystems throughout much of Atlantic Canada.

The coyote became established in New Brunswick during the 1970s, and by the early 1980s breeding territories were most likely established throughout all favourable forested-agricultural habitats. The sequence in Nova Scotia appears to have been 6-8 years later than in New Brunswick (i.e., colonization throughout the 1980s). The first coyotes arrived from northern Maine and perhaps southeastern Quebec, having probably been raised by adults which fed mainly on snowshoe hare and white-tailed deer, especially in winter. White-tailed deer were abundant in both New Brunswick and Nova Scotia, their population increase promoted by favourable winter climate and an abundance of early successional hardwood browse (food) created by expanding forest harvest operations. In many areas winter deer yards were identified and afforded protection. Annual physical condition and reproductive indices and the sex and age structure of autumn harvests suggested a healthy population which had not surpassed the "magical carrying capacity" limits of the range.

Important to our discussion here is that white-tailed deer in the northeast had developed in a "predator-free environment." The eastern timber wolf, historically the dominant large predator of the region, had been absent for over a century, and the only other natural predator of note was the bobcat. (Not to ignore the presence of the eastern panther, but historic low numbers and uncertain distribution suggest that the influence of that predator on deer populations was probably minimal.) Although the bobcat does kill deer, it has never been identified as influencing deer numbers, or even representing a serious predator. (In some southwestern regions, bobcats can be serious predators on new-born fawns.)

The regulated harvest by hunters removed a portion of the deer population each autumn, but those removed represented more of a stimulus to herd productivity than a serious threat to population decline. It is very unlikely that the annual legal harvests removed more than 20-25% of provincial deer herds, and given the measured productivity for northeastern deer, a removal rate of that magnitude, especially in the autumn, should not cause population declines. Also, a certain proportion of the deer removed by hunting in the autumn is compensatory; i.e., those animals would have succumbed to other sources of mortality through the winter. Thus, there are no substantive data to suggest that provincial deer populations were approaching the "carrying capacity" threshold of their range prior to the recent region-wide numerical declines.

Colonizing coyotes found white-tailed deer in abundance, and these "predator-free" populations had not developed, or perhaps had lost, behavioural patterns which increase survival within a forested environment containing significant numbers of natural predators, e.g., timber wolves or coyotes. For most of the year, coyotes in spruce-fir forests depend upon snowshoe hare for much of their diet, supplemented with any other additional foods they are able to obtain (e.g. carrion, small mammals, birds, fruits, and berries). Even in winter, prior to the deep snows, coyotes continue to seek out small game and the unhampered white-tailed deer remain difficult to capture. As snows accumulate through January and February, deer become more restricted in their activities and patterns of distribution, and in northern portions of their range, they often move into traditional areas of winter deer concentration. These "deer yards" usually contain a canopy of mature spruce, fir, and pine which prevents deep snows from accumulating on the forest floor. Deer yards are frequently located on south facing slopes along stream valleys. (Southern exposures enhance solar warmth and help regulate body temperature.) In regions of low snow accumulation (e.g. south-western Nova Scotia) deer remain more widely distributed in winter and are less restricted in their mobility. However, most coyotes still have access to deer in winter, even if their opportunities for killing deer are less than in more northern regions. All evidence, both direct and circumstantial, suggests that coyotes preyed heavily in winter on the abundant and naive white-tailed deer in central and northern New Brunswick throughout the 1980s. Even approximate measures of the magnitude of that predation are difficult to assess, but there can be little doubt that it was sustained and significant. In contrast to the autumn harvest of deer by hunters, when much of the removal is compensatory, the late winter and early spring loss to coyotes is largely additive. If we assume a maximum spring population of 12,000 coyotes (0.15/km^2) in New Brunswick during the mid-1980s (it may well have been higher), and an average of 2 deer per coyote per year (probably minimal given the abundance and availability of deer), coyotes could have removed 25,000-30,000 deer annually, very similar to the legal harvest at that time. While coyotes in southern New Brunswick may have consumed less, those in the north may have consumed more, so the average of 2 deer per coyote per year seems reasonable.

A radio-collared adult female coyote and her two pups which my colleagues and I followed through the winter of 1983-84 in northern New Brunswick killed at least 10 deer during January through March. That total represents deer carcasses that we found during tracking of those 3 coyotes for 3 months only and most certainly does not represent the total killed throughout the year. In wolf and white-tailed deer predator-prey systems in northern forested habitats, each wolf may kill up to 15 deer per year.[76] Realizing that an unmeasured but significant number of deer are shot illegally each year, the total loss of deer to all sources of predation (human and natural) was substantial, and apparently sufficient to cause a fairly rapid population decline. The same scenario most likely applied to Nova Scotia, although predation rates may have been less, given the reduced severity of winter weather throughout most of that province.

A popular misconception is that deer outside of regions of heavy snowfall and prolonged and deep winter snow cover are free from predation from coyotes. Rates of predation in late winter may be less, but one or two significant snowfalls can quickly create conditions, although perhaps temporary, which can cause substantive losses of deer. A study of coyotes in Kejimkujik National Park in southwestern Nova Scotia provides an interesting observation.[77] This area of the Maritime Provinces experiences mild to moderate winters, and climate has not been considered a major factor in deer mortality. If snow depths are the main factor contributing to winter predation by coyotes on deer in the northeast, predation here would be expected to be minimal or negligible. Following a heavy snowfall in mid-March 1993, a group of 3 or 4 coyotes killed 5 deer (probably within the same hour) which were bedded down and severely restricted by the deep snow. A sixth deer was killed several days later by this same group of coyotes. The group consisted of an adult male (radio-collared), an adult female, and 1 or 2 coyotes of unknown sex and age (perhaps pups of the adult pair). The coyotes fed on only one of the first 5 deer and consumed most of the sixth. They did not return to any of the kills. Much predation by coyotes on deer is by chance (such as the incident in Kejimkujik Park); i.e., one or more coyotes happen to intercept a deer, and if the deer hesitates or does not detect the danger in time, the chase can be short and final. Lack of snow, or shallow snow depths, does not necessarily exclude predation on deer.

A question often asked is, if coyotes significantly impact upon deer in parts of the northeast, how can states like Mississippi (twice the size of Nova Scotia) support 400,000 coyotes and maintain high populations and harvests of deer? The most likely reasons include: 1) an absence of the severe winters that serve not only to concentrate deer and restrict their mobility and movements (facilitating predation) but also to limit access by coyotes to alternate food sources, 2) the availability of more abundant and diverse sources of alternate prey, especially hares, rabbits and rodents, and 3) different behavioural patterns developed in response to those differences in environment and food availability.

In southern latitudes, lack of cold temperatures and snow cover in winter not only allows deer greater mobility and aids escape from predators but also enhances herd productivity (more young produced and greater overall survival), thus reducing the numerical response of deer herds to coyote predation. Coyotes may prey on deer in the south but much of that predation is on young fawns. In highly productive deer populations, a moderate loss of fawns to coyote predation would prove insignificant to overall herd dynamics. Probably more significant to the ability of a region to support both high densities of deer and coyotes is the year-round availability of an abundant supply of alternate food, including rodents, hares, rabbits, fruit, berries, carrion, domestic stock and various forms of human garbage. The northern spruce-fir forests of New Brunswick in February represent a far different environment to both deer and coyotes than the food-rich agricultural hardwood forests, swamps, and savannahs of the southern United States.

9 PREDATORS AND PREDATION

"Nature is really a predator-prey arena, for most living things eat others and are in turn eaten. This is the strategy of life in nature....[It] is not easy to immediately recognize the significance of the concept that death is necessary for, and a part of, life."[1]

The colonization of eastern North America by the coyote would have received far less attention if coyotes did not kill and eat deer and sheep. In fact, without the growing controversy and debate which has developed with the arrival of the eastern coyote, I probably wouldn't have written this book. I know of no other animal, predator or prey, which has created such depth and intensity of public feeling, from those who will accept nothing less than total removal to those who advocate that humans abstain from interference of any kind in the natural state of wild ecosystems. Surely the best path lies somewhere in between. To identify the most appropiate course of management for the eastern coyote, it is necessary to assess the role of this new predator in the eastern forested ecosystem objectively. In earlier chapters I have provided the reader with information on the biology and ecology of the eastern coyote, as best we know it, and a historical summary of colonization and taxonomy. I will now review some of the early and current thought on predation in general and consider how it may apply to the eastern coyote and white-tailed deer in particular.

A lack of information, or even worse, a profusion of misinformation, has been responsible for much of the "great debate" over the coyote throughout its range in eastern North America. Having said that, there are also the overriding socio-aesthetic and socio-economic considerations which influence how each of us views the coyote and most of the other wild creatures with which we share the planet. These considerations (i.e., individual beliefs and philosophies; dollar values) further cloud the issue with emotional biases and personal prejudices. It may give us pleasure to see a coyote run across a field, unless we have lambs in the pasture. It may be spiritually rewarding to hear the chorus of coyotes at day's end, but that twilight song may sound different to the farmer who lost a prize ewe to those same coyotes the previous evening. So it is with the cross-country skier who receives a large measure of personal reward from seeing coyote tracks in the snow, or perhaps catching a fleeting glimpse of a pair of coyotes crossing the trail ahead. Those same tracks in the snow leaving a secluded deer yard have different meaning to the game officer who just examined a deer carcass left by the female and her mate. It is the game officer who must answer to the local Fish and Game Association when they ask why the deer populations are declining and what is being done about it. Wildlife that provides one person recreation or sport may, at the same time, be a serious competitor or agricultural pest to another.

It is equally reasonable to some that the killing of wild game for sport can no longer be condoned in an affluent and civilized society with changing social norms and moral values. A coyote kills a deer to survive; most hunters kill deer as a supplement to a diet already rich in animal protein. Some have a strong personal conviction against killing for sport. This moral attitude towards wildlife and the consumptive use of wildlife, given our unique role as animals capable of rational thought, advocates abstinence or a moratorium on all forms of killing for sport. It is difficult to argue against that philosophy on moral grounds but the argument is less convincing on biological grounds.

The first issue to be identified, debated, and resolved is that of natural versus unnatural, or human-influenced, ecosystems. There are few ecosystems in eastern North America which have not been influenced to some extent by human development and disturbance, and in many cases that disturbance has been substantial. Today there are few remaining stands of old-growth forests in the northeast. Changes to the forests from timber harvest and intensive silviculture has accelerated rapidly in recent years, and, contrary to what some people suggest, "unnatural" changes to the forest system (large scale forest harvest and replanting) do not mimic natural long-term rotations in forest stands created by fire and disease. We must therefore recognize that most populations of wildlife in northeastern forests are developing within an environment which is far different from pre-European forest systems. We are most likely seeing species and populations struggling within ecosystems which are influenced and controlled by new or greatly modified environmental forces and stresses. It is somewhat naive to suggest a hands-off (natural) course of management for wildlife species which are themselves surviving and evolving within an ecosystem greatly modified by human disturbances (unnatural). Thus, the first issue is "to manage or not to manage." A not-to-manage strategy is very simple (do nothing), but the consequences, which are uncertain, may be complex and far-reaching. The question may be asked, "If humans have taken away most of the natural defences from his domesticated livestock, is there no moral responsibility to protect them from being inhumanely killed by predators?" Questions of moral values and judgements represent part of the overall philosophical discussion, but other than to give cause for thought, I will pursue them no further here.

White-tailed deer expanded their range into the spruce-fir forests of the northeastern United States and eastern Canada as a result of abundant forage created by forest harvesting during the latter part of the past century. Other factors which contributed to that expansion were less severe winters (perhaps) and the absence of wolves. The creation of forest openings allowed the development of early successional plant communities which supported an abundance of stems and twigs of hardwood trees and shrubs, the preferred winter forage of white-tailed deer in the northeastern forests. Other than humans, the deer lived within a relatively predator-free environment. For the past 100 years, therefore, white-tailed deer populations in the northeast have lived within an unnatural forest system, i.e., one which has been extensively modified through forest harvesting, and one free of natural predators, especially the genus *Canis*, the natural predator of ungulates in forest systems in eastern North America. This unnatural forest and white-tailed deer system that humans have developed in the northeast must be kept in mind during discussion of ungulate-habitat and ungulate-predator systems.

First, what population controls operated the "predator-free" deer-habitat model prior to the arrival of the eastern coyote? Graeme Caughley described a hypothetical model where, free of climatic or predator constraints, ungulates (hoofed mammals, usually plant-eating) introduced into a previously unoccupied area increase to a peak density and then crash steeply to a considerably lower level.[2] Subsequent population changes are heavily dampened and density finally steadies well below the initial peak. The vegetation may follow a similar trajectory, first falling in abundance as the population rises, increasing again as the animals crash, and finally settling at a density and rate of production at equilibrium with a relatively constant pressure of grazing. This simple ungulate-habitat model is not totally applicable in the northeast where deer reproduction and mortality are significantly influenced by climatic stress, and the abundance and distribution of winter food is influenced by changes to the forest habitat from timber harvest and management.

The "carrying capacity" of a unit of habitat is usually accepted as the maximum density of plant-eating animals that can be sustained indefinitely without reducing the quantity or quality of vegetation. In more temperate situations, where winter stress is minimal or absent, the goal of wildlife management is to maintain populations just below the carrying limits of its habitat. Thus, by regulating harvests and manipulating population growth, a maximum number of animals could be removed annually, while maintaining a high rate of reproduction and juvenile survival without reducing the habitat's inventory of food by overuse. In this rather hypothetical world, the theory of harvesting dynamics rests on the assumption that, at least after the first year of life, hunting mortality and natural mortality are exactly compensatory – the harvesting of one individual reduces natural mortality by one (i.e., the harvested animal would have died from some natural cause).[3] If hunting mortality and natural mortality exactly compensate, the resources made available by the death of one animal are released for use by others. Caughley cautions that the rules implied by exactly compensatory mortality have never been recorded for any ungulate population. Rates of natural mortality, however, are certainly less for low than high ungulate populations, but it is never negligible. Thus, in theory, a greater rate of harvest can be sustained by deer populations at high densities than by those at low densities. How does this conceptual model of deer, habitat, carrying capacity, natural mortality and compensatory mortality relate to the white-tailed deer in northeastern spruce-fir forests? Probably not very well at all, especially with the additional mortality from predation introduced by the eastern coyote.

Deer harvest records for New Brunswick and Nova Scotia (and many other provinces or states in the northeast) show that populations, as indicated by numbers harvested, have been dynamic; their numbers have fluctuated through time in an environment free of significant natural predation (*Figure 14*). It is almost certain, and quite generally accepted, that significant population changes were driven by changes in mortality caused by climate-related stress in winter rather than by legal harvest (we know very little about the significance of illegal harvest to total mortality but in some areas it is estimated to be equal to the legal harvest.) Mortality from severe overuse of food resources may have occurred at local levels during initial population expansion, but, due to extensive forest harvest operations and the subsequent abundance of a "standing crop" of winter deer forage, overuse of range has not likely influenced regional trends of white-tailed deer in the recent past. There is a definite distinction between "standing crop" of forage and "availability" of forage in winter, the latter influenced by winter severity (depth, consistency and duration of winter snow and ambient temperatures). Thus, white-tailed deer populations fluctuated within an "unnatural" forest system where densities were influenced most by winter climatic conditions and where deaths from malnutrition and starvation often surpassed annual recruitment.

A series of wolf-ungulate models have been proposed which are worth reviewing for their possible application to the coyote and white-tailed deer predator-prey model now developing in parts the northeast.[4] The analogy between the role of the eastern coyote and that of the timber wolf as predators upon white-tailed deer in the spruce-fir forests of the northeast appears real. Although the role of the coyote as a predator on deer has been reviewed earlier, it is appropriate to make further mention here.

But first, how effective are wolves in influencing numerical trends in white-tailed deer populations? Not surprisingly, like most predator-prey questions, the extent to which wolves limit white-tailed deer populations remains unclear. David Mech provides a good review of past and current scientific thought on wolf-ungulate predator-prey interactions[5] and explains that the frontier mentality of dead wolves meaning live deer failed to consider the concept of compensatory mortality and compensatory reproduction. If a wolf (or coyote) kills a deer which would have soon died from some other cause, such as starvation during a harsh winter, does the predator actually have a negative effect on the population? If predation increases the productivity or survival of remaining members of a deer population, is it really harmful? The pendulum began to swing in favour of the predator. The possibility that losses to predators and to hunting could be compensated for by fewer prey lost to other forms of natural mortality (e.g., disease and parasites, old age, accidents) fascinated the scientist, the hunter, and the general public alike. Predators maintained healthy prey populations in balance and harmony with their environment. This new thought about predator-prey systems developed a backlash against predator control.

However, no two systems are exactly alike, and the precise mechanisms driving one predator-prey model may be quite different from another. Deep snows in northern

Figure 14: A 50-year record of deer harvest in New Brunswick and Nova Scotia. A region-wide decline in deer which began in the mid-1950s in Nova Scotia and during the early 1960s in New Brunswick occurred prior to colonization by the eastern coyote. Such broad regional declines in deer populations were probably initiated by mortality and reduced herd productivity from severe winters and consequent reduced availability of food. Predation by coyotes may now prevent deer populations in many parts of the northeast from reaching such high densities and may accelerate population declines during times of extreme winter stress.

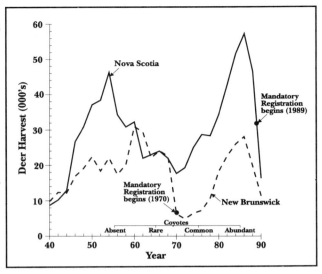

Figure 15: Annual snowfall at Moncton, and 25-year deer harvest for the province of New Brunswick.

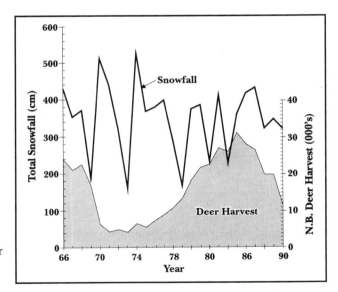

New Brunswick and Maine may lead to significant losses of deer to coyotes in late winter, and those losses to coyotes may be additive to other forms of mortality, so may contribute to population decline. In contrast, lower winter severity in most of Nova Scotia, southern New Brunswick, and much of the northeastern states may allow deer greater mobility in winter and provide coyotes greater access to alternate sources of prey (small mammals, snowshoe hare). Predation on deer there may be largely compensatory, with periods of significant predation limited to a few brief periods of severe winter snows. However, as suggested by the recent studies of Brent Patterson in Kejimkujik National Park, and described earlier, coyotes may rely heavily on deer for food, both winter and summer, even in southwestern Nova Scotia. This behaviour may indicate low availability of buffer prey species or factors which we know little or nothing about.

Two facts are becoming clear: 1) predator/prey ratios may vary considerably between systems, and 2) the predator/prey ratio is critical in determining the degree to which predators may limit prey.[6] Recent studies (several mentioned earlier) have shown that winter severity and human harvest may influence prey density, alter predator/prey ratios, and influence the effect of predator upon prey. David Mech sees a trend of the pendulum of public perception towards predator-prey systems swinging back to where it was, i.e., the belief that predators can significantly influence prey populations and that reduction of predators (reduced predator/prey ratios) can, under certain conditions, contribute positively to maintaining or enhancing prey populations. Mech hopes that the pendulum does not reach the other extreme again, as that position is clearly unwarranted, and the public should realize that refinements are as necessary in wildlife management as in any other science.

> "In the northern part of its range, the whitetail's need to contend with snow and low temperatures adds significantly to its vulnerability. Hindered mobility in deep snow (46 cm or more), reduced food intake, increased exposure to cold (and resulting weight loss) each winter may kill some individuals outright or, under less extreme conditions, greatly dispose them to predation. In addition, since fawns are in utero [developing within the female] throughout this energetically stressful period, those born following severe winters have a low viability."

Mech concludes that, under certain circumstances, coyotes can influence deer numbers.

> "...The possible additive effect of coyote predation on deer populations also must be considered. Thus, even though a coyote density may not be high enough in a particular area by itself to affect deer numbers seriously, when added to the noncompensatory mortality caused by bears, bobcats, domestic dogs, weather, accidents, drowning, etc., coyote predation may have a significant impact."

Recognizing the evidence which suggests that coyotes, under certain conditions, can control deer numbers, Mech also comments on why similar situations are less evident in wolf-white-tailed deer systems.

> "... It is reasonable to ask why a full-time predator such as the wolf cannot necessarily limit deer numbers when a part-time predator, such as the coyote, can. The answer is that coyotes, which weigh about half what wolves weigh, can achieve densities perhaps five times as high as the usual wolf densities. Also, coyote numbers can be subsidized by a multitude of alternate types of prey, whereas the wolf depends much more exclusively on deer, especially in winter when there are few alternative food sources. Thus, if the wolf overexploits its primary food supply, its own population must decline... which tends to relieve pressure on deer numbers."[7]

The single-prey versus multiple-prey systems are important for understanding coyotes and their prey in the northeast. The wolf (single-prey system) is less able to maintain numbers when white-tailed deer populations decline beyond a specific level. The coyote (multiple-prey system) can maintain viable populations (at reduced levels) following declines in deer numbers by switching to alternate prey. In northeastern spruce-fir forests in winter, the snowshoe hare represents the only reliable alternate source of food, and in times of hare scarcity, and white-tailed deer decline, coyote numbers could be seriously reduced. At such times, coyotes may make greater use of agricultural habitat, and greater use of carrion from domestic stock (as discussed elsewhere). David Mech refers to the ability of wolves to kill white-tailed deer most readily when snow conditions in late winter hinder travel by deer but allow the support of wolves. This situation has also been identified as the time when predation by coyotes on white-tailed deer is greatest in the northeast.

There is substantial debate on whether the recent decline in deer populations in New Brunswick and Nova Scotia was a function of winter severity alone or a combination of winter severity, predation, illegal hunting, and loss of forested winter cover from timber harvest operations. Again, what do the winter weather records show? In the absence of deep winter snows which restrict deer mobility, temperature has little effect on survival of deer. I have chosen to examine total snowfall as the indicator of winter severity, and have selected the records for Moncton, New Brunswick, the approximate geographical centre of the Maritimes, as the data set to compare with the deer harvest in New Brunswick. There are other measures of winter severity, of which snowfall is only one part, but over the long term, total snowfall is perhaps the most significant factor influencing deer survival during winter in northern forested wilderness habitats.

The long-term (25 years: 1966-1990) average annual snowfall at the Moncton airport as measured by Atmospheric Environment Service, Environment Canada was 348 cm (*Figure 15*). The harvest of deer in New Brunswick (and Nova Scotia) began a 5-fold increase from the early 1970s through the mid-1980s during which time the annual snowfall at Moncton was greater than the long-term average in 8 of 12 years (1974 through 1985). The harvest of deer declined through the next 5 years (1986 through 1990) during which time the annual snowfall was greater than the long-term average in 3 of those 5 years. A closer look at *Figure 15* shows an interesting trend, which may or may not be real. As the annual deer harvest approached 20,000 in the early 1980s, total snowfall appeared to influence the numbers of deer killed the next hunting season. Above-average snowfalls in 1980 and 1981 slowed the increase in deer, whereas a low snowfall in 1982 was followed by a 20% increase in the harvest in the fall of 1983. Snowfall in 1983 was greater than in any of the previous 10 years, and the harvest of deer subsequently declined in 1984. The heavy snowfall of 1983 was followed by the second lowest in 10 years, followed by a record harvest of deer in the province in the fall of 1985. Life was good for the deer hunter. Then came 3 consecutive winters of above average snowfall. In 1987 more snow fell than in any of the previous 12 years, and the deer herd entered a free fall.

Was snowfall alone responsible for the decline in deer? No one knows for certain.

Severe winters can inflict direct mortality on deer as well as reduce productivity of females the following spring. A look at *Figure 15* does show, however, that when the deer harvest began to increase in the mid-1970s there were above average snowfalls 4 consecutive years (1974-1977), while the greatest snowfall in the past 25 years occurred in 1974. However, when deer numbers are low the response of deer populations to environmental stress is less evident, although the magnitude of that response relative to population size may be similar. A decline in the deer harvest from 6,000 to 3,000 would be of less concern than a decline from 30,000 to 15,000 although both represent a 50% reduction. (Note: The reader should be aware that adjustments in the lengths of hunting seasons and bag limits have influenced the intensities of changes to harvest statistics.)

A 50-year record of deer harvests for Nova Scotia and New Brunswick shows 2 very distinct peaks each followed by sharp declines (*Figure 14*). The one major difference in the two declines is that the earliest (1955-1970 in Nova Scotia; 1962-1972 in New Brunswick) occurred when coyotes were rare or absent, and the latest (mid- to late-1980s to the present) occurred when coyotes were abundant. The severity of the most recent declines, and results from research which show moderate to high rates of consumption of deer in winter by coyotes in many parts of the northeast, suggest that predation by coyotes served to amplify a decline initiated by environmental stress. The predator-prey scales were tipped in favour of the predator, and deer populations tumbled. (Timber harvesting, which caused the progressive loss of older-aged softwood stands required by deer for shelter during winters of high snowfall may also have played a part in this decline.)

Although history shows that deer in predator-free northeastern forests have experienced population changes due to severe winters and restricted food availability, predation by the eastern coyote can now accelerate those declines and suppress population recovery. Confirmation of the latter claim will require longer monitoring of coyote-white-tailed deer systems in the northeast. However, given the evidence at hand and studies of predator-prey systems from other northern forested regions, and assuming that coyotes will maintain viable although reduced breeding populations in spite of reduced numbers of white-tailed deer, many parts of the northeast may never again see deer densities comparable to those which existed prior to colonization by the eastern coyote. What remains to be established are the numerical limits within which deer populations will fluctuate relative to this new predator-prey system. Doug Pimlott and Lloyd Keith both suggest that a limiting effect by predators can be viewed as an evolutionary norm for ungulates.[8] This further suggests that the effects of coyotes on white-tailed deer in the northeast, whatever they may be, should be viewed as a natural system rather than as an unnatural predator-free and food limiting system.

Descriptive models for wolf-ungulate (deer, moose, caribou) systems (mentioned earlier) have been proposed; they help identify situations where wolf control may or may not increase ungulate numbers.[9] Given the similarity of the evolving coyote-white-tailed deer model in the spruce-fir forests of the northeast to wolf-ungulate models in other northern forested systems, it may be useful to examine the applicability of those models to the situation in the northeast. Seven of 18 studies of wolf-ungulate interactions in North America concluded that predation by wolves was the major limiting factor of the ungulate populations, 6 concluded that weather, forage and human harvest complicated the predator-prey interaction, and 5 concluded that wolves were not limiting their ungulate prey.[10] The models showed the interactions of an ungulate population with its "nutrition/climate" level and predators. The predator-prey model in the northeast is probably still evolving, so it is difficult to ascribe any of the models to the current and possibly temporary situation, i.e., *coyotes are now creating a predator-prey model for this region.* The ultimate model will resemble one where ungulate (white-tailed deer) populations are kept well below the regional nutrition/climate level by a predator (coyote) which maintains a viable breeding population at reduced levels of deer by taking advantage of a variety of other (buffer) food sources.

Alternate or buffer prey species may influence coyote-deer systems in one of two ways: 1) buffer species may allow coyotes to maintain densities which exert additional mortality on a declining deer population, or 2) increasing alternate prey may reduce predation on the deer population, thus allowing numerical stability or increase.[11] Either situation may apply in coyote-white-tailed deer-snowshoe hare systems in the northeast, depending upon an array of influencing variables (e.g., relative densities of coyotes, deer, and hares; winter severity; quantity and quality of deer habitat; hunting pressure). A probable coyote-white-tailed deer model for the spruce-fir forests of the northeast is shown in *Figure 16* where the loss of deer biomass from a pre-coyote, unnatural, food-limited model to a post-coyote, natural, coyote-deer model might best be referred to as a "predator pit" (the gap between the upper numerical limits of deer populations with and without predators).

Figure 16: Colonization of the northeast by the coyote has introduced a new and important predator into the forested ecosystem. The unnatural predator-free system which the white-tailed deer occupied has been replaced by a natural predator/prey system, one where numbers of deer will be kept lower than before the arrival of the coyote, population changes will be less robust, and winter severity will influence predation by coyotes and short-term population trends.

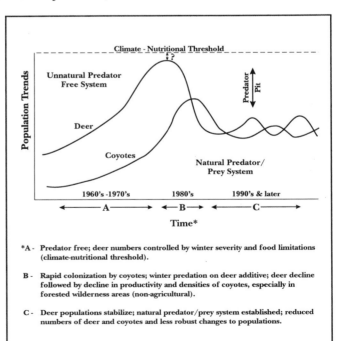

*A - Predator free; deer numbers controlled by winter severity and food limitations (climate-nutritional threshold).

B - Rapid colonization by coyotes; winter predation on deer additive; deer decline followed by decline in productivity and densities of coyotes, especially in forested wilderness areas (non-agricultural).

C - Deer populations stabilize; natural predator/prey system established; reduced numbers of deer and coyotes and less robust changes to populations.

151

White-tailed deer on the Gaspé Peninsula of Quebec live in spruce-fir forests and face winter conditions similar to deer in northern New Brunswick. Coyotes colonized most of the Gaspé Peninsula during the 1970s and 1980s in steps similar to the sequence of colonization by coyotes in New Brunswick. Michel Crête addressed the interactions of coyotes and white-tailed deer on the Gaspé Peninsula at a recent conference in Halifax, Nova Scotia.

> "Harvest of deer bucks dropped from 1,094 in 1986 to 143 in 1991 during a sequence of harsh winters, which reflected population size. Hunting ceased in 1992 and a program to stimulate coyote harvest by trappers was set up. We studied coyote ecology between 1988 and 1992. Deer made up 98% of the food of coyotes using one of the last deer wintering areas in 1992, and they seemingly killed [more than] 20% of the deer ... in the area at the beginning of the winter although the season was mild. In the centre of the province, coyotes ate a variety of food, dominated by fruits, microtines [a subfamily of rodents which includes voles and lemmings], hare, and woodchuck during the snow-free period, but the feeding habits changed between 1988 and 1991. Coyotes were territorial in the boreal forest of the interior during summer, but left the area in winter; ... habitat used in winter was unknown, but it is suspected that coyotes migrated to deer wintering areas or close to human settlements."[12]

During 33 days in the Bonaventure deer yard on the Gaspé Peninsula in the winter of 1991-92, biologists found 37 deer carcasses. The deaths of at least 32 of the deer were directly attributed to predation by coyotes. All the deer had been in good physical condition, and the mortality to coyotes was considered to be additive.[13]

> "Coyote populations should decrease on the peninsula in the future because of the scarcity of the main winter food item, deer. On the other hand, it is not certain that white-tailed deer can persist because of frequent harsh winters coupled with the presence of coyotes. I propose that the boreal forest of the interior constitutes a sink habitat for coyotes [i.e., areas of low coyote productivity], but that some source habitat [i.e., areas of high coyote productivity] will persist around human settlements. Variation in winter severity should create fluctuations in the deer/coyote system."[14]

There is no other predator-prey system to compare with what is presently developing between coyotes and deer in the northeast. Higher densities of coyotes and their ability, at least seasonally, to switch their diet from ungulates to smaller prey sets this smaller but more efficient canid predator apart from the larger, more specialized, and more vulnerable wolf. It is this uncertainty of how successful the coyote may be in maintaining viable populations in spite of declining white-tailed deer that makes predictions of final predator-prey ratios in the northeast risky. The importance of fluctuating snowshoe hare populations to the maintenance of coyote densities and the suppressive impact that coyotes may have on population increases of that species (see "Prey Dependency") further complicates an already complex predator-prey system.

10 PREDATOR CONTROL

"Because predators kill game it has been assumed that any reduction in predator numbers will create a corresponding increase in game. It is this basic premise that is open to question."[1]

These words were penned 50 years ago by Aldo Leopold, the father of modern-day wildlife management. Have we progressed in our attitude towards, and in our under-standing of, predators and predation over the past half century? The conflict between man (the steward and herder of domestic animals) and predators developed as part of the pastoral industry, and as chronicled from earliest biblical times the loyal shepherd stood guard to protect his flock from the evil intent of beast, bird, or man. In North America the war on predators began with early European settlement – the first bounty law was passed by colonial lawmakers of Massachusetts in 1630. As the dwindling wild herds of plains bison were replaced by sheep and cattle, the removal of large carnivores became an important issue. It wasn't long before numbers of grizzly bear, mountain lion, wolf, and even the golden eagle became decimated throughout large portions of early pre-settlement range. The one predator which showed as much resolve for survival, and even expansion, as humans showed for its extermination was the coyote. This small wild canid was first ignored as farmers and ranchers were preoccupied with their battle against the larger and more dangerous predators. As the wolves, bears, and mountain lions fell before the onslaught and became locally exter-minated, or greatly reduced in numbers, and their perceived threat to the settlers largely eliminated, the ubiquitous coyote inherited the role as "public enemy number 1" and became the target of extensive and costly programs of predator control.

In the early 1900s, coyotes and wolves continued to inflict unacceptable losses to sheep and cattle ranchers in the western United States. Between 1907 and 1914 the Bureau of Biological Survey of the United States Department of Agriculture conducted numerous studies and published many bulletins and manuals on methods for their control. To address mounting public pressure for some form of government intervention to stop or reduce those losses, the United States Congress appropriated $125,000 in 1915 for the Bureau of Biological Survey to enter directly into predator control activities. This responsibility was later transferred to the Division of Wildlife

Services in the Bureau of Sport Fisheries and Wildlife. These federal efforts were complemented by programs initiated by many states and predator control efforts reached a peak in the 1930s and 1940s.

Research, however, began to show evidence which questioned predator control as an effective method for reducing predator populations, at least to the extent that reductions significantly reduced losses of wild game populations. And here lies the root of much of the controversy and misunderstanding about predation and the effectiveness of predator control. *The objective of early predator control efforts was to protect domestic livestock* and to that end, along with better methods of fencing and herding, those efforts proved quite effective. Early programs of wildlife management, in efforts to restore many of the populations of game species devastated by human intervention, introduced predator control as one of the more visible, and perhaps more easily measured, methods to achieve their objectives. The large carnivores, which had been largely eliminated from rangeland and had become limited to pockets of wilderness, were further pursued and persecuted under the guise of game management in efforts to increase populations of "useable" wildlife species.

While the value of local predator control efforts could be measured and evaluated by reduced losses of sheep and cattle, it was more difficult to use that measure to justify the control of predators in wild natural ecosystems. Wildlife research began to learn more about the complex interrelationships between predators, prey, and their habitat. The concept of compensatory mortality, made popular by such early conservationists as Paul Errington, redefined the "eye for an eye" philosophy of predator removal, and introduced a whole new dimension to the study of natural, and unnatural, ecosystems.

As mentioned earlier, the pendulum began to swing in favour of the predator. If mortality from predation was largely compensated for by reduced losses from other sources (e.g. disease, accidents, malnutrition) then mortality from hunting should be equally compensated for. The concept that mortality from hunting might be largely compensatory became especially popular in the field of waterfowl management. Large banding and recovery data sets were subjected to sophisticated statistical analyses (although that was not the original intent of the waterfowl banding program) and many scientific papers were published to prove or disprove the theory of compensatory mortality. Without an extended review of those studies here, suffice to say that the issue remains unresolved. Most population ecologists agree, however, that the extent which mortality from predation and hunting may be compensatory is a matter of degree. Low levels of mortality from predation and/or hunting may be largely compensatory, and breeding populations may be unaffected. As the proportion of a population lost to predation or hunting increases, so does the possibility that part of the loss is additive, i.e., it adds to the total annual mortality. Thus, each predator-prey situation must be assessed individually; generic management prescriptions are seldom applicable.

Paul Errington recognized habitat conditions as the primary determinant of population levels among prey animals.[2] He recognized a "threshold of vulnerability" – a level of numbers below which prey animals in a given habitat are relatively secure from predation and above which they are readily taken by predators. This concept relates to the influence of predator-prey ratios on rates of predation and how populations of predators often "track" populations of prey. This all becomes part of the theory that predation is one of the density-dependent mortality factors that interact to limit the numbers of prolific plant-feeding prey animals to levels where they do not destroy their food resources. We are gradually becoming aware of the complexities of predator-prey systems. Vulnerability of prey has been greatly oversimplified, and the old rule that predators feed only on the sick and weak is no longer universally accepted. Although prey vulnerability may involve pathology, it can also result from abnormal behaviour, weather extremes, overpopulation, or simply chance.

A 1978 study by the United States Fish and Wildlife Service provides a review of the application of the concept of predator control in the United States.[3] A summary of the main points from that study include the following:

1) Most game populations are subject to predation as one of several limiting or regulatory influences. Predator control, or protection from predation, therefore merits consideration as a possible management option whenever increased game production is desired.

2) Predators can limit game populations and are most likely to do so when the ratio of predators to prey is high.

3) Predator food studies reveal little about the impact of predators on prey populations.

4) Mortality studies in game populations frequently show predation to be a major cause of loss but leave unresolved the question of whether or not predation actually limits prey numbers.

5) Predation is not limited to inferior or sick prey individuals whose death is imminent; healthy animals are taken as well. Predation is frequently selective for certain age or sex classes of the prey, such as fawns and adult males.

6) The declines of game due to habitat deterioration or overuse cannot be reversed by predator control.

7) When predator control is not followed by increased game production, one would usually conclude that predation was not the limiting factor in that case. But ineffectiveness can also result from a failure to remove enough predators or the problem individuals.

8) Predator control, at times, may provide long-range benefits for the predator that is being controlled.

9) Because predation can be limiting under some circumstances but not others, general principles are hard to apply to specific cases. Each situation must be judged on its own merits, using the best data and expertise available.

A model developed to simulate population dynamics of western coyotes showed that the primary effect of killing coyotes is to reduce the density of the population thereby stimulating density-dependent changes in birth and natural mortality rates.[4] This example of the potential implications of coyote population reduction is frequently referred to when choosing to illustrate the futility of control efforts unless very large proportions of populations are removed. Tests of varying levels of removal show that a coyote population can maintain itself and even increase its numbers except at the very highest levels of control. If 75% of the coyotes are killed each year, the population can be exterminated in slightly over 50 years! (Note: This model was developed with data from western coyote populations and direct application to eastern coyotes may be inappropiate. Most trappers in the northeast who specialize in harvesting coyotes report substantial reductions in numbers caught following several years of removal.) A rationale to guide decisions for or against the use of predator control in specific big-game management situations was subsequently proposed.[5]

Wildlife managers must decide that the game to be protected is more desirable or more valuable than the predators to be removed. To justify predator control, the game managers must show that hunters will be able to use the increased production of game, that the habitat will support more game, that predator control will permit the game to increase, and that predator control is economically feasible and acceptable in terms of its ecological impact. The functional response of coyote populations to reduced prey availability has been demonstrated in wild coyote predator-prey systems. Thus, a similar response by coyote populations to reduced densities from predator control and the creation of artificially reduced predator-prey ratios should be expected.

There are two basic approaches to predator control: 1) removal of predators at the time and place of the problem (trouble-shooting), preferably only the individual animals actually causing trouble, and 2) a much larger and more extensive program aimed to reduce the size and density of the predator population. The trouble-shooting approach requires techniques that can be aimed at specific individuals. Extensive programs of control require methods which can be applied over large areas with a minimum of manpower and distribution cost.

Most studies recommend that, if coyotes must be reduced, removal would be most effective after dispersal (October-January) and immediately prior to the whelping season (March in the northeast). Reductions would then be additive and would remove part of the reproductive effort. Removal in the late winter and early spring would be prior to lambing, calving, and fawning seasons and could contribute to declines in coyote predation on young during that vulnerable period. In the forested northeast, January through March can be the period of increased predation on deer in winter yards, and removal at that time would prove most feasible.

A frequently used and efficient system of predator control relies on some form of extension activity. This management approach involves the training or instruction of farmers and ranchers to solve their own problems with wild animals. A small number of professionals are employed to respond to requests for assistance. It is more likely that control will be confined in time and space if the farmer and rancher assume responsibility for removing the offending predators. Missouri was one of the first states to adopt the extension approach to predator control, and for this reason it is often referred to as the "Missouri system." It was adopted by that state in 1945 in response to public dissatisfaction with the control of predators by state employees. Missouri recorded the early results of the program, which showed an 81% reduction in the costs of predator control over an 8-year period. The "extension" system of predator control has been widely adopted by many of the eastern states and several provinces where coyotes have recently become established and predation on livestock has become a concern.

Coyotes received recognition as a wild furbearer in the state of Maine in 1972.[6] Prior to that coyotelike canids could be killed by the public without penalty, and people were often encouraged to do so. The first formal coyote control effort was initiated in 1979 when government wardens trapped and snared coyotes in deer yards. A team of specially trained wardens was discontinued in 1983 in an effort to reduce departmental spending and was replaced with a formal Animal Damage Control (ADC) program. This program was established to hire and pay trappers to control coyotes in and around winter deer yards.

Fourteen ADC agents were initially employed in 1983. This core of paid control agents was supplemented by a much larger number of highly skilled volunteers. Volunteers received additional training by the Maine Department of Inland Fish and Wildlife (MDIFW). Of 240 certified control agents in 1989, only 38 reported coyote control activity. From 1983 through 1989, ADC coyote captures accounted for only 15% of the annual harvest. However, a large proportion of those coyotes removed by the ADC were real or potential problem coyotes and the value of their removal cannot be truly measured as a proportion of the total harvest. It is interesting that complaints of sheep losses declined significantly over that 8-year period. Henry Hilton emphasized the emotional "relief valve effect" of predator removal even though the biological merits of the program may be less apparent. Although the benefits of predator removal to the sheep industry can be adequately measured, its effectiveness in deer management strategies is less clear.

> "No form of coyote control is included in Maine's formal deer management system ... even though coyote predation, in all likelihood, plays some role in the dynamics of deer populations in Maine. Coyote population reduction is not considered feasible over large areas ... and even the focused removal of damage-causing coyotes to benefit 'preferred' wild species carries its own costs and ethical concerns. However, discussions continue both within and outside MDIFW about the potential benefits to deer, and costs to people, of reducing predator losses....
>
> The role of effective coyote control to meet deer management objectives in Maine has not been fully debated. Under the present deer management system, manipulation of the legal harvest of antlerless deer is considered the only realistic means of regulation currently available. Discussions about the relative merits of coyote control in achieving deer management objectives continue."[7]

Any discussion on predators and predator removal would be incomplete if it did not give some attention to the controversial issue of bounties as an effective and economical means of predator control. Few, if any, of the studies in the literature about bounties conclude that they are useful for controlling predator populations of any kind. A 35-year data set on the numbers and costs of coyotes bountied in Michigan shows that $1,899,280 was paid for 111,569 coyotes from 1935 through 1970. After 35 years of continuous bounties on coyotes, only 5 fewer were killed in 1970 (3,021) than in 1935 (3,026). The apparent inability of bounties to reduce coyotes in Michigan is similar to the results of efforts in other states which introduced the bounty system in sincere but misdirected efforts to control predators on a state-wide basis.

Reasons for the failure of bounties to achieve real declines in numbers of most predators, especially coyotes, are many. Bounty hunters go where predators are abundant, which may or may not be where the damage is occurring. Many of the bountied predators are killed incidental to other activities such as hunting and highway driving and contribute little additional to population reduction. Most states and provinces have discontinued the payment of bounties in recognition of the failure of bounties to achieve original objectives.

The bounty system has not been restricted to the United States. The Quebec Department of Agriculture paid a $35 bounty on coyotes from 1967 to 1971 and Nova Scotia implemented a $50 bounty on coyotes from 1982 to 1986. Don Dodds reviewed the Nova Scotia data for that 5-year period and concluded that:

> *"Nova Scotia spent thousands between 1982 and 1986 on bounties and the policy was ineffective. Any further bounty expenditure will doubtless be just as ineffective and if the efforts result in more coyotes rather than fewer, as may happen, we would certainly not be doing sheep farmers or hunters a favour.... A reasonable approach to the problem should be selective toward target animals and target areas and efficient taking of the appropriate animals."* [8]

This trouble-shooting approach to coyote control is similar to that practised in many states and provinces, with minor variations, and if history is to have any influence on coyote management in the northeast, that strategy appears to be the most practical. Province or state-wide control, especially in forested habitat, has never proven effective. Because coyote productivity is often influenced by food supply and coyote densities, the futility of extensive and costly programs of control is obvious. The bounty system has *never* been shown to be effective in controlling coyotes. Even if a measure of reduction could be achieved, the resiliency of coyote populations to increased mortality and their potential for emigration and rapid recolonization would make necessary extensive, sustained, and very expensive operations. If decades of aerial gunning, poisons, traps, bounties, and sundry other attempts at coyote control have proven ineffective on the open prairies, why should anyone think a similar effort in the thick spruce-fir forests of the northeast would ever prove otherwise?

Public perception and the values assigned to wildlife (and other public resources) are changing. The "consumptive user" concept towards wildlife (and forest) resources developed and embraced during an earlier era when humans fought the elements to survive is being replaced by a "non-consumptive" appreciation for wildlife enjoyed by a growing segment of an affluent society. Should we equate a coyote in a deer yard with a mink in a chicken coop? The mink kills chickens which the farmer (and consumer) depends upon for a livelihood, and it must be removed to prevent further losses of chickens and to avoid economic losses. The same can be said for removing certain insects from a vegetable garden. But in a natural system with untethered wildlife upon which few people actually depend for all or part of their livelihood, do we have the right to decide which animals should be abundant and which few, merely because we perceive one as being useful (to us) and the other a nuisance or a threat?

These considerations are not unique to wildlife, and they are becoming more important in the development of management strategies for many other natural resources, including the forests themselves. They are considerations which we must all respect, if not endorse, and future management decisions for public resources will become more a product of public debate and consensus than of authoritative pronouncement.

11 INTERSPECIFIC INTERACTIONS

Some form of partitioning of resources often allows carnivores to share a common space or prey base. This sharing of resources can be accomplished by using different habitats within a commonly used space, or by using the same habitats at different times. (The latter assumes sufficient prey to serve both predators.) Predators can also share the same space at the same time by using different prey. Conflict and direct competition between and among predators occurs when they are unable to adequately partition space and food.

> "...Sympatric carnivores partition prey according to body size. Convergence on limited food resources is less likely in southern latitudes where prey populations are more diverse. In northern regions, interference competition has resulted in an apparent dominance hierarchy among canids. Gray wolves are dominant over coyotes, and red foxes are subordinate to coyotes.... Coyotes and lynx are spatially segregated as a result of differing morphological adaptations to snow.... Interference competition between coyotes and bobcats is apparently restricted to female and juvenile bobcats because of their small body size.... [Exploitation] competition among all sex/age classes of [bobcat and coyotes] may be more influential in determining the composition of their local populations, especially in northern latitudes where prey diversity is limited and bobcats are under climatic stress."[1]

COYOTES AND WOLVES

As noted above, an ecological rule of thumb is that the more similar 2 species are in appearance, size, behaviour, or living habits, the less tolerant they are of one another. Normally the larger or more aggressive of the two "displaces" the other. This appears to be the situation with wolves, coyotes and red foxes. It also appears to apply to bobcat and lynx (bobcat displacing lynx). Among northern populations of canids, wolves dominate coyotes and coyotes dominate red foxes.[2] If this is true, how can hybridization between the wolf and coyote be said to play an important role in the development of the eastern coyote? There are exceptions to every rule, and who would argue that sex has not often been involved when rules of normal behaviour have been broken at one time or another. Hybridization between wolves and coyotes is not common, and when it does occur, it is most often at the limits of coyote and/or wolf ranges. At low densities, where competition between the two species is less, coyotes and wolves may coexist and this may result in periodic interbreeding.[3] This also applies to coyote-domestic dog hybridization and the subsequent development of coy-dogs.

As coyotes colonized southern Ontario and the northern Lake States, they entered the southern range limits of the gray wolf. In the southern states, dispersing coyotes came into contact with relic populations of red wolves. Most early coyote dispersers were females; during breeding season, in the absence of male coyote suitors, they sometimes cross-bred with wolves and domestic dogs. (Note: DNA analysis shows that hybridization occurs most frequently between a male wolf and a female coyote. See "Taxonomy).” As coyotes increase and territories become established, interbreeding with wolves and dogs becomes less frequent. On established ranges, where coyotes and wolves overlap, such as in Alaska, the Prairie Provinces and central Ontario, wolves show little tolerance for coyotes and will sometimes kill them.[4] A study of radio-marked wolves and coyotes in northeastern Alberta indicated coyotes occurred primarily where the chance of encountering wolf packs was low; that was often at the periphery of wolf territories, areas (buffer zones) infrequently used by wolves to avoid encounters with adjacent wolf packs.[5] Coyotes that were encountered by wolves were frequently killed.

Ludwig Carbyn, a research scientist with Canadian Wildlife Service, radio-marked coyotes and wolves in Riding Mountain National Park in Manitoba and studied their movements and interactions from 1974 to 1979.

> *"Twenty-two wolves and 34 coyotes were radio-collared and radio tracked. Home range overlap of four coyotes and three wolves was studied. Abundance indices obtained from howling surveys indicated that as wolf densities declined coyotes increased. Seven known or suspected wolf-killed coyotes were examined. Two of four radio-collared coyotes in one wolf pack territory were killed by wolves, and two coyotes may have been killed by wolves. Average survival from time of capture for the four radio-collared coyotes was 145 days. Wolves did not consume coyotes. Coyote survival along wolf territory edges was greatest at moderate wolf densities."[6]*

Carbyn made other interesting observations of wolf-coyote interactions in Riding Mountain National Park. Although coyotes did not always avoid wolves, avoidance was greatest in late winter. He attributed that to greater difficulty in deep snow by coyotes, and thus greater vulnerability to mortality from wolf attacks. He also found that in winter coyotes often trailed wolves, albeit at a safe distance, most likely to facilitate travel in deep snow or in anticipation of scavenging on wolf kills. (Coyotes scavenge on moose killed by wolves in Alaska.) Wolf-related mortality was highest when wolf densities were high.

"Different behavior and activity patterns of wolves and coyotes probably are important and should be studied further. Wolf packs often rest in mid-day and there are suggestions ... that wolves avoid areas close to humans during daylight hours. Coyotes may then adjust their movements in relation to wolf activities. The ability to do so, however, could be related to snow thickness, so animals less capable of avoiding wolves would perish first."[7]

David Mech, one of the most knowledgeable authorities on North American wolves, attributed the extirpation of coyotes on Isle Royale in Lake Superior to the arrival of wolves.

"Since coyotes and wolves are closely related and since wolves are strongly territorial, it is not unlikely that on a limited range, such as Isle Royale, wolves would chase and probably kill every coyote encountered."[8]

William Berg and Robert Chesness studied the ecology of radio-collared coyotes in northern Minnesota from 1970 to 1975; this state is also home to an expanding population of gray wolves.

"Only six coyotes have been trapped during the study period in the area identified as being occupied by wolves, and radioed coyotes inhabiting the adjacent areas generally avoided the wolf-occupied range. Evidence of wolves chasing coyotes has been found, one fight between a wolf and a coyote has been seen from an aircraft, and two coyotes, one radioed, have been killed by wolves during the study period."[9]

Dick Dekker studied wolves, coyotes, and foxes in Jasper National Park, Alberta, from 1980 to 1989.

"The reasons for the fluctuation [from 1980 to 1989] in coyote sightings are not clear, but the highest counts of 1983-1984 coincided with the disappearance of the local denning wolf pack ... possibly as a result of control measures on adjacent provincial grazing leases....

Even if wolves remain common in Jasper National Park, coyotes will probably not disappear because (1) they concentrate in areas of low wolf occurrence, and (2) they disperse into the park from settled lands to the east."[10]

The intolerance of wolves towards coyotes has little relevance throughout most of the present range of the eastern coyote. It does, however, add credibility to the earlier discussion of possible reasons for the historic expansion of the coyote throughout most of North America south of forested range occupied by the gray wolf.

COYOTES AND RED FOXES

Coyotes and red foxes share a common range throughout much of North America. However, there appears to be an inverse relationship between densities of coyotes and foxes. High densities of coyotes tend to limit both the distribution of fox territories and their numbers. Trappers and biologists in the northeast have noted declines in foxes following colonization by eastern coyotes and increases in their populations.

Studies from the Yukon Territory to Wyoming and from Alberta to Maine have verified this intolerance of coyotes towards red foxes. Both the coyote and the longer established red fox use the same major prey species in the Yukon. In true boreal situations, coyotes are more dependent on snowshoe hare than are red foxes,[11] and foxes may persist there when hares decline, because of their ability to exploit alternative prey. This scenario sounds very much like the coyote and wolf versus white-tailed deer "exploitation competition" often found in more southern latitudes. In the Yukon, where deer are not widely distributed, coyotes and foxes both depend upon snowshoe hare (interference competition).

"... Our study provides evidence that in exploitation competition, foxes may persist because of elasticity in their choice of prey, but in interference competition, coyotes may persist by dominating edges. This manner of balancing competitive abilities may play an important role in allowing foxes and coyotes to coexist in mixed lowland habitats of the southwest Yukon."[12]

Strong spatial segregation also existed between coyotes and foxes in Jasper National Park, with coyotes occupying the prey-rich valley bottoms and foxes common only on the mountainsides.[13] Foxes were unable to utilize valley bottoms because of the presence of coyotes.

"On 18 June 1975, I saw a coyote crouch and wait for an approaching fox which dodged the coyote's rush and escaped. On eight occasions, I observed foxes follow and bark at coyotes that were within 0.8 km from a fox den with pups. The coyotes repeatedly chased the foxes, which dodged and fled until the coyotes gave up. Murie saw foxes follow and bark at wolves (Canis lupus) near fox dens in Alaska. On 16 June 1974, I saw a fox approach and bark at two coyotes, each of which briefly chased the fox. Eventually, the coyotes entered the woodlot, until the second coyote emerged and took over. Eventually, this coyote gave up too, but the fox didn't return. The total distance of the chase was about 1 km. On 21 June 1977, I was observing four fox pups sleeping near a field den, when suddenly a coyote ran towards them. Some distance away, the vixen barked a warning and the pups bolted into the den in the nick of time.... Coyotes may be a serious danger to red foxes, especially the young, and foxes avoid coyotes by spatial segregation. In central Alberta, red foxes occur mainly near human habitation and roads. I have found them denning in the immediate vicinity of farms with large dogs, which appeared to keep coyotes away. Rural residents of the ... region told me of three cases where foxes hid their pups under buildings in their yard.... Red foxes have only quite recently established themselves on the farmlands of central Alberta [early 1970s], perhaps by taking advantage of a depressed coyote population decimated during the late 1960s by snowmobile hunters. Foxes will probably continue to exist on the Alberta farmlands, but only locally in areas where coyotes are scarce or absent."[14]

Spatial avoidance by coyotes and foxes in Alberta has also been observed in other regions of North America. In North Dakota resident red foxes avoid large central portions of coyote family territories and thus avoid interspecific encounters.[15]

Similarly in Ontario, red foxes avoid areas where coyotes traditionally travel and raise pups.[16] The mechanics of coyote-induced declines in red fox populations are largely unknown, but various hypotheses have been advanced.

> "...Young foxes are probably most vulnerable to mortality from coyotes, especially when dispersing, because they are inexperienced and travel through unfamiliar terrain, including coyote territoties.... We suggest that coyotes are largely unintimitated by red foxes and will establish family territories in areas occupied by foxes but that the opposite is much less likely to occur. Few resident foxes in areas recently invaded by coyotes will abandon their territories even though by remaining close to coyotes, individual foxes risk coyote-inflicted mortality. Territory adjustment is likely the way most resident foxes cope with invading coyotes.... Local red fox populations are maintained primarily by immigration of dispersing juveniles ... but dispersing foxes tend to avoid establishing residency in areas occupied by coyotes. Hence, through attrition of resident adult foxes, gradual displacement of fox territories away from coyote territory cores, rejection of coyote-occupied areas by dispersing foxes, and limited coyote-inflicted mortality, a red fox population would gradually decline as the coyote population increased. Eventually, if coyotes became sufficiently abundant, red foxes may no longer be present. Because the hypothesized mechanism is largely interspecific avoidance, population changes could occur with little direct evidence of coyote involvement.... The establishment of coyotes in an area occupied solely by red foxes may appear to have no immediate impact on the density of red foxes.... Visibility of foxes in the overall area may remain unchanged or possibly increase as the foxes begin to adjust to the coyotes by living in increasingly closer association with people. The effect would be especially noticeable during spring and summer when ... many fox rearing dens would be located near well-travelled roads and farms."[17]

Here in the northeast, a long-term study of the interactions of coyotes, red foxes, and bobcats was conducted in Maine from 1979 to 1984 by scientists at the Department of Wildlife at the University of Maine and the Maine Cooperative Wildlife Research Unit.[18]

> "Foxes and coyotes were not found to overlap spatially. The observed arrangement of fox ranges abutting, but not overlapping, traditional coyote ranges is believed to be the result of biological processes.... Coyotes apparently have displaced red foxes from some areas through interference competition."[19]

> "This spatial segregation likely reduces the potential for aggressive encounters between foxes and coyotes.... Foxes used habitats adjacent to streams, rivers, and lakeshores intensively.... Riparian and lakeshore habitats act as natural boundaries between coyote territories. These boundary areas provide suitable habitats for foxes that are external to core portions of coyote family territories."[20]

Direct mortality by coyotes on red foxes has been observed. It was reported earlier that Dekker observed coyotes chasing red foxes in Alberta, and Voigt and Earle reported that trappers in Ontario frequently found foxes in traps that were killed by coyotes. There have been 4 instances of predation on radio-collared foxes in northern Maine.[21] Given the very real competition between coyotes and red foxes, what are the management implications for red fox in the northeast?

"The presence of resident coyotes in eastern Maine limits the available habitat and carrying capacity for red foxes; however, the ability of foxes to persist in boundary areas prevents complete displacement from regions occupied by coyotes. Management for red foxes should be reevaluated in areas of eastern North America where coyotes have become established. Coyote-induced declines in red fox densities may require reductions in allowable fox harvests in some areas. Effects of coyotes on fox numbers will vary according to the density of coyote territories and the availability of refugia from coyotes."[22]

COYOTES AND BOBCATS

Although sympatric [inhabiting the same range] coyotes and bobcats have been studied in Arizona, Oklahoma, and Oregon,[23] this brief review is restricted to two recent studies in Maine. In western Maine radio-collared coyotes and bobcats were followed from 1979 to 1982, and these authors suggested that competition between coyotes and bobcats for deer might be important.

"Bobcats could conceivably have lower hunting success where deer also are preyed upon by coyotes. A detailed study of these questions would be useful in assessing the potential effects of exploitation competition between coyotes and bobcats, as well as provide information on the effects of predators on deer.... We found no evidence for interference competition between coyotes and bobcats. They occurred in the same habitats, occupied overlapping home ranges simultaneously, and ate many of the same foods, including using some deer carcasses in common. We found no instances of avoidance or aggression, and analysis of spacing patterns showed no displacement. The evolution and taxonomic separation between canids and felids... is apparently sufficient to permit peaceful coexistence."[24]

A second study of bobcat-coyote niche relationships was conducted from 1979 to 1984 in eastern Maine where regional patterns of bobcat and coyote abundance suggested that these two species might be competitors, with coyotes dominant over bobcats.

"During periods of extensive use of toxicants to reduce coyote abundance in the western United States, bobcat populations increased as coyote densities were reduced.... After reduction efforts were relaxed, coyotes increased in number and bobcat densities declined."

These authors reasoned that because bobcats in Maine are at the northern edge of their distribution range and because the abundance and variety of prey in Maine is limited and bobcat survival is influenced by winter prey availability, increasing abundance of coyotes would have a negative effect upon bobcats. They also used radio-telemetry to study activity patterns and habitat use of both coyotes and bobcats. Overlap in seasonal habitat use was relatively high among bobcats and coyotes although distribution patterns did vary between species. Bobcats preferred hardwood-dominated stands with dense understories, perhaps reflecting their high dependence upon snowshoe hares. Use of thick undercover by bobcats may also

> *"be a function of their characteristic felid hunting technique of concealment, stalk, and sudden attack, in contrast to the open-area pursuit method of canids."*[25]

One bobcat was found killed by coyotes. Seasonal use of habitat by coyotes was more varied than for bobcats, probably a function of the greater diversity in coyote diet. Competition for food was lowest during summer and autumn when coyotes frequently consumed fruits. A comparison of food habits of bobcats before and after the arrival of coyotes showed a greater dependency on snowshoe hares and less on white-tailed deer, although there are no data to directly implicate the coyote in this change. The authors did not observe any spatial displacement of bobcats by coyotes but suggested rather that coyotes have reduced the ability of habitat in eastern Maine to support bobcats by reducing the availability of prey.

> *"...Bobcats probably will not be displaced because they are a more effective predator in areas with dense understories and abundant snowshoe hare populations. Therefore, bobcat numbers may stabilize at levels below those that occurred before the colonization of the area by coyotes."*[26]

Because of different feeding strategies and habitat use, the bobcat and lynx (shown here) appear to be less affected by the presence of coyotes than the red fox (G. Parker).

COYOTES AND HUMANS

Attacks by coyotes on humans are rare. However there have been such unfortunate encounters and I will present several of them here. Perhaps the first and only known fatality was that of a 3-year-old child killed by coyotes in Los Angeles County, California.[27] That fatal attack, and other non-fatal encounters in the same locale, were attributed to the location of residential areas in mountain canyons near shrubby vegetation. This promoted coyote-human encounters, often involving children and coyotes which had become used to handouts and urban environments. These are the same circumstances which often lead to most unfortunate human-wildlife encounters at many provincial, state, and federal parks.

There are other substantiated accounts of human-coyote encounters and several have been documented by Ludwig Carbyn of the Canadian Wildlife Service. Carbyn summarized information from warden reports in Banff and Jasper National Parks in western Canada and in Yellowstone National Park in northwestern Wyoming. He compiled a list of 10 attacks which resulted in minor injuries and 4 attacks which produced major injuries. The following are descriptions of the 4 major attacks.

The first occurred in Yellowstone National Park in November, 1960.

"... A 1.5-year-old child was moved from a car to a stroller on the porch and left unattended for a short time. A neighbour saw a coyote attacking the child and came to the rescue with a broom. Only after persistent shouting and attacks by 3 adults did the coyote leave. The child received 21 stitches in the face and had bruises on her back and arms, but was generally protected by a heavy snowsuit."

The second incident occurred on August 30, 1985, in a Jasper National Park campground. It involved a 4-year-old girl who was playing out of sight of her parents but only a short distance away.

"Screaming from the child attracted her parents, who threw rocks at the coyote to scare it off. The child was rushed to hospital with numerous lacerations on the face."

Helen Flewelling killed this coyote with an iron bar as it raided her chickens near Saint John, New Brunswick (*Telegraph Journal*, Saint John).

167

The most serious attack that Carbyn investigated occurred in the townsite of Jasper in mid-April 1985.

"A mother sent her 2-year-old daughter to the backyard to play with a friend. After approximately 10 minutes, the mother went to see the children only to find a coyote dragging the limp body of her child uphill. The coyote's jaws appeared to be clamped around the throat and neck of the child. The coyote dropped the child as her parents rushed toward the animal. The unconscious child was rushed to a nearby hospital with extensive injuries around the face, neck, and throat. However, the child recovered."

The final attack reported by Carbyn occurred near Creston, British Columbia.

"On 30 July 1988, an 18-month-old girl was walking along a trail at a highway stop with her 10-year-old sister. A coyote attacked the smaller girl, and shortly thereafter the parents arrived. The coyote was biting the neck and head region while the child was lying face down. As the father picked up the child, the coyote moved back only a few paces. It remained in the area until shot by police within about an hour. Rabies tests were negative. Injuries to the child's face, head, and arms were extensive, but generally superficial. More than 200 stitches were required to close the wounds, but there was no permanent muscle or nerve damage."

Carbyn concluded that most attacks by coyotes on humans were predatory in nature – the coyotes appeared to have lost fear of humans and regarded children as prey. He compares most coyote-human encounters with bear-human encounters, where both predators become habituated to food sources associated with humans. It is significant that serious attacks involved infants, most likely because of their small size and vulnerability. In situations where coyotes lose their normal fear of humans, such as at campgrounds in provincial, federal, and state parks, they may perceive humans as just another potential food item. Carbyn also told of other unusual behaviour of coyotes towards humans.

"In Riding Mountain National Park, Manitoba, 1 coyote repeatedly chased cars and snapped at tires. In the same park a coyote repeatedly slashed tents in a campground. Similarly, in July 1988, there were several coyote attacks in Banff National Park on campers that were sleeping or resting in sleeping bags.... There was no evidence to suggest that any of the attacks summarized in this paper were acts of diseased coyotes..."[28]

I recently read the following August 29, 1993 *Canadian Press* story of strange behaviour by a coyote – like wild canid near Cambridge, Ontario.

"A wild dog bit off a woman's finger, hung by its teeth from the neck of a cow and took police on a merry chase Friday through this southwestern Ontario city.... The animal, which at one point lunged at a moving car, was finally bludgeoned to death by a shovel-wielding homeowner whose own dog had been attacked.... 'We're really not sure what it is-part-dog, part-wolf, part-coyote,' said Sgt. Ken Boult of Waterloo region police. 'But it is no longer with us.'

In Atlantic Canada a young girl visiting Cape Breton Highlands National Park was "attacked" by a coyote on August 25, 1988.

"A young visitor at the park ... was walking from the washroom ... to the Visitor Centre parking lot when she noticed the coyote walking towards her. She did not approach the animal but kept walking without paying attention to it. The animal approached from behind, jumped up and bit the girl on the left side, then bit her on the ankle.... [A] park employee chased the coyote with a broom and notified [a] warden who attended the scene and shot the animal which had not left the area. Investigation revealed that the coyote had been seen in and around the ... campground several times. The animal was a young female of about 15 pounds with no apparent fear of humans and had become accustomed to human food and handouts.... [The girl] was taken to the hospital ... where she was treated for minor puncture wounds. Rabies testing on the coyote proved negative."[29]

Several other persons have been "nipped" in Cape Breton Highlands National Park when attempting to feed coyotes which had become accustomed to tourists and free handouts. Such ill advised behaviour is strictly prohibited by Parks Canada.

Coyotes are known to kill domestic cats and dogs.[30] Owners, especially in rural areas, should be aware of this potential danger to free-ranging pets. The following account of an encounter between a coyote, a cat, and the cat's owner near Germantown in southeastern New Brunswick serves to illustrate the reason for concern.

"It was hard to tell who was more frightened during a confrontation on the back steps of a house in Germantown. A showdown occurred between a coyote, a pet cat the coyote had in its jaws and a widow in her 70s. The coyote lost. Frances Crilly yelled at the coyote to drop her cat Smudge - and it did. Smudge limped back into the house, apparently none the worse for wear. Forest ranger Brian Betts said he had no local reports of coyotes eating family pets. He said they mostly eat field mice."[31]

In summary, then, the presence of the eastern coyote throughout the northeast does present a potential risk to humans, especially children, but that risk is slight when weighed against other dangers to human health. Parents can reduce that risk by following simple precautions. As with other forms of wildlife, especially predators, intentional encounters, such as feeding or close photography, should be avoided. Small children should not be left unattended when in wilderness areas, especially campgrounds where coyotes may be especially bold. Farmers can reduce problem coyotes by removing carcasses of domestic stock or other sources of food which coyotes might find attractive. Given the choice, most wild animals will go to great lengths to avoid contact with humans. The public should not consider the coyote reason for avoiding wilderness areas, but rather should treat the coyote with the caution and respect due all wild animals, especially those that have the potential to cause bodily harm and personal injury.

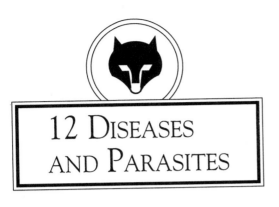

12 DISEASES AND PARASITES

"Wild canids of North America harbour a wide variety of external and internal parasites. One recent study concluded that coyotes and wolves are reported hosts for ... 8 viral, 4 rickettsial, 9 bacterial, 2 mycotic, 8 protozoan, 9 trematode, 17 cestode, 2 acanthocephalan, 25 nematode, 2 mite, 3 louse, 15 tick, and 30 flea infections."[1]

Most information on host-parasite relationships for coyotes comes from traditional ranges west of the Mississippi River in the United States and from the Prairie Provinces in Canada. The swiftness of eastern colonization and the potential implications of the coyote in the natural ecosystems here has limited most research to the task of addressing basic ecological concerns. The less glamourous task of describing parasites and diseases associated with these new predators, although perhaps of equal importance, is often considered a more academic pursuit. A detailed account of the wide assortment of diseases and parasites that the eastern coyote may play host to is beyond the scope of this general ecological review. In the absence of detailed analyses of specimens from the northeast, any assumptions on presence and prevalence of diseases based on western studies may be premature. However, I will provide a short review of a few of the more common parasites most likely associated with the eastern coyote and of some which, for various reasons (one of which is human health), may be of interest to the reader. I have drawn extensively on the two reviews of host-parasite relationships in the wild canids of North America presented by D. B. Pence and J. W. Custer at the Worldwide Furbearer Conference held at Frostburg, Maryland in 1980.

VIRAL INFECTIONS

ORAL PAPILLOMATOSIS

Typified by lesions, from 1 to several mm in diameter, confined to the lips, tongue, and buccal cavity (in the mouth). Infected coyotes may appear healthy but are often emaciated and weak. This disease has been reported in coyotes from Texas, Saskatchewan, Manitoba, Alberta, and Kansas.[2] Frequency of infection varies with region. Five of 277 (1.8%) and 23 of 473 (4.8%) coyotes were infected in Alberta, although only 1 of 1,500 (.06%) and none of 1,000 specimens from Texas showed symptoms of the disease.[3] Experimental inoculation of infected tissue from coyotes has produced lesions in domestic dogs, but the danger of such transmissions in the wild appears minimal.

DISTEMPER

This disease is common among many carnivores but is most often associated with canids, especially coyotes, wolves, and foxes. The disease is transmitted principally through aerosol or contact with nasal exudate and saliva.[4] Symptoms of the disease include thirst and a hot dry nose, listlessness, anorexia, emaciation, diarrhea, and laboured breathing and cough. Distemper is most prevalent in juveniles and appears more frequently with increases in densities of host populations (density dependence). Mortality of coyotes from distemper can be severe, especially among juveniles. Prevalence of distemper in wild coyote populations varies by region and coyote densities. Eleven of 30 coyotes from Texas tested positive.[5] Mortality in wild coyote populations from canine distemper can become important when compounded with other environmental factors such as overpopulation, malnutrition and parasitism. A coyote which attacked 3 toy poodles on Cape Breton Island in April 1994 and was subsequently shot, suffered from canine distemper.

INFECTIOUS CANINE HEPATITIS

This viral disease is very similar to distemper. Clinical symptoms may vary from nil to anorexia, listlessness, convulsions, paralysis, and muscular twitching.[6] Eleven of 86 (13%) coyotes from Texas showed positve blood tests for this virus.[7]

RABIES

Although coyotes are known to become infected with rabies, the incidence of rabid coyotes in the wild is relatively low, certainly less than the rate of infection in foxes. Of 9,943 confirmed cases of rabies reported in 1977 from the United States, Canada, and Mexico, there were only two cases involving coyotes, one in Canada and one from Mexico. Of the 8,598 reported cases of rabies in Ontario from 1961 to 1969, only 35 (0.41%) involved coyotes and/or wolves.[8] It is generally agreed that coyotes are not nearly as susceptible to rabies as foxes, skunks, bats, or raccoons.

PARASITIC FLATWORMS (TREMATODES)

ALARIA SPP.

There are a number of intestinal flatworms (flukes) of this genus which commonly infect wolves and coyotes throughout North America. These parasites can also be found in domestic dogs without producing adverse clinical symptoms. The number of these worms per infected animal can be considerable, with as many as 673 reported from one coyote from Manitoba, apparently with no pathologic effects.[9] The area of infection is commonly restricted to the duodenum region of the small intestine. The life history of trematodes can be complex, with aquatic snails and vertebrates (frogs, fish) acting as intermediate hosts. Rates of infection in samples of coyotes from various regions were: Alberta, 33%; Manitoba, 37%; south Texas, 100%; west Texas, 12%.[10] Although the effect of these intestinal flatworms on wild coyote populations is unknown, obvious clinical symptoms are rare.

LIVER FLUKES

Another type of internal flatworm is commonly restricted to the liver region of varying proportions of wild canids throughout most regions of North America. The life cycle of these flukes is also complex with certain species of aquatic snails and fish acting as intermediate hosts. One sample of coyotes from Alberta found a rate of infection of 7% with intensities of individual infection ranging from 1 to over 900 worms.[11] The clinical manifestations of liver fluke infections on wild canid populations is little understood.

Other trematodes identified in wild canids include lung and pancreatic flukes, but the frequency of occurrence in regional populations is normally low; little is known of their distribution among populations of eastern coyotes.

TAPEWORMS (CESTODES)

Wild canids are host to a variety of tapeworms, which can represent a major component of the internal load of helminth parasites. Although hundreds of tapeworms may be found within the viscera of individual coyotes, little is known of their pathogenicity. In domestic dogs, adult tapeworms do not appear to be very harmful, and symptoms of infection are rare except in young animals with high rates of infection where alternating bouts of diarrhea and constipation may occur.

Tapeworms require intermediate hosts to complete their life cycle, and these larval stages of the parasite most often infect various species of rodents, rabbits and hares, and deer. Typically, eggs from an infected canid are passed in the faeces. Eggs ingested by a suitable alternate host, which can occasionally include humans, develop into larval stages which, depending upon the species of tapeworm, become distributed in various organs and tissues. The life cycle is normally completed when a wild canid kills an infected alternate host and ingests mature larvae. Humans can become infected with the larvae stages of tapeworms by accidentally ingesting eggs passed in the faeces of canids infected with adult tapeworms. This most often involves infected domestic dogs rather than wild canids. This might occur in rural areas where dogs run free in the forests and become infected and children are allowed to play in areas where dog faeces accumulate. I describe several of the more common forms of tapeworms which may be associated with coyotes and certain species of prey in the northeast. Information on these species comes from the 1964 publication by the government of Ontario entitled *Manual of Common Parasites, Diseases and Anomalies of Wildlife in Ontario*.[12]

TAENIA HYDATIGENA (THIN-NECKED BLADDERWORM)

The adult stage of this tapeworm is found in the intestinal tract of wolves, coyotes, and dogs. Certain herbivores, such as deer, elk, moose, caribou, and reindeer become infected by eating eggs passed in the faeces of infected canids. The larval stage of the parasite (*Cysticercus tenuicollis*) occurs in a bladder-like cyst in the liver and abdominal cavity of the infected herbivore. Infestations in herbivores are usually light with only slight, localized damage in the liver. Cysts are about 1.27 cm (1/2 inch) in diameter containing one active larval tapeworm each. The parasite is not transmissible to humans and the meat of infected herbivores is considered safe for human consumption. Obviously infected entrails should not be fed to dogs or left available for wild carnivores.

TAENIA PISIFORMIS

The cysts (*Cysticercus pisiformis*) or intermediate larval stages of this common tapeworm of coyotes and domestic dogs are frequently found in the abdominal cavity among the organs of hares, rabbits, and less frequently, mice. Wolves and foxes may also serve as final hosts. Infestations do not normally lead to mortality in either the primary or secondary hosts. This parasite is not transmissible to humans and the meat of infected hares and rabbits is considered safe for human consumption. Infected viscera should not be fed to dogs.

TAENIA KRABBEI (MUSCLE CYSTICERCOSIS)

The larval or cystic stage of this tapeworm, *Cysticercus tarandi*, occurs in the heart and skeletal muscle of wild herbivores such as deer, moose, caribou, and reindeer. The adult of this tapeworm has been reported in wolves, coyotes, bobcats, and dogs. The larval cyst measures only about 0.63 cm (1/4 of an inch) or less in length and is yellowish-white in colour. Each bladder like cyst contains one larval tapeworm. The adult tapeworm has never been reported in humans and meat from infected herbivores is considered safe for human consumption. As with other forms of tapeworm larvae, infected meat and organs should not be fed to domestic dogs.

MULTICEPS SERIALIS

The adult tapeworm is an intestinal parasite of the wolf, coyote, fox, and dog. Larval stages of this parasite occur as bladder like sacs or cysts under the skin and between the muscles of hares, rabbits, and squirrels. Each cyst may contain the heads of numerous developing tapeworms. Cysts may be as large as a hen's egg and are normally obvious to anyone handling the carcass of an infected hare or rabbit. The parasite does not normally lead to death of the infected alternate host. As the parasite is not transmissible to humans, the meat from an infected hare or rabbit is considered safe for consumption. If numerous cysts are present in the meat, however, the carcass should be destroyed.

ECHINOCOCCUS GRANULOSUS (HYDATID DISEASE)

The adult stage of this tapeworm is found in a carnivore, and the larval stage develops in a herbivore. The adult tapeworm is most commonly found in northern wolf populations and the larval stage, referred to as a hydatid cyst, is most commonly found in elk, moose, caribou, and reindeer, although deer can also serve as a suitable alternate host. In Ontario 20% of a sample of 520 timber wolves were infected but only 0.5% of 339 coyotes.[13] Although the occurrence of this tapeworm in eastern coyote populations would be rare, it is listed here because of the susceptibility of humans as suitable alternate hosts. Infected herbivores develop cysts, usually in the lungs, which can vary from the size of a pin head to that of a football, each cyst containing fluid and the heads of thousands of developing tapeworms. Humans may serve as the alternate host by ingesting eggs passed in the faeces of infected canids, most often domestic dogs (see *Figure 17*). Humans cannot serve as a suitable host for the adult tapeworm and cannot become infected by handling or eating hydatid cysts from infected herbivores. Most harm probably occurs in the intermediate hosts where larval stages of certain tapeworm species can produce considerable pathology in rodents, rabbits and hares, and cervids (e.g., deer).

This photograph shows hydatid cysts in the lung of a moose. Although the hydatid tapeworm is most commmon in northern wolves, coyotes and domestic dogs may act as hosts for this parasite, once cysts containing immature tapeworms are ingested (Fyvie, 1964).

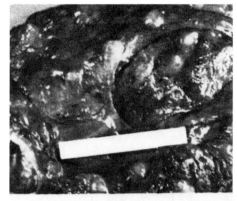

Hydatid cysts in portion of moose lung.

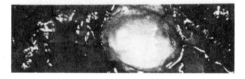

NEMATODE (ROUNDWORM) INFECTIONS

Nematodes are one of the most frequently reported forms of internal parasites of wild canids, and include a wide variety of lungworms and hookworms. As many as 27 species have been reported in North American coyotes.[14] Some lungworms are restricted in distribution by the geographic range of specific alternate hosts. The following is a selection of the more common nematodes identified mainly from coyotes and which may or may not be prevalent in eastern coyote populations.

CAPILLARIA AEROPHILA

This is a widely distributed form of lungworm commonly found in coyotes of the western United States and western Canada. Its distribution and prevalence within coyote populations may be dependent upon the distribution of earthworms which are believed to serve as the normal intermediate host. Infection normally occurs from the trachea to the lungs and in heavily infected animals produces a thick mucous. Severe infections are seldom reported in wild coyote populations.

TRICHINELLA SPIRALIS

This nematode is responsible for the disease commonly referred to as trichinosis, infections of which occasionally occur in humans from ingestion of raw or poorly cooked pork or bear meat. Wild carnivores most often acquire the infection from ingesting rodents. Infective larvae then develop into adult nematodes in the intestine, which can then reproduce and provide new infective larvae which can become encysted in the host's muscle tissue. Infected carnivores are normally considered poor reservoirs of transmission. However, larvae passed in the faeces of infected carnivores can be ingested by other potential hosts, such as swine.

DIOCTOPHYMA RENALE (GIANT KIDNEY WORM)

The giant kidney worm is a widespread parasite of many carnivores, including domestic and wild canids. It is rarely reported in humans. It is one of the largest parasitic nematodes, often reaching lengths of 100 cm. The worm is bright red in colour and can occur in the kidney or the abdominal cavity. The life cycle of the giant kidney worm like so many other parasitic worms, is complex. Eggs are passed in the urine of the infected host and subsequently ingested by aquatic nematode worms. The eggs hatch within the aquatic worms and develop to an infective larval stage; if this stage is eaten by a carnivore, including the coyote, it develops into an adult giant kidney worm. If an infected aquatic worm is eaten by a fish, the larvae become encysted and can infect the carnivore which feeds on the fish. The giant kidney worm has been reported in coyotes from California to Alberta and Ontario. Symptoms of kidney worm infections may include weight loss, frequent urination, nervous trembling, and anemia. Presence of the giant kidney worm results in complete kidney destruction although rarely are both kidneys infected.

PHYSALOPTERA SPP.(STOMACH WORMS)

The dog stomach worm (*P. rara*) is the most frequently reported species from wild canids. Stomach worms have been reported in coyotes from a wide geographical range including most western states, and in Canada, Manitoba. Certain beetles and insects serve as intermediate host for this worm including the cockroach and field cricket. Adult coyotes with individual loads of several hundred worms do not seem to be adversely affected.

DIROFILARIA IMMITIS (DOG HEARTWORM)

Canine heartworm disease is one of the most serious diseases of domesticated wild canids. Heartworm infection has been reported from all species of wild canids in North America and is widely distributed in coyote populations. Infection is transmitted by several species of mosquito. Coyote populations in certain western states are considered the primary reservoir for canine heartworm disease; in certain southern states, this disease is considered an important factor in morbidity and mortality of coyotes.

TOXASCARIS LEONINA (INTESTINAL NEMATODE)

This internal parasite is a common intestinal worm of wild canids. It has been reported in western coyote populations from Utah, Texas, Montana, Louisiana, Kansas, and other states, and from Manitoba, Alberta, the Yukon, and the Northwest Territories in Canada. This parasite lives in the small intestine and has a direct life cycle; i.e., infection occurs through direct ingestion of eggs from fecal-contaminated soil, food, or water, or of rodents which have picked up the eggs and contain developing larvae. Clinical manifestations are usually restricted to juveniles and include anorexia, vomiting, bloating, diarrhea, and a rough coat.

OSLERUS OSLERI (TRACHEAL WORM)

Tracheal worms are widespread among continental coyote populations, having been

The giant kidney worm, one of the largest parasitic roundworms, has been isolated from coyotes in the northeast (Fyvie, 1964).

Figure 17: The hydatid tapeworm, *Echinococcus granulosus*, although uncommon in coyotes, is of interest because humans may serve as host to hydatid cysts if eggs from infected canids (wolves, coyotes or domestic dogs) are accidentally ingested. **A.** Eggs from an infected canid are passed in the feces. **B.** Moose, caribou or deer (cervids) accidentally eat eggs when feeding on ground vegetation. **C.** Larvae circulate to lungs and encyst. **D.** Larvae reproduce asexually in cyst. **E.** Canid kills infected cervid and eats cyst. **F.** Larvae mature into adult tapeworms and live in canids's intestine. Hydatid tapeworms and cysts are most common in wolves, moose and caribou of northern Canada (Mech, 1966).

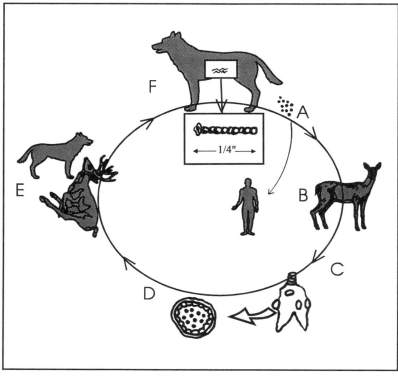

reported in most western states, as well as in Minnesota, and in Canada, from Alberta and Manitoba. Infection is believed to result directly from ingestion of infective larvae. Most infections occur in animals over 2 years of age. Most studies have concluded that the effects of tracheal worm infections in coyote populations are of little consequence.

ANCYLOSTOMA CANINUM (COMMON DOG HOOKWORM)

Although there are several species of hookworms which have been isolated from coyotes, the common dog hookworm appears to be the most prevalent. This parasite has been recorded from southern Canada to the tropics. Eggs are passed in the faeces. Hatched larvae, when ingested, migrate up the trachaea, are swallowed, and mature into adult worms in the small intestine. Infection is usually more severe in juveniles than in adults. As hookworms utilize the blood of their host, severe infections may include progressive anemia, emaciation, diarrhea, and general weakness sometimes resulting in death. Female coyotes with light hookworm infections can cause severe infections in pups, especially at den sites with moist soils which allow a high survival of infective larvae. Such conditions can lead to pup mortality.

ARTHROPOD INFECTIONS

SARCOPTIC MANGE (CANINE MANGE)

Sarcoptic mange is often considered the most serious disease of wild canids. This disease is caused by the mite *Sarcoptes scabiei* var. *canis*. During periods of severe and widespread infection, referred to as epizootics, as much as 70% of a population may carry the disease, and mortality can be high. The disease normally becomes severe during periods of high coyote densities, and in this respect it can be considered a form of population control. The disease is highly contagious and transmission is by direct contact. The female mite burrows into the skin and lays eggs. Eggs hatch into larvae which in turn develop into nymphs and finally adults, all on a single canid host. Although the disease is transmissible to humans it is usually not severe, and generally appears as a reddish rash for several weeks. Clinical symptoms of severe infections of sarcoptic mange include crusted hemorrhagic lesions over much of the body resulting in extensive hair loss.

TICKS

Ticks are not common in most of the northeast, and although coyotes can be carriers, they are not known to be exceptionally vulnerable to heavy tick infestations. The adult female tick requires blood to ensure viable eggs and tick infestations are most severe in spring and early summer. After feeding, adult ticks fall off the host and lay eggs in the soil. Light to moderate tick infestations do not normally affect the host animal. In Atlantic Canada the eastern wood tick (*Dermacentor variabilis*), originally imported from New England, is now common over much of southern Nova Scotia and would be frequent on coyotes there, as it is on most other wild mammals.

FLEAS

The coyote flea (*Pulex simulans*) is a common external parasite of coyotes.

Although a number of other species of fleas have been identified, most appear to be from incidental transmissions from prey species and do not successfully reproduce on coyotes.

"*Fleas apparently are more an irritating nuisance to coyotes than a real health hazard, although there is some indication that certain fleas may be vectors of tularemia, bubonic plague, equine encephalitis, and possibly other diseases. Infestations of 100 to 400 fleas per coyote are not uncommon, but the continuity of infestations, reproductive success of the fleas, or health effects on the coyote can only be surmised.*"[15]

LICE

The only louse which is known to successfully parasitize coyotes in temperate and northern regions is the common dog louse (*Trichodectes canis*). Incidences of infection appear to be extremely low, and like mange, become more prevalent in populations that are stressed from extremes in weather and nutrition. Only 2 of 2,000 coyotes examined in the western United States between 1948 and 1963 were infested with lice.[16]

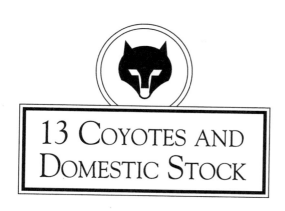

13 Coyotes and Domestic Stock

"No predator-control problem has attracted more attention, churned up more human emotions, aroused more political furor, and demanded more unwarranted expenditures than the one involving the predators that prey on livestock.... When all the polite considerations are stripped from the controversy of livestock depredation, there remains the classic confrontation of the coyote as the predator and the sheep as the prey. All socioeconomic conflicts of other species scale down from this end of the predator-prey spectrum."[1]

Measuring the impact of predation by coyotes on domestic livestock, and developing and evaluating means for eliminating or mitigating those losses have been the focus of surveys and research by a great many people and organizations for many years. These efforts have historically been most intense on the traditional sheep and coyote ranges in the western United States. However, with the rapid colonization of most of eastern North America by the coyote in the past 30 years, depredation by this new predator on domestic livestock here has become a very real concern.

The issue in the east is further complicated by the fact that the eastern coyote, for reasons not fully understood but reviewed earlier, has developed behavioural and morphological modifications which enhance its ability to successfully prey on larger animals and survive in northern forested wilderness landscapes. Thus, the larger and more social eastern coyote is not only adept at preying on physically larger wild animals but also conceivably more capable of preying on larger domestic prey. The issue in northeastern North America, of course, is further complicated by the real or perceived ability of coyotes to impact upon white-tailed deer populations. The eastern coyote, therefore, has received the wrath of both the farmer and the sportsman, and calls for its control have been both frequent and intense. As the novelty of this new predator waned, however, so did the vociferous intensity of public concern, and a general mood of adversarial defiance has been replaced by one of begrudging tolerance. This growing public acceptance of the eastern coyote as a member of our wildlife community permits a more logical and objective assessment of the many real and potential ecological implications, and allows us to develop means of living with our new neighbour rather than to plot and scheme futile ways for its control and eradication.

But first let us consider a sample of studies from more traditional western ranges which have assessed the impact of coyote predation on domestic livestock there, especially on sheep. We will then review progress in the development of means to mitigate losses of livestock to coyotes and how those developments might apply to situations in the northeast. There have been many studies, some with conflicting results, and we will restrict our review here to only a sampling to gain an appreciation of the problems and possible solutions.

ASSESSING THE PROBLEM

There is not universal accord that reductions in densities of coyotes are consistent with reduced losses of sheep to predation. Not all coyotes kill sheep, and many of the coyotes removed are not the offenders. Sterner and Shumake provide a good review of the results of a sampling of surveys in the western United States designed to estimate the extent of predation by coyotes on sheep.[2] Those surveys were classified into three types: 1) questionnaire, 2) interview, and 3) biological.

QUESTIONNAIRE
Sheep ranchers in Colorado, Montana, Texas, and Wyoming were sampled by questionnaire from 1966 through 1969. That survey included ranchers who collectively herded approximately 16 million sheep. The total annual percent lost to all causes varied by state from 15% to 36%; the percent lost to coyotes varied from 3% to 5%. Coyotes accounted for about 70% of all losses to predators. A second survey in Idaho in the early 1970s found total annual losses were 12% to 14%, the percent lost to coyotes 2-3%, and the proportion of losses to predators attributed to coyotes 74-82%.

A comprehensive questionnaire survey was conducted by the United States Department of Agriculture's Economic Research Service in 1974. A total of 8,910 responses were received from 38,000 sheep producers surveyed in 15 western states. That survey showed an overall average of 8.1% loss of lambs to coyotes and 11.4% loss of lambs to all predators. Of the adult sheep 2.5% were killed by coyotes and 3.4% by all predators.[3] These and other surveys indicate that predation is a much more serious problem for some producers than for others, with some 20% to 25% of producers sustaining annual losses in excess of 10%.

INTERVIEWS
Additional sampling of sheep ranchers in California and Utah were conducted by interviews from 1969 through 1974. These interviews supported the results from questionnaire sampling, implicating the coyote in the loss of 1-5% of all sheep, and identifying the coyote as responsible for 78-88% of all losses to predators.

A 1974 survey of sheep producers in Alberta showed that province-wide predation losses averaged 1.6% of the ewes and 2.8% of the lambs.[4] Interestingly, rates of predation varied considerably by landtype, from 0.8% loss of lambs and ewes in southern parklands to 3.2% of ewes in the northern parkland and 6.8% of the lambs in the mixed forest. The authors attributed increases in predation among landscapes to increasing forested habitats adjacent to sheep pastures. Other factors likely contributing to varying rates of predation included flock size, management practices, accessibility of flocks to coyotes, and alternate food supplies for coyotes. Predation accounted for 24% and 18% of the total annual mortality of lambs and ewes respectively. Larger flocks were more susceptible to predation than smaller flocks. Coyotes were responsible for 88% of losses to predation.

Coyotes are often attracted to farms where carcasses of livestock are left exposed. Once carcasses have been consumed, coyotes may turn to killing live animals (G. Connolly).

BIOLOGICAL

A series of ground searches on selected sheep ranges in the western United States from 1972 through 1976 perhaps provided the most unbiased measure of the extent of coyote predation on sheep. This sample of 8 surveys involved daily searches for dead sheep and examinations of sheep carcasses to determine cause of death. Losses due solely to coyotes varied from 4% with coyote control to 21% with restricted control. In 4 of 6 cases, coyotes were responsible for over 90% of all losses to predators.

The 1970s was a period when a great deal of effort was expended by state and federal agencies in the United States in estimating rates of predation by coyotes on sheep. This interest had much to do with the 1972 president's executive order banning the use of poisons on federal land. The problem had to be quantified, and alternate methods of reducing losses to predation had to be developed. The following examples serve to illustrate how most studies showed much the same result.

Donald Henne of the Montana Cooperative Wildlife Research Unit documented causes of mortality suffered by domestic sheep on a 3,393 ha western Montana ranch from March 15, 1974 through March 14, 1975.[5] There was no coyote control during the first 7 months of the study. Eighty-five percent of field mortality over the

12-month period was the result of predators. Predators killed 21% of the original herd and 29% of the 1974 lamb crop exposed to predation. Coyotes were responsible for 436 of 449 predator kills (97%). Seventy-five percent of the sheep lost to predation were healthy compared to 73% of a sample shot for comparison (coyotes were apparently not selecting for sick or diseased animals). Coyotes killed 72% of the sheep by neck-throat bites. Feeding on sheep ranged from none (9%) to very light (11%), light (28%), moderate (38%), and extensive (14%). Henne found that coyotes seldom returned to carcasses, and the leaving of carcasses had no measureable effect on the number of new kills.

A study in Nebraska measured the impact of predation on livestock in 22 western states from 1971 through 1973. Percentage losses of sheep and lambs were 7.2, 7.9, and 8.1 for the three years, respectively. The estimated monetary losses of livestock increased from $105 million in 1971 to $170 million in 1973. In 1973 alone, losses of cattle and calves totalled $80 million, sheep and lambs $53 million, chickens $32 million, and pigs $5 million.

"For all species, the coyote was by far the most important predator."[6]

The coyote was also the most important predator in a study of predation and the sheep industry in California during 1972-1974, being responsible for 82% of all losses to predators. (Dogs accounted for 14% of predation.) Coyotes were responsible for 93% of all predator-killed lambs and ewes in a study of mortality associated with sheep operations in Idaho in 1973-74, 91% of losses to predation in northeastern Nevada, and 77% of losses to predation on 5 southern Wyoming ranches in 1973-75. Predation accounted for 62% of total lamb loss on 10 sheep ranches in western Utah in 1972-1975 and coyotes were responsible for 94% of all predator kills.[7]

A survey of 1,251 questionaire respondents in Iowa reported that 41% had sheep killed by coyotes or dogs in 1975. Three percent of all sheep owned by respondents were killed by coyotes. Surprisingly perhaps, 1% were killed by dogs. Also, dogs killed more sheep per incident and sheep per operator than did coyotes. Eighty percent of losses to coyotes occurred from May through September.

"The sheep industry in Iowa is confronted with a predator problem similar to that of western states. A large number of the sheep producers are losing significant percentages of their flocks to predators."[8]

A personal interview survey of 20% of range-sheep operators in the state of Utah who collectively owned approximately 135,000 ewes, was conducted in 1969.[9] Coyotes were responsible for 81% of the losses of lambs and 71% of the losses of ewes to predation. Sheep ranchers in Utah lost over $1.1 million to predation in 1969.

"Losses of domestic livestock to coyotes ... and dogs were investigated from claims filed at county courthouses in Iowa between 1960 and 1974. A total of 5,800 claims was examined, representing losses of 18,309 sheep, 826 cattle, 2,257 swine, and 6,839 chickens, turkeys, geese, and ducks. For all reported sheep losses, 49 percent were attributed to dogs and 36 percent to coyotes. The proportions of cattle, swine, and poultry killed by dogs also were greater than those attributed to coyotes. Since 1960, the proportion of the predator loss

attributed to coyotes has increased, although there has been no change in the total magnitude of predation losses.... Traditional management tools that result in the taking of coyotes primarily in the fall and winter (hunting, trapping and bounties) have little effect on coyotes during the season when the greatest livestock losses are occurring."[10]

In summary, results of most surveys showed that the coyote was the main predator of sheep in western North America and that losses to coyotes were often significant. The general trend appeared to be that most ranchers experienced a few losses, while a few ranchers received moderate to high losses. Also, far more lambs were lost than ewes. Although coyote predation on sheep has received the greatest attention and media coverage, coyotes can also be a significant predator of cattle, goats, hogs, and poultry and can cause damage to various crops such as melons and fruits. The Economics, Statistics, and Cooperative Services, USDA, included questions on cattle losses to predators as part of a comprehensive survey of the beef breeding industry.[11] The population of beef cattle producers was defined as all those in major feeder cattle regions of the continental United States with 20 or more beef breeding cows who marketed feeder calves or yearlings during 1975. The population as defined for estimating losses to predators included 80% of total beef breeding cows in the 50 states.

Predators killed less than one-tenth of one percent of the January 1 inventory of beef cattle in 1975. Most losses were attributed to predators other than coyotes and dogs. The reported rate of calf losses to predators was higher than that of cattle losses but it was still minor compared to other causes. Losses of calves ranged from 0.4% to 0.8%. By comparison, calf losses to theft, disease, and other causes ranged from 3.6% to 9.1%. If calves can get through the first 6-8 weeks of life the probability of predation decreases to nearly 0 by weaning time.[12] The total economic loss of sheep and cattle to coyotes in the United States in 1977 was approximately $39 million. A recent report by the United States National Agricultural Statistics Service estimated that coyotes were responsible for the predation of 84,500 sheep, 227,400 lambs, and 64,900 goats in the United States in 1990, for a total economic loss of $16.4 million.[13]

Coyotes were responsible for 35% of all confirmed losses of cattle to predation in Alberta from 1974-1978.[14] Predation of cattle by coyotes peaked during March-June. Coyotes selected calves over adults and adults over yearlings. The Animal Damage Control (ADC) program in the United States provides services to the public consisting primarily of direct predator control and technical assistance. Although estimates by the ADC of damage to domestic livestock by predators are based on reports from the public and are considered much lower than the actual damage and losses, the ADC estimated that coyotes damaged nearly 17,000 poultry and fowl valued at $351,000 in 1990. The most significant poultry damage was to turkeys, which accounted for more than $300,000 of the reported loss to poultry and fowl.[15]

In Nova Scotia provincial records show that compensation was paid for the loss of 317 sheep to coyotes in 1986. That figure increased to 1,016 in 1988, at which time the government paid out $73,715 as compensation to farmers for those losses,[16] and decreased to 580 by 1990, the last year that compensation was paid. Reasons for the decline might include a greater awareness of the growing problem, better herd-

Coyotes frequently attack sheep with bites to the head and neck; death is often caused by strangulation (G. Connolly).

ing practices, the increased use of guard dogs and donkeys and other means of improved stewardship, as well as a decline in the number of sheep farms (many producers were driven out of business by the predation of coyotes) and decreasing numbers of coyotes in core sheep areas. The loss in 1988 represented 3.4% of an estimated provincial sheep populaton of 30,000, very similar to average losses of sheep to coyotes in the western United States and the 3% loss of sheep to coyotes in Maine.[17] Most losses in Nova Scotia represent lambs in spring although losses of lambs and ewes in autumn are not uncommon. There is some concern in Nova Scotia over losses of beef calves to coyotes in spring, although the reported "kills" may not all be from direct predation by coyotes. Coyotes may feed on young calves that have died or been weakened from other causes.

The New Brunswick Department of Agriculture has compensated for losses of sheep to coyotes since 1979. Most losses occur from mid-summer through autumn, especially when young coyotes begin travelling and hunting with the adults. The number of sheep killed by coyotes in New Brunswick increased from 89 in 1989 to a high of 325 in 1992. The numbers fluctuated during this 14-year period from 57 in 1981 to 312 in 1984 and down to 105 in 1987. The loss to coyote predation averages 2-4% of the total provincial population of approximately 8,000 breeding ewes and lambs. Compensation averages $100 per loss and total annual compensation has varied from a low of $4,465 in 1981 to $24,413 in 1990.[18]

The way coyotes kill sheep appears similar throughout its range. Guy Connolly and his colleagues studied the behaviour of captive coyotes killing sheep in California and found differences in which of the captive coyotes actually did the killing. The coyotes attacking sheep most frequently were 2-year old males, and females paired with those males. Yearling males attacked less frequently and unpaired females did not attack.

> *"Each coyote clamped its teeth in or near the larynx region of the sheep and held on until the sheep succumbed. This technique left characteristic tooth marks and hemorrhaging. The sheep appeared to die primarily of suffocation. Killing time averaged 13 minutes..... The body parts most frequently eaten from kills were digestive organs and muscle from the hind leg, neck, shoulder, and head."*[19]

PREVENTIVE MANAGEMENT

It seems only reasonable that if so much effort has been devoted to estimating the magnitude of losses of livestock to predators, an equal or greater effort would be devoted to developing preventive measures to reduce those losses. This has certainly been the case, and I will now review a selection of those efforts. First I will consider some of the early research which evaluated various methods of preventive management options, and then I will provide a summary of which methods are commonly used for specific domestic species.

Basically there are two ways to reduce losses of livestock to coyotes: 1) remove the offending coyotes, or 2) discourage them by keeping predator and livestock apart.[20] We will limit our discussion here to the second option, i.e., preventive management.

CONDITIONED AVOIDANCE OF PREY

Some of the earliest research on reducing loss of sheep to coyotes (in the absence of wide-scale programs of poisoning coyotes) experimented with means of developing conditioned avoidance of sheep by coyotes.

> *"If consumption of a particular substance is followed by illness, an animal often decreases consumption of that substance on a subsequent exposure."*[21]

Experimental trials injected sheep carcasses with chemicals which, when ingested by coyotes, caused unpleasant reactions that the coyotes would, hopefully, associate with sheep. It was assumed that once so conditioned, coyotes would avoid further predation on sheep. The drug most often used in these trials was lithium chloride (LiCl), a naturally occurring, nonlethal salt which is inexpensive and invokes rapid onset of illness which is not long lasting.[22] In coyotes, reaction to LiCl is vomiting which begins approximately ½ hour after ingestion. In theory ranchers would position LiCl laced sheep carcasses at the edges of pastures to intercept coyotes and develop conditioned avoidance behaviour towards sheep.

Carl Gustavson of North Dakota State University first claimed success with aversive conditioning in coyotes and documented up to 60% reductions in losses of sheep during 4 field trials.[23] One potential problem was that the highly developed sense of smell in coyotes allowed them to detect the presence or absence of the salty chemical and thus they did not always associate invoked sickness with live "unscented" sheep. Further trials suggested that:

> *"even if an effective chemical could be found for lacing dead sheep, the killing of*

live sheep would continue or perhaps even increase as coyotes begin to avoid dead sheep remains (which might be laced) and switch over to live sheep."[24]

Subsequent studies questioned the positive taste aversive results of earlier research and the utility of widescale field application.[25] In 1982 John Bourne and Michael Dorrance concluded from studies in Alberta and a review of the literature that:

"To date, no definitive field study has shown that LiCl baits reduce predation losses of domestic sheep."[26]

There was some effort in the mid-1970s to use odour as a repellent for reducing predation, but those experiments proved inconclusive.[27]

ANTIPREDATOR FENCING

"Total exclusion of coyotes by fencing is impractical because they might dig deeper, climb or jump higher, or wait until the fence is damaged or inoperable (with electric fences) to pass through. But it is possible to fence out coyotes with reasonable effectiveness. Important factors in accomplishing this include cost, motivation for dealing with the problem of predation, and willingness to take the long-term view necessary to justify the investment involved in fencing."[28]

Fencing appears to be the most effective means of reducing, or in many instances eliminating, predation by coyotes on domestic sheep. Conventional types of fencing have been used to deter coyotes since at least the 1890s.[29] However, fencing must be done properly and only after an objective long-term cost-benefit assessment. Details for construction of conventional and electric exclusion fences are available from most state and provincial agriculture and/or wildlife extension services.

Conventional (non-electric and usually netwire) fences can effectively reduce predation losses to coyotes. Although coyotes can dig under, jump over, and go through fences (they can fit through openings as small as 15 cm (6 inches) on a side) coyote-proof fences are possible. The most effective conventional fences should be 1.5-1.8 m (5-6 feet) high, made of woven-wire galvanized mesh, with a 0.61-m (2-foot) apron turned outward at the ground to discourage coyotes from digging under. A 45.7-cm (18-inch) outward facing overhang provides additional protection. Regular fence maintenance allows identification of potential access points and sites coyotes may be frequenting or where they may be digging. Removal of coyotes from such sites may be feasible. Electric fences have been shown to be most effective at excluding coyotes.

"The use of electric fencing to deter coyotes was discussed by W. L. McAtee as early as 1939. In past years, a few Kansas sheep producers have used standard single or double-wire electric fences in attempts to exclude coyotes, with some apparent success. It was not until recent revolutionary developments in electric fence technology and design, however, that this technique became an effective and economically practical method for excluding predators from livestock.

The development of new, low-impedance energizers (chargers) in new Zealand and Australia has prompted renewed interest in the utilization of electrified fences for protecting livestock from predators.

Proper fencing remains one of the most effective means for keeping coyotes away from livestock (G. Connolly).

Because coyotes are very agile, any fence protecting livestock should be at least 1.5-1.8 m (5-6 feet) high (G. Connolly).

Coyotes can squeeze through openings as small as 15 cm (6 inches) on a side (G. Connolly).

These fences utilize high tensile strength, smooth wire stretched to a tension of 150 to 250 pounds [68 to 113 kg]. This tension helps to maintain the proper wire spacings and assures that any animal attempting to force its way between wires will make strong contact."

The most practical fencing arrangement appears to be a 5-strand electrified design with alternating hot and ground wires and 15-cm (6-inch) spacings (beginning at ground) between the first 3 strands followed by 20- and 25-cm (8- and 10-inch) spacings [total height approximately 0.91 m (3 feet)]. Tests in Kansas by the Denver Wildlife Research Center, USFWS, have shown that:

"where existing woven wire fences are in reasonably good condition, sheep can

187

be protected from coyotes by adding 4 or 5 off-set electric wires. [Note: some agencies recommend only 1 or 2 off set electric wires]. In that case, all of the electric wires were charged and the existing fence was used as a ground. More or less wires might be required for a particular fence, depending on the net wire spacings and the habits of depredating coyotes."

Electric fences have been field tested to measure their success at reducing predation by coyotes.

"In 1979, predator research biologists from the Denver Wildlife Research Center, USFWS, interviewed sheep producers in the West who were using electric fences or wires to protect sheep from coyotes. Twenty-three producers were interviewed in Kansas, Oklahoma and Texas and 14 in California, Oregon and Washington. Fourteen producers provided adequate information to permit a comparison before and after they erected their electric fences and wires. Before fencing, losses to coyotes by all 14 producers over an aggregate total of 271 months and 27 lambing seasons totaled 1,064 sheep. Losses after fences or electric wires were installed, over a period of 228 months and 22 lambing seasons, totaled 51 sheep. This represents a reduction of about 94 percent in reported predator losses after the installation of electric fences or wires. Of 34 respondents, 23 (68%) rated their fences as very effective and 11 (32%) as fairly effective for controlling predation. All but one or two of 34 producers said that their fences were a good investment, that they would install more electric fence or additional wires if losses in the future were high, and that they would recommend electric fencing as a predator damage control technique to other producers."[30]

A study in Alberta confirmed the effectiveness of electric fencing in deterring coyote predation on sheep within forested and agricultural landscape similar to the conditions throughout much of the northeast.

"... Our tests ran throughout 1 ½ - 2 ½ grazing seasons under conditions typical of most domestic sheep operations in northern Alberta, and are probably applicable to most of the forested areas of Canada....

Predation losses on these farms declined dramatically after electric fences were completed [from 60 in 1974 to 6 in 1976]....

Demand for lethal control has declined markedly since electric fences became operational and consequently, number of predators taken in control operations have also declined. At least 46 coyotes were killed in 1975, and 30 ... in 1976, prior to completion of electric fences. In contrast, only four coyotes were killed during 1976-78, after fences were completed."[31]

Livestock Protection Animals

The 1972 ban on the use of toxicants for controlling predators in the United States led to producers and researchers searching for alternate methods of predator management. One popular and aesthetically appealing method has been the use of certain animals either bred and/or trained to guard livestock, especially sheep, against predators. We will review the use and effectiveness of two such animals here: the dog and the donkey.

GUARD DOGS

"The livestock protection breeds are among the most ancient of dogs. Indeed, the role of flock guardian may have been one of the first uses man found for the domesticated dog. Livestock protection dogs probably originated in the Middle East and Asia.... By the time of Christ, this use for dogs seems to have been widespread.... It seems certain that, from the earliest of times, livestock protection dogs served as a shepherd's first line of defense from wild animals....

Livestock protection dogs share many characteristics. All are possessed of an independent, aloof personality, the ability to think for themselves, unabiding loyalty and undaunting courage. Many of the dogs are white, which is probably the result of selective breeding. It has been theorized that white dogs "blend in" with sheep and are more easily distinguished from predators by both sheep and shepherds."[32]

Readers should not confuse livestock guarding dogs with livestock herding dogs. Herding dogs, such as border collies, are kept busy chasing, biting, and barking to control and direct the movement of livestock, especially sheep. They work closely with the handler, responding to hand and verbal signals. Guard dogs most often do their job independently and are discouraged from biting, barking, or otherwise disturbing the sheep. Their job is to protect the sheep, not to herd them. Guard dogs are often intolerant of other dogs near "their" sheep and do not work well with herding dogs.[33]

There are a variety of guard dog breeds available in North America, and for details on the care and training of the most popular breeds I refer the reader to the following publications.

Guarding Dogs Protect Sheep from Predators by Jeffrey Green and Roger Woodruff (Agriculture Information Bulletin #455, USDA, Dubois, Idaho, 1983, 27pp.)

Livestock Protection Dogs by David Sims and Orysia Dawydiak (Fort Payne, Alabama: OTR Publications, 1990, 128 pp.)

The following are several of the most popular and dependable breeds.

THE AKBASH

A western Turkey working dog essential in that country for the protection of flocks from wolves, wild dogs, bears, and jackals. Considered one of the most beautiful of guard dogs, it combines elegance with power. Mature males may weigh 54 kg (120 pounds). In North America it has proven effective in deterring coyotes, feral dogs, and other predators.[34]

THE ANATOLIAN SHEPHERD

The most popular of Turkish breeds in North America. A big, burly, powerful dog [males can weigh 45 kg (100 pounds)] but combined with a lionlike grace and tremendous agility.

"The Anatolian has proven to be an excellent dog for livestock protection and as a home guardian."

THE GREAT PYRENEES

Originating in the Great Pyrenees Mountains of France this breed has proven to be the most popular of livestock guarding dogs in North America. It was the earliest of livestock protecting dogs brought to this country and is equally suited as watchdog and trusted companion.

> *"He is as serious in play as in work, adapting and molding himself to the moods, desires and even the very life of his human companions, through fair weather and foul, through leisure hours and hours fraught with danger, responsibility and extreme exertion; he is the exemplification of gentleness and docility with those he knows, of faithfulness and devotion for his master even to the point of self-sacrifice; and of courage in the protection of the flock placed in his care and of the ones he loves."*

THE KOMONDOR

The dog frequently depicted in movies and cartoons as the faithful guardian of sheep from the big bad wolf. This breed is distinctive by its long corded white coat and formidable stature. The Komondor has been used to guard flocks from predators on the windswept steppes of Hungary for more than 1,000 years. The long, thick, and corded coat serves as protection from both the elements and the teeth and claws of predators. It is perhaps the most powerful, rugged, and hardy of all the breeds of livestock protection dogs.

> *"Perhaps the most serious problem encountered by some producers is one of a personal disillusionment in the use of guarding dogs. Some think that the purchase of a guard dog will immediately solve their predator problems. Unfortunately, this is rarely the case, especially on the range....*
>
> *Guard dogs cannot be turned on and off at will, and possible benefits offered by the dog are generally not realized without an initial investment of time and patience....*
>
> *Some become good livestock guardians and others do not. After a certain point it appears that no amount of proper training and early exposure will guarantee that a dog will become a good guardian. Instinctive ability must be present in the successful dog."*[35]

Surveys of sheep producers in the United States and Canada have shown that the use of guard dogs offers a reasonable and passive method of deterring predation.[36]

> *"Once established, dogs can often be viewed as a first line of defense to be supplemented with other methods of control as necessary. However, not all dogs are effective, and not all predator problems will be solved by dogs."*[37]

William Andelt, Department of Fishery and Wildlife Biology at Colorado State University, evaluated the effectiveness of livestock guarding dogs for reducing predation on domestic sheep in Colorado.

> *"Domestic ewe and lamb mortality from all causes and from predators were estimated from surveys of producers with and without livestock guarding dogs in Colorado during 1986. In general, producers without guarding dogs lost a greater*

Young livestock protection dogs should be acquainted with livestock at an early age, but owners should be careful that the puppies are not injured or badly frightened (USDA).

proportion of their ewes and lambs from all causes and from coyotes than did producers with guarding dogs. Twenty of 22 producers that used guarding dogs in 1986 rated their dogs' predator control performance as excellent or good.... The majority of producers also indicated that guarding dogs reduced their reliance on other predator control techniques and on predator control agencies."[38]

As he does when using other potential means for limiting losses of sheep to predation, a producer must measure the potential benefits of livestock guarding dogs to his operation relative to current and projected losses without such protection.

"Mean first-year cost for 1 guarding dog including cost of purchase, shipping, feed, health care, travel associated with care and training of the dog, damage caused by the dog, and miscellaneous totalled $834. Subsequent mean-annual expenses for feed, travel, health care, and miscellaneous totaled $286. A mean of 9 hours/month labor was required to train and maintain a dog.... Our research ... indicates that more dogs work well than fail, and there are few limits to the type of conditions under which a good dog can be a benefit....

To some producers, the peace of mind of knowing a dog is on duty 24 hours/ day is a significant benefit. Because predation is episodic, some producers may suffer significant losses only once or twice in a several year period."[39]

Some points for consideration by producers thinking of purchasing livestock guarding dogs include the following.[40]

(1) There is no one breed of dog currently thought to be the best for predator control.

(2) Dogs should be purchased from a reputable breeder—one who knows about the dogs he or she sells.

(3) Given a choice, buy dogs from a working parentage.

(4) Start the dogs with livestock at an early age (8-12 weeks) and be sure that the livestock won't injure the young puppy or frighten it badly.

(5) Put the pups immediately where you want them to work. (Don't raise a pup for several months in your home or yard and then later expect it to stay near the barn with your sheep.)

(6) Be patient. Large working dogs may not mature until 2 or 3 years of age, so expect puppy problems (such as playing with sheep) for some time. However, be swift to correct any bad behaviour of the dog, especially as regards playing with or harrassing livestock. The dog must know that harrassing the stock is unacceptable.

(7) Give the dog some basic obedience training (come, sit, stay, no, etc.) and be able to reasonably control it.

(8) Even though a pup is of a guarding breed, it may not necessarily perform the livestock guarding task well.

(9) Don't expect miracles, presumably the guarding is instinctive, but be prepared to teach the dog what you expect it to do. (Where it is to guard and what it is to guard.)

(10) Opinion varies as to the degree of affection that should be given a guarding dog. The best approach is probably to give the dog affection when it is where it is supposed to be, and when it is doing what it is supposed to be doing. This positive enforcement will produce better results than physical abuse.

The Komondor, shown here in mock battle with a coyote, is distinctive by its long, corded, white coat and formidable stature (J. S. Green).

Producers interested in purchasing one or more guarding dogs would be well advised to thoroughly research the topic. This would include knowing the availability of reputable breeders, the economics of guard dogs to their particular operation, the breed most compatible with their needs and objectives and a realistic assessment of the time required to ensure that the guard dog option becomes a positive investment to their business.

GUARD DONKEYS

"Donkeys are small asses, and like their close relatives, horses, they come in all sizes and colors.... The name 'donkey,' is derived from the English word 'dun,' which describes the usual color.... Males are known as 'jacks,' females as 'jennets' or 'jennys.' Burros are the small so-called native asses of North America, having been brought here by early Spanish expeditions. They are a blend of many breeds originating in Europe and the Middle East. The Spanish translation of 'donkey' is 'burro.' Thus the terms donkey and burro are used interchangeably."[41]

In the United States feral donkeys are found in Arizona, Nevada, California, Oregon, and Utah, and populations are managed by The Bureau of Land Management and the U.S. Forest Service under the 1971 Wild Free-Roaming Horse and Burro Act. A feral donkey management plan was introduced in 1988 and a reduction of the wild populations was advised. Feral donkeys are periodically removed from the wild and sold to the public.[42] This program is the source of most donkeys used for livestock protection in Canada and the United States.

There have been studies to measure the effectiveness and utility of donkeys for protecting livestock. Some results and recommendations from those studies include the following.[43]

(1) Use only a jenny or a gelded jack (john). Intact jacks are too aggressive and may injure livestock. Some jennys may also injure livestock.

(2) Use only one donkey per group of sheep. When 2 or more adult donkeys are together or with a horse, they usually stay together, not necessarily near the sheep. Also avoid using donkeys in adjacent pastures since they may fraternize across the fence and ignore the sheep.

(3) Allow about 4-6 weeks for a naive donkey to bond to the sheep. Stronger bonding may occur when a very young donkey is raised from birth with sheep.

(4) Remove the donkey during lambing, particularly if lambing in confinement, as a precaution against accidental or intentional injuries to lambs or disruption of the lamb-ewe bond.

Other suggestions for prospective guard donkey users include:[44]

(5) Guard donkeys should be selected from medium- to large-sized stock. Do not use extremely small or miniature donkeys.

(6) Test a new donkey's guarding response by challenging the donkey with a dog in a corral or small pasture.

(7) Raise guard donkeys away from dogs. Avoid or limit the use of herding dogs around donkeys.

(8) Use donkeys in small [242 ha (less than 600 acres)] open pastures with not more than 200 head of sheep or goats.

(9) Do not allow donkeys access to feed containing Rumensin, urea, or other products intended only for ruminants (cattle, sheep, goats).

Donkeys respond to intruding dogs and coyotes by braying, baring of the teeth, and chasing with attempts to kick and bite the intruder. The reaction of guarding donkeys to canids appears to be more of a sheer dislike for the intruder than an act of protection towards the flock. Benefits of guarding donkeys over guarding dogs include longevity (20 years or more) and less cost for feed, maintenance, and care.[45]

One of the largest breeders of donkeys in Atlantic Canada is Don James of Apohaqui, New Brunswick. When I spoke with Don at his Great White North Donkey and Mule Company in August 1994 he had 35 head of miniature, standard, and mammoth stock. He sells donkeys for both pets and guarding livestock, and I would suggest that anyone wishing to learn more about the art of raising donkeys should visit Don at his secluded farm in the rolling hills of southern New Brunswick just outside of Sussex. Some suggestions from Don for those interested in donkeys for protecting livestock include the following:

"Some donkeys, regardless of their size, are naturals as guard donkeys. Most guard donkeys are made, however—that is bonded with their charges when young. We suggest putting the donkey at weaning age, 4-6 months, in the barn or corral, close to his/her new charges, and allowing them to bond. Donkeys love company and seem to bond readily with sheep or cattle. An advantage over a dog is that they readily eat the same as their charges, apart from certain feeds, and quite happily stay with the flock/herd....

Even minatures or small standards can be quite protective - it all depends on the individual donkey....

Standard size donkeys cost in the region of $750, miniature jacks $850. Ongoing costs include regular worming and hoof care. Otherwise, they are relatively inexpensive to keep."

Don James breeds and sells mammoth, standard, and minature donkeys for pets and to protect livestock from predators (G. Parker).

Like guard dogs, donkeys should be considered a tool to minimize losses of livestock and not a substitute for good livestock management, which can include improved fencing, better herding and lambing practices, and proper disposal of dead livestock.

PREDATOR FRIGHTENING DEVICES

An assortment of devices and methods for frightening or otherwise deterring coyotes from approaching sheep have been tried with varying levels of success. Most can only be effective when sheep are in corrals or closely confined in small pasturages. It is important to understand that coyotes soon become accustomed to frightening devices; producers should vary their positions, frequencies, and intensities, and the combinations of use.

Mercury vapour lights with electric-eye sensors above corrals which automatically turn on at dusk and off at dawn have been used with success. Lighted corrals also provide the owner the opportunity to stake out and shoot the offending animals. Less successful are propane exploders which produce explosions at timed intervals. Coyotes soon become accustomed to such devices and their use should be temporary until more effective preventive actions can be implemented. There is some evidence that sheep wearing bells are less prone to attack by coyotes than sheep without bells, although there have been few studies to measure their effectiveness. Vehicles, radios, or other distractions placed near or among sheep may also help to deter predation.

HUSBANDRY PRACTICES

The single most important preventive management option available to the sheep producer is penning sheep at night.

> *"Sheep that are regularly penned soon learn to come into the corrals or nearby vicinity in the evening where they can be shut in with a minimal amount of time and effort. Even if the corral fence is not 'coyote proof,' the mere fact that the sheep are confined reduces the predation risk. Upgrading corral or pasture fences with predator resistant fences and adding lights can further reduce the risk of loss."*[46]

Prior to the arrival of the coyote in the northeast, many livestock producers disposed of carcasses in wooded areas adjacent to pastures. It is now evident that such practices can lead to increased predation by coyotes on pastured livestock. There are two apparent reasons for this. First, coyotes which feed on sheep carrion, for example, become accustomed to a diet of sheep, and when the carrion has been consumed, they turn to killing pastured live animals. Second, there is evidence from Alberta that in winter coyotes may roam considerable distances to obtain food, and those coyotes can concentrate in areas where agricultural carrion is available.[47] In Alberta, coyotes which breed in the forests may move to agricultural lands in winter in search of food, further increasing the risks of coyote concentrations at carrion disposal sites.

In the northeast, lambing normally takes place in barns and sheds, so the need for special protection from predators at this very vulnerable period is removed. However, ewes and young lambs are often pastured soon after lambing, and producers should exercise due caution. A relatively small, open, and tightly fenced pasture that can be kept under close surveillance is recommended. Cow-calf operators may wish to take similar precautions, especially if predation by coyotes on young calves has occurred in the past.

The keeping of detailed records by producers on counts of sheep and when and where losses do occur can prove important for identifying trends and patterns of predation and for making decisions on the type and intensity of predator damage control and preventive management. When pasture availability allows, producers may distribute stock in a manner which reduces predation. Records may show that certain pastures are susceptible to predation at certain times of the year, and appropriate adjustments in grazing schedules can prove useful.

Finally, a producer should be certain of the source of mortality when a carcass is examined. Wrongly attributing death to predation by coyotes can lead to unjustified and expensive programs of preventive management or to costly efforts of coyote removal.

> "... The herd should be examined for signs of disease, birthing problems, or other conditions that could lead to weakness or death."[48]

14 COYOTE MANAGEMENT

"Man has become a worldwide and master predator, exploiting many animal resources and eliminating competing predators. His mastery is increasingly secure by virtue of his numbers, technology, and innovations in husbandry. His intolerance, however, towards other predatory animals-contesting them to the death-continues largely unabated. From childhood, man's legends, art, religion, and literature steep him too well in fear and enmity of the larger predatory species..... A predator is an animal that kills another and more often than not eats its prey. If the prey species is abundant and of no economic or recreational value, the public does not become excited except perhaps to regard the predator as a repugnant killer. Repugnant or not, a predator must kill in order to survive, a detail often overlooked by the layman who feels revulsion at the sight of blood and body parts."[1]

These words by Robert McCabe and Edward Kozicky on predator management, although penned nearly a quarter of a century ago, seem appropriate for introducing this discussion on management of the eastern coyote. The recent establishment of coyotes in the northeast has certainly influenced the abundance, habitat use, geographical distribution, and amplitude of population change of many native wildlife species. We have reviewed the interactions of coyotes with several wildlife species in the northeast. To a great many people the most important of these is the influence of coyotes on white-tailed deer. Many hunters refer to deer and wildlife as one and the same, i.e., wildlife = white-tailed deer, even though the white-tailed deer is a relative newcomer to many parts of the northeast and the deep winter snows of the spruce-fir forests represent an unnatural and often hostile environment. Would there be such concern about the coyote if it ate porcupines rather than deer in the forests, or mice rather than sheep in the pastures? The answer is most certainly not, so the problem lies with the coyote being man's competitor for both wild and domestic animals. Hardly a revolutionary thought, but one certainly worth establishing at the outset before methods of, and justifications for, coyote management are discussed.

"To manage any animal group implies efforts to increase, decrease, or to hold stable the group in question. In the case of predators, the greatest emphasis is usually placed on reduction of numbers and only rarely on increasing or maintaining predator populations." [2]

Most of us manage one thing or another, whether it be our bank account, grocery supplies, or our temper. Some are better managers than others. But how do you "manage" wildlife species or populations? I have reviewed some of the basic principles and challenges of managing white-tailed deer, especially in the northeast, where population levels are often influenced by environmental stress, especially the depth and duration of winter snow. At the local level, winter cover and food requirements of deer can be maintained or enhanced through properly designed patterns of forest harvest. Populations can also be influenced by flexible regulations which distribute the harvest in accordance with regional densities of deer and hunting pressures. Management options are more limited for many other wildlife species, and the coyote may well be one of the most difficult of all to manage. Few sportsmen would question a management goal for white-tailed deer of maintaining populations that provide the highest hunting success to the greatest number of hunters without reducing the "carrying capacity" of the habitat. With coyotes there is no such agreement on just what the present or future management objectives should be. Do we set population goals for coyotes and develop management plans to reach those goals? For coyotes, population targets have traditionally been downward, and management has been one of control, if not eradication.

A symposium on the coyote held in Colorado in 1978 featured a session on management. [3] The papers in the management session dealt exclusively with assessing the damage to domestic animals by coyotes and reviewing measures for controlling that damage and reducing the numbers of coyotes. To my knowledge there has never been a management strategy for coyotes with a goal to increase populations. Proactive coyote management strategies have therefore traditionally consisted of means for reducing losses of domestic animals to coyotes, usually accomplished through campaigns of coyote control.

"The known number of coyotes removed by the Federal-Cooperative Animal Damage Control Program from 1916 through 1975 was 3,973,558.... This is a minimum estimate because many of those destroyed by toxicants were probably not found. Even greater numbers may have been taken by ranchers, sport hunters, and fur trappers. In addition, many State and local governmental agencies conducted predator control work outside the auspices of the Federally supervised program. In 1974 at least 295,000 coyotes were killed in the 17 western states.... Some 71,000 of these were taken by the Federal Animal Control Program and the remainder by sport hunters, fur trappers, and local control or bounty programs....[F]or each coyote taken by Federal agents at least three more were killed by others." [4]

Coyote management throughout most of this century has consisted of removing large numbers as cheaply and efficiently as possible. Sheep ranching is not a large industry in northeastern North America and although eastern coyotes continue to kill sheep here, the problem is not as unmanageable as it is on the open western prairies where hundreds of thousands of sheep spend much of the year on large acreages exposed to predators.

Most wildlife agencies in the northeast now accept the eastern coyote as an established component of the wildlife fauna, and management strategies are developed accordingly. We may not all agree with the *fait accompli* of that recognition but the success of colonization by the eastern coyote suggests that we would be wise to do so. The coyote is also generally placed within the furbearer category of consumptive wildlife, and the trapping of coyotes is confined to regulated harvests like that of other furbearers such as foxes, bobcats, and pine marten. Most state and provincial wildlife agencies in the northeast also allow the killing of coyotes during deer and small game hunting seasons or by the purchase of a special licence when other hunting seasons are closed. Except under a few local laws at the county or state level, the bounty system is no longer, or never was, recognized as a practical means to control or reduce coyotes. The following review should serve to acquaint readers with the general status and recognition given the eastern coyote by a selected number of states and provinces; readers interested in regulations which apply to coyotes in their area should refer to game regulations for their specific jurisdiction or consult with local game department officials.

Bounties were the traditional means of "managing" coyotes in Iowa. The state of Iowa does not support the practice, but because bylaw bounties are paid from county taxes, the bounty system is still in effect in that state. However, few bounties have been paid on coyotes over the years, because of the fraud associated with such payments and because of very tight county budgets. In 1970 the coyote was defined as a furbearer and game species. Coyotes can be hunted year-round and trapped during regular autumn fur harvest seasons. Landowners can remove problem coyotes at any time with traps or other means. In 1991 the state was attempting to establish a full-time animal control agent. Good livestock husbandry techniques have proven the most effective means for coping with sheep predation by coyotes.[5]

The state of Tennessee recognizes the coyote as a furbearer, and as such it is protected by law, but for a person with the proper licence, the hunting and trapping season is year-round with no limit. The state has never used bounties; several bounty bills introduced in the legislature were defeated. Although the state is not directly involved with coyote control, technical assistance is provided to help landowners control nuisance coyotes.[6]

"Bounties for coyotes were paid by several county administrations in Ohio for a short time but have been withdrawn. Control measures in stock damage situations are performed by the United States Department of Agriculture. Reparations are paid to farmers with verified damage by the Ohio Department of Agriculture. Inspections have shown that feral dogs cause three times as much stock damage as coyotes. The coyote was added to the furbearer list in the early 1980s.... We currently have no closed season for coyotes although they cannot be taken by snare. We have facilitated contact between stockmen with depredation problems

and volunteer coyote hunters and trappers. A list of cooperators has been developed [in 1991] by the Ohio State Trappers Association to provide this cooperation to selectively remove problem animals and to reduce local problems....The Division of Wildlife does not support bounties. They have proven to be ineffective in alleviating problems and financially wasteful. We encourage people with depredation problems to revise their stock practices and to selectively remove problem animals."[7]

There was no management strategy for coyotes in Illinois prior to 1973 when they first came under the protection of state wildlife laws. Coyotes are now classified as a protected furbearer and can be hunted year-round except for the annual firearms deer season. Most coyotes are harvested from November through February. The present management program is designed to reduce coyotes below their present levels but, because of depressed pelt value, it has achieved little success. Coyote bounties have never been supported by the state of Illinois. A few counties paid bounties in the 1970s but most, if not all, have now been dropped....

"Almost no work on coyote damage control as it relates to livestock production has been accomplished in the state of Illinois. Usually livestock producers employ confinement facilities which totally eliminate losses to predators. The problems occur when a farmer tries to farrow his sows in the 40-acre woodlot down by the creek. Others use improper disposal methods for dead stock and coyotes become habituated to feeding on the critters the farmers are trying to protect. The best approach is usually to remove the offending animal by trapping."[8]

In Michigan, coyote management has progressed from bounty, to year-round seasons, to a liberal season. Depressed fur prices have discouraged the public from actively hunting and trapping coyotes, although the season is open from mid-July to mid-April. Coyotes do not normally cause a problem with livestock. Coyotes in Kentucky can be hunted legally year-round and trapped during the regular furbearer trapping season of approximately 75 days. The state has no bounty and landowners are encouraged to deal with coyote problems themselves. There are no state personnel paid to trap or hunt coyotes. In North Carolina, where coyotes only recently became established, the current management strategy is one of complete lack of protection. Coyotes are not recognized as either a furbearer or game species in West Virginia, and can be hunted and trapped in accordance with prevailing seasons and regulations for the harvesting of other species of wildlife. As in several other states, although West Virginia does not support the bounty, local governments have occasionally established bounties on coyotes. Selective removal of problem animals is the practice when game species are bothered by coyotes.[9]

There is no present strategy for management of the coyote in Rhode Island. Although recognized as a furbearer, the coyote can be shot at any time of the year, but pelts must be tagged prior to sale. There has never been a bounty on coyotes in that state. The present status of the coyote in New York state is that of a protected game species and furbearer which may be taken by the possessor of a valid licence for either small game or trapping. Coyotes taken in a lawful manner during the open season must be tagged with a possession tag. Coyote depredation on livestock in New York is considered insignificant. It has been illegal to pay bounties in the state of New York by any level of government since 1972. The law does allow property owners to kill coyotes which are injuring livestock or property.[10]

As coyotes became established in Connecticut, liberal regulations were established for both hunting and trapping.

> "Coyotes may now be trapped during the regular trapping season with no season bag limit. Coyotes may be hunted throughout the year except for the approximate one month period of spring turkey hunting and for a two week period immediately preceeding the opening of fall small game seasons. The coyote is considered a furbearer.... Preventive measures [for sheep] vary but electric or woven wire fence is most common.... If a coyote problem continues ... we may issue permits to allow trappers or hunters to attempt to remove the offending animal(s).... There is no bounty system in Connecticut nor would they be supported by our Division."[11]

The coyote was listed as a game animal in New Jersey with a closed season in the 1975-76 wildlife regulations. In 1980 it was listed as a furbearer, with a trapping season from mid-November to mid-March. In 1986 farmers were given permission to kill coyotes that were causing damage to livestock, crops, or property at any time of the year. Electric fencing is the preventive measure recommended in all cases of livestock depredation. Coyotes in Massachusetts received complete protection when they first arrived in that state. They are still protected but managed as a furbearer with both hunting and trapping seasons. Massachusetts has never had a bounty on coyotes.[12]

> "The coyote is not listed as a furbearer nor is it protected in New Hampshire. The coyote take climbed from 13 in 1972 peaking at 291 in 1986. The take has declined the last three years [1988-1990] probably largely due to low pelt prices and lack of hunter/trapper interest.... Our state does not support bounties and has helped kill past legislative proposals for them."[13]

Coyotes have been common in Maine at least since the 1960s and although they held no specific management status their exploitation was encouraged. The coyote was listed as a furbearer in 1972, but due to restrictions on trapping to protect other furbearers such as bobcat and fisher, seasons were soon shortened from most of the winter to one month. Special licences continued to permit the hunting of coyotes, and in 1983 a night hunting permit was introduced to expand and increase the efficiency of hunting opportunities. As coyotes increased and deer decreased through the late 1970s and early 1980s, and a concerned public demanded increased measures of control, the Maine Department of Inland Fisheries and Wildlife adopted a formal coyote control policy. Most control was focused on and around deer concentration areas in late winter. Although a bounty on coyotes was strongly advocated by a large segment of the public, government biologists opposed it as a highly questionable appropiation of limited state revenues. Although a form of incentive program was introduced in 1989, it was soon discontinued when it received little public support. Many small sheep-producers suffered high losses from coyotes due to poor security against predation when the problem first developed in the late 1970s and early 1980s. Those producers that survived early losses improved protection of stock by installing electric fences, improving herding practices and using guard animals. The state provided assistance to those producers who continued to sustain losses to coyotes.[14]

In the province of Quebec a bounty of $35 had been paid on coyotes by the Quebec Department of Agriculture from 1967 to 1971. In 1972 all payment of bounties for predators ceased although the Quebec Department of Wildlife administered a predator control program until 1981. In 1975-76 the coyote was specifically mentioned as a furbearer, but the trapping season, like the hunting season, was open year-round with no limits. A season for trapping coyotes, from mid-October to mid-March, was established in 1980, and a restricted season for hunting, from late October through February, was established in 1984. The hunting season was adjusted in 1986 from late September through April. In 1988 hunting and trapping seasons for coyotes both began in mid-October and ended on March 1. In 1994-95, however, in response to public concern over coyote predation on deer and sheep, the hunting season was extended to March 31. The harvest of coyotes in Quebec peaked at 4,086 in 1991.[15] Because of recent declines in numbers of white-tailed deer in northern regions, it is expected that numbers of coyotes will also continue to decline.

All four Atlantic Provinces now recognize the coyote as a furbearer and/or game animal, and as such the hunting and trapping of coyotes is regulated under provincial legislation. Coyotes in New Brunswick were first subject to provincial fur harvesting seasons in 1976. By 1992-93 coyotes could be trapped and/or snared during autumn seasons by holders of a fur harvesting licence. Coyotes could also be shot by holders of a small game and/or big game hunting licence, a spring bear hunting licence, or a special varmint licence (extended season through February). A "special coyote control permit" also allowed the holder of a valid fur harvester's licence to hunt, trap and/or snare coyotes during a 30-day period in a specific region of the province. In 1992-93 154 coyotes were taken on 33 of these special permits. Landowners could also obtain a licence to remove coyotes to prevent damage to property or injury to occupants of occupied land.

In Nova Scotia coyotes were first managed as a furbearer under the Lands and Forests Act when their presence in the province was recognized in 1976. Although they could be harvested year-round by legal means, trapping and snaring were only permitted by licenced fur harvesters (in 1992 the season for trapping coyotes was October 15 to February 28) or with a special Nuisance Wildlife Permit. As mentioned earlier, Nova Scotia implemented a $50 bounty on coyotes in 1982. The futility of that politically motivated venture soon became clear and the bounty was discontinued in 1987. In 1989 a Coyote Hunting Permit allowed hunting of coyotes with a centre fire rifle and a bullet of 80 grains or less from the end of the deer season to the end of March. In 1991 the bullet weight was raised to 100 grains and a questionnaire was added to allow an assessment of hunter success rates.

On Prince Edward Island coyotes were declared both game and furbearing animals under the Fish and Game Protection Act in 1987, shortly after the first coyote was trapped in that province in 1983. Hunting coyotes with radio-collared dogs has become popular with a few houndsmen and a special season was extended in 1993 until the end of February for that activity. In 1992 special seasons for calling and stalking coyotes were also extended until the end of March.

In Newfoundland the trapping and snaring of coyotes is permitted with a provincial fur harvesting licence. To date only 30 coyotes have been harvested on the island since the first one was killed in 1987.

In contrast to the unresolved conflict between coyotes and sheep in the west, the impact of coyotes on sheep in the northeast, although often a problem, is nevertheless, manageable. I have reviewed a selection of preventive management options available to the smaller sheep producers in the northeast, and in some instances government compensation buffers direct losses of livestock to coyotes. Most concern over the coyote in the extreme northeastern portions of its range, however, is due to its impact upon other wildlife species, especially the white-tailed deer.

"Man, the consummate predator, is covetous of all other creatures that impinge on his predatory prerogative. Thus, even though his predatory instincts are often recreational, as in fishing and hunting, he protects his potential prey by efforts to eliminate competition from other predators."[16]

Not everyone agrees that human beings should interfere in natural predator-prey systems for the sole reason of retaining more prey for their sporting pleasure. However, as both coyotes and deer now inhabit much of the northeast *because of* changes to the environment from human disturbance, the present coyote-deer predator-prey model might be considered unnatural. In that respect perhaps man not only has the right but the responsibility to ensure the viability of all wildlife populations in this unnatural environment caused by his meddling, including both deer and coyotes. This is a philosophical debate, and one for which there is no definitive right or wrong answer. However, the reader should understand and respect the way others may view the role of the coyote in the predator-prey systems of the northeast, whether these systems be perceived as natural or unnatural.

James Cardoza, a wildlife biologist with the Massachusetts Division of Fisheries

Lloyd Duncanson and Chet Brown with pelts from coyotes trapped in the Annapolis Valley area of Nova Scotia (L. Duncanson).

and Wildlife, offered these reflections on coyotes and predators in general, pointing out how polarized human perceptions of predation often fail to understand the real interactions between predator and prey or the functioning of the ecosystem in general.

> "In 1930 the Journal of Mammalogy referred to the coyote as the 'archpredator of our time.' Attitudes towards predators have become more tolerant since then, although extremist viewpoints still prevail. Emotional diatribes between sharply polarized factions hinder effective cooperation in resolving real problems and engender suspicions and antagonisms that carry over into other environmental issues. Despite some protectionist allegations, coyote predation is real and can be substantial.... Some predator control is unquestionably necessary some of the time. The mixture of lethal and nonlethal methods that may be used depends on the nature of the problem, the legality and practicality of the methods under consideration, and the knowledge and sensitivity of the persons implementing control.... Ultimately, interactions between humans and wildlife will be influenced by our capacity of understanding-of wildlife species, of ecosystems, and of each other. Those who see coyotes as a mysterious, benign Erdgeist ("earth spirit") and those who see a malevolent archpredator are both distorting the real coyote, a unique, adaptable wild creature filling a particular communal niche. Coyote problems can only be resolved by coming to terms with that reality."[17]

What have we learned of the role of the coyote as a predator in ecological systems across North America? We have certainly learned that the coyote is highly adaptable and capable of adjusting its food habits, behaviour, reproduction and even its size relative to the prevailing environment and available prey species. We have learned that populations, especially in northern forests, are influenced most by the availability of food. That food might be black-tailed deer fawns in Washington, snowshoe hare in Alberta, or white-tailed deer in Nova Scotia, but the influence of food on the population dynamics of coyotes is remarkably similar. We have also learned that the feeding habits of coyotes can vary between forested and agricultural habitats in the same geographical area, and just as all coyotes probably do not kill sheep, it is equally probable that all coyotes do not kill deer. Coyotes often adjust their diet throughout the year, feeding on those food sources most readily available. A diversified diet of mice, hares, birds and plants in the summer may change to one dominated by berries in the fall, snowshoe hare in the early winter, and white-tailed deer in late winter.

We have also learned that most efforts of extensive coyote control have met with limited success. Costly campaigns of poison control on the prairies did effectively reduce populations of coyotes, but they also reduced many other non-target species such as foxes, ferrets, and eagles. Such misguided efforts under the guise of "coyote management" are gone forever. Coyotes must now be recognized as one component of a complex and dynamic ecological system.

Deer populations in the northeast, in the absence of wild canid predators, have been controlled by winter weather and food availability. Recent declines in deer populations in southeastern Quebec, northern Maine, New Brunswick, and Nova

Scotia may have been initiated by environmental factors but were intensified by additive mortality from predation by coyotes in late winter. Because the decline has been so swift and extensive, it is doubtful that landscape change from forestry operations has been responsible, although it may have been a contributing factor.

The colonization and growth of coyote populations in forested wilderness regions of the northeast and concurrent declines in numbers of white-tailed deer may have been a real cause-effect relationship or a remarkable coincidence. We may never know for certain. Even if there were agreement on the cause-effect theory, what new or innovative management strategies would be most appropriate? Can any management plan satisfy those polarized factions mentioned earlier? Probably not, but the evolution of coyote management in many jurisdictions from bounty, to no protection, to recognition as a game animal and furbearer should tell us something. The most practical and effective program of coyote management in the northeast would appear to be one which encourages public use (trapping, hunting) and control, when necessary, through government extension services which encourage farmers and ranchers to solve their own problems. Public education should emphasize preventive management where potential problems between livestock and coyotes are identified before the conflict and damage occurs.

We have reviewed the interactions of coyotes and deer across the continent, and only in forested wilderness areas of the northeast do coyotes appear to have a serious impact on deer populations, predation there being most serious during periods of deep snow in late winter. What form of coyote "management" could best address that problem? Not everyone agrees that this new but natural predator-prey model developing between deer and coyotes in the northeast is a problem. The knee-jerk reaction for militancy against the coyote with calls for campaigns of control and removal, although attractive to many, has never proven successful. It is also probably somewhat premature to enter into any long-term management commitments until deer and coyotes settle on a final predator-prey model for the region. Through adaptive strategies discussed earlier, deer will evolve and cope with this new predator, and coyote populations will be controlled (through mechanisms previously reviewed) by available food resources within that predator-prey system, one where the densities of deer will be lower than in pre-coyote times, and coyote densities will be lower than when they first arrived and found deer in abundance.

EPILOGUE

We began our journey on the trail of the coyote from the open prairies and grasslands of western United States to the shores of Bay of Fundy over 100 years ago, a mere tick in the geological clock but more than a lifetime for most of us. Can the lessons learned in this journey help us better understand and accept the coyote for what it represents and the role that it is assuming in the forests and fields of northeastern North America? I have discovered through my research and writing over the past several years that our first lesson might be to understand that the coyote has assumed the role as the dominant large predator in the forest system, a role which has been empty since timber wolves were driven from the land over a century ago. This role is not necessarily a facsimile of that of the wolf, but because of some very special physical and behaviour features and adaptations, and a radically changed landscape with a unique wild and domestic fauna, the coyote is developing its own distinctive role in the forested ecosystem.

The coyote and white-tailed deer are shaping a predator-prey model in tune with the environment of the northern spruce-fir forests. Pre-coyote white-tailed deer populations struggled within a system where numerical thresholds were set by available food resources but controlled by winter weather. It was an unnatural system where predation by wild canids, the controlling and self-regulating mechanism for most natural ungulate populations in forested habitats, was absent.

The eastern coyote is a medium-sized and highly adaptable multiple-prey predator. For that reason, and because of the radical changes inflicted by humans upon the northeastern forest system, and because of the proven adaptability of white-tailed deer themselves, a generic coyote-white-tailed deer predator-prey model for the northeast is not possible. The coyote has not evolved over the past thousands of years to prey exclusively on deer. It is a medium-sized canid that evolved to prey on rabbits, hares, and rodents of the open plains. Although the eastern coyote is larger than its prairie ancestors, perhaps due to hybridization with wolves and perhaps adapting to the forest environment, it still remains a medium-sized predator, and given the choice, I suggest that it still prefers medium-sized prey. Significant predation on deer in the northeast appears to be limited to late winter, and prey switching from hares to deer is probably a response by coyotes to alternative winter food and stressful environmental conditions. Given a choice, coyotes most likely prefer a continued diet of hares, rodents, carrion, and perhaps occasional human garbage. In areas of agricultural farmland and moderate winters, deer and coyotes may cohabit in moderate numbers. In more remote wilderness regions with reduced sources of alternate food and more severe winters, this relationship may not be possible, and both deer and coyotes eventually reach and maintain low levels. I have proposed a coyote-white-tailed deer model which may be developing in much of the forested landscape of the northeast, one where maximum levels of deer are maintained well below the pre-coyote nutritional-climate threshold which served to control deer populations in the absence of a natural predator. Many of us grew up in that unnatural predator-free system when the deer were more abundant and the deer hunter more happy. The reader may find some consolation in knowing that, for better or for worse, what we have now is more what the Creator intended, and if that fails to console, concerns should be directed to a level considerably above that of the Fish and Wildlife Branch.

Our bookshelves and newspapers are filled with the facts, statistics, and just plain horror stories of a human legacy of environmental insults. This animal of rational thought but irrational behaviour has historically measured the worth of other creatures in terms of their value to him (her). If it tastes good, grow it, and keep out the weeds. We brought wild animals to our homes, eliminated all natural means of self-defence through domestication, then declared war on all predators that did not understand that these were our animals for our own personal use. How stupid of those predators! Many of us feel that the coyote has no right here, that somehow it should have remained on the western prairies, or that someone, somehow, should have seen that it did so. There is no one to blame in this story, there is no scape goat who must account for this change in the way we must now perceive the northern forest and the animals that live here. Not unless we wish to blame our forefathers who pushed back the frontier, opened up the forests and worked hard to create the materialistic society that we so value today.

Even if we chose to influence the direction and intensity of population changes of deer and coyotes in the northeast, would our efforts be misdirected, or do we have the knowledge base and technology to adjust and redefine the natural patterns of change and evolvement in ecological systems? The message is quite clear that we do not, especially with coyotes, and our meddling and tinkering with biological processes, which we are far from understanding completely, would serve us little good. The reproductive capacity and resiliency of coyotes has evolved to address the very situation that we set about to create. We may temporarily reduce the predator: prey ratio by expensive programs of coyote control, but reduced densities of coyotes stimulates higher coyote productivity. Increased productivity of those coyotes not removed, and the mobility of juveniles and transients, ensures that vacant territories do not remain empty for long. Our efforts to control coyotes on the western prairies, although successfully reducing populations on occasion, were well intentioned but very ill conceived. We could never expect to achieve even a fraction of that success by massive campaigns of coyote control in the forested northeast.

Society is moving away from the philosophy of "man, the consumptive user of wildlife." For many people a woodpecker is given equal value to a white-tailed deer in the forest ecosystem, a system which consists of the sum of its parts. The coyote has now become one part of that system, and a rather important one at that. It is at the upper level of the food chain, and because of that, has come into conflict with humans, a predator with which it must share that role. Let us conclude this study of the eastern coyote with the following passage by Stanley Young, the early North American naturalist with whom we began our journey.

"From civilized man's selfish point of view, predators are commonly looked upon as pests or outlaws with almost every hand raised against them. In fairness to these animals, it should always be kept in mind that their destructive habits cannot be due to any criminal intent, but are due wholly to their efforts to gain a livelihood by the only means that nature has provided through untold ages of evolution."[1]

THE EASTERN COYOTE

The cold wind cut through his ragged coat
The snow drifted round and deep
And the old male nestled his snout in his tail
As he drifted off back into sleep

He lay neath a spruce above Trinity Bay
Having finished an evening meal
Not one of grouse or hare or deer
But one of turre and seal

He had come to this island cross the frigid strait
From the slopes of Lac Bras D'or
And across the ice he undauntingly marched
Till he reached this frozen shore

And here the trail ended, in this northern land
Far from the heat and the sun
Which scorched the plains that his kin had left
Having fought the trap and the gun

His father had crossed the Canso Strait
From the tides of the Fundy sea
And he fed on sheep at the Margaree
And on deer near the Miramichi

He knew not why he followed the eastern sky
Nor why the autumn brought chill
But he knew the ways of the grouse and the hare
And of the stalk, the chase, and the kill

The coyote stirred as the raven called
It told of hate and fear
And he sniffed the breeze from the village below
And the dangers that lurked so near

That foul-smelling predator is apart from the rest
It kills for the sport and the thrill
And despises the coyote for entering this land
With its strength, its cunning and skill

This creature that kills with poison and gun
Has declared war on any that dare
Compete for game that he hunts for sport
But to others means life or despair

The snow has stopped, the stars shine bright
As the lone stranger turns to the moon
And a cold chill grips those souls below
Who hear his mournful tune

Eyes peer out past the glow of the lamp
A dog utters a plaintive whine
The heart beats faster, sweat beads the brow
Old fears race through the mind

Ancient fears run deep, they cloud the thought
As survival becomes the will
From a time long past when with club and stone
Man scavenged for spoils of the kill

So here lies the clue, a glimpse from our past
When wild dog, bear and man
Competed for survival in a hostile world
With the dog having the upper hand

With return of light aroused fears subside
Courage buoyed by the warmth of the sun
They'll hunt down this intruder who invaded their land
With machine and trap and gun

The bullet strikes deep, he draws his last breath
As the snowmobiles circle about
And the old male stumbles never to rise
Of his fate there was no doubt

But there once was a time with tables turned
When naked, cold and still
Man cowered neath the stars as the dogs circled bout
Waiting to make the kill

So take time to reflect before casting that stone
And rushing to lay the blame
For the conflict is old and fears run deep
And it's not yet the end of the game

G. Parker

ENDNOTES

INTRODUCTION

[1] Howard J. Stains, "Distribution and taxonomy of the Canidae," in M.W. Fox, ed., *The Wild Canids* (New York: Van Nostrand Reinhold, 1975), 3-4.

[2] H. T. Gier, "Ecology and behavior of the coyote (*Canis latrans*)," in M.W. Fox, ed., *The Wild Canids* (New York: Van Nostrand Reinhold, 1975), 247.

[3] S. P. Young and H. H. T. Jackson, *The Clever Coyote* (Lincoln and London: University of Nebraska Press, 1951), 229.

[4] Ibid., 6.

[5] Ibid., 232.

[6] Ronald M. Nowak, "Evolution and taxonomy of coyotes and related *Canis*," in M. Bekoff, ed., *Coyotes: Biology, Behavior, and Management* (New York: Academic Press, 1978), 5-6.

[7] Gier, 247.

[8] G. C. Moore and G. R. Parker, "Colonization by the eastern coyote, *Canis latrans*," in A. H. Boer, ed., *Ecology and Management of the Eastern Coyote* (Fredericton: University of New Brunswick Press, 1992), 23-37.

CHAPTER 1. TAXONOMY

[1] P. S. Gipson, J. A. Sealander, and J. E. Dunn, "The taxonomic status of wild *Canis* in Arkansas," *Systematic Zoology* 23 (1974), 8.

[2] S. P. Young and H. H. T. Jackson, *The Clever Coyote* (Lincoln and London: University of Nebraska Press, 1951), 266.

[3] Ibid., 266.

[4] Ibid., 269.

[5] W. E. Berg and R. A. Chesness, "Ecology of coyotes in northern Minnesota," in M. Bekoff, ed., *Coyotes: Biology, Behavior, and Management* (New York: Academic Press, 1978), 229.

[6] Henry Hilton, "Systematics and ecology of the eastern coyote," in M. Bekoff, ed., *Coyotes: Biology, Behavior, and Management* (New York: Academic Press, 1978), 209.

[7] Ibid., 212.

[8] W. E. Howard, "A means to distinguish skulls of coyotes and domestic dogs," *Journal of Mammalogy* 30 (1949), 169-171.

[9] Hilton, 212.

[10] Ibid., 214.

[11] L. R. Dice, "A family of dog-coyote hybrids," *Journal of Mammalogy* 23 (1942), 186-192.

[12] H. Silver and W. T. Silver, "Growth and behavior of the coyote-like canid of northern New England with observations on canid hybrids," *Wildlife Monographs* 17 (1969).

[13] B. Lawrence and W. H. Bossert, "Multiple character analysis of *Canis lupus, latrans* and *familiaris*, with a discussion of the relationships of *Canis niger*," *American Zoologist* 7 (1967), 223-232.

[14] B. Lawrence and W. H. Bossert, "The cranial evidence for hybridization in New England *Canis*," *Breviora* 330 (1969), 1-13

[15] R. M. Mengel, "A study of dog-coyote hybrids and implications concerning hybridization in *Canis*," *Journal of Mammalogy* 52 (1971), 316-336.

[16] J. J. Kennelly and J. D. Roberts, "Fertility of coyote-dog hybrids," *Journal of Mammalogy* 50 (1969), 830-831.

[17] G. B. Kolenosky, "Hybridization between wolf and coyote," *Journal of Mammalogy* 52 (1971), 446-449.

[18] Hilton, 214.

[19] H. J. McGinnis, "Pennsylvania coyotes and their relationship to other wild *Canis* populations in the Great Lakes region and northeastern United States," M.Sc. thesis (Pennsylvania State University, University Park, 1979).

[20] O. J. Schmitz and G. B. Kolenosky, "Wolves and coyotes in Ontario: morphological relationships and origins," *Canadian Journal of Zoology* 63 (1985), 1130-1137.

[21] Silver and Silver; Lawrence and Bossert (1967; 1969).

[22] O. J. Schmitz and D. M. Lavigne, "Factors affecting body size in sympatric Ontario *Canis*," *Journal of Mammalogy* 68 (1987), 92-99.

[23] J. M. Thurber and R. O. Peterson, "Changes in body size associated with range expansion in the coyote (*Canis latrans*)," *Journal of Mammalogy* 72 (1991), 750-755.

[24] S. Larivière and M. Crête, "The size of eastern coyotes (*Canis latrans*): a comment," *Journal of Mammalogy* 74 (1993), 1073.

[25] Robert K. Wayne and Niles Lehman, "Mitochondrial DNA analysis of the eastern coyote: origins and hybridization," in A. H. Boer, ed., *Ecology and Management of the Eastern Coyote* (Fredericton: University of New Brunswick Press, 1992), 9-22.

[26] Kolenosky, 446-449.

[27] Young and Jackson, 271.

[28] P. S. Gipson, "Coyotes and related *Canis* in the southeastern United States with a comment on Mexican and Central American *Canis*," in M. Bekoff, ed., *Coyotes: Biology, Behavior, and Management* (New York: Academic Press, 1978), 191.

[29] Young and Jackson, 274.

[30] H. McCarley, "The taxonomic status of wild *Canis* (Canidae) in the South Central United States," *The Southwestern Naturalist* 7 (1962), 227-235.

[31] J. Paridiso, "Canids recently collected in east Texas, with comments on the taxonomy of the red wolf," *American Midland Naturalist* 80 (1968), 529-534; Nowak, 1967; R. M. Nowak, "Report on the red wolf," *Defenders of Wildlife News* 45 (1970), 82-94; Gipson et al., 1974; J.W. Goertz, L. V. Fitzgerald and R. M. Nowak, "The status of wild *Canis* in Louisiana," *American Midland Naturalist* 93 (1975), 215-218.

[32] T. W. French and J. L. Dusi, "Status of the coyote and red wolf in Alabama," *Journal of the Alabama Academy of Sciences* 54 (1979), 220-224; Gipson, 1978.

[33] M. K. Phillips and V. G. Henry, "Comments on red wolf taxonomy," *Conservation Biology* 6 (1992), 597.

[34] C. Lydeard and M. L. Kennedy, "Morphologic assessment of recently founded populations of the coyote, *Canis latrans*, in Tennessee," *Journal of Mammalogy* 69 (1988), 773-781.

CHAPTER 2. COLONIZATION

[1] Ronald M. Nowak, "Evolution and taxonomy of coyotes and related *Canis*," in M. Bekoff, ed., *Coyotes: Biology, Behavior, and Management* (New York: Academic Press, 1978), 12.

[2] S. P. Young and H. H. T. Jackson, *The Clever Coyote* (Lincoln and London: University of Nebraska Press, 1951), 11.

[3] P. S. Gipson, "Coyotes and related *Canis* in the southeastern United States with a comment on Mexican and Central American *Canis*," in M. Bekoff, ed., *Coyotes: Biology, Behavior, and Management* (New York: Academic Press, 1978), 196.

[4] F. L. Stewart, "Coyote in New Brunswick during prehistoric times," *Nature Canada* 5 (1976), 27.

[5] Young and Jackson, 7.

[6] H. T. Gier, "Ecology and behavior of the coyote *(Canis latrans)*," in M. W. Fox. ed., *The Wild Canids* (New York: Van Nostrand Reinhold, 1975), 247.

[7] Ibid., 248.

[8] Brian Slough, Furbearer Biologist, Yukon Territory, pers. comm.

[9] A. L. Rand, "Mammals of Yukon, Canada," *National Museum of Canada Bulletin* No. 100 (1945), 36.

[10] Phil Koehl, Department of Fish and Game, Alaska, pers. comm.

[11] Winthrop Staples, Kenai National Wildlife Refuge, Alaska, pers. comm.

[12] Ken Reynolds, Delaware Department of Natural Resources and Environmental Control, pers. comm.

[13] S. P. Young and E. A. Goldman, *The Wolves of North America* (New York: Dover Publications, 1964), 478.

[14] B. Lawrence and W. H. Bossert, "Multiple character analysis of *Canis lupus, latrans and familiaris,* with a discussion of the relationship of *Canis niger,*" *American Zoologist* 7 (1967), 230; L. D. Mech, *The Wolf: The Ecology and Behaviour of an Endangered Species* (New York: The Natural History Press, 1970), 22-25.

[15] J. L. Paradiso, "Canids recently collected in east Texas, with comments on the taxonomy of the red wolf," *American Midland Naturalist* 80 (1968), 529-534.

[16] Rollin H. Baker, *Michigan Mammals* (East Lansing: Michigan State University Press, 1983), 393.

[17] D. F. Hoffmeister, *Mammals of Illinois* (Urbana and Chicago: University of Illinois Press, 1989), 272; G. Hubert, Illinois Division of Wildlife Resources, pers. comm.

[18] R. E. Mumford, *Distribution of the Mammals of Indiana,* (Indianapolis: The Indiana Academy of Science, 1969), 85; L. E. Lehman, "Coyote vocal responsiveness to broadcast auditory stimuli in south central Indiana," *Proceedings of the Indiana Academy of Science* 97 (1987), 253.

[19] K. Fruth, "The coyote *(Canis latrans),*" *Wisconsin Department of Natural Resources, Bureau of Wildlife Management* PUBL-WM-148.86 (1986), 3; Baker, 393; Hoffmeister, 272; J. L. Weeks, G. M. Tori, and M. C. Shieldcastle, "Coyotes *(Canis latrans)* in Ohio," *Ohio Journal of Science* 90 (1990), 142-145; Lehman, 253.

[20] G. B. Kolenosky, D. R. Voigt, and R. O. Standfield, "Wolves and coyotes in Ontario," *Ontario Ministry of Natural Resources,* (1978), 13.

[21] E. C. Cross and J. R. Dymond, "The mammals of Ontario," *Royal Ontario Museum of Zoology Handbook* No. 1 (1929), 18-19.

[22] O. J. Schmitz and G. B. Kolenosky, "Wolves and coyotes in Ontario: morphological relationships and origins," *Canadian Journal of Zoology* 63 (1985), 1131.

[23] G. B. Kolenosky and R. O. Standfield, "Morphological and ecological variation among gray wolves *(Canis lupus)* of Ontario, Canada," in M. W. Fox, ed., *The Wild Canids* (New York: Van Nostrand Reinhold, 1975), 63.

[24] Schmitz and Kolenosky, 1135.

[25] Young and Jackson, 32.

[26] L. A. Lord, "Un envahisseur importun au Québec: le coyote," *Les Carnets de Zoologie* 21 (1961), 6-7.

[27] Serge Larivière et Michel Crête, "Causes et conséquences de la colonisation du Québec par le coyote *(Canis latrans),*" *Québec Ministère du Loisir, de la Chasse et de la Pêche* SP 1935-07-92 (1992), 1-39.

[28] Stan Georges, "A range extension of the coyote in Quebec," *The Canadian Field-Naturalist* 90 (1976), 78.

[29] René Lafond, Coordonnateur animaux à fourrure, Gouvernement du Québec, pers. comm.

[30] C. W. Severinghaus, "Notes on the history of wild canids in New York," *New York Fish and Game Journal* 21 (1974), 117.

[31] C. M. Aldous, "Coyotes in Maine," *Journal of Mammalogy* 20 (1939), 104-106.

[32] Severinghaus, 124; Aldous, 104-106.

[33] H. J. McGinnis, "Pennsylvania coyotes and their relationship to other wild *Canis* populations in the Great Lakes region and northeastern United States," M.Sc. thesis (Pennsylvania State University, University Park, 1979), iii-iv.

[34] Severinghaus, 120.

[35] A. J. Godin, *Wild Mammals of New England* (Baltimore: The Johns Hopkins University Press, 1977), 199.

[36] R. C. Lund, "New wolf for an old niche, "*New Jersey Outdoors* Jan-Feb (1976), 2.

[37] Georges, 78.

[38] Severinghaus, 120, 122-124.

[39] V. B. Richins and R. D. Hugie, "Distribution, taxonomic status, and characteristics of coyotes in Maine," *Journal of Wildlife Management* 38 (1974), 447-454.

[40] Severinghaus, 120.

[41] H. Hilton, "Systematics and ecology of the eastern coyote," in M. Bekoff, ed., *Coyotes: Biology, Behavior, and Management* (New York: Academic Press, 1978), 212.

[42] L. P. Pringle, "Notes on coyotes in southern New England," *Journal of Mammalogy* 41 (1960), 278; E. Orff, State of New Hampshire Fish and Game Department, pers. comm.

[43] Pringle, 278; T. Decker, Massachusetts Division of Fisheries and Wildlife, pers. comm.

[44] P. Rego, Wildlife Division, State of Connecticutt, pers. comm.

[45] P. Jane, Maryland Department of Natural Resources, pers. comm.

[46] F. A. Uhmer, "Recent records of coyotes in Pennsylvania and New Jersey," *Journal of Mammalogy* 30 (1949), 435-436.

[47] P. McConnell, Division of Fish, Game and Wildlife, State of New Jersey, pers. comm.

[48] McGinnis, iv.

[49] C. Brown, Department of Natural Resources, State of West Virginia, pers. comm.

[50] Weeks et al., 142-145.

[51] W. A. Squires, "The mammals of New Brunswick," *The New Brunswick Museum, Monographic Series* No. 5, (1968), 35.

[52] *The Kings County Record*, Vol. 72, No. 14, p.1. January 1, 1959.

[53] David J. Cartwright, "The appearance of the eastern coyote," *Canadian Wildlife Administration* 1 (1975), 34.

[54] Mike O'Brian, "The coyote - a new mammal, new challenges," *Conservation* 7 (1983), 6.

[55] H. H. Thomas and R. L. Dibblee, "A coyote, *Canis latrans*, on Prince Edward Island," *Canadian Field-Naturalist* 100 (1986), 565.

[56] Randy Dibblee, Prince Edward Island Wildlife Division, pers. comm.

[57] Oscar Forsey, Newfoundland Wildlife Division, pers. comm.

[58] T. W. French and J. L. Dusi, "Status of the coyote and red wolf in Alabama," *Journal of the Alabama Academy of Science* 54 (1979), 222.

[59] P. S. Gipson, J. A. Sealander and J. E. Dunn, "The taxonomic status of wild *Canis* in Arkansas," *Systematic Zoology* 23 (1974), 1-11.

[60] Ibid., 8, 10.

[61] E. P. Hill., P. W. Sumner, and J. B. Wooding, "Human influences on range expansion of coyotes in the southeast," *Wildlife Society Bulletin* 15 (1987), 522.

[62] D. I. Hall and J. D. Newsom, "The coyote in Louisiana," *Louisiana Agriculture* 21 (1978), 4.

[63] S. C. Dellinger and J. D. Black, "Notes on Arkansas mammals," *Journal of Mammalogy* 21 (1940), 187-191; Lawrence and Bossert, 229; Gipson et al., 8; J. A. Sealander, Jr., "A provisional check-list and key to the mammals of Arkansas (with annotations)," *American Midland Naturalist* 56 (1956), 257-296.

[64] Gipson et al., 8.

[65] E. A. Jones and E. P. Hill, "Coyotes in Mississippi," *Wildlife Sport Fisheries Management* 85-3 (1985), 3.

[66] W. Bourne, "Coyotes come calling on the south," *Southern Outdoors* Feb (1991), 72.

[67] J. B. Wooding, P. W. Sumner and E. P. Hill, "Coyotes in Alabama," *Alabama Conservation* 55 (1985), 20.

[68] French and Dusi, 220.

[69] Ibid., 222.

[70] French and Dusi, 222.

[71] F. B. Golley, *Mammals of Georgia*, (Athens: University of Georgia Press, 1962), 172.

[72] H. H. Bailey, "Coyotes (*Canis latrans*) in Florida," Bailey Museum and Library, *Natural History Bulletin*, Miami, (1933); J. R. Bradley and W. H. Campbell, "Distribution of coyotes in Florida," *Florida Field Naturalist* 11 (1983), 40-41.

[73] J. B. Wooding and T. S. Hardisky, "Coyote distribution in Florida," *Florida Field Naturalist* 18 (1990), 12 -13.

[74] B. Baker, South Carolina Wildlife and Marine Resources Department, pers. comm.

[75] M. L. Kennedy, "Status of coyote research," *Tennessee Wildlife Resources Agency, Technical Report* 89-2 (1989), 2.

[76] Tom Edwards, Kentucky Department of Fish and Wildlife Resources, pers. comm.

CHAPTER 3. PHYSICAL CHARACTERISTICS

[1] W. B. Grange, *The Way To Game Abundance*. (New York: Charles Scribner's Sons, 1949), 5.

[2] C. Hart Merriam, "Revision of the coyotes or prairie wolves, with description of new forms," *Proceedings of the Biological Society of Washington* 11 (1897), 23.

[3] Stanley P. Young, "Part 1, Its history, life habits, economic status, and control," in Stanley P. Young and Hartley H. T. Jackson, *The Clever Coyote* (Lincoln and London: University of Nebraska Press, 1951), 3.

[4] Ibid., 48.

[5] Ibid., 50, 52-53.

[6] Ronald D. Andrews and Edward K. Boggess, "Ecology of coyotes in Iowa," in M. Bekoff, ed., *Coyotes: Biology, Behavior, and Management* (New York: Academic Press, 1978), 251-252.

[7] Ibid., 252; H. T. Gier, "Coyotes in Kansas," *Kansas Agricultural Experimental Station Bulletin* 393 (1957), 40.

[8] V. M. Hawthorne,"Coyote movements in Sagehen Creek Basin, northeastern California," *California Fish and Game* 57 (1971), 157; V. B. Richens and R. D. Hugie, "Distribution, taxonomic status, and characteristics of coyotes in Maine," *Journal of Wildlife Management* 38 (1974), 447.

[9] D. R. Voigt and W. E. Berg, "Coyote," in M. Novak, J. A. Baker, M. E. Olbard, and B. Malloch, eds., *Wild Furbearer Management and Conservation in North America* (Ontario Ministry of Natural Resources, 1987), 345.

[10] Henry Hilton, "The physical characteristics, taxonomic status and food habits of the eastern coyote in Maine," M.Sc. thesis (University of Maine, Orono, 1976), 25.

[11] P. S. Gipson," Coyotes and related *Canis* in the southeastern United States with a comment on Mexican and Central American *Canis*," in M. Bekoff, ed., *Coyotes: Biology, Behavior, and Management* (New York: Academic Press, 1978), 199.

[12] J. D. Black, "Mammals of northwestern Arkansas," *Journal of Mammalogy* 17 (1936), 31.

[13] Gipson, 200.

[14] W. E. Berg and R. A. Chesness, "Ecology of coyotes in northern Minnesota," in M. Bekoff, ed., *Coyotes: Biology, Behavior, and Management* (New York: Academic Press, 1978), 245.

[15] D. F. Hoffmeister, *Mammals of Illinois* (Urbana and Chicago: University of Illinois Press, 1989), 270.

[16] E. K. Boggess and F. R. Henderson, "Regional weights of Kansas coyotes," *Transactions of the Kansas Academy of Science* 80 (1977), 79-80.

[17] J. R. Lorenz, "Physical characteristics, movement and population estimate of the eastern coyote in New England," M.Sc. thesis (University of Massachusetts, Amherst, 1978), 12.

[18] Henry Hilton, "Systematics and ecology of the eastern coyote," in M. Bekoff, ed., *Coyotes: Biology, Behavior, and Management* (New York: Academic Press, 1978), 212-213.

[19] G. C. Moore and J. S. Millar, "Food habits and average weights of a fall-winter sample of eastern coyotes, *Canis latrans*," *Canadian Field-Naturalist* 100 (1986), 106.

[20] J. D. McNearney, "A study of colonizing eastern coyotes (*Canis latrans thamnos*) in Nova Scotia," *Typewritten report for Special Problems in Biology*, (Acadia University, Wolfville, Nova Scotia, 1982), 7.

[21] S. G. Tell, "Coyote (*Canis latrans thamnos*) in Nova Scotia," *Typewritten report for Special Problems in Biology* (Acadia University, Wolfville, Nova Scotia, 1987), 20.

[22] Barry Sabean, "Coyote carcass collections," *Nova Scotia Trappers Newsletter* 29 (1993), 10.

[23] R. Dibblee, Furbearer Biologist, Prince Edward Island Fish and Wildlife Branch, pers. comm.

[24] Newfoundland and Labrador Wildlife Division files.

CHAPTER 4. FOOD HABITS

[1] J. F. Dobie, *The Voice of the Coyote* (Boston: Little, Brown and Company, 1949), 107.

[2] R. M. Bond, "Coyote food habits on the Lava Beds National Monument," *Journal of Wildlife Management* 3 (1939), 183-185.

[3] T. J. Ogle, "Predator-prey relationships between coyotes and white-tailed deer," *Northwest Science* 45 (1971), 216.

[4] D. Holle, "Food habits of coyotes in an area of high fawn mortality," *Proceedings of the Oklahoma Academy of Science* 58 (1978), 12; J. A. Litvaitis and J. H. Shaw, "Coyote movements, habitat use and food habits in southwestern Oklahoma," *Journal of Wildlife Management* 44 (1980), 65; J. T. Springer and J. S. Smith, "Summer food habits of coyotes in central Wyoming," *Great Basin Naturalist* 41 (1981), 451; J. G. MacCracken and D. W. Uresk, "Coyote foods in the Black Hills, South Dakota," *Journal of Wildlife Management* 48 (1984), 1421.

[5] P. S. Gipson, "Food habits of coyotes in Arkansas," *Journal of Wildlife Management* 38 (1974), 851; D. I. Hall and J. D. Newsom, "The coyote in Louisiana," *Louisiana Agriculture* 21 (1978), 5; M. K. Phillips and G. F. Hubert, Jr., "Winter food habits of coyotes in southeastern Illinois," *Transactions of the Illinois State Academy of Science* 73 (1980), 82.

[6] J. J. Ozoga and E. M. Harger, "Winter activities and feeding habits of northern Michigan coyotes," *Journal of Wildlife Management* 30 (1966), 814-816; T. J. Niebauer and O. J. Rongstad, "Coyote food habits in northwestern Wisconsin," in R. L. Phillips and C. Jonkel, eds., *Proceedings of the 1975 Predator Symposium* (Missoula: University of Montana Printing Department, 1975), 245; C. N. Huegel, "Winter ecology of coyotes in northern Wisconsin," M.Sc. thesis (University of Wisconsin, Madison, 1979), 8.

[7] Ozoga and Harger, 818.

[8] Niebauer and Rongstad, 245.

[9] Huegel, 10; Ozoga and Harger, 816.

[10] Niebauer and Rongstad, 247, 248.

[11] W. J. Hamilton, Jr., "Food habits of the coyote in the Adirondacks," *New York Fish and Game Journal* 21 (1974), 177.

[12] Ibid., 181.

[13] R. H. Brocke, "A taste for venison," *Natural History* (May, 1992), 51.

[14] Ibid., 51.

[15] R. E. Chambers, "Diets of Adirondack coyotes and red foxes," *Transactions of the Northeast Section of the Wildlife Society* 44 (1987), 90.

[16] Brocke, 51.

[17] Henry Hilton, "The physical characteristics, taxonomic status and food habits of the eastern coyote in Maine." M. Sc. thesis (University of Maine, Orono, 1976), 6.

[18] V. B. Richens and R. D. Hugie, "Distribution, taxonomic status, and characteristics of coyotes in Maine." *Journal of Wildlife Management* 38 (1974), 450, 453-54.

[19] Hilton, 61-62.

[20] Ibid., 51, 53-55.

[21] D. J. Harrison and J. A. Harrison, "Foods of adult Maine coyotes and their known-aged pups," *Journal of Wildlife Management* 48 (1984), 922-926 (quotation, 925).

[22] J. T. Major and J. A. Sherburne, "Interspecific relationships of coyotes, bobcats and red foxes in western Maine," *Journal of Wildlife Management* 51 (1987), 606-616.

[23] F. J. Dibello, S. M. Arthur, and W. B. Krohn, "Food habits of sympatric coyotes, *Canis latrans*, red foxes, *Vulpes vulpes*, and bobcats, *Lynx rufus*, in Maine," *Canadian Field-Naturalist* 104 (1990), 403-408.

[24] A. F. O'Connell, Jr., D. J. Harrison, B. Connery, and K. B. Anderson, "Food use by an insular population of coyotes," *Transactions of the Northeast Section of the Wildlife Society* 49 (1992), 36-42.

[25] J. M. Bergeron and P. Demers, "Le régime alimentaire du Coyote (*Canis latrans*) et du chien errant (*C. familiaris*) dans le sud Québec," *Canadian Field-Naturalist* 95 (1981), 172-177.

[26] M. K. Phillips and V. G. Henry, "Comments on red wolf taxonomy," *Conservation Biology* 6 (1992), 596-599.

[27] G. R. Lavigne, "Sex/age composition and physical condition of deer killed by coyotes during winter in Maine," in A. H. Boer, ed., *Ecology and Management of the Eastern Coyote* (Fredericton: University of New Brunswick Press, 1992) 142.

[28] Ibid., 141.

[29] L. E. LaPierre, "Fall and winter food habits of the eastern coyote (*Canis latrans*) in southeastern New Brunswick, Canada," *Proceedings of the Nova Scotia Institute of Science* 35 (1985), 71-74.

[30] G. C. Moore and J. S. Millar, "Food habits and average weights of a fall-winter sample of eastern coyotes, *Canis latrans*," *Canadian Field-Naturalist* 100 (1986), 105-106.

[31] G. R. Parker, "The seasonal diet of coyotes, *Canis latrans*, in northern New Brunswick," *Canadian Field-Naturalist* 100 (1986), 74-77.

[32] G. R. Parker and J. W. Maxwell, "Seasonal movements and winter ecology of the coyote, *Canis latrans*, in northern New Brunswick," *Canadian Field-Naturalist* 103 (1989), 1-11.

[33] L. D. Morton, "Winter ecology of the eastern coyote," M.Sc. thesis (University of New Brunswick, Fredericton, 1988).

[34] D. Smith, "The determination of coyote (*Canis latrans*) food habits from the contents of scats," *Typewritten report for Special Problems in Biology,* (Acadia University, Wolfville, 1990).

[35] D. Ekiai, "The diet of coyotes (*Canis latrans*) as determined by scat analysis," *Typewritten report for Special Problems in Biology,* (Acadia University, Wolfville, 1990).

[36] B. Patterson, "Ecology of the eastern coyote in Kejimkujik National Park," M.Sc. thesis (Acadia University, Wolfville, 1995).

[37] R. Hall, "Winter tracking of coyotes," *Nova Scotia Department of Lands and Forests Technical Note No. 44* (1987), 1-3.

[38] Barry Sabean, "Coyote winter tracking update," *Conservation* 14 (1990), 4.

[39] Barry Sabean, "Tracking coyotes in winter," *Conservation* 17 (1993), 11-12.

[40] C. Kohler, "Ages and percent femur fat of coyote-killed deer in eastern New Brunswick," B. Sc. thesis (University of New Brunswick, Fredericton, 1987), 1-17.

[41] Ibid., ii.

[42] Newfoundland and Labrador Wildlife Division files.

CHAPTER 5. REPRODUCTION

[1] W. B. Grange, *The Way To Game Abundance* (New York: Charles Scribner's Sons, 1949), 14.

[2] C. Elton and M. Nicholson, "The ten-year cycle in numbers of the lynx in Canada," *Journal of Animal Ecology* 11 (1942), 215-244.

[3] Jack K. Saunders, Jr., "Food habits of the lynx in Newfoundland," *Journal of Wildlife Management* 27 (1963), 384-390; C. J. Brand, L. B. Keith, and C. A. Fischer, "Lynx responses to changing snowshoe hare densities in central Alberta," *Journal of Wildlife Management* 40 (1976), 416-428; C. J. Brand and L. B. Keith, "Lynx demography during a snowshoe hare decline in Alberta," *Journal of Wildlife Management* 43 (1979), 827-849; G. R. Parker, J. W. Maxwell, L. D. Morton, and G. E. J. Smith, "The ecology of lynx (*Lynx canadensis*) on Cape Breton Island," *Canadian Journal of Zoology* 61 (1983), 770-786.

[4] S. L. Caturano, "Habitat and home range use by coyotes in eastern Maine," M.Sc. thesis (University of Maine, Orono, 1983), 6.

[5] Stanley Young and Hartley H. T. Jackson, *The Clever Coyote* (Lincoln and London: University of Nebraska Press, 1951), 79.

[6] H. T. Gier, "Coyotes in Kansas," *Kansas Agricultural Experimental Station Bulletin* 393 (1957), 6.

[7] Ibid., 37.

[8] H. T. Gier, "Ecology and behavior of the coyote (*Canis latrans*)," in M.W. Fox, ed., *The Wild Canids* (New York: Van Nostrand Reinhold, 1975), 251-254.

[9] J. J. Kennelly, "Coyote reproduction," in M. Bekoff, ed., *Coyotes: Biology, Behavior, and Management* (New York: Academic Press, 1978), 74-75.

[10] Ibid., 83-85.

[11] E. M. Gese, "Reproductive activity in an old-age coyote in southeastern Colorado," *The Southwestern Naturalist* 35 (1990), 101-102.

[12] Robert E. Chambers, "Reproduction of coyotes in their northeastern range," in A. H. Boer, ed., *Ecology and Management of the Eastern Coyote* (Fredericton: University of New Brunswick Press, 1992), 39.

[13] Henry Hilton, "Systematics and ecology of the eastern coyote," in M. Bekoff, ed., *Coyotes: Biology, Behavior, and Management* (New York: Academic Press, 1978), 220.

[14] B. Patterson, "Ecology of the eastern coyote in Kejimkujik National Park," M.Sc. thesis, (Acadia university, Wolfville, Nova Scotia, 1995).

[15] H. Silver and W. T. Silver, "Growth and behavior of the coyote-like canid of northern New England with observations on canid hybrids," *Wildlife Monographs* 17 (1969), 8; Gier, 1957, 37; Kennelly, 86.

[16] D. J. Harrison, D. W. May, and P. W. Rego, "Distribution, productivity and food habits of a recently established coyote population in Connecticut, " *Transactions of the Northeast Fish and Wildlife Conference* 46 (1989) (Abstracts only); Y. Jean and J. M. Bergeron, "Productivity of coyotes, *Canis latrans* from southern Quebec, Canada," *Canadian Journal of Zoology* 62 (1984), 2242.

[17] Gary Moore, "A comparative study of colonizing and longer established eastern coyote (*Canis latrans* var) populations," M.Sc. thesis, (University of Western Ontario, London, 1981).

[18] Henry Hilton, "Systematics and ecology of the eastern coyote," in M. Bekoff, ed., *Coyotes: Biology, Behavior, and Management* (New York: Academic Press, 1978), 220.

[19] Stanley P. Young, "Part 1, Its history, life habits, economic status, and control," in S. P. Young and H. H. T. Jackson, *The Clever Coyote* (Lincoln and London: University of Nebraska Press, 1951), 82-83.

[20] Gier, 1975, 254.

[21] Ibid., 255.

[22] Gier, 1957, 41.

[23] W. C. Lemm, "Coyote denning as a method of damage conrol," *Proceedings of the Great Plains Wildlife Damage Control Workshop*, (Manhatten: Kansas State University, 1973), 40.

[24] Gier, 1957, 42.

[25] W. F. Andelt, D. P. Althoff, and P. S. Gipson, "Movements of breeding coyotes with emphasis on den site relationships," *Journal of Mammalogy* 60 (1979), 570.

[26] M. L. Kennedy, "Status of coyote research," *Tennessee Wildlife Resources Agency Technical Report* 89-2 (1989), 17.

[27] K. Fruth, "The coyote (*Canis latrans*)," *Wisconsin Department of Natural Resources, Bureau of Wildlife Management* PUBL-WM-148. 86 (1986), 1.

[28] D. J. Harrison and J. R. Gilbert, "Denning ecology and movements of coyotes in Maine during pup rearing," *Journal of Mammalogy* 66 (1985), 714; D. L. Hallett, "Post-natal mortality, movements, and den sites of Missouri coyotes," M.Sc. thesis (University of Missouri, Columbia, 1977); G. B. Kolenosky, D. R. Voigt, and R. O. Standfield, "Wolves and coyotes in Ontario," *Ontario Ministry of Natural Resources* (1978), 15.

[29] See Harrison and Gilbert, 714; D. J. Sherburne and G. J. Matula, Jr., "Predator habitat utilization studies, Dickey-Lincoln School Lakes Project," *Maine Cooperative Wildlife Research Unit Unpublished Report* (1981); B. Patterson, pers. comm.

[30] Young and Jackson, 80-81.

[31] Gier, 1975, 255.

[32] See F. F. Knowlton, "Preliminary interpretations of coyote population mechanics with some management implications," *Journal of Wildlife Management* 36 (1972), 372-373; J. T. Springer and C. R. Wenger, "Interactions between, and some ecological aspects of coyotes and mule deer in central Wyoming," *Wyoming Department of Wildlife, Wildlife Technical Report* No. 1981 (1981), 79; F. W. Clark, "Influence of jackrabbit density on coyote population change," *Journal of Wildlife Management* 36 (1972), 343-356; E. M. Gese, O. J. Rongstad, and W. R. Mytton, "Population dynamics of coyotes in southeastern Colorado," *Journal of Wildlife Management* 53 (1989), 176; B. R. Mahan and H. T. Gier, "Age structure and reproductive success of coyotes (*Canis latrans*) in Illinois," *Transactions of the Illinois State Academy of Science* 70 (1977), 239; G. F. Hubert, Jr., "Population trends and characteristics: canid investigations," *Illinois Department of Conservation, Job Completion Report* No. W-49-R (25), (1978), 4; Fruth, 1; Kennedy, 13; W. H. Longley, "Coyote collection," *Minnesota Game Research Project Quarterly Progress Report* 30 (1970), 60; K. T. Atkinson and D. M. Shackleton, "Coyote, *Canis latrans*, ecology in a rural-urban environment," *Canadian Field-Naturalist* 105 (1991), 50.

[33] C. H. Nellis and L. B. Keith, "Population dynamics of coyotes in central Alberta, 1964-68," *Journal of Wildlife Management* 40 (1976), 389-398; A. W. Todd, L. B. Keith, and C. A. Fischer, "Population ecology of coyotes during a fluctuation of snowshoe hares," *Journal of Wildlife Management* 45 (1981), 629-640; A. W. Todd and L. B. Keith, "Coyote demography during a snowshoe hare decline in Alberta," *Journal of Wildlife Management* 47 (1983), 394-404.

[34] State of Connecticut, "Furbearer population monitoring-carcass collections and necropsies," *Project Performance Report* No.W-49-R-11, Period 10/1/85 - 9/30/86 (1987), 137-142; D. J.

Harrison, "Coyotes in the northeast: their history, origin and ecology," *Appalachia* 46 (1986), 38; Jean and Bergeron, 2242; Gary C. Moore and John S. Millar, "A comparative study of colonizing and longer established eastern coyote populations," *Journal of Wildlife Management* 48 (1984), 691-699.

[35] S. B. Anderson, "The coyote bounty in Nova Scotia 1982-1986," *Nova Scotia Department of Lands and Forests Technical Note* 52 (1988), 1-4.

[36] B. Patterson, pers. comm.

[37] Harrison and Gilbert, 715-16.

[38] Ibid., 717.

[39] Lemm, 39.

[40] Silver and Silver, 8.

[41] Gier, 1975, 255.

[42] C. Snow, "Some observations on the behavioral and morphological development of coyote pups," *American Zoologist* 7 (1967), 353.

[43] Hilton, 220.

[44] Silver and Silver, 10, 19-20.

[45] Ibid., 9-12, 21-22.

[46] Gier, 1975, 255.

[47] Ibid., 256.

[48] Young and Jackson, 86, 88.

[49] Gier, 1975, 257.

[50] Kolenosky, et al., 15.

[51] B. Patterson, pers. comm.

[52] See Gier, 1975, 257.

[53] W. E. Berg and R. A. Chesness, "Ecology of coyotes in northern Minnesota," in M. Bekoff, ed., *Coyotes: Biology, Behavior, and Management* (New York: Academic Press, 1978), 241.

[54] Nellis and Keith, 389-399.

[55] W. B. Robinson and M. V. Cummings, "Movements of coyotes from and to Yellowstone National Park," *United States Department of Interior, Special Scientific Report, Wildlife No.* 11 (1951), 1-17; Knowlton, 378; E. K. Boggess, R. D. Andrews and R. A. Bishop, "Iowa coyote ecology studies," *Coyote Research Newsletter* 3 (1975), 2.

[56] Nellis and Keith, 393.

[57] Gese et al., 176.

[58] D. R. Voigt and W. E. Berg, "Coyote," in M. Novak, J. A. Baker, M. E. Olbard, and B. Malloch, eds., *Wild Furbearer Management and Conservation in North America* (Ontario Ministry of Natural Resources, 1987), 348-349.

[59] J. R. Lorenz, "Physical characteristics, movement and population estimate of the eastern coyote in New England," M.Sc. thesis (University of Massachusetts, Amherst, 1978), 42-43.

[60] D. J. Harrison, "Dispersal characteristics of juvenile coyotes in Maine," *Journal of Wildlife Management* 56 (1992), 132, 135.

[61] Ibid., 128.

[62] L. D. Morton, "Winter ecology of the eastern coyote," M.Sc. thesis (University of New Brunswick, Fredericton, 1988).

[63] L. D. Morton, pers. comm.

[64] D. J. Harrison, "Social ecology of coyotes in northeastern North America: relationships to dispersal, food resource, and human exploitation," in A.H. Boer, ed., *Ecology and Management of the Eastern Coyote* (Fredericton: University of New Brunswick Press, 1992), 53-72.

Chapter 6. Population Dynamics

1 W. B. Grange, *The Way To Game Abundance* (New York: Charles Scribner's Sons, 1949), 16-17.

2 F. F. Knowlton and L. C. Stoddart, "Coyote population mechanics: another look," in F. L. Bunnell, D. S. Eastman, and J. M. Peck, eds., *Symposium on the Natural Regulation of Wildlife Populations* (University of Idaho, Moscow, 1983), 93-111.

3 F. W. Clark, "Influence of jackrabbit density on coyote population change," *Journal of Wildlife Management* 36 (1972), 343.

4 F. F. Knowlton, "Preliminary interpretations of coyote population mechanics with some management implications," *Journal of Wildlife Management* 36 (1972), 371.

5 See Henry Hilton, "Coyotes in Maine: a case study," in A. H. Boer, ed., *Ecology and Management of the Eastern Coyote* (Fredericton: University of New Brunswick Press, 1992), 184; D. F. Hoffmeister, *Mammals of Illinois* (Urbana and Chicago: University of Illinois Press, 1989), 271; K. Fruth, "The coyote (*Canis latrans*)," *Wisconsin Department of Natural Resources, Bureau of Wildlife Management* PUBL-WM-148.86 (1986), 3.

6 W. Bourne, "Coyotes come calling on the south," *Southern Outdoors* Feb. (1991), 72.

7 Henry Hilton, "Eastern Coyote assessment-1985, Planning for Maine's Inland Fish and Wildlife," *Maine Department of Inland Fisheries and Wildlife Report* (1986), 543.

8 S. B. Linhart and F. F. Knowlton, "Determining age of coyotes by tooth cementum layers," *Journal of Wildlife Management* 31 (1967), 119-124.

9 See Knowlton, 379; Y. Jean and J. M. Bergeron, "Productivity of coyotes, *Canis latrans*, from southern Quebec, Canada," *Canadian Journal of Zoology* 62 (1984), 2241; H. J. Mathwig, "Food and population characteristics of Iowa coyotes," *Iowa State Journal of Research* 47 (1973), 187; C. E. Adams, "Ages of hunter-killed coyotes in southeastern Nebraska," *Journal of Wildlife Management* 42 (1978), 425.

10 R.D. Pastuck, "Some aspects of the ecology of the coyote (*Canis latrans*) in southwestern Manitoba," M.Sc. thesis (University of Manitoba, Winnipeg, 1974), 150-151; B. R. Mahan and H. T. Gier, "Age structure and reproductive success of coyotes (*Canis latrans*) in Illinois," *Transactions of the Illinois State Academy of Science* 70 (1977), 239.

11 See Knowlton, 375.

12 See C. H. Nellis and L. B. Keith, "Population dynamics of coyotes in central Alberta, 1964-68," *Journal of Wildlife Management* 40 (1976), 389-399; A. W. Todd, L. B. Keith, and C. A. Fischer, "Population ecology of coyotes during a fluctuation of snowshoe hares," *Journal of Wildlife Management* 45 (1981), 629-640; A. W. Todd and L. B. Keith, "Coyote demography during a snowshoe hare decline in Alberta," *Journal of Wildlife Management* 47 (1983), 394-404; A. W. Todd, "Demographic and dietary comparisons of forest and farmland coyote, *Canis latrans*, populations in Alberta," *Canadian Field-Naturalist* 99 (1985), 163-171; Clark, 343-356.

13 Todd and Keith, 394.

14 D. R. Voigt, "The adaptable coyote," *Ontario Fish and Game Review* 16 (1977), 4.

15 S. B. Anderson, "The coyote bounty in Nova Scotia 1982-1986," *Nova Scotia Department of Lands and Forests Technical Note* No. 52 (1988), 1-4.

16 J. Mills, "Sex, age and reproductive condition from coyotes (*Canis latrans*) in Nova Scotia (during 1992-93)," *Typewritten report for Special Problems in Biology* (Acadia University, Wolfville, 1993), 1-13.

17 See E. M. Gese, O. J. Rongstad, and W. R. Mytton, "Population dynamics of coyotes in southeastern Colorado," *Journal of Wildlife Management* 53 (1989), 176; Adams, 426; W. P. Meinzer, D. N. Ueckert and J. T. Flinders, "Foodniche of coyotes in the rolling plains of Texas," *Journal of Range Management* 28 (1975), 26; W. E. Berg and R. A. Chesness, "Ecology of coyotes in northern Minnesota," in M. Bekoff, ed., *Coyotes: Biology, Behavior, and Management* (New York: Academic Press, 1978), 244.

[18] Knowlton, 375.

[19] R. H. Manville, "Longevity of the coyote," *Journal of Mammalogy* 34 (1953), 390.

[20] See S. P. Young and H. H. T. Jackson, *The Clever Coyote* (Lincoln and London: University of Nebraska Press, 1951), 78 and 79.

[21] Meinzer et al., 26.

[22] Knowlton, 377-378.

[23] Gese, et al., 177.

[24] Nellis and Keith, 389-399.

[25] Todd and Keith, 401.

[26] S. P. Wetmore, C. H. Nellis and L. B. Keith, "A study of winter coyote hunting in Alberta with emphasis on use of snowmobiles," *Alberta Department of Lands and Forests, Wildlife Technical Bulletin* 2 (1970), 1-22.

[27] Todd et al., 632.

[28] Todd, 99.

[29] See L. D. Mech, "Disproportionate sex ratios of wolf pups," *Journal of Wildlife Management* 39 (1975), 737-740; D. G. Kleiman and C. A. Brady, "Coyote behavior in the context of recent canid research: problems and perspectives," in M. Bekoff, ed., *Coyotes: Biology, Behavior, and Management* (New York: Academic Press, 1978), 172.

[30] J. R. Lorenz, "Physical characteristics, movement and population estimate of the eastern coyote in New England," M.Sc. thesis (University of Massachusetts, Amherst, 1978), 32.

[31] G. C. Moore and J. S. Millar, "A comparative study of colonizing and longer established eastern coyote populations," *Journal of Wildlife Management* 48 (1984), 693.

[32] J. D. MacNearney, "A study of colonizing eastern coyotes (*Canis latrans thamnos*) in Nova Scotia," *Typewritten report for Special Problems in Biology*, (Acadia University, Wolfville, 1982).

[33] Anderson, 1-4.

[34] Mills, 1-13.

[35] See Nellis and Keith, 395-396; H. T. Gier, "Coyotes in Kansas," *Kansas Agricultural Experimental Station Bulletin* 393 (1957), 60; D. L. Hallett, "Post-natal mortality, movements, and den sites of Missouri coyotes," M.Sc. thesis (University of Missouri, Columbia, 1977); J. J. Knudson, "Demographic analysis of a Utah-Idaho coyote population," M.Sc. thesis (Utah State University, Logan, 1976); F. F. Knowlton and L. C. Stoddart, "Coyote population dynamics: another look," in F. L. Bunnell, D. S. Eastman, and J. M. Peek, eds., *Symposium on the Natural Regulation of Wildlife Populations* (Moscow: University of Idaho, 1983), 93-111.

[36] H. T. Gier, "Ecology and behavior of the coyote (*Canis latrans*)," in M. W. Fox, ed., *The Wild Canids* (New York: Van Nostrand Reinhold, 1975), 258; Nellis and Keith, 395-396;

[37] Knowlton and Stoddart, 93-111.

[38] Wetmore et al., 1-22.

[39] S. J. Hibler, "Coyote movement patterns with emphasis on home range characteristics," M.Sc. thesis (Utah State University, Logan, 1977).

[40] Knowlton, 375.

[41] Ibid., 379.

[42] L. A. Windberg, H. L. Anderson, and R. M. Engeman, "Survival of coyotes in southern Texas," *Journal of Wildlife Management* 49 (1985), 303.

[43] See R. P. Davison, "The effect of exploitation on some parameters of coyote populations," Ph.D. diss. (Utah State University, Logan, 1980); Knudson; W. M. Tzilkowski,, "Mortality patterns of radio-marked coyotes in Jackson Hole, Wyoming." Ph.D. diss. (University of Massachusetts, Amherst, 1980).

[44] Gese, et al., 174; W. F. Andelt, "Behavioral ecology of coyotes in south Texas," *Wildlife Monograph* 94 (1985).

[45] Nellis and Keith, 396.

[46] H. Hilton, "The physical characteristics, taxonomic status and food habits of the eastern coyote in Maine," M.Sc. thesis (University of Maine, Orono, 1976).

[47] Knowlton and Stoddart, 99.

[48] Gese et al., 176.

[49] Windberg et al., 304.

[50] See Knudson; Tzilkowsky.

[51] D. Pyrah, "Social distribution and population estimates of coyotes in north-central Montana," *Journal of Wildlife Management* 48 (1984), 687.

[52] Clark, 354.

[53] R. D. Andrews and E. K. Boggess, "Ecology of coyotes in Iowa," in M. Bekoff, ed., *Coyotes: Biology, Behavior, and Management* (New York: Academic Press, 1978), 262.

[54] D. J. Harrison, "Dispersal characteristics of juvenile coyotes in Maine," *Journal of Wildlife Management* 56 (1992), 134.

[55] E. W. Pearson, "A 1974 coyote harvest estimate for 17 western states," *Wildlife Society Bulletin* 6 (1978), 27.

[56] R. Grimes, "The coyote that outfoxed a state," *National Wool Grower* 62 (1972), 16-17, 32.

[57] L. B. Keith, *Wildlife's Ten-year Cycle* (Madison: University of Wisconsin Press, 1963).

[58] Gier, 1957; L. J. Korschgen, "Food habits of the coyote in Missouri," *Journal of Wildlife Management* 21 (1957), 424-435; Clark, 343-356.

[59] Todd and Keith, 403.

[60] Todd (1985), 163-171.

[61] A. W. Todd and L. B. Keith, "Responses of coyotes to winter reductions in agricultural carrion," *Alberta Wildlife Technical Bulletin* 5 (1976), 1-32; Todd and Keith (1983), 403.

[62] Todd, 171.

[63] Ibid., 165.

[64] F. H. Wagner and L. C. Stoddart, "Influence of coyote predation on black-tailed jackrabbit populations in Utah," *Journal of Wildlife Management* 36 (1972), 341.

[65] Clark, 343-356 (quotation, 355).

[66] F. F. Knowlton and L. C. Stoddart, "Some observations from two coyote-prey studies," in A. H. Boer, ed., *Ecology and Management of the Eastern Coyote* (Fredericton: University of New Brunswick Press, 1992), 105-117.

Chapter 7. Home range and Movements

[1] E. T. Seton, *Life Histories of Northern Animals* Vol. 1. (New York: Charles Scribner's Sons, 1909).

[2] M. Bekoff and M. C. Wells, "The social ecology of coyotes," *Scientific American* 242 (1980), 136.

[3] J. W. Laundre and B. L. Keller, "Home-range size of coyotes: a critical review," *Journal of Wildlife Management* 48 (1984), 137-138.

[4] D. J. Harrison, "Social ecology of coyotes in northeastern North America: relationships to dispersal, food resources, and human exploitation," in A. H. Boer, ed., *Ecology and Management of the Eastern Coyote* (Fredericton: University of New Brunswick Press, 1992), 53-72.

[5] D. K. Person, "Home range, activity, habitat use, and food habits of eastern coyotes in the Champlain Valley region of Vermont," M.Sc. thesis (University of Vermont, Burlington, 1988); D. K. Person and D. H. Hirth, "Home range and habitat use of coyotes in a farm region of Vermont," *Journal of Wildlife Management* 55 (1991), 433-441.

[6] Harrison, 66.

[7] See F. J. Camenzind, "Behavioral ecology of coyotes on the National Elk Refuge, Jackson, Wyoming," in M. Bekoff, ed., *Coyotes: Biology, Behavior, and Management* (New York: Academic Press, 1978), 267-294; Bekoff and Wells, 130-148.

[8] D. Pyrah, "Social distribution and population estimates of coyotes in north-central Montana," *Journal of Wildlife Management* 48 (1984), 688.

[9] Ibid., 689-690.

[10] E. M. Gese, O. J. Rongstad, and W. R. Mytton, "Population dynamics of coyotes in southeastern Colorado," *Journal of Wildlife Management* 53 (1989), 178.

[11] Camenzind, 267-294; Bekoff and Wells, 130-148; W. F. Andelt and P. S. Gipson, "Home range, activity, and daily movements of coyotes," *Journal of Wildlife Management* 43 (1979), 944-951.

[12] L. A. Windberg and F. F. Knowlton, "Management implications of coyote spacing patterns in southern Texas," *Journal of Wildlife Management* 52 (1988), 638-639.

[13] Ibid., 632.

[14] S. Holzman, M. J. Conroy, and J. Pickering, "Home range, movements, and habitat use of coyotes in southcentral Georgia," *Journal of Wildlife Management* 56 (1992), 142; L. A. Windberg, H. L. Anderson, and R. M. Engeman, "Survival of coyotes in southern Texas," *Journal of Wildlife Management* 49 (1985), 301.

[15] J. T. Springer, "Movement patterns of coyotes in south central Washington," *Journal of Wildlife Management* 46 (1982), 191.

[16] See P. W. Sumner, E. P. Hill, and J. B. Wooding, "Activity and movements of coyotes in Mississippi and Alabama," *Proceedings of the Annual Conference of Southeast Fish and Wildlife Agencies* 38 (1984), 174; A. B. Sargeant, S. H. Allen, and J. O. Hastings, "Spatial relations between sympatric coyotes and red foxes in North Dakota," *Journal of Wildlife Management* 51 (1987), 285; R. A. Woodruff and B. C. Keller, "Dispersal, daily activity, and home range of coyotes in south-eastern Idaho," *Northwest Science* 56 (1982), 199; L. L. Edwards, "Home range of the coyote in southern Idaho," M.Sc. thesis (Idaho State University, Pocatello, 1975), 25-27; Andelt and Gipson, 945; E. M. Gese, O. J. Rongstad, and W. R. Mytton, "Home range and habitat use of coyotes in southeastern Colorado," *Journal of Wildlife Management* 52 (1988), 640.

[17] D. P. Althoff and P. S. Gipson, "Coyote family spatial relationships with reference to poultry losses," *Journal of Wildlife Management* 45 (1981), 647.

[18] J. A. Litvaitis and J. H. Shaw, "Coyote movements, habitat use and food habits in southwestern Oklahoma," *Journal of Wildlife Management* 44 (1980), 64.

[19] Andelt (1985), 1-45.

[20] See K. Preece, "Home range, movements, and social behavior of denning female coyotes in north-central Minnesota," *Minnesota Wildlife Research Quarterly* 38 (1978), 163; J. J. Ozoga and E. M. Harger, "Winter activities and feeding habits of northern Michigan coyotes," *Journal of Wildlife Management* 30 (1966), 811; D. R. Voigt, "The adaptable coyote," *Ontario Fish and Game Review* 16 (1977), 4.

[21] S. L. Caturano, "Habitat and home range use by coyotes in eastern Maine," M.Sc. thesis (University of Maine, Orono, 1983), 7-8.

[22] J. T. Major and J. A. Sherburne, "Interspecific relationships of coyotes, bobcats and red foxes in western Maine," *Journal of Wildlife Management* 51 (1987), 610-611.

[23] G. R. Parker and J. W. Maxwell, "Seasonal movements and winter ecology of the coyote, *Canis latrans*, in northern New Brunswick," *Canadian Field-Naturalist* 103 (1989), 1-11.

[24] L. S. Mills and F. F. Knowlton, "Coyote space use in relation to prey abundance," *Canadian Journal of Zoology* 69 (1991), 1516-1521.

[25] J. T. Springer and C. R. Wenger, "Interactions between, and some ecological aspects of coyotes and mule deer in central Wyoming," *Wyoming Department of Wildlife Technical Report* No. 1981 (1981), 67.

[26] Bekoff and Wells, 138.

[27] W. B. Robinson and E. F. Grand, "Comparative movements of bobcats and coyotes as disclosed by tagging," *Journal of Wildlife Management* 22 (1958), 122.

[28] V. M. Hawthorne, "Coyote movements in Sagehen Creek Basin, northeastern California," *California Fish and Game* 57 (1971), 154.

[29] P. W. Sumner, E. P. Hill, and J. B. Wooding, "Activity and movements of coyotes in Mississippi and Alabama," *Proceedings of the Annual Conference of Southeast Fish and Wildlife Agencies* 38 (1984), 174.

[30] Ibid., 199.

[31] Andelt and Gipson, 945.

[32] Litvaitis Shaw, 64.

[33] Andelt (1985), 1-45.

[34] Parker and Maxwell, 1-11.

[35] Bekoff and Wells, 138-139.

CHAPTER 8. COYOTES AND WHITE-TAILED DEER

[1] D. L. Allen, *Our Wildlife Legacy* (New York: Funk and Wagnalls Company, 1954), 234.

[2] R. E. McCabe and T. R. McCabe, "Of slings and arrows: an historical retrospection," in L. K. Halls, ed., *White-tailed Deer: Ecology and Management* (Harrisburg: Wildlife Management Institute, Stackpole Books, 1984), 19-22.

[3] E. T. Seton, *Lives of Game Animals*, Vol. 3, Part 1, (Garden City: Doubleday, 1929).

[4] H. Silver, "History," in H. R. Siegler, ed., "The white-tailed deer of New Hampshire," *New Hampshire Fish and Game Survey Report* No.10 (1968), 18.

[5] Ibid., 21 and 22.

[6] T. J. Allen and J. I. Cromer, "White-tailed deer in West Virginia," *West Virginia Department of Natural Resources Bulletin* No.7 (1977), 4-7.

[7] B. L. Dahlberg and R. C. Guettinger, "The white-tailed deer in Wisconsin," *Wisconsin Conservation Department, Technical Wildlife Bulletin* No. 14 (1956), 13-41.

[8] D. D. Anderson, "The status of deer in Kansas," *University of Kansas Miscellaneous Publication* No. 39 (1964), 7.

[9] McCabe and McCabe, 66, 68, 70.

[10] E. T. Seton, *Life Histories of Northern Mammals*, Vol. 1 (New York: Charles Scribner's Sons, 1909).

[11] McCabe and McCabe, 72.

[12] D. A. Benson and D. G. Dodds, "The deer of Nova Scotia," *Nova Scotia Department of Lands and Forests*, 1977, 1.

[13] J. S. Erskine, quoted in Benson and Dodds, 1-2.

[14] Benson and Dodds, 24, 38.

[15] R. M. Nowak, "A perspective on the taxonomy of wolves in North America," in L. N. Carbyn, ed., *Wolves in Canada and Alaska* (Canadian Wildlife Service Report Series No. 45, 1983), 17-18.

[16] J. A. Allen, "The former range of some New England carnivorous mammals," *American Naturalist* 10 (1876), 710.

[17] W. A. Squires, "A naturalist in New Brunswick," *The New Brunswick Museum*, Saint John (1972), 118-20, 122.

[18] J. Bernard Gilpin, "On the Mammalia of Nova Scotia," *Transactions of the Nova Scotia Institute of Natural Science* No 1 (1864), 8.

[19] See C. W. Severinghaus, "Notes on the history of wild canids in New York," *New York Fish and Game Journal* 21 (1974), 117-125.

[20] R. M. Bond, "Coyote food habits on the Lava Beds National Monument," *Journal of Wildlife Management* 3 (1939), 180-198.

[21] V. M. Hawthorne, "Coyote food habits in Sagehen Creek Basin, Northeastern California," *California Fish and Game* 58 (1972), 11.

[22] T. J. Ogle, "Predator-prey relationships between coyote and white-tailed deer," *Northwest Science* 45 (1971), 216.

[23] A. F. Halloran and B. P. Glass, "The carnivores and ungulates of the Wichita Mountains Wildlife Refuge, Oklahoma," *Journal of Mammalogy* 40 (1959), 363; J. A. Litvaitis and J. H. Shaw, "Coyote movements, habitat use and food habits in southwestern Oklahoma," *Journal of Wildlife Management* 44 (1980), 65.

[24] D. Holle, "Food habits of coyotes in an area of high fawn mortality," *Proceedings of the Oklahoma Academy of Science* No. 58 (1978), 13.

[25] J. T. Springer and J. S. Smith, "Summer food habits of coyotes in central Wyoming," *Great Basin Naturalist* 41 (1981), 452; J. G. MacCracken and D. W. Uresk, "Coyote foods in the Black Hills, South Dakota," *Journal of Wildlife Management* 48 (1984), 1421-1422.

[26] P. S. Gipson, "Food habits of coyotes in Arkansas," *Journal of Wildlife Management* 38 (1974), 849; D. I. Hall and J. D. Newsom, "The coyote in Louisiana," *Louisiana Agriculture* 21 (1978), 5.

[27] K. M. Blanton and E. P. Hill, "Coyote use of white-tailed deer fawns in relation to deer density," *Proceedings of the Annual Conference of Southeast Association Fish and Wildlife Agencies* 43 (1989), 470.

[28] See T. J. Niebauer and O. J. Rongstad, "Coyote food habits in northwestern Wisconsin," in R. L. Phillips and C. Jonkel, eds., *Proceedings of the 1975 Predator Symposium* (Missoula: University of Montana Printing Department, 1975), 237-251; C. N. Huegel, "Winter ecology of coyotes in northern Wisconsin," M.Sc. thesis (University of Wisconsin, Madison, 1979), 24; J. J. Ozoga and E. M. Harger, "Winter activities and feeding habits of northern Michigan coyotes," *Journal of Wildlife Management* 30 (1966), 815.

[29] W. J. Hamilton, Jr., "Food habits of the coyote in the Adirondacks," *New York Fish and Game Journal* 21 (1974), 179; D. J. Harrison, D. W. May, and P. W. Rego, "Distribution, productivity and food habits of a recently established coyote population in Connecticut," *Transactions of the Northeast Fish and Wildlife Conference* 46 (1989), Abstracts only; State of Connecticut, "Furbearer population monitoring-carcass collections and necropsies," *Project Performance Report* No.W-49-R-11, Period 10/1/85 - 9/30/86 (1987), 137-142.

[30] V. B. Richens and R. D. Hugie, "Distribution, taxonomic status, and characteristics of coyotes in Maine," *Journal of Wildlife Management* 38 (1974), 450; H. Hilton, "The physical characteristics, taxonomic status and food habits of the eastern coyote in Maine," M.Sc. thesis (University of Maine, Orono, 1976), 44; D. J. Harrison and J. A. Harrison, "Foods of adult Maine coyotes and their known-aged pups," *Journal of Wildlife Management* 48 (1984), 924-925.

[31] J .T. Major, "Ecology and interspecific relationships of coyotes, bobcats and red foxes in western Maine," Ph.D. diss., (University of Maine, Orono, 1984); J. T. Major and J. A. Sherburne, "Interspecific relationships of coyotes, bobcats and red foxes in western Maine," *Journal of Wildlife Management* 51 (1987), 606-616; F. J. Dibello, S. M. Arthur, and W. B. Krohn, "Food habits of sympatric coyotes, *Canis latrans*, red foxes, *Vulpes vulpes*, and bobcats, *Lynx rufus*, in Maine," *Canadian Field-Naturalist* 104 (1990), 403-408.

[32] See Major; Major and Sherburne, 606-616.

[33] F. Messier, C. Barrette, and J. Huot, "Coyote predation on a white-tailed deer population in southern Quebec, Canada," *Canadian Journal of Zoology* 64 (1986), 1134.

[34] J. M. Bergeron and P. Demers, "Le régime alimentaire du Coyote (*Canis latrans*) et du chien errant (*C. familiaris*) dans le sud du Québec," *Canadian Field-Naturalist* 95 (1981), 172-177.

[35] L. E. LaPierre, "Fall and winter food habits of the eastern coyote (*Canis latrans*) in southeastern New Brunswick, Canada," *Proceedings of the Nova Scotia Institute of Science* 35 (1985), 71-74.

[36] G. C. Moore and J. S. Millar, "Food habits and average weights of a fall-winter sample of eastern coyotes, *Canis latrans*," *Canadian Field-Naturalist* 100 (1986), 105-106.

[37] L. D. Morton, "Winter ecology of the eastern coyote," M.Sc. thesis (University of New Brunswick, Fredericton, 1988), 11.

[38] G. R. Parker, "The seasonal diet of coyotes, *Canis latrans*, in northern New Brunswick," *Canadian Field-Naturalist* 100 (1986), 74-77.

[39] R. Hall, "Winter tracking of coyotes," *Nova Scotia Lands and Forests Technical Note* 44 (1978), 2.

[40] See D. Smith, "The determination of coyote (*Canis latrans*) food habits from the contents of scats," *Typewritten report for Special Problems in Biology* (Acadia University, Wolfville, 1990); D. Ekkiai, "The diet of coyotes (*Canis latrans*) by scat analysis," *Typewritten report for Special Problems in Biology* (Acadia University, Wolfville, 1990).

[41] B. Patterson, "Ecology of the eastern coyote in Kejimkujik National Park," M.Sc. thesis (Acadia University, Wolfville, 1994).

[42] Ozoga and Harger, 809-819.

[43] C. N. Huegel, 1-32.

[44] Hilton, 1-67.

[45] G. R. Parker and J. W. Maxwell, "Seasonal movements and winter ecology of the coyote, *Canis latrans*, in northern New Brunswick," *Canadian Field-Naturalist* 103 (1989), 1-11.

[46] Morton, 16-20.

[47] Hall, 1-3.

[48] Barry Sabean, "Coyote winter tracking update," *Conservation* 14 (1990), 4 and 8.

[49] Barry Sabean, "Tracking coyotes in winter," *Conservation* 17 (1993), 11-12.

[50] Messier et al., 1135.

[51] B. Patterson, pers. comm.

[52] Mitchell J. Willis, "Impacts of coyote removal on pronghorn fawn survival," *Proceedings of the Pronghorn Antelope Workshop* 13, (1988), 60.

[53] J. R. Udy, "Effects of predator control on antelope populations," *Utah State Department of Fish and Game Publication* No. 5 (1953), 1-48.

[54] Ibid., 44.

[55] R. H. Smith, D. J. Neff, and N. G. Woolsey, "Pronghorn response to coyote control-a benefit: cost analysis," *Wildlife Society Bulletin* 14 (1986), 226-231 (quotation, 230).

[56] O. N. Arrington and A. E. Edwards, "Predator control as a factor in antelope management," *Transactions of the North American Wildlife Conference* 16 (1951), 179-193.

[57] Smith et al., 226-231.

[58] K. E. Menzel, "Improved survival of pronghorn fawns with coyote control," *Biennial Pronghorn Antelope Workshop* 15 (1992).

[59] M. Crête and A. Desrosiers, "L'invasion du coyote (*Canis latrans*) menace la survie de la population relique de caribous (*Rangifer tarandus*) du Parc de la Gaspésie," *Québec Ministère du Loisir, de la Chasse et de la Pêche*, (1993), 1-31.

[60] Ibid., 13.

[61] E. R. Brown, "The black-tailed deer of western Washington," *Washington State Game Department Biological Bulletin* No. 13 (1961), 44.

[62] J. G. Kie, M. White, and F. F. Knowlton, "Effects of coyote predation on population dynamics of white-tailed deer," in D. L. Drawe, ed., *Proceedings of the Welder Wildlife Foundation Symposium* 1 (1979), 65-82.

[63] S. L. Beasom, "Relationships between predator removal and white-tailed deer productivity," *Journal of Wildlife Management* 38 (1974), 854-859.

[64] G. G. Stout, "Effects of coyote reduction on white-tailed deer productivity on Fort Sill,

Oklahoma," *Wildlife Society Bulletin* 10 (1982), 329.

[65] D. D. Austin, P. J. Urness, and M. L. Wolfe, "The influence of predator control on two adjacent wintering deer herds," *Great Basin Naturalist* 37 (1977), 101-102.

[66] See F. Messier, F. Potvin, and F. Duchesneau, "Faisabilité d'une réduction expérimentale du coyote dans le but d'accroître une population de cerfs de Virginie," *Le Naturaliste Canadien* 114 (1987), 477-486.

[67] Ibid., 477.

[68] Charles Trainer, "Direct causes of mortality in mule deer fawns during summer and winter periods on Steens Mountain, Oregon - a progress report," *Proceedings of the Annual Conference of Western Association State Game and Fish Commissioners* 55 (1975), 163; Paul N. Ebert, "Recent changes in Oregon's mule deer population and management," *Proceedings of the Annual Conference of Western Association State Game and Fish Commissioners* 56 (1976), 411.

[69] G. W. Garner, "Mortality of white-tailed deer fawns in the Wichita Mountains, Comanche County, Oklahoma," Ph.D. diss. (Oklahoma State University, Stillwater, 1976), 3.

[70] K. L. Hamlin, S. J. Riley, D. Pyrah, A. R. Dood, and R. J. Mackie, "Relationships among mule deer fawn mortality, coyotes, and alternate prey species during summer," *Journal of Wildlife Management* 48 (1984), 489-499 (quotations, 495, 498).

[71] K. L. Hamlin et al., 489-499 (quotations 495, 498).

[72] T. A. Decker, W. M. Healy, and S. A. Williams, "Survival of white-tailed deer fawns in western Massachusetts," *Northeast Wildlife* 49 (1992), 28-35.

[73] B. K. Carroll and D. L. Brown, "Factors affecting neonatal fawn survival in southcentral Texas," *Journal of Wildlife Management* 41 (1977), 63-69 (quotation, 68).

[74] R. S. Cook, M. White, D. D. Trainer, and W. C. Glazener, "Mortality of young white-tailed deer fawns in South Texas," *Journal of Wildlife Management* 35 (1971), 47-56 (quotations, 47, 55).

[75] J. G. Teer, D. L. Drawe, T. L. Blankenship, W. F. Andelt, R. S. Cook, J. G. Kie, F. F. Knowlton, and M. White, "Deer and coyotes: the Welder experiments," *Transactions of the North American Wildlife and Natural Resources Conference* 56 (1991), 550-560 (quotations, 555-56, 558-59).

[76] L. D. Mech, "Predators and predation," in L. K. Halls, ed., *White-tailed Deer: Ecology and Management*. (Harrisburg: Wildlife Management Institute, Stackpole Books, 1984), 189-190.

[77] B. Patterson, pers. comm.

CHAPTER 9. PREDATORS AND PREDATION

[1] W. E. Howard, "The biology of predator control," *An Addison-Wesley Module in Biology* No. 11 (1974), 8.

[2] G. Caughley, "Wildlife management and the dynamics of ungulate populations," *Applied Biology* 1 (1976), 197.

[3] Ibid., 227.

[4] J. B. Therberge and D. A. Gauthier, "Models of wolf-ungulate relationships: when is wolf control justified?" *Wildlife Society Bulletin* 13 (1985), 449-458.

[5] L. D. Mech, "Predators and predation," in L. K. Halls, ed., *White-tailed Deer: Ecology and Management*. (Harrisburg: Wildlife Management Institute, Stackpole Books, 1984), 189-190.

[6] Ibid., 189; G. E. Connolly, "Predators and predator control," in J. L. Schmidt and D. L. Gilbert, eds., *Big Game of North America* (Harrisburg: Stackpole Books, 1978), 389; L. B. Keith, "Population dynamics of wolves," in L. N. Carbyn, ed., *Wolves in Canada and Alaska* (Canadian Wildlife Service Report Series No. 45, 1983), 66-77.

[7] Mech, 190-191, 194, 196.

[8] D. H. Pimlott, "Wolf predation and ungulate populations," *American Zoologist* 7 (1967), 267-278; L. B. Keith, "Population dynamics of mammals," *International Congress of Game Biologists* 11 (1974), 17-57.

[9] Theberge and Gauthier, 449-458.

[10] Ibid., 451.

[11] Connolly, 390.

[12] M. Crête, "Population dynamics of coyotes colonizing the boreal forest of eastern Quebec," *International Union of Game Biologists XXI Congress*, Dalhousie University, Halifax, Nova Scotia, August 15-20, 1993 (abstract only).

[13] M. L. Poulle, R. Lemieux, M. Crête, and J. Huot, "Régime alimentaire du coyote et sélection des proies dans un ravage de cerfs de Virginie en fort déclin:le ravage de Bonaventure (Gaspésie)," *Québec Ministère du Loisir, de la Chasse et de la Pêche* (1992).

[14] M. Crête, (abstract only).

CHAPTER 10. PREDATOR CONTROL

[1] A. S. Leopold, "The predator in wildlife management," *Sierra Club Bulletin* 39 (1954), 34.

[2] P. W. Errington, "Predation and vertebrate populations," *The Quarterly Review of Biology* 21 (1946), 144-177, 221-245; P. W. Errington, *Of Predation and Life*, (Ames: Iowa State University Press, 1967).

[3] U. S. Fish and Wildlife Service, "Predator damage in the West: a study of coyote management alternatives," *U.S. Department of the Interior*, Washington, D.C., (1978).

[4] G. E. Connolly and W. M. Longhurst, "The effects of control on coyote populations," *University of California Division of Agricultural Science Bulletin* No. 1872 (1975), 1-37.

[5] G. E. Connolly, "Predators and predator control," in J. L. Schmidt and D. Gilbert, eds., *Big Game of North America* (Harrisburg: Wildlife Management Institute, Stackpole Books, 1978), 392.

[6] H. Hilton, "Coyotes in Maine: a case study," in A. H. Boer, ed., *Ecology and Management of the Eastern Coyote* (Fredericton: University of New Brunswick Press, 1992), 183-194.

[7] Ibid., 188, 191.

[8] D. G. Dodds, "A price on their heads," *Eastern Woods and Waters* April/May (1988), 48.

CHAPTER 11. INTERSPECIFIC INTERACTIONS

[1] J. A. Litvaitis, "Niche relations between coyotes and sympatric carnivora," in A. H. Boer, ed., *Ecology and Management of the Eastern Coyote* (Fredericton: University of New Brunswick Press, 1992), 73.

[2] Ibid., 73.

[3] G. B. Kolenosky and R. O. Standfield, "Morphological and ecological variation among gray wolves (*Canis lupus*) of Ontario, Canada," in M. W. Fox, ed., *The Wild Canids* (New York: Van Nostrand Reinhold, 1975), 62-72.

[4] W. E. Berg and R. A. Chesness, "Ecology of coyotes in northern Minnesota," in M. Bekoff, ed., *Coyotes: Biology, Behavior, and Management* (New York: Academic Press, 1978), 242.

[5] T. K. Fuller and L. B. Keith, "Non-overlapping ranges of coyotes and wolves in northeastern Alberta," *Journal of Mammalogy* 62 (1981), 403-405.

[6] L. N. Carbyn, "Coyote population fluctuations and spatial distribution in relation to wolf territories in Riding Mountain National Park, Manitoba," *Canadian Field-Naturalist* 96 (1982), 176.

[7] Ibid., 182.

[8] L. D. Mech, "The wolves of Isle Royale," *U.S. National Park Service*, Fauna Series No. 7 (1966), 160.

[9] Berg and Chesness, 242.

[10] D. Dekker, "Population fluctuations and spatial relationships among wolves, *Canis lupus*, coyotes, *Canis latrans*, and red foxes, *Vulpes vulpes*, in Jasper National Park, Alberta," *Canadian Field-Naturalist* 103 (1989), 263.

[11] See A. Murie, "The wolves of Mount McKinley," *Fauna of the National Parks of the United States*, Fauna Series No. 5 (Washington: United States Printing Office, 1944): J. B. Theberge and C. H. R. Wedeles, "Prey selection and habitat partitioning in sympatric coyote and red fox populations in southwest Yukon, Canada," *Canadian Journal of Zoology* 67 (1989), 1289.

[12] Ibid., 1289.

[13] Dekker, 262.

[14] D. Dekker, "Denning and foraging habits of red foxes, *Vulpes vulpes*, and their interactions with coyotes, *Canis latrans*, in central Alberta, 1972-1981," *Canadian Field-Naturalist* 97 (1983), 306.

[15] A. B. Sargeant, S. H. Allen, and J. O. Hastings, "Spatial relations between sympatric coyotes and red foxes in North Dakota," *Journal of Wildlife Management* 51 (1987), 291.

[16] D. R. Voigt and B. D. Earle, "Avoidance of coyotes by red fox families," *Journal of Wildlife Management* 47 (1983), 856.

[17] Sargeant et al., 292.

[18] J. T. Major, "Ecology and interspecific relationships of coyotes, bobcats and red foxes in western Maine," Ph.D. diss. (University of Maine, Orono, 1984); D. J. Harrison, "Coyote dispersal, mortality, and spatial interactions with red foxes in Maine," Ph. D. diss. (University of Maine, Orono, 1986); J. T. Major and J. A. Sherburne, "Interspecific relationships of coyotes, bobcats and red foxes in western Maine," *Journal of Wildlife Management* 51 (1987), 606-616.

[19] Major and Sherburne, 615.

[20] D. J. Harrison, J. A. Bissonette, and J. A. Sherburne, "Spatial relationships between coyotes and red foxes in eastern Maine," *Journal of Wildlife Management* 53 (1989), 184.

[21] J. A. Sherburne and G. J. Matula, Jr., "Predator habitat utilization studies, Dickey-Lincoln chool Lakes Project," *Maine Cooperative Wildlife Research Unit, Unpublished Report*, University of Maine, Orono, (1981).

[22] Harrison et al., 185.

[23] R. L. Small, "Interspecific competition among three species of Carnivora on the Spider Ranch, Yavapai County, Arizona," M.Sc. thesis (University of Arizona, Tuscon, 1971); J. A. Litvaitis, "A comparison of coyote and bobcat food habits in the Wichita Mountains, Oklahoma," *Proceedings of the Oklahoma Academy of Sciences* 61 (1981), 81-82; G. W. Witmer and D. S. deCalesta, "Resource use by unexploited sympatric bobcats and coyotes in Oregon," *Canadian Journal of Zoology* 64 (1986), 2333-2338.

[24] Major and Sherburne, 606-616, (quotations, 614, 615).

[25] J. A. Litvaitis and D. H. Harrison, "Bobcat-coyote niche relationships during a period of coyote population increase," *Canadian Journal of Zoology* 67 (1989), 1180-1188, (quotations, 1181, 1185).

[26] Ibid., 1187.

[27] R. G. Howell, "The urban coyote problem in Los Angeles County," *Proceedings of the Vertebrate Pest Conference* 10 (1982), 21-22.

[28] L. N. Carbyn, "Coyote attacks on children in western North America," *Wildlife Society Bulletin* 17 (1989), 444-446.

[29] B. Sabean, pers. comm.

[30] J. R. Bider and P. G. Weil, "Dog, *Canis familiaris*, killed by a coyote, *Canis latrans*, on Montreal Island, Quebec," *The Canadian Field-Naturalist* 98 (1984), 498-499.

[31] A Canadian Press story which appeared in the July 23, 1994 edition of *The Halifax Chronicle-Herald*, p. D22.

CHAPTER 12. DISEASES AND PARASITES

[1] D. B. Pence and J. W. Custer, "Host-parasite relationships in the wild Canidae of North America. 2. Pathology of infectious diseases in the genus *Canis*," in J. A. Chapman and D. Pursley, eds., *Proceedings of the Worldwide Furbearer Conference*, Frostburg, Maryland (1981), 760.

[2] See D. O. Trainer, F. F. Knowlton, and L. Karstad, "Oral papillomatosis in the coyote," *Bulletin of Wildlife Disease Association* 4 (1968), 52-54; E. Broughton, F. E. Graesser, L. N. Carbyn, and L. P. E. Choquette, "Oral papillomatosis in the coyote in western Canada," *Journal of Wildlife Diseases* 6 (1970), 180-181; A. S. Greig and K. M. Charlton, "Electron microscopy of the virus of oral papillomatosis in the coyote," *Journal of Wildlife Diseases* 9 (1973), 359-361; Broughton, et. al., 180-181; C. H. Nellis, "Prevalence of oral papilloma-like lesions in coyotes in Alberta," *Canadian Journal of Zoology* 51 (1973), 900; W. M. Samuel, G. A. Chalmers, and J. R. Gunson, "Oral papillomatosis in coyotes (*Canis latrans*) and wolves (*Canis lupus*) of Alberta," *Journal of Wildlife Diseases* 14 (1978a), 165-169; H. T. Gier, S. M. Kruckenberg, and R. J. Marler, "Parasites and diseases of coyotes," in M. Bekoff, ed., *Coyotes: Biology, Behavior, and Management* (New York: Academic Press, 1978), 37-71.

[3] See Nellis, 900; Samuel, et al., (1978a), 165-169; Gier, et al., 37-71; Pence and Custer, 762.

[4] J. R. Gorham, "The epizootiology of distemper," *Journal of the American Veterinary Medical Association* 149 (1966), 610-622.

[5] D. O. Trainer and F. F. Knowlton, "Serologic evidence of diseases in Texas coyotes," *Journal of Wildlife Management* 32 (1968), 981-983.

[6] R. G. Green, N. R. Ziegler, W. E. Carlson, J. E. Shillinger, S. H. Tyler, and E. T. Dewey, "Epizootic fox encephalitis. V, General and pathogenic properties of the virus," *American Journal of Hygiene* 19 (1934), 343-361.

[7] Trainer and Knowlton, 981-983.

[8] D. H. Johnston and M. Beauregard, "Rabies epidemiology in Ontario," *Bulletin of Wildlife Disease Association* 5 (1969), 357-370.

[9] W. M. Samuel, S. Ramalingam, and L. N. Carbyn, "Helminths of coyotes (*Canis latrans* Say), wolves (*Canis lupus* L.) and red foxes (*Vulpes vulpes* L.) of southwestern Manitoba," *Canadian Journal of Zoology* 56 (1978), 2614-2617.

[10] See J. C. Holmes and R. Podesta, "The helminths of wolves and coyotes from the forested regions of Alberta," *Canadian Journal of Zoology* 46 (1968), 1193-1204; Samuel, et al., (in *Canadian Journal of Zoology*, 2614-2617); J. E. Thorton, R. R. Bell, and M. J. Reardon, "Internal parasites of the coyote in southern Texas," *Journal of Wildlife Diseases* 10 (1974), 232-236; D. B. Pence and W. P. Meinzer, "Helminth parasitism in the coyote, *Canis latrans*, from the Rolling Plains of Texas," *International Journal of Parasitology* 9 (1979), 339-344.

[11] Holmes and Podesta, 1193-1204.

[12] A. Fyvie, "Manual of common parasites, diseases and anomalies of wildlife in Ontario," *Ontario Department of Lands and Forests, Research Branch* (1964).

[13] R. S. Freeman, A. Adorjan, and D. H. Pimlott, "Cestodes of wolves, coyotes and coyote-dog hybrids in Ontario," *Canadian Journal of Zoology* 39 (1961), 527-532.

[14] Pence and Custer, 796-819.

[15] Gier, et al., 46.

[16] Ibid., 43.

CHAPTER 13. COYOTES AND DOMESTIC STOCK

[1] R. A. McCabe and E. L. Kozicky, "A position on predator management," *Journal of Wildlife Management* 36 (1972), 390.

[2] R. T. Sterner and S. A. Shumake, "Coyote damage-control research: a review and analysis," in M. Bekoff, ed., *Coyotes: Biology, Behavior, and Management* (New York: Academic Press, 1978), 297-325.

[3] U. S. Fish and Wildlife Service, "Predator damage in the west: a study of coyote management alternatives," *U.S. Department of Interior*, Washington, D.C., (1978).

[4] M. J. Dorrance and L. D. Roy, "Predation losses of domestic sheep in Alberta," *Journal of Range Management* 29 (1976), 457-460.

[5] D. R. Henne, "Domestic sheep mortality on a western Montana ranch," in R. L. Phillips and C. Jonkel, eds., *Proceedings of the 1975 Predator Symposium* (Missoula: University of Montana Printing Dept., 1977), 133-146.

[6] C. E. Terrill, "Livestock losses to predators in western states," in R. L. Phillips and C. Jonkel, eds., *Proceedings of the 1975 Predator Symposium* (Missoula, University of Montana Printing Dept., 1977), 157-162 (quotation, 159).

[7] See G. E. Nesse, W. M. Longhurst, and W. E. Howard, "Predation and the sheep industry in California," *University of California, Division of Agricultural Sciences Bulletin* No. 1878 (1976), 7; R. D. Nass, "Mortality associated with sheep operations in Idaho," *Journal of Range Management* 30 (1977), 253; D. A. Klebenow and K. McAdoo, "Predation on domestic sheep in northeastern Nevada," *Journal of Range Management* 29 (1976), 96; J. R. Tigner and G. E. Larson, "Sheep losses on selected ranches in southern Wyoming," *Journal of Range Management* 30 (1977), 244; R. G. Taylor, J. P. Workman, and J. E. Bowns, "The economics of sheep predation in southwestern Utah," *Journal of Range Management* 32 (1979), 317.

[8] J. M. Schaefer, R. D. Andrews, and J. J. Dinsmore, "An assessment of coyote and dog predation on sheep in southern Iowa," *Journal of Wildlife Management* 45 (1981), 883, 892-93.

[9] D. Nielson and D. Curle, "Predator costs to Utah's range sheep industry," *National Wool Grower* 60 (1970), 14-16.

[10] E. K. Boggess, R. D. Andrews, and R. A. Bishop, "Domestic animal losses to coyotes and dogs in Iowa," *Journal of Wildlife Management* 42 (1978), 362.

[11] Economics, Statistics and Cooperative Service, "Cattle and calf losses in feeder cattle production," *United States Department of Agriculture, unpublished report* (1978).

[12] U. S. Fish and Wildlife Service, 34.

[13] National Agricultural Statistics Service (Nass), "Sheep and goat predator loss," *United States Department of Agriculture, Agricultural Statistics Board Report* Lv Gn 1 (4-91) (1991), 1-12.

[14] M. J. Dorrance, "Predation losses of cattle in Alberta," *Journal of Range Management* 35 (1982), 690-692.

[15] G. E. Connolly, "Coyote damage to livestock and other resources," in A. H. Boer, ed., *Ecology and Management of the Eastern Coyote* (Fredericton: University of New Brunswick Press, 1992), 161-169.

[16] Barry Sabean, "The eastern coyote in Nova Scotia," *Conservation* 13 (1989), 5-8.

[17] H. Hilton, "Coyotes in Maine: a case study," in A. H. Boer, ed., *Ecology and Management of the Eastern Coyote* (Fredericton: University of New Brunswick Press, 1992), 183-194.

[18] Brian Trenholm, New Brunswick Department of Agriculture, pers. comm.

[19] G. E. Connolly, R. M. Timm, W. E. Howard, and W. M. Longhurst, "Sheep killing behavior of captive coyotes," *Journal of Wildlife Management* 40 (1976), 400.

[20] F. A. Servello, T. L. Edwards, and B. U. Constantin, "Managing coyote problems in Kentucky," *University of Kentucky, Cooperative Extension Service* FOR-37, (1989), 3.

[21] S. W. Horn, "An evaluation of predatory suppression in coyotes using lithium chloride-induced illness," *Journal of Wildlife Management* 47 (1983), 999.

[22] S. R. Ellins and G. C. Martin, "Olfactory discrimination of lithium chloride by the coyote (*Canis latrans*)" *Behavioral and Neural Biology* 29 (1980), 215.

[23] C. R. Gustavson, J. Garcia, W. G. Hawkins, and K. W. Rusiniak, "Coyote predation control by aversive conditioning," *Science* 184 (1974), 581-583; C. R. Gustavson, "An experimental evaluation of aversive conditioning for controlling coyote predation: a critique," *Journal of Wildlife Management* 43 (1979), 209.

[24] M. M. Conover, J. G. Francik, and D. E. Miller, "An experimental evaluation of aversive conditioning for controlling coyote predation," *Journal of Wildlife Management* 41 (1977), 778.

[25] See R. E. Griffiths, Jr., G. E. Connolly, R. J. Burns, and R. T. Sterner, "Coyotes, sheep and lithium chloride," *Proceedings of the Vertebrate Pest Conference* 8 (1978), 190-196; M. R. Conover, J. G. Francik, and D. E. Miller, "Aversive conditioning in coyotes: a reply," *Journal of Wildlife Management* 43 (1979), 209-211; R. J. Burns and G. E. Connolly, "Lithium chloride bait aversion did not influence prey killing by coyotes," *Proceedings of the Vertebrate Pest Conference* 9 (1980), 200-204; R. J. Burns, "Microencapsulated lithium chloride bait aversion did not stop coyote predation on sheep," *Journal of Wildlife Management* 47 (1983), 1016.

[26] J. Bourne and M. J. Dorrance, "A field test of lithium chloride aversion to reduce coyote predation on domestic sheep," *Journal of Wildlife Management* 46 (1982), 239.

[27] P. N. Lehner, R. Krumm, and A. T. Cringan, "Tests for olfactory repellents for coyotes and dogs," *Journal of Wildlife Management* 40 (1976), 145-150.

[28] M. Shelton and N. L. Gates, "Antipredator fencing," in J. S. Green, ed., *Protecting livestock from coyotes: a synopsis of research of the Agricultural Research Service*, USDA, Beltsville, Md. (1987), 30.

[29] F. R. Henderson and C. W. Spaeth, "Managing predator problems: practices and procedures for preventing and reducing livestock losses," *Kansas State University, Cooperative Extension Service* C-620, (1980), 9.

[30] Ibid., 9-11.

[31] M. J. Dorrance and J. Bourne, "An evaluation of anti-coyote electric fencing," *Journal of Range Management* 33 (1980), 385-387.

[32] D. E. Simms and O. Dawydiak, *Livestock Protection Dogs* (Fort Payne: OTR Publications, 1990), 17-18.

[33] J. S. Green and R. A. Woodruff, "Guarding dogs protect sheep from predators," *U.S. Department of Agriculture, Information Bulletin* No. 455 (1983), 8.

[34] Sims and Dawydiak, 20-21, 22, 27-28.

[35] Green and Woodruff, 3.

[36] W. F. Andelt, "Effectiveness of livestock guarding dogs for reducing predation on domestic sheep," *Wildlife Society Bulletin* 20 (1992), 55-62; J. S. Green, R. A. Woodruff, and T. T. Tueller, "Livestock-guarding dogs for predator control: costs, benefits, and practicality," *Wildlife Society Bulletin* 12 (1984), 44-50.

[37] Green, et al., 49.

[38] Andelt, 61-62.

[39] Green, et al., 49-50.

[40] Henderson and Spaeth, 16-17.

[41] J. S. Green, "Donkeys for predator control," *Proceedings of the 4th Eastern Wildlife Damage Control Conference*, Madison,Wi., (1989), 1.

[42] Ibid., 2.

[43] Ibid., 2-3.

[44] M. T. Walton and G. A. Field, "Use of donkeys to guard sheep and goats in Texas," *Proceedings of the 4th Eastern Wildlife Damage Control Conference*, Madison, Wi., (1989), 7-8.

[45] Green, 4.

[46] Henderson and Spaeth, 6.

[47] A. W. Todd and L. B. Keith, "Responses of coyotes to winter reductions in agricultural carrion," *Alberta Fish and Wildlife Division, Wildlife Technical Bulletin* No. 5 (1976), 1-32.

[48] Henderson and Spaeth, 8.

Chapter 14. Coyote Management

[1] R. A. McCabe and E. L. Kozicky, "A position on predator management," *Journal of Wildlife Management* 36 (1972), 382-83.

[2] Ibid., 383.

[3] See M. Bekoff, ed., *Coyotes: Biology, Behavior, and Management,* (New York: Academic Press, 1978).

[4] G. E. Connolly, "Predator control and coyote populations: a review of simulation models," in M. Bekoff, ed., *Coyotes: Biology, Behavior, and Management* (New York: Academic Press, 1978), 328.

[5] Ronald Andrews, Iowa Department of Natural Resources, pers. comm.

[6] Ed Warr, Tennessee Wildlife Resources Agency, pers. comm.

[7] John Weeks, Ohio Department of Narural Resources, pers. comm.

[8] George Hubert, Jr., Illinois Department of Conservation, pers. comm.

[9] Personal communications from John Stuht, Michigan Department of Natural Resources; Tom Edwards, Kentucky Department of Fish and Wildlife Resources; Perry Sumner, North Carolina Resources Commission; and Clifford Brown, State of West Virginia Department of Natural Resources.

[10] Personal communication from Michael Lapisky, Rhode Island Department of Environmental Management; and Ben Tullar, New York Department of Environmental Conservation.

[11] Paul Rego, State of Connecticut Department of Environmental Protection, pers. comm.

[12] Personal communication from Patricia McConnell, State of New Jersey Department of Environmental Protection; and Thomas Decker, Massachusetts Division of Fisheries and Wildlife.

[13] Eric Orff, State of New Hampshire Fish and Game Department, pers. comm.

[14] H. Hilton, "Coyotes in Maine: a case study," in A. H. Boer, ed., *Ecology and Management of the Eastern Coyote* (Fredericton: University of New Brunswick Press, 1992), 183-194.

[15] René Lafond, Coordonnateur animaux à fourrure, Gouvernement du Québec, Ministère du Loisir, de la Chase et de la Pêche, pers. comm.

[16] McCabe and Kozicky, 384.

[17] James Cardoza, "Coyotes in Massachusetts," *Massachusetts Audubon Society, Public Service Information* No. 8/89/TP/500 (1989), 4.

Epilogue

[1] S.P. Young and H. H. T. Jackson, *The Clever Coyote* (Lincoln and London: University of Nebraska Press, 1951), 225.

BIBLIOGRAPHY

Adams, C. E. "Ages of hunter-killed coyotes in southeastern Nebraska." *Journal of Wildlife Management* 42, 1978.

Aldous, C.M. "Coyotes in Maine." *Journal of Mammalogy* 20, 1939.

Allen, D.L. *Our Wildlife Legacy.* New York: Funk and Wagnalls Company, 1954.

Allen, J.A. "The former range of some New England carnivorous mammals." *American Naturalist* 10, 1876.

Allen, T.J., and J.I. Cromer. "White-tailed deer in West Virginia." *West Virginia Department of Natural Resources Bulletin* No. 7, 1977.

Althoff, D.P., and P.S. Gipson. "Coyote family spatial relationships with reference to poultry losses." *Journal of Wildlife Management* 45, 1981.

Andelt, W.F. "Behavioral ecology of coyotes in south Texas." *Wildlife Monograph* 94, 1985.

Andelt, W.F. "Coyote predation." in M. Novak, J.A. Baker, M.E. Obbard, and B. Malloch, eds., *Wild Furbearer Management and Conservation in North America,* pp. 128-140. Ontario Ministry of Natural Resources, 1987.

Andelt, W.F. "Effectiveness of livestock guarding dogs for reducing predation on domestic sheep." *Wildlife Society Bulletin* 20, 1992.

Andelt, W.F., D.P. Althoff, and P.S. Gipson. "Movements of breeding coyotes with emphasis on den site relationships." *Journal of Mammalogy* 60, 1979.

Andelt, W.F., and P.S. Gipson. "Home range, activity, and daily movements of coyotes." *Journal of Wildlife Management* 43, 1979.

Anderson, D.D. "The status of deer in Kansas." *University of Kansas Miscellaneous Publication* No. 39, 1964.

Anderson, S.B. "The coyote bounty in Nova Scotia 1982-1986." *Nova Scotia Department of Lands and Forests Technical Note* No. 52, 1988.

Andrews, R.D., and E.K. Boggess. "Ecology of coyotes in Iowa." in M. Bekoff, ed., *Coyotes: Biology, Behavior, and Management,* pp. 249-265. New York: Academic Press, 1978.

Arrington, O.N., and A.E. Edwards. "Predator control as a factor in antelope management." *Transactions of the North American Wildlife Conference* 16, 1951.

Atkinson, K.T., and D.M. Shackleton. "Coyote, *Canis latrans*, ecology in a rural-urban environment." *Canadian Field-Naturalist* 105, 1991.

Austin, D.D., P.J. Urness, and M.L. Wolfe. "The influence of predator control on two adjacent wintering deer herds." *Great Basin Naturalist* 37, 1977.

Babb, J.G. and M.L. Kennedy. "An estimate of minimum density for coyotes in western Tennessee." *Journal of Wildlife Management* 53, 1989.

Bailey, H.H. "Coyotes (*Canis latrans*) in Florida. "*Bailey Museum and Library, Natural History Bulletin*, Miami. 1933.

Baker, R.H. *Michigan Mammals.* East Lansing: Michigan State University Press, 1983.

Beasom, S.L. "Relationships between predator removal and white-tailed deer productivity." *Journal of Wildlife Management* 38, 1974.

Bekoff, M. "Social behavior and ecology of the African Canidae: a review," in M.W. Fox, ed., *The Wild Canids,* pp.120-142. New York: Van Nostrand Reinhold, 1975.

Bekoff, M., ed. *Coyotes: Biology, Behavior, and Management.* New York: Academic Press, 1978.

Bekoff, M., and M.C. Wells. "The social ecology of coyotes." *Scientific American* 242, 1980.

Benson, D.A., and D.G. Dodds. *The Deer of Nova Scotia.* Nova Scotia Department of Lands and Forests, 1977.

Berg, W.E., and R.A. Chesness. "Ecology of coyotes in northern Minnesota." in M. Bekoff, ed., *Coyotes: Biology, Behavior, and Management,* pp. 229-247. New York: Academic Press, 1978.

Bergeron, J.- M., and P. Demers. "Le régime alimentaire du Coyote (*Canis latrans*) et du chien errant (*C. familiaris*) dans le sud du Québec." *Canadian Field-Naturalist* 95, 1981.

Bider, J.R., and P.G. Weil. "Dog, *Canis familiaris*, killed by a coyote, *Canis latrans*, on Montreal Island, Quebec." *The Canadian Field-Naturalist* 98, 1984.

Black, J.D. "Mammals of northwestern Arkansas." *Journal of Mammalogy* 17, 1936.

Blanton, K.M., and E.P. Hill. "Coyote use of white-tailed deer fawns in relation to deer density." *Proceedings of the Annual Conference of Southeast Association Fish and Wildlife Agencies* 43, 1989.

Boer, A. H., ed., *Ecology and Management of the Eastern Coyote*. Fredericton: University of New Brunswick Press, 1992.

Boggess, E.K., R.D. Andrews, and R.A. Bishop. "Iowa coyote ecology studies." *Coyote Research Newsletter* 3, 1975.

Bogess, E.K., R.D. Andrews, and R.A Bishop, "Domestic animal losses to coyotes and dogs in Iowa," *Journal of Wildlife Management* 42, 1978.

Boggess, E.K., and F.R. Henderson. "Regional weights of Kansas coyotes." *Transactions of the Kansas Academy of Science* 80, 1977.

Bond, R. M. "Coyote food habits on the Lava Beds National Monument." *Journal of Wildlife Management* 3, 1939.

Bourne, W. "Coyotes come calling on the south." *Southern Outdoors*, February 1991.

Bourne, J., and M.J. Dorrance. "A field test of lithium chloride aversion to reduce coyote predation on domestic sheep." *Journal of Wildlife Management* 46, 1982.

Bowen, W.D. "Home range and spatial organizations of coyotes in Jasper National Park, Alberta." *Journal of Wildlife Management* 46, 1982.

Bradley, J.R., and W.H. Campbell. "Distribution of coyotes in Florida." *Florida Field Naturalist* 11, 1983.

Brand, C.J., L.B. Keith, and C.A. Fischer. "Lynx responses to changing snowshoe hare densities in central Alberta." *Journal of Wildlife Management* 40, 1976.

Brand, C.J., and L.B. Keith. "Lynx demography during a snowshoe hare decline in Alberta." *Journal of Wildlife Management* 43, 1979.

Brocke, R.H. " A taste for venison." *Natural History*, May 1992.

Broughton, E., F.E. Graesser, L.N. Carbyn, and L.P.E. Choquette, "Oral papillomatosis in the coyote in western Canada." *Journal of Wildlife Diseases* 6, 1970.

Brown, E.R. "The black-tailed deer of western Washington." *Washington State Game Department Biological Bulletin* No. 13, 1961.

Burns, R.J. "Microencapsulated lithium chloride bait aversion did not stop coyote predation on sheep," *Journal of Wildlife Management* 47, 1983.

Burns, R.J., and G.E. Connolly, "Lithium chloride bait aversion did not influence prey killing by coyotes," *Proceedings of the Vertebrate Pest Conference* 9, 1980.

Camenzind, F.J. "Behavioral ecology of coyotes on the National Elk Refuge, Jackson, Wyoming." in M. Bekoff, ed., *Coyotes: Biology, Behavior, and Management*. pp. 267-294. New York: Academic Press, 1978.

Carbyn, L.N. "Coyote population fluctuations and spatial distribution in relation to wolf territories in Riding Mountain National Park, Manitoba." *Canadian Field-Naturalist* 96, 1982.

Carbyn, L.N, "Coyote attacks on children in western North America." *Wildlife Society Bulletin* 17, 1989.

Cardoza, James E. "Coyotes in Massachusetts." *Massachusetts Audubon Society, Public Service Information* No. 8/89/TP/500, 1989.

Carroll, B.K., and D.L. Brown. "Factors affecting neonatal fawn survival in southcentral Texas." *Journal of Wildlife Management* 41, 1977.

Cartwright, D.J. "The appearance of the eastern coyote." *Canadian Wildlife Administration* 1, 1975.

Caturano, S.L. "Habitat and home range use by coyotes in eastern Maine." M.Sc thesis, University of Maine, Orono, 1983.

Caughley, G. "Wildlife management and the dynamics of ungulate populations." *Applied Biology* 1, 1976.

Chambers, R.E. "Diets of Adirondack coyotes and red foxes." *Transactions of the Northeast Section Wildlife Society* 44, 1987.

Chambers, R.E. "Reproduction of coyotes in their northeastern range," in A.H. Boer, ed., *Ecology and Management of the Eastern Coyote*, pp. 39-52. Fredericton: University of New Brunswick Press, 1992.

Clark, F.W. "Influence of jackrabbit density on coyote population change." *Journal of Wildlife Management* 36, 1972.

Connolly, G.E. "Predators and predator control." in J.L. Schmidt, and D.L. Gilbert, eds., *Big Game of North America*, pp. 369-394. Harrisburg: Wildlife Management Institute, Stackpole Books, Inc., 1978a.

Connolly, G.E. "Predator control and coyote populations: a review of simulation models." in M. Bekoff, ed., *Coyotes: Biology, Behavior, and Management*, pp. 327-345. New York: Academic Press, 1978b.

Connolly, G.E. "Coyote damage to livestock and other resources." in A.H. Boer, ed., *Ecology and Management of the Eastern Coyote*, pp. 161-169. Fredericton: University of New Brunswick Press, 1992.

Connolly, G.E., and W.M. Longhurst. "The effects of control on coyote populations." *University of California, Division of Agricultural Science Bulletin* No. 1872, 1975.

Connolly, G.E., R.M. Timm, W.E. Howard, and W.M. Longhurst. "Sheep killing behavior of captive coyotes." *Journal of Wildlife Management* 40, 1976.

Conover, M.R., J.G. Francik, and D.E. Miller, "An experimental evaluation of aversive conditioning for controlling coyote predation." *Journal of Wildlife Management* 41, 1977.

Conover, M.R., J.G. Francik, and D.E. Miller, "Aversive conditioning in coyotes: a reply." *Journal of Wildlife Management* 43, 1979.

Cook, R.S., M. White, D.D. Trainer, and W.C. Glazener. "Mortality of young white-tailed deer fawns in South Texas." *Journal of Wildlife Management* 35, 1971.

Crête, M. "Population dynamics of coyotes colonizing the boreal forest of eastern Quebec." *International Union of Game Biologists XXI Congress*, Dalhousie University, Halifax, Nova Scotia, August 15-20, 1993 (Abstract only).

Crête, M., et A. Desrosiers. "L'invasion du coyote (*Canis latrans*) menace la survie de la population relique de caribous (*Rangifer tarandus*) du Parc de la Gaspésie." *Québec Ministère du Loisir, de la Chasse et de la Pêche*, 1993.

Cross, E.C., and J.R. Dymond. "The mammals of Ontario." *Royal Ontario Museum of Zoology Handbook* No.1, 1929.

Crowe, D.M., and M.D. Strickland. "Population structures of some mammalian predators in southeastern Wyoming." *Journal of Wildlife Management* 39, 1975.

Dahlberg, B.L., and R.C. Guettinger. "The white-tailed deer in Wisconsin." *Wisconsin Conservation Department, Technical Wildlife Bulletin* No. 14, 1956.

Davison, R.P. "The effect of exploitation on some parameters of coyote populations." Ph.D. diss., Utah State University, Logan, 1980.

Decker, T.A., W.M. Healy, and S.A. Williams. "Survival of white-tailed deer fawns in western Massachusetts," *Northeast Wildlife* 49, 1992.

Dekker, D. "Denning and foraging habits of red foxes, *Vulpes vulpes*, and their interactions with coyotes, *Canis latrans*, in central Alberta, 1972-1981." *Canadian Field-Naturalist* 97, 1983.

Dekker, D. "Population fluctuations and spatial relationships among wolves, *Canis lupus*, coyotes, *Canis latrans*, and red foxes, *Vulpes vulpes*, in Jasper National Park, Alberta. *Canadian Field-Naturalist* 103, 1989.

Dellinger, S.C., and J.D. Black. "Notes on Arkansas mammals," *Journal of Mammalogy* 21, 1940.

Dibello, F.J., S.M. Arthur, and W.B. Krohn. "Food habits of sympatric coyotes, *Canis latrans*, red foxes, *Vulpes vulpes*, and bobcats *Lynx rufus*, in Maine." *Canadian Field-Naturalist* 104, 1990.

Dice, L.R., "A family of dog-coyote hybrids." *Journal of Mammalogy* 23, 1942.

Dobie, J.F. *The Voice of the Coyote.* Boston, Massachusetts: Little, Brown and Company, 1949.

Dodds, D.G. "A price on their heads." *Eastern Woods and Waters*, April/May, 1988.

Dorrance, D.G. "Predation losses of cattle in Alberta." *Journal of Range Management* 35, 1982.

Dorrance, M.J., and L.D. Roy. "Predation losses of domestic sheep in Alberta." *Journal of Range Management* 29, 1976.

Dorrance, M.J., and J. Bourne. "An evaluation of anti-coyote electric fencing." *Journal of Range Management* 33, 1980.

Ebert, P.N. "Recent changes in Oregon's mule deer population and management." *Proceedings of the Annual Conference of Western Association State Game and Fish Commissioners* 56, 1976.

Economics, Statistics, and Cooperatives Service. "Cattle and calf losses in feeder cattle production." *United States Department of Agriculture*, Unpubl. Report, 1978.

Edwards, L.L. "Home range of the coyote in southern Idaho." M.Sc. thesis, Idaho State University, Pocatello, 1975.

Ekiai, D. "The diet of coyotes (*Canis latrans*) as determined by scat analysis." *Typewritten report for Special Problems in Biology Course*, Acadia University, Wolfville, Nova Scotia, 1990.

Ellins, S.R., and G.C. Martin. "Olfactory discrimination of lithium chloride by the coyote (*Canis latrans*)." *Behavioral and Neural Biology* 29, 1980.

Ellis, R.J. "Food habits and control of coyotes in northcentral Oklahoma." *Oklahoma State University Publication* 56, 1959.

Elton, C., and M. Nicholson. "The ten-year cycle in numbers of the lynx in Canada." *Journal of Animal Ecology* 11, 1942.

Errington, P.W. "Predation and vertebrate populations." *The Quarterly Review of Biology* 21, 1946.

Errington, P.W. *Of Predation and Life.* Ames: Iowa State University Press, 1967.

Freeman, R.S., A. Adorjan, and D.H. Pimlott. "Cestodes of wolves, coyotes and coyote-dog hybrids in Ontario." *Canadian Journal of Zoology* 39, 1961.

French, T.W., and J.L. Dusi. "Status of the coyote and red wolf in Alabama." *Journal of the Alabama Academy of Sciences* 54, 1979.

Fruth, K. "The coyote (*Canis latrans*)." *Wisconsin Department of Natural Resources, Bureau of Wildlife Management* PUBL-WM-148.86, 1986.

Fuller, T.K "Population dynamics of wolves in north-central Minnesota." *Wildlife Monographs* 105, 1989.

Fuller, T.K., and L.B. Keith. "Non-overlapping ranges of coyotes and wolves in northeastern Alberta." *Journal of Mammalogy* 62, 1981.

Fyvie, A. "Manual of common parasites, diseases and anomalies of wildlife in Ontario." *Ontario Department of Lands and Forests, Research Branch*, 1964.

Garner, G.W. "Mortality of white-tailed deer fawns in the Wichita Mountains, Comanche County, Oklahoma." Ph.D. diss., Oklahoma State University, Stillwater, 1976.

Georges, Stan. "A range extension of the coyote in Quebec." *The Canadian Field-Naturalist* 90, 1976.

Gese, E.M. "Reproductive activity in an old-age coyote in southeastern Colorado." *The Southwestern Naturalist* 35, 1990.

Gese, E.M., O.J. Rongstad, and W.R. Mytton. "Home range and habitat use of coyotes in southeastern Colorado." *Journal of Wildlife Management* 52, 1988.

Gese, E.M., O.J. Rongstad, and W.R. Mytton. "Population dynamics of coyotes in southeastern Colorado." *Journal of Wildlife Management* 53, 1989.

Gier, H.T. " Coyotes in Kansas." *Kansas Agricultural Experimental Station Bulletin* 393, 1957.

Gier, H.T. "Ecology and behavior of the coyote (*Canis latrans*)." in M.W. Fox, ed., *The Wild Canids*, pp. 247-262. New York: Van Nostrand Reinhold, 1975.

Gier, H.T., S.M. Kruckenberg, and R.J. Marler. "Parasites and diseases of coyotes." in M. Bekoff, ed., *Coyotes: Biology, Behavior, and Management*, pp 37-71. New York: Academic Press, 1978.

Gilpin, J.B. "On the Mammalia of Nova Scotia." *Transactions of the Nova Scotia Institute of Natural Science* 1, 1864.

Gipson, P.S. "Food habits of coyotes in Arkansas." *Journal of Wildlife Management* 38, 1974.

Gipson, P.S., J.A. Sealander, and J.E. Dunn. "The taxonomic status of wild *Canis* in Arkansas." *Systematic Zoology* 23, 1974.

Gipson, P.S. "Coyotes and related *Canis* in the Southeastern United States with a comment on Mexican and Central American *Canis*." in M. Bekoff, ed., *Coyotes: Biology, Behavior, and Management*, pp. 191-208. New York: Academic Press, 1978.

Goertz, J.W., L.V. Fitzgerald, and R.M. Nowak. "The status of wild *Canis* in Louisiana." *American Midland Naturalist* 93, 1975.

Godin, A.J. *Wild Mammals of New England.* Baltimore: The Johns Hopkins University Press, 1977.

Golley, F.B. *Mammals of Georgia.* Athens: University of Georgia Press, 1962.

Gorham, J.R. "The epizootiology of distemper." *Journal of American Veterinary Medical Association* 149, 1966.

Grange, W. B. *The Way to Game Abundance.* New York: Charles Scribner's Sons, 1949.

Green, J.S. "Donkeys for predator control." *Proceedings of the 4th Eastern Wildlife Damage Control Conference*, Madison, Wisconsin, 1989.

Green, J.S., and R.A. Woodruff. "Guarding dogs protect sheep from predators." *United States Department of Agriculture, Information Bulletin* No. 455, 1983.

Green, J.S., R.A. Woodruff, and T.T. Tueller. "Livestock-guarding dogs for predator control: costs, benefits, and practicality." *Wildlife Society Bulletin* 12, 1984.

Green, R.G., N.R. Ziegler, W.E. Carlson, J.E. Shillinger, S.H. Tyler, and E.T. Dewey. "Epizootic fox encephalitis. V. General and pathogenic properties of the virus." *American Journal of Hygiene* 19, 1934.

Greig, A.S., and K.M. Charlton. "Electron microscopy of the virus of oral papillomatosis in the coyote." *Journal of Wildlife Diseases* 9, 1973.

Griffiths, R.E. Jr., G.E. Connolly, R.J. Burns, and R.T. Sterner. "Coyotes, sheep and lithium chloride." *Proceedings of the Vertebrate Pest Conference* 8, 1978.

Grimes, R. "The coyote that outfoxed a state." *National Wool Grower* 62, 1972.

Gustavson, C.R. "An experimental evaluation of aversive conditioning for controlling coyote predation: a critique." *Journal of Wildlife Management* 43, 1979.

Gustavson, C.R., J. Garcia, W.G. Hawkins, and K.W. Rusiniak. "Coyote predation control by aversive conditioning." *Science* 184, 1974.

Hall, R. "Winter tracking of coyotes." *Nova Scotia Lands and Forests Technical Note* No. 44, 1987.

Hall, D.I., and J.D. Newsom. "The coyote in Louisiana." *Louisiana Agriculture* 21, 1978.

Hallett, D.L. "Post-natal mortality, movements, and den sites of Missouri coyotes." M.Sc. thesis, University of Missouri, Columbia, 1977.

Halloran. A.F., and B.P. Glass. "The carnivores and ungulates of the Wichita Mountains Wildlife Refuge, Oklahoma." *Journal of Mammalogy* 40, 1959.

Hamilton, W.J., Jr. "Food habits of the coyote in the Adirondacks." *New York Fish and Game Journal* 21, 1974.

Hamlin, K.L., S.J. Riley, D. Pyrah, A.R. Dood, and R.J. Mackie. "Relationships among mule deer fawn mortality, coyotes, and alternate prey species during summer." *Journal of Wildlife Management* 48, 1984.

Harrison, D.J., "Denning ecology, movements, and dispersal of coyotes in eastern Maine." M.Sc. thesis, University of Maine, Orono, 1983.

Harrison, D.J. "Coyote dispersal, mortality, and spatial interactions with red foxes in Maine." Ph.D. diss., University of Maine, Orono, 1986.

Harrison, D.J. "Coyotes in the northeast: their history, origin and ecology." *Appalachia* 46, 1986.

Harrison, D.J., D.W. May, and P.W. Rego. "Distribution, productivity and food habits of a recently established coyote population in Connecticut." *Transactions of the Northeast Fish and Wildlife Conference* (Abstracts only) 46, 1989.

Harrison, D.J. "Social ecology of coyotes in northeastern North America: relationships to dispersal, food resources, and human exploitation." in A.H. Boer, ed., *Ecology and Management of the Eastern Coyote*, pp. 53-72. Fredericton: University of New Brunswick Press, 1992a.

Harrison, D.J. "Dispersal characteristics of juvenile coyotes in Maine." *Journal of Wildlife Management* 56, 1992b.

Harrison, D.J., and J.A. Harrison. "Foods of adult Maine coyotes and their known-aged pups." *Journal of Wildlife Management* 48, 1984.

Harrison, D.J., and J.R. Gilbert. "Denning ecology and movements of coyotes in Maine during pup rearing." *Journal of Mammalogy* 66, 1985.

Harrison, D.J., J.A. Bissonette, and J.A. Sherburne. "Spatial relationships between coyotes and red foxes in eastern Maine." *Journal of Wildlife Management* 53, 1989.

Hawthorne, V.M. "Coyote movements in Sagehen Creek Basin, northeastern California." *California Fish and Game* 57, 1971.

Hawthorne, V.M. "Coyote food habits in Sagehen Creek Basin, Northeastern California." *California Fish and Game* 58, 1972.

Henderson, F.R., and C.W. Spaeth. "Managing predator problems: practices and procedures for preventing and reducing livestock losses." *Kansas State University, Cooperative Extension Service* C-620, 1980.

Henne, D.R. "Domestic sheep mortality on a western Montana ranch." in R.L. Phillips, and C. Jonkel, eds., *Proceedings of the 1975 Predator Symposium*, pp. 133-146. Missoula: University of Montana Printing Department, 1977.

Hibler, S.J. "Coyote movement patterns with emphasis on home range characteristics." M.Sc. thesis, Utah State University, Logan, 1977.

Hill, E.P., P.W. Sumner, and J.B. Wooding. "Human influences on range expansion of coyotes in the southeast." *Wildlife Society Bulletin* 15, 1987.

Hilton, H. "The physical characteristics, taxonomic status and food habits of the eastern coyote in Maine." M.Sc. thesis, University of Maine, Orono, 1976.

Hilton, H. "Systematics and ecology of the eastern coyote." in M. Bekoff, ed., *Coyotes: Biology, Behavior, and Management*, pp. 209-228. New York: Academic Press, 1978.

Hilton, H. "Eastern coyote assessment-1985. Planning for Maine's Inland Fish and Wildlife," *Maine Department of Inland Fisheries and Wildlife*, Augusta, 1986.

Hilton, H. "Coyotes in Maine: a case study." in A.H. Boer, ed., *Ecology and Management of the Eastern Coyote*, pp. 183-194. Fredericton: University of New Brunswick Press, 1992.

Hoffmeister, D.F. *Mammals of Illinois*. Urbana and Chicago, University of Illinois Press, 1989.

Holle, D. "Food habits of coyotes in an area of high fawn mortality." *Proceedings of the Oklahoma Academy of Science* 58, 1978.

Holmes, J.C., and R. Podesta. "The helminths of wolves and coyotes from the forested regions of Alberta." *Canadian Journal of Zoology* 46, 1968.

Holzman, S., M.J. Conroy, and J. Pickering. "Home range, movements, and habitat use of coyotes in southcentral Georgia." *Journal of Wildlife Management* 56, 1992.

Horn, S.W. "An evaluation of predatory suppression in coyotes using lithium chloride-induced illness." *Journal of Wildlife Management* 47, 1983.

Howard, W. E. "A means to distinguish skulls of coyotes and domestic dogs." *Journal of Mammalogy* 30, 1949.

Howard, W. E. "The biology of predator control." *An Addison-Wesley Module in Biology* No. 11, 1974.

Howell, R. G. "The urban coyote problem in Los Angeles County." *Proceedings of the Vertebrate Pest Conference* 10, 1982.

Hubert, G.F., Jr., "Population trends and characteristics: canid investigations." *Illinois Department of Conservation, Job Completion Report* No. W-49-R(25), 1978.

Huegel, C.N. "Winter ecology of coyotes in northern Wisconsin." M.Sc. thesis, University of Wisconsin, Madison, 1979.

Jean, Y., and J.M. Bergeron. "Productivity of coyotes, *Canis latrans*, from southern Quebec, Canada." *Canadian Journal of Zoology* 62, 1984.

Johnston, D.H., and M. Beauregard. "Rabies epidemiology in Ontario." *Bulletin of Wildlife Disease Association* 5, 1969.

Jones, E.A., and E.P. Hill. "Coyotes in Mississippi." *Wildlife Sport Fisheries Management* 85-3, 1985.

Keith, L.B., *Wildlife's Ten-Year Cycle*. Madison: University of Wisconsin Press, 1963.

Keith, L.B. "Population dynamics of mammals." *International Congress of Game Biologists* 11, 1974.

Keith, L.B. "Population dynamics of wolves." in L.N. Carbyn, ed., *Wolves in Canada and Alaska*, pp. 66-77. Canadian Wildlife Service Report Series No. 45, Edmonton, 1983.

Kennedy, M.L. "Status of coyote research." *Tennessee Wildlife Resources Agency Technical Report* 89-2, 1989.

Kennelly, J.J. "Coyote reproduction." in M. Bekoff, ed., *Coyotes: Biology, Behavior, and Management*, pp. 73-93. New York: Academic Press, 1978.

Kennelly, J.J., and J.D. Roberts. "Fertility of coyote-dog hybrids." *Journal of Mammalogy* 50, 1969.

Kie, J.G., M. White, and F.F. Knowlton. "Effects of coyote predation on population dynamics of white-tailed deer." in D.L. Drawe, ed., *Proceedings of the Welder Wildlife Foundation Symposium* 1, pp. 65-82. Corpus Christi, Texas, 1979.

Klebenow, D.A., and K. McAdoo. "Predation on domestic sheep in northeastern Nevada." *Journal of Range Management* 29, 1976.

Kleiman, D.G., and C.A. Brady. "Coyote behavior in the context of recent canid research: problems and perspectives." in M. Bekoff, ed., *Coyotes: Biology, Behavior, and Management*, pp. 163-188. New York: Academic Press, 1978.

Knowlton, F.F. "Preliminary interpretations of coyote population mechanics with some management implications." *Journal of Wildlife Management* 36, 1972.

Knowlton, F.F., and L.C. Stoddart. "Coyote population mechanics: another look." in F.L. Bunnell, D.S. Eastman, and J.M. Peck, eds., *Symposium on the Natural Regulation of Wildlife Populations*, pp. 93-111. University of Idaho, Moscow, 1983.

Knowlton, F.F., and L.C. Stoddart. "Some observations from two coyote-prey studies." in A.H. Boer, ed., *Ecology and Management of the Eastern Coyote*, pp. 101-121. Fredericton: University of New Brunswick Press, 1992.

Knudson J.J. "Demographic analysis of a Utah-Idaho coyote population." M.Sc. thesis, Utah State University, Logan. 1976.

Kohler, C. "Ages and percent femur fat of coyote-killed deer in eastern New Brunswick." B.Sc. thesis (forestry), University of New Brunswick, Fredericton, 1987.

Kolenosky, G.B. "Hybridization between wolf and coyote." *Journal of Mammalogy* 52, 1971.

Kolenosky, G.B., and R. O. Standfield. "Morphological and ecological variation among gray wolves (*Canis lupus*) of Ontario, Canada." in M.W. Fox, ed., *The Wild Canids*, pp.62-72. New York: Van Nostrand Reinhold, 1975.

Kolenosky, G.B., D.R. Voigt, and R.O. Standfield. "Wolves and coyotes in Ontario." *Ontario Ministry of Natural Resources*, 1978.

Korschgen, L.J. "Food habits of the coyote in Missouri." *Journal of Wildlife Management* 21, 1957.

LaPierre, L.E. "Fall and winter food habits of the eastern coyote (*Canis latrans*) in southeastern New Brunswick, Canada." *Proceedings of the Nova Scotia Institute of Science* 35, 1985.

Larivière, S., and M. Crête. "Causes et conséquences de la colonisation du Québec par le coyote (*Canis latrans*)." *Québec Ministère du Loisir, de la Chasse et de la Pêche*, 1992.

Larivière, S., and M. Crête. "The size of eastern coyotes (*Canis latrans*): a comment." *Journal of Mammalogy* 74, 1993.

Laundre, J.W., and B.L. Keller. "Home-range size of coyotes: a critical review." *Journal of Wildlife Management* 48, 1984.

Lavigne, G.R. "Sex/age composition and physical condition of deer killed by coyotes during winter in Maine." in A.H. Boer, ed., *Ecology and Management of the Eastern Coyote*, pp. 141-159. Fredericton: University of New Brunswick Press, 1992.

Lawrence, B., and W.H. Bossert. "Multiple character analysis of *Canis lupus, latrans* and *familiaris*, with a discussion of the relationships of *Canis niger*." *American Zoologist* 7, 1967.

Lawrence, B., and W.H. Bossert. "The cranial evidence for hybridization in New England *Canis*." *Breviora* 330, 1969.

Lehman, L.E. "Indiana fur harvests 1700-1980." *Indiana Department of Natural Resources Pitman-Robertson Bulletin* No. 13, 1982.

Lehman, L.E. "Coyote vocal responsiveness to broadcast auditory stimuli in south central Indiana." *Proceedings of the Indiana Academy of Science* 97, 1987.

Lehner, P.N., R. Krumm, and A.T. Cringan. "Tests for olfactory repellents for coyotes and dogs." *Journal of Wildlife Management* 40, 1976.

Lemm, W.C. "Coyote denning as a method of damage control." *Proceedings of the Great Plains Wildlife Damage Control Workshop*, Kansas State University, Manhattan, 1973.

Leopold, A.S. "The predator in wildlife management." *Sierra Club Bulletin* 39, 1954.

Letourneau, G. *America's New "Wolf."* Portland, Maine: Guy Gannett Publishing Co., 1984.

Linhart, S.B., and F.F. Knowlton. "Determining age of coyotes by tooth cementum layers." *Journal of Wildlife Management* 31, 1967.

Litvaitis, J.A. "A comparison of coyote and bobcat food habits in the Wichita Mountains, Oklahoma." *Proceedings of the Oklahoma Academy of Sciences* 61, 1981.

Litvaitis, J.A. "Niche relations between coyotes and sympatric carnivora." in A.H. Boer, ed., *Ecology and Management of the Eastern Coyote*, pp. 73-85. Fredericton: University of New Brunswick Press, 1992.

Litvaitis, J.A., and J.H. Shaw. "Coyote movements, habitat use and food habits in southwestern Oklahoma." *Journal of Wildlife Management* 44, 1980.

Litvaitis, J.A., and D.J. Harrison. "Bobcat-coyote niche relationships during a period of coyote population increase." *Canadian Journal of Zoology* 67, 1989.

Longley, W.H. "Coyote collection." *Minnesota Game Research Project Quarterly Progress Report* 30, 1970.

Lord, L.A. "Un envahisseur importun au Québec: le coyote." *Les Carnets de Zoologie* 21, 1961.

Lorenz, J.R. "Physical characteristics, movement and population estimate of the eastern coyote in New England." M.Sc. thesis, University of Massachusetts, Amherst, 1978.

Lund, R.C. "New wolf for an old niche." *New Jersey Outdoors* Jan-Feb, 1976.

Lydeard, C., and M.L. Kennedy. "Morphologic assessment of recently founded populations of the coyote, *Canis latrans*, in Tennessee." *Journal of Mammalogy* 69, 1988.

MacCracken, J.G., and D.W. Uresk. "Coyote foods in the Black Hills, South Dakota." *Journal of Wildlife Management* 48, 1984.

MacNearney, J.D. "A study of colonizing eastern coyotes (*Canis latrans thamnos*) in Nova Scotia." *Typewritten report for Special Problems in Biology*, Acadia University, Wolfville, Nova Scotia, 1982.

Mahan, B.R., and H.T. Gier. "Age structure and reproductive success of coyotes (*Canis latrans*) in Illinois." *Transactions of the Illinois State Academy of Science* 70, 1977.

Major, J.T. "Ecology and interspecific relationships of coyotes, bobcats and red foxes in western Maine. Ph.D. diss., University of Maine, Orono, 1984.

Major, J.T., and J.A. Sherburne. "Interspecific relationships of coyotes, bobcats and red foxes in western Maine." *Journal of Wildlife Management* 51, 1987.

Manville, R.H. "Longevity of the coyote." *Journal of Mammalogy* 34, 1953.

Mathwig, H.J. 1973. "Food and population characteristics of Iowa coyotes." *Iowa State Journal of Research* 47, 1973.

McCabe, R.A., and E.L. Kozicky. "A position on predator management." *Journal of Wildlife Management* 36, 1972.

McCabe, R.E., and T.R. McCabe. "Of slings and arrows: an historical retrospection." in L.K. Halls, ed., *White-tailed Deer: Ecology and Management*, pp. 19-72. Harrisburg: Wildlife Management Institute, Stackpole Books, 1984.

McCarley, H. "The taxonomic status of wild *Canis* (Canidae) in the South Central United States." *The Southwestern Naturalist* 7, 1962.

McGinnis, H.J. "Pennsylvania coyotes and their relationship to other wild *Canis* populations in the Great Lakes region and northeastern United States." M.Sc. thesis, Pennsylvania State University, University Park, 1979.

Mech, L.D. "The wolves of Isle Royale." *United States National Park Service, Fauna Series* No. 7, 1966.

Mech, L.D. *The Wolf: The Ecology and Behavior of an Endangered Species*. New York: The Natural History Press, 1970.

Mech, L.D. "Disproportionate sex ratios of wolf pups." *Journal of Wildlife Management* 39, 1975.

Mech, L.D. "Predators and predation." in L.K. Halls, ed., *White-tailed Deer: Ecology and Management*, pp. 189-200. Harrisburg: Wildlife Management Institute, Stackpole Books, 1984.

Meinzer, W.P., D.N. Ueckert, and J.T. Flinders. "Foodniche of coyotes in the rolling plains of Texas." *Journal of Range Management* 28, 1975.

Mengel, R.M. "A study of dog-coyote hybrids and implications concerning hybridization in *Canis*." *Journal of Mammalogy* 52, 1971.

Menzel, K.E. "Improved survival of pronghorn fawns with coyote control." *Biennial Pronghorn Antelope Workshop* 15, 1992. (Proceedings not yet published).

Merriam, C.H. "Revision of the coyotes or prairie wolves, with description of new forms." *Biological Society of Washington* 11, 1897.

Messier, F., C. Barrette, and J. Huot. "Coyote predation on a white-tailed deer population in southern Quebec, Canada." *Canadian Journal of Zoology* 64, 1986.

Messier, F., F. Potvin, and F. Duchesneau. "Faisabilité d'une réduction expérimentale du coyote dans le but d'accroître une population de cerfs de Virginie." *Le Naturaliste Canadien* 114, 1987.

Michaelson, K.A., and J.W. Goertz. "Food habits of coyotes in northwest Louisiana." *Louisiana Academy of Science* XL: 1975.

Mills, J. "Sex, age and reproductive condition from coyotes (*Canis latrans*) in Nova Scotia (during 1992-93)." *Typewritten report for Special Problems In Biology*, Acadia University, Wolfville, Nova Scotia, 1993.

Mills, L.S., and F.F. Knowlton. "Coyote space use in relation to prey abundance." *Canadian Journal of Zoology* 69, 1991.

Moore, G.C. "A comparative study of colonizing and longer established eastern coyote (*Canis latrans* var.) populations. M.Sc. thesis, University of Western Ontario, London, 1981.

Moore, G.C., and J.S. Millar. "A comparative study of colonizing and longer established eastern coyote populations." *Journal of Wildlife Management* 48, 1984.

Moore, G.C., and J.S. Millar. 1986. "Food habits and average weights of a fall-winter sample of eastern coyotes, *Canis latrans*." *Canadian Field-Naturalist* 100, 1986.

Moore, G.C., and G.R. Parker. "Colonization by the eastern coyote (*Canis latrans*)." in A.H. Boer, ed., *Ecology and Management of the Eastern Coyote*, pp. 23-37. Fredericton: University of New Brunswick Press, 1992.

Morton, L.D. "Winter ecology of the eastern coyote." M.Sc. thesis, University of New Brunswick, Fredericton, 1988.

Mumford, R.E. *Distribution of the Mammals of Indiana*. Indianapolis: The Indiana Academy of Science, 1969.

Munoz, J.R. "Causes of sheep mortality at the Cook Ranch, Florence, Montana 1975-76."M.Sc. thesis, University of Montana, Missoula, 1977.

Murie, A. "The wolves of Mount McKinley." *Fauna of the National Parks of the United States, Fauna Series* No. 5, 1944.

National Agricultural Statistics Service (NASS). "Sheep and goat predator loss." *United States Department of Agriculture, Agricultural Statistics Board Report* Lv Gn 1 (4-91), Washington, D.C., 1991.

Nass, R.D. "Mortality associated with sheep operations in Idaho." *Journal of Range Management* 30, 1977.

Nellis, C.H. "Prevalence of oral papilloma-like lesions in coyotes in Alberta." *Canadian Journal of Zoology* 51, 1973.

Nellis, C.H., and L.B. Keith. "Population dynamics of coyotes in central Alberta, 1964-68." *Journal of Wildlife Management* 40, 1976.

Nesse, G.E., W.M. Longhurst, and W.E. Howard. "Predation and the sheep industry in California." *University of California, Division of Agricultural Sciences Bulletin* No. 1878, 1976.

Niebauer, T.J., and O.J. Rongstad. "Coyote food habits in northwestern Wisconsin." in R.L. Phillips and C. Jonkel, eds., *Proceedings of the 1975 Predator Symposium*, pp. 237-251. Missoula: University of Montana Printing Department, 1977.

Nielson, D., and D. Curle. "Predator costs to Utah's range sheep industry." *National Wool Grower* 60, 1970.

Novak, M., J.A. Baker, M.E. Obbard, and B. Malloch, eds., *Wild Furbearer Management and Conservation in North America*. Ontario Ministry of Natural Resources, 1987.

Nowak, R.M. "Report on the red wolf." *Defenders of Wildlife News* 45, 1970.

Nowak, R.M. "Evolution and taxonomy of coyotes and related *Canis*." in M. Bekoff, ed., *Coyotes: Biology, Behavior, and Management*, pp. 3-16. New York: Academic Press, 1978.

Nowak, R.M. "A perspective on the taxonomy of wolves in North America." in L.N. Carbyn, ed., *Wolves in Canada and Alaska*, pp. 10-19. Canadian Wildlife Service Report Series No. 45, 1983.

O'Brien, M. "The coyote-a new mammal, new challenges." *Conservation* 7, 1983.

O'Connell, A.F., D.J. Harrison, B. Connery, and K.B. Anderson. "Food use by an insular population of coyotes." *Transactions of the Northeast Section of The Wildlife Society* 49, 1992.

Ogle T.J. "Predator-prey relationships between coyote and white-tailed deer." *Northwest Science* 45, 1971.

Ozoga, J.J., and E.M. Harger. "Winter activities and feeding habits of northern Michigan coyotes." *Journal of Wildlife Management* 30, 1966.

Paridiso, J. "Canids recently collected in east Texas, with comments on the taxonomy of the red wolf." *American Midland Naturalist* 80, 1968.

Parker, G.R. "The seasonal diet of coyotes, *Canis latrans*, in northern New Brunswick." *Canadian Field-Naturalist* 100, 1986.

Parker, G.R., J.W. Maxwell, L.D. Morton, and G.E.J. Smith. "The ecology of lynx (*Lynx canadensis*) on Cape Breton Island." *Canadian Journal of Zoology* 61, 1983.

Parker, G.R., and J.W. Maxwell. "Seasonal movements and winter ecology of the coyote, *Canis latrans*, in northern New Brunswick." *Canadian Field-Naturalist* 103, 1989.

Pastuck, R.D. 1974. "Some aspects of the ecology of the coyote (*Canis latrans*) in southwestern Manitoba." M.Sc. thesis, University of Manitoba, Winnipeg, 1974.

Patterson, B. "Ecology of the eastern coyote in Kejimkujik National Park," M.Sc. thesis, Acadia University, Wolfville, 1995.

Pearson, E.W. "A 1974 coyote harvest estimate for 17 western states." *Wildlife Society Bulletin* 6, 1978.

Pence, D.B., and J.W. Custer. "Host-parasite relationships in the wild Canidae of North America. 2. Pathology of infectious diseases in the genus *Canis*." in J.A. Chapman and D. Pursley, eds., *Proceedings of the Worldwide Furbearer Conference*, pp. 760-845. Frostburg, Maryland, 1981.

Pence, D.B., and W.P. Meinzer. "Helminth parasitism in the coyote, *Canis latrans*, from the Rolling Plains of Texas." *International Journal of Parasitology* 9, 1979.

Person, D.K. "Home range, activity, habitat use, and food habits of eastern coyotes in the Champlain Valley region of Vermont." M.Sc. thesis, University of Vermont, Burlington, 1988.

Person, D.K., and D.H. Hirth. "Home range and habitat use of coyotes in a farm region of Vermont." *Journal of Wildlife Management* 55, 1991.

Phillips, M.K., and G.F. Hubert, Jr. "Winter food habits of coyotes in southeastern Illinois." *Transactions of the Illinois State Academy of Science* 73, 1980.

Phillips, M.K., and V.G. Henry. "Comments on red wolf taxonomy." *Conservation Biology* 6, 1992.

Pimlott, D.H. "Wolf predation and ungulate populations." *American Zoologist* 7, 1967.

Poulle, M.L., R. Lemieux, M. Crête, et J. Huot. "Régime alimentaire du coyote et sélection des proies dans un ravage de cerfs de Virginie en fort déclin: le ravage de Bonaventure (Gaspésie)." *Québec Ministère du Loisir, de la Chasse et de la Pêche*, Unpublished Report, 1992.

Preece, K. "Home range, movements, and social behavior of denning female coyotes in north-central Minnesota." *Minnesota Wildlife Research Quarterly* 38, 1978.

Pringle, L.P. "Notes on coyotes in southern New England." *Journal of Mammalogy* 41, 1960.

Pyrah, D. "Social distribution and population estimates of coyotes in north-central Montana." *Journal of Wildlife Management* 48, 1984.

Rand, A.L., "Mammals of Yukon, Canada." *National Museum of Canada Bulletin* No. 100, 1945.

Richens, V.B., and R.D. Hugie. "Distribution, taxonomic status, and characteristics of coyotes in Maine." *Journal of Wildlife Management* 38, 1974.

Robinson, W.B., and M.V. Cummings. "Notes on behavior of coyotes." *Journal of Mammalogy* 28, 1947.

Robinson, W.B., and M.V. Cummings. "Movements of coyotes from and to Yellowstone National Park." *United States Department of Interior, Special Scientific Report. Wildlife* No. 11, 1951.

Robinson, W.B., and E.F. Grand. "Comparative movements of bobcats and coyotes as disclosed by tagging." *Journal of Wildlife Management* 22, 1958.

Rogers, J.G., Jr. "Analysis of the coyote population of Dona Ana County, New Mexico." M.Sc thesis, New Mexico State University, 1965.

Rue, L.L III. *The World of the White-tailed Deer*. Philadelphia and New York: J.B. Lippincott Company, 1962.

Sabean, B. "The eastern coyote in Nova Scotia." *Conservation* 13, 1989.

Sabean, B. "Coyote winter tracking update." *Conservation* 14, 1990.

Sabean, B. "Tracking coyotes in winter." *Conservation* 17, 1993.

Sabean, B. "Coyote carcass collections." *Nova Scotia Trappers Newsletter* 29, 1993.

Samuel, W.M., G.A. Chalmers, and J.R. Gunson. "Oral papillomatosis in coyotes (*Canis latrans*) and wolves (*Canis lupus*) of Alberta." *Journal of Wildlife Diseases* 14, 1978.

Samuel, W.M., S. Ramalingam, and L.N. Carbyn. "Helminths of coyotes (*Canis latrans* Say), wolves (*Canis lupus* L.) and red foxes (*Vulpes vulpes* L.) of southwestern Manitoba." *Canadian Journal of Zoology* 56, 1978.

Sargeant, A.B., S.H. Allen, and J.O. Hastings. "Spatial relations between sympatric coyotes and red foxes in North Dakota." *Journal of Wildlife Management* 51, 1987.

Saunders, J.K., Jr. "Food habits of the lynx in Newfoundland." *Journal of Wildlife Management* 27, 1963.

Schaaf, L.E., and T. Edwards. "Coyotes in Kentucky." *Unpublished report by Kentucky Wildlife Division*, 1987.

Schaefer, J.M., R.D. Andrews, and J.J. Dinsmore. "An assessment of coyote and dog predation on sheep in southern Iowa." *Journal of Wildlife Management* 45, 1981.

Schladweiler, P. "Effects of coyote predation on his game population in Montana. Coyote densities, small mammal population indices, and his game farm production and survival in the various study areas." *Job Progress Report, Research Project Segment* W-120-R-8, NG-47-1, 1977.

Schmitz, O.J., and G.B. Kolenosky. "Wolves and coyotes in Ontario: morphological relationships and origins." *Canadian Journal of Zoology* 63, 1985.

Schmitz, O.J., and D.M. Lavigne. "Factors affecting body size in sympatric Ontario *Canis*." *Journal of Mammalogy* 68, 1987.

Sealander, J.A., Jr. "A provisional check-list and key to the mammals of Arkansas (with annotations)." *American Midland Naturalist* 56, 1956.

Servello, F.A., T.L. Edwards, and B.U. Constantin. "Managing coyote problems in Kentucky." *University of Kentucky, Cooperative Extension Service* FOR-37, 1989.

Seton, E.T. *Life Histories of Northern Mammals.* Vol.1. New York: Charles Scribner's Sons, 1909.

Seton, E.T. *Lives of Game Animals.* Vol. 3, Part 1, Garden City, Doubleday, Doran and Co., Inc., 1929.

Severinghaus, C.W. "Notes on the history of wild canids in New York." *New York Fish and Game Journal* 21, 1974.

Shelton, M., and N.L. Gates. "Antipredator fencing," in J.S. Green, ed., *Protecting livestock from coyotes: a synopsis of research of the Agricultural Research Service*, pp. 30-37. USDA, Beltsville, Md., 1987.

Sherburne, D.J., and G.J. Matula, Jr. "Predator habitat utilization studies, Dickey-Lincoln School Lakes Project." *Maine Cooperative Wildlife Research Unit*, University of Maine, Orono, 1981.

Silver, H. "A history of New Hampshire game and furbearers." *New Hampshire Fish and Game Department Survey Report* 6, 1957.

Silver, H. "History." in H.R. Siegler, ed., *The White-tailed Deer of New Hampshire*, pp. 15-28. New Hampshire Fish and Game Department, Survey Report No. 10, 1968.

Silver, H., and W.T. Silver. "Growth and behavior of the coyote-like canid of northern New England with observations on canid hybrids." *Wildlife Monographs* 17, 1969.

Simms, D.E., and O. Dawydiak. *Livestock Protection Dogs.* Fort Payne: OTR Publications, 1990.

Small, R.L. "Interspecific competition among three species of Carnivora on the Spider Ranch, Yavapai County, Arizona." M.Sc. thesis, University of Arizona, Tuscon, 1971.

Smith, D. "The determination of coyote (*Canis latrans*) food habits from the contents of scats." *Typewritten report for Special Problems in Biology*, Acadia University, Wolfville, Nova Scotia, 1990.

Smith, R.H., D.J. Neff, and N.G. Woolsey. "Pronghorn response to coyote control-a benefit cost analysis." *Wildlife Society Bulletin* 14, 1986.

Snow, C. "Some observations on the behavioral and morphological development of coyote pups." *American Zoologist* 7, 1967.

Springer, J.T. "Movement patterns of coyotes in south central Washington." *Journal of Wildlife Management* 46, 1982.

Springer, J.T., and J.S. Smith. "Summer food habits of coyotes in central Wyoming." *Great Basin Naturalist* 41, 1981.

Springer, J.T., and C.R. Wenger. "Interactions between, and some ecological aspects of coyotes and mule deer in central Wyoming." *Wyoming Department of Wildlife Technical Report* No. 1981, 1981.

Squires, W.A. "The mammals of New Brunswick." *The New Brunswick Museum Monograph Series* No. 5, 1968.

Squires, W.A. "A naturalist in New Brunswick." *The New Brunswick Museum*, 1972.

Stains, H. J. "Distribution and taxonomy of the Canidae." in M.W. Fox, ed., *The Wild Canids*, pp. 3-26. New York: Van Nostrand Reinhold, 1975.

State of Connecticut, "Furbearer population monitoring - carcass collections and necropsies." *Project Performance Report* No. W-49-R-11, Period 10/1/85 - 9/30/86, 1987.

Sterner, R.T., and S.A. Shumake. "Coyote damage - control research: a review and analysis." in M. Bekoff, ed., *Coyotes: Biology, Behavior, and Management*, pp. 297-325. New York: Academic Press, 1978.

Stewart, F.L. "Coyote in New Brunswick during prehistoric times." *Nature Canada* 5, 1976.

Stout, G.G. "Effects of coyote reduction on white-tailed deer productivity on Fort Sill, Oklahoma." *Wildlife Society Bulletin* 10, 1982.

Sumner, P.W., E.P Hill, and J.B. Wooding. "Activity and movements of coyotes in Mississippi and Alabama." *Proceedings of the Annual Conference of Southeast Fish & Wildlife Agencies* 38, 1984.

Taylor, R.G., J.P. Workman, and J.E. Bowns. "The economics of sheep predation in southwestern Utah." *Journal of Range Management* 32, 1979.

Taylor, R.W., C.L. Counts, III, and S.B. Mills, "Occurrence and distribution of the coyote, *Canis latrans* Say, in West Virginia." *Proceedings of the West Virginia Academy of Science* 48, 1976.

Teer, J.G., D.L. Drawe, T.L. Blankenship, W.F. Andelt, R.S. Cook, J.G. Kie, F.F. Knowlton, and M. White. "Deer and coyotes: the Welder experiments." *Transactions of the North American Wildlife and Natural Resources Conference* 56, 1991.

Tell, S.G. "Coyote (*Canis latrans thamnos*) in Nova Scotia." *Typewritten report for Special Problems in Biology*, Acadia University, Wolfville, Nova Scotia, 1987.

Terrill, C.E. "Livestock losses to predators in western states." in R.L. Phillips and C. Jonkel, eds., *Proceedings of the 1975 Predator Symposium*, pp. 157-162. Missoula: University of Montana Printing Department, 1975.

Therberge, J.B., and D.A. Gauthier. "Models of wolf-ungulate relationships: when is wolf control justified?" *Wildlife Society Bulletin* 13, 1985.

Theberge, J.B., and C.H.R. Wedeles. "Prey selection and habitat partitioning in sympatric coyote and red fox populations in southwest Yukon, Canada." *Canadian Journal of Zoology* 67, 1989.

Thomas H.H., and R.L. Dibblee. "A coyote, *Canis latrans*, on Prince Edward Island." *Canadian Field-Naturalist* 100, 1986.

Thornton, J.E., R.R. Bell, and M.J. Reardon. "Internal parasites of the coyote in southern Texas." *Journal of Wildlife Diseases* 10, 1974.

Thurber, J.M., and R.O. Peterson. "Changes in body size associated with range expansion in the coyote (*Canis latrans*)." *Journal of Mammalogy* 72, 1991.

Tigner, J.R., and G.E. Larson. "Sheep losses on selected ranches in southern Wyoming." *Journal of Range Management* 30, 1977.

Todd, A.W. "Demographic and dietary comparisons of forest and farmland coyote, *Canis latrans*, populations in Alberta." *Canadian Field-Naturalist* 99, 1985.

Todd, A.W., and L.B. Keith. "Responses of coyotes to winter reductions in agricultural carrion." *Alberta Fish and Wildlife Division, Technical Bulletin* No 5, 1976.

Todd, A.W., L.B. Keith, and C.A. Fischer. "Population ecology of coyotes during a fluctuation of snowshoe hares." *Journal of Wildlife Management* 45, 1981.

Todd, A.W., and L.B. Keith. "Coyote demography during a snowshoe hare decline in Alberta." *Journal of Wildlife Management* 47, 1983.

Trainer, C. "Direct causes of mortality in mule deer fawns during summer and winter periods on Steens Mountain, Oregon-a progress report." *Proceedings of the Annual Conference of Western Association State Game and Fish Commissioners* 55, 1975.

Trainer, D.O., and F.F. Knowlton. "Serologic evidence of diseases in Texas coyotes." *Journal of Wildlife Management* 32, 1968.

Trainer, D.O., F.F. Knowlton, and L. Karstad. "Oral papillomatosis in the coyote." *Bulletin of Wildlife Disease Association* 4, 1968.

Trefethen, J.B. *An American Crusade for Wildlife*. New York: Winchester Press, 1975.

Tzilkowski, W.M. "Mortality patterns of radio-marked coyotes in Jackson Hole, Wyoming." Ph.D. diss., University of Massachusetts, Amherst, 1980.

Udy, J.R. "Effects of predator control on antelope populations." *Utah State Department of Fish and Game Publication* No. 5, 1953.

Uhmer, F.A. "Recent records of coyotes in Pennsylvania and New Jersey." *Journal of Mammalogy* 30, 1949.

United States Fish and Wildlife Service. "Predator damage in the west: a study of coyote management alternatives." *United States Department of the Interior*, Washington, D.C., 1978.

Voigt, J.R. "The adaptable coyote." *Ontario Fish and Game Review* 16, 1977.

Voigt, D.R., and B.D. Earle. "Avoidance of coyotes by red fox families." *Journal of Wildlife Management* 47, 1983.

Voigt, D.R. and W.E. Berg. "Coyote." in M. Novak, J.A. Baker, M.E. Obbard, and B. Malloch., eds., *Wild Furbearer Management and Conservation in North America*, pp. 344-357. Ministry of Natural Resources, Ontario, 1987.

Wagner, F.H., and L.C. Stoddart. "Influence of coyote predation on black-tailed jackrabbit populations in Utah." *Journal of Wildlife Management* 36, 1972.

Walton, M.T., and G.A. Field. "Use of donkeys to guard sheep and goats in Texas." *Proceedings of the Eastern Wildlife Damage Control Conference* 4, 1989.

Wayne, R.K., and S.M. Jenks. "Mitochondrial DNA analysis implying extensive hybridization of the endangered red wolf." *Nature* 351, 1991.

Wayne, R.K., and N. Lehman. "Mitochondrial DNA analysis of the eastern coyote: origins and hybridization." in A.H. Boer, ed., *Ecology and Management of the Eastern Coyote*, pp. 9-22. Fredericton: University of New Brunswick Press, 1992.

Weaver, J.L. "Coyote-food base relationships in Jackson Hole, Wyoming." M.Sc. thesis, Utah State University, Logan, 1977.

Weeks, J.L., G.M. Tori, and M.C. Shieldcastle. "Coyotes (*Canis latrans*) in Ohio." *Ohio Journal of Science* 90, 1990.

Wetmore, S.P., C.H. Nellis, and L.B. Keith. "A study of winter coyote hunting in Alberta with emphasis on use of snowmobiles." *Alberta Department of Lands and Forests, Wildlife Technical Bulletin* 2, 1970.

Willis, M. J. "Impacts of coyote removal on pronghorn fawn survival." *Proceedings of the Pronghorn Antelope Workshop* 13, 1988.

Windberg, L.A., H.L. Anderson, and R.M. Engeman. "Survival of coyotes in southern Texas." *Journal of Wildlife Management* 49, 1985.

Windberg, L.A., and F.F. Knowlton. "Management implications of coyote spacing patterns in southern Texas." *Journal of Wildlife Management* 52, 1988.

Witmer, G.W., and D.S. deCalesta. "Resource use by unexploited sympatric bobcats and coyotes in Oregon." *Canadian Journal of Zoology* 64, 1986.

Wooding, J.B., P.W. Sumner, and E.P. Hill. "Coyotes in Alabama." *Alabama Conservation* 55, 1985.

Wooding, J.B., and T.S. Hardisky. "Coyote distribution in Florida." *Florida Field Naturalist* 18, 1990.

Woodruff, R.A., and B.C. Keller. "Dispersal, daily activity, and home range of coyotes in southeastern Idaho." *Northwest Science* 56, 1982.

Young, S.P., and H.H.T. Jackson. *The Clever Coyote.* Lincoln: University of Nebraska Press, 1951.

Young, S.P. and E.A. Goldman. *The Wolves of North America.* New York: Dover Publications, 1964.

INDEX

Adirondacks, coyote behavioural patterns, 77; early colonization of, 25–26; feeding habits of coyotes in, 47–48; use of deer in winter, 46–48, 117.

Age structure, 82–85; Alberta, 85; definition of, 82; determination of, 82–84; influence of food availability, 84, 85; life expectancy, 85; Nova Scotia, (Table 5, 88), 85; samples from across North America, (Table 4, 83).

Alabama, colonization of, 33; releases in, 34; daily movement patterns, 106.

Alberta, attacks on humans, 167–168; coyote densities, (Table 3, 80), 80–81; electric fencing for sheep, 188; interaction between coyotes and wolves, 161, between coyotes and red foxes, 163; predation on sheep, 180–181; snowshoe hare influencing coyote densities, 80–81; 94–96; mortality rates, 89–90; 10–year cycle, 94–95.

Alaska, arrival of coyotes, 17–19; eating salmon, 19; mortality from wolves, 19; reliance by coyotes on garbage, 19; moose carcasses 19.

Albinism, frequency of, 38–39.

Arkansas, confusion in coyote taxonomy, 32.

Atlantic Canada, colonization of, 28–32.

Bobcats, interaction with coyotes in Maine, 165–166.

Body size, 39–42.

Bounties, ineffectiveness of, 157–158; in Nova Scotia, 158.

Breeding season, 59–63; in Kansas, 60–61; New York, 62; Maine, 62; Nova Scotia, 62; length of, 59– 63.

Brocke, Ranier, 77.

Brundige, Gary, 47–48.

Brush wolf, 7.

Canidae, Family, 6.

Canis, history of genus in southeast, 13–15.

Canis latrans, 3, *C.L. frustror*, 13–15, interbreeding with red wolves, 14; *C. l. thamnos*, 7, 13–15; *C. l. var.*, 10, 15.

Canis rufus, 6, 14.

Cartwright, Dave, 30.

Cattle, predation on, 183.

Chambers, Robert, 62.

Colonization, by eastern coyotes, 16–34; early expansion, 17–20; northern front of, 22–32; southern front of, 32–35.

Connolly, Guy, 9, 184–85.

Coyote, age structure, 82–85; as a control on deer populations, 119–125, 151–152; breeding, 59–63; dens, 63–66; classification of, 2–3; control of, 153–159; densities, 77–82; diseases, 170–178; stock, 179–196; food habits, 43–57; early expansion east, 17–20; evolution, 4; home ranges, 99–105; interaction with wolves, 160–162, red foxes, 162–165, bobcats, 165–166, humans, 167–169; management, 197–205; mortality, 89–93; origin of name, 4; pregnancy, length of, 9, 62–63; pre–settlement distribution, 16–17; prey dependency, 94–98; releases, 21–22, in: Georgia, 34, Florida, 34, New York, 26, North Carolina, 34, southeast, 32; pup development, 70–74; pup dispersal, 75–77; reproduction, 58–77; sex ratios, 86–89; studies of deer–coyote interactions, 123–142; survival, 89–93; taxonomy, 6–15; weights of, 36–52.

Coyote–dog (Coy–dog), advanced breeding season, 9–10, 11; early abundance in Adirondacks, 26; in New England, 26-27; mortality of young, 10–11; parental care, 10–11.

Densities, across North America, 79–82; definition of, 78; in the northeast, 81–82; post–1900, 81; pre– 1900, 81; increase from north to south, 80, 97–98.

Dens, descriptions of, 63–66.

Diseases and parasites, review of, 170–178; distemper, 171; mange, 177; rabies, 171; tapeworms, 172–174.

Domestic dog, breeding cycle, 9; interbreeding with coyote, 9; lack of reproductive synchrony with coyotes, 10.

Duncanson, Lloyd, 41.

Eastern coyote, behaviour, 9–10; breeding pattern, 9–10; characteristics of, 9–11; fossil remains of, 17; increased size in Ontario, 11–12; pregnancy, length of, 9, 62–63; taxonomy, 6–15; theory for larger size, 12.